MW00606699

John W. Smith

Betty Jo,

I hope you enjoy this account of a great team & wonderful sport. Best wishes & Cowboy up!

David Parrish
Jan 2010

OKLAHOMA HORIZONS SERIES

cowboy up

John Smith Leads the Legendary Oklahoma State Wrestlers to Their Greatest Season Ever

by Kim D. Parrish

FOREWORD BY JOHN SMITH

Series Editor:
GINI MOORE CAMPBELL

OKLAHOMA
HERITAGE
ASSOCIATION
Oklahoma City

To S.L.and Caroline
—*Kim Parrish*

OKLAHOMA HORIZONS SERIES
Copyright 2007 by Oklahoma Heritage Association

All rights reserved. No part of this book may be reproduced or utilized in any form or by any means, electronic or mechanical, including photocopying and recording, by any information storage and retrieval system, without permission of the publisher.

"Cowboy Up" used with permission of Christine Lynn Andersson and The National Football League.

Printed in the United States of America by Bart Baker Group, LLC & Jostens, Inc.
405.503.3207
ISBN 10: 1-885596-61-8   ISBN 13: 978-1-885596-61-1
Library of Congress Catalog Number 2007928202
Cover and contents designed by Sandi Welch/2WDesignGroup.com

OKLAHOMA HERITAGE ASSOCIATION

Glen D. Johnson, Oklahoma City
Chairman of the Board

Tom McDaniel, Oklahoma City
Chairman-Elect of The Board

Roxana Lorton, Tulsa
Chairman Emeritus of the Board

Vice Chairman of the Board
Calvin Anthony, Stillwater
Nevyle Cable, Okmulgee
Ken Fergeson, Altus
Ike Glass, Newkirk
David Kyle, Tulsa
Paul Massad, Norman
Meg Salyer, Oklahoma City
Justice Steve Taylor, McAlester

At Large Executive Committee Members
Clayton I. Bennett, Oklahoma City
Bond Payne, Oklahoma City
David Rainbolt, Oklahoma City

Becky Frank, Tulsa
Corporate Secretary

Roger Collins, Bristow
Treasurer

Shannon Nance, Oklahoma City
President

Directors
Bill Anoatubby, Ada
Wanda Bass, McAlester
Jim Bellatti, Stillwater
Ed Boynton, Durant
Bob Burke, Oklahoma City
G. Bridger Cox, Ardmore
Andy Coats, Oklahoma City
Betty Crow, Altus

Ford Drummond, Bartlesville
Cy Elmburg, Miami
Clyde Estes, Henryetta
Patti Evans, Ponca City
Christy Everest, Oklahoma City
John Feaver, Chickasha
Vaughndean Fuller, Tulsa
Gilbert "Gib" Gibson, Lawton
C. Hubert Gragg, Newcastle
Jean Harbison, Lawton
Fred Harlan, Okmulgee
Pat Henry, Lawton
Ernest L. Holloway, Langston
Jane Jayroe, Oklahoma City
Larry Lee, Tulsa
Duke Ligon, Oklahoma City
Dave Lopez, Oklahoma City
John Massey, Durant
J.W. McLean, Frisco, Texas
Mary Mélon, Oklahoma City
John W. Nichols, Oklahoma City
C.D. Northcutt, Ponca City
Suzanne O'Brien, Tulsa
Deane H. Oven, Tulsa
Leslie Paris, Tulsa
Gregory E. Pyle, Durant
Carl R. Renfro, Ponca City
Sharon Shoulders, Henryetta
Lee Allan Smith, Oklahoma City
Stan Stamper, Hugo
Mark Stansberry, Edmond
G. Lee Stidham, Checotah
Harold Stuart, Jensen Beach, FL
Chuck Thompson, Norman
Ty Tyler, Oklahoma City
J. Blake Wade, Oklahoma City
Peter M. Walter, Tulsa
Hardy Watkins, Oklahoma City

OKLAHOMA HERITAGE ASSOCIATION
1400 CLASSEN DRIVE
OKLAHOMA CITY, OKLAHOMA 73106

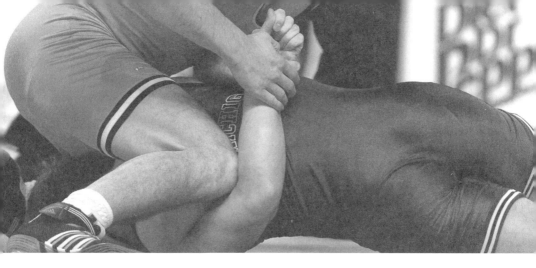

table of contents

acknowledgments

I START WITH COACH JOHN SMITH, who granted me unfettered access to his team's practices, meetings, coaches' conferences, hotel hallway admonitions, locker room talks, and countless other encounters, for an entire season. He sat patiently for hours as I asked questions. He did so, I believe, because of his love of the sport, his devotion to his alma mater, and his belief in the project. I am forever grateful.

Almost without exception, each and every member of the Cowboy wrestling family availed themselves and helped tell this story. This group included Cowboy wrestlers Rusty Blackmon, Michael Christian, Eric Dabbs, Ryan Davis, Ronnie Delk, Jake Duke, Zack Esposito, Derrick Fleenor, Ryan Freeman, Daniel Frishkorn, Johny Hendricks, Taylor Hosick, B. J. Jackson, Jack Jensen, Clay Kehrer, Ethan Kyle, Sam Lewnes, Brandon Mason, Newly McSpadden, Steve Mocco, Nathan Morgan, Brett Munson, Brent Parkey, Chris Pendleton, Justin Porter, Jake Rosholt, Coleman Scott, Clark Shouse, Derek Stevens, and Kevin Ward; media relations coordinator for wrestling Chris Matthews; team physician Dr. Tom Allen; team manager Randy Pogue; strength and conditioning coach Gary Calcagno; head trainer Chris Pickering and assistant trainer Sarah Tackett; Cowboy assistant head coach and assistant coaches Mark Branch, Eric Guerrero and Pat Smith; and administrative staff members Jessi King, Melissa White, and Maggie White.

Special thanks goes to Brandy Baker, Director of Operations for Cowboy wrestling, as this project hit the home stretch. Along with the

Cowboy wrestlers, coaches, and staff, the following sat for interviews or engaged in conversations with the author: Joe Azevado, Kami Barcini, Daniel Cormier, George Day, Ron Good, Congressman Jim Jordan, Colin Kuchinic, Muhammed Lawal, Tyrone Lewis, Dan McCool, Joe Mocco, Joe Mocco Jr., Roger Moore, Teague Moore, Larry Morgan, Mike Moyer, Shane Roller, Lee Roy Smith Jr., Lee Roy Smith III, and Johnny Thompson. I also give hearty thanks to the unnamed fans, wrestlers, officials and members of the wrestling culture whose ear I bent as the Cowboys traveled the nation.

Chris Matthews, media relations coordinator par excellent, was in on this deal from literally the first moment. I was only one of a very large group whom he assisted and helped through a very busy season. He was unflappable, organized and professional in all of our dealings.

Manager and operations specialist Randy Pogue allowed me to tag along and observe how things got done behind the scenes. Many people help set the table before the Cowboys take the mat, and Randy was always on point for Coach Smith and the entire team. If gold medals were awarded in his field, he would join many multi-winners in the Cowboy wrestling room.

Dr. Tom Allen, Chris Hoffman, Chris Pickering and George Shenold made the long bus rides manageable, and countless after-match meals enjoyable and interesting.

Several friends and wrestling fans reviewed the manuscript, but two in particular stand out. No one has a better eye for the story and heart for the sport than *Stillwater News Press* Sports Editor and Cowboy wrestling beat-writer Roger Moore. Broadcasting legend J. Carl Guymon may be properly described as a national treasure of wrestling knowledge, particularly as it relates to Oklahoma State. These two friends offered perspective and corrections that the author would never have snagged.

Oklahoma State Assistant Athletic Director Scott Williams reviewed the manuscript and provided helpful suggestions.

Jim Bowen, Dr. Jeremy Cook and Mika Metzer snap thousands of pictures each season of Cowboy wrestling, and they made their trove of pictures available for this work. Also providing pictures were Del City, Oklahoma High School journalism teacher Brook Bullock, Jeffrey G. Nolan, Northern

Iowa University, the University of Minnesota, and Brian Ballweg (Hofstra University Athletics).

I am indebted to Gini Moore Campbell of the Oklahoma Heritage Association for her skillful copy-editing of the manuscript, which has saved me from innumerable infelicities.

Quotations at the beginning of each chapter are from Kathy Etling's *The Quotable Cowboy* (Guilford, Connecticut: The Lyons Press, 2002).

I am also grateful for the love and support throughout the process received from my wife Sarah Lee and our daughter Caroline. They became college wrestling fans along the way—and each giggled at this project from day one, partially because of the delight I took in it.

The O.S.U. wrestling White Jacket Club's support throughout the years has helped the Cowboys compete at the highest level. Particular thanks for their assistance on this endeavor.

Finally, my gratitude to the Rev. Dr. Greg Headington, whose passion and generosity made the project possible.

—KIM D. PARRISH

foreword

by John W. Smith

FEW UNDERSTAND THE SACRIFICES college wrestlers make to attain the highest echelons of their sport. That is one reason I allowed Judge Parrish to travel with the 2004-2005 Cowboy wrestling squad, and prepare a behind-the-scenes account of a complete season—the highs and the lows— to be documented and presented to the general public in book form. The story of Oklahoma State wrestling needs to be told time and again. What a story it is.

There have been some great Oklahoma State teams. Coach Gallagher's 1928 squad crowned four national champions, and captured the first NCAA team title ever awarded. In the ensuing seventy-seven seasons, OSU has won an unbelievable 34 NCAA team championships. Five of those Cowboy teams crowned four individual champions, but the 2004-2005 Oklahoma State team may be the greatest in our history. That team was 21-0 in duals, won the NWCA National Duals and the Big 12 championship, captured the NCAA team title by seventy points, and crowned an unprecedented five national champions. It represented a unique blend of talent and chemistry, along with a heavy dose of perhaps the most important ingredient necessary in the heart of a champion—the ability to respond to adversity. *Cowboy Up* chronicles that process.

From my time as a small boy from Del City, Oklahoma, where I was pinned in my first five matches, wrestling has meant so much to me. The sport provided me with a college education, allowed me to travel the world representing my country, provided a framework for my family to support and love one another, introduced me to fellow competitors in countries across the globe, and now has allowed me to help carry on the Cowboy wrestling tradition for my alma mater.

No one has ever compiled a comprehensive story of a Cowboy wrestling team the way Judge Parrish has. Through thoughtful questions posed while we sat on buses, airplanes and vans, in locker rooms, hotel lobbies and wrestling rooms across America, he looked behind won-loss records, and delved into motivations, thought-processes, and methods, as I made the sometimes-painful transition from competitor to coach.

My favorite part of *Cowboy Up* might be each individual wrestler's story along the way, both mentally and physically, as the student-athlete absorbed the most challenging and invigorating chapter of his life. Believe me—every recruit comes into our program with a distinct set of talents and challenges—and this book tells those wonderful and sometimes heartbreaking stories with diligence, sensitivity and acute observation.

Cowboy Up reveals a good number of the coaching philosophies I have learned, through a process of trial and error, over the past eighteen seasons. Collegiate wrestling has continued to become more and more competitive, and some coaches are understandably reluctant to share what they have learned. It is my conviction that United States wrestling benefits if we coaches harness our collective capability to spur innovation, growth and success in our sport at all levels of competition. I think of my own wrestling coaches—from grade school through the Olympics—and the fine coaches I have competed against, who taught me important lessons along the way. I am particularly mindful of the late Tommy Chesbro, my first college coach, who served as my mentor, teacher, motivator and friend. In many areas, particularly in teaching techniques, he set the standard.

In my wrestling life, and in the careers of my wrestlers, the line between being a champion and one who never sees his dreams come true is such a fragile and delicate wrinkle—and it often involves mental processes more than physical brawn. *Cowboy Up* sheds light on the unfathomable mysteries of that process.

—JOHN W. SMITH
Head Wrestling Coach
Oklahoma State University
Stillwater, Oklahoma
April 2007

I WAS CURIOUS what it was like behind the scenes of the most successful athletic program in intercollegiate sports history…especially in a sport considered by those who know it as the toughest competition in college athletics. I wrestled in high school, and the sport taught me a bit about engaging in a process with an end in mind, taking personal responsibility for my mistakes and failures, and facing difficult tasks, if only for the most remote and unpromised hope of a glorious payoff. I read stories about United States Senators, an award-winning writer, industrialists, an astronaut, the author of the Emancipation Proclamation, and a Nobel Prize winner who seemed to regard competitive wrestling as the pivotal experience of their young lives. There was something to this sport that seemed to seep into people and stain their souls with glorious ink.

So I asked John Smith, the legendary head wrestling coach of the Oklahoma State University Cowboys, if I could travel with his team for a season and record my observations in book form. Much to my surprise, he said "yes." So I tagged along the next 18 weeks, as the Cowboys traveled almost 16,000 miles by bus, plane, van, and automobile to 12 different states, through four time zones, in and out of 10 hotels as they wrestled 21 dual matches and four tournaments against bone-hard competition.

The team saw the sun rise over New York City and slip behind a golden Pacific horizon. It felt the biting winter wind knife through Cleveland and tramped through wet snow in Lincoln. It found rest on an airport carpet in Reno and in a bus hurling across the winter-crusted plains of Iowa.

I witnessed countless afternoon practices in the Cowboy wrestling room while the team gathered a collective identity as a distinctive culture where deeds trumped words, and special opportunity took on the form of facing the common enemies of fear, hunger, history, and desperate opponents.

The team sat in stuffy hotel hallways, dank locker rooms, and darkened buses as Coach Smith talked about the privilege of being the hunted ones. I watched and took notes as the wrestlers trained, traveled, pulled weight, studied, bled, starved, fought, prayed, cried, competed, slept, waited, worried, laughed, screamed, cursed, whispered, and held onto hope. All for only one end in mind.

I am trained as a lawyer and not a journalist. My eye is for detail and patterns and not story lines and drama. But to my great surprise, the process lent itself to both. It is a story of newcomers getting their chance and veterans losing their way. It is a story of brotherly love and family betrayal. It is about the power of expectations and the blunt, cold truth of not measuring up. It is a tale about boys becoming men, a coach becoming a teacher, and a group becoming a team. But most of all, it is a story that needs to be told.

Wrestling is a sport devoid of self-indulgence, empty talk, and misrepresentation. Weaknesses cannot be swept under the rug, and no counterfeit champions are crowned. False impressions and shoddy goods are quickly and ruthlessly revealed. There is an attention to detail which demands discipline and objectivity. Longfellow described the craftsmen of old who cut no corners, even on those details and form others would not notice.

In the elder days of art
Builders wrought with greatest care
Each minute and unseen part
For the Gods are everywhere[1]

Such are the wrestlers who correlate deed and word, true to particulars as well as context, who bleed for truth and strain for victory.

This is one version of their story by one who has seen.

—KIM D. PARRISH
Oklahoma City, Oklahoma
November 2006

YOU'VE GOT TO GET THE JOB DONE,
WHATEVER IT TAKES—
THAT'S THE COWBOY WAY.

—Cody Lambert, quoted in *Gold Buckle* (1995)

<h1 style="text-align:center">one</h1>

03.19.05

THE LEFT UPPER HEMISPHERE of his scraped, gaunt face carried the purple hue of a ripened plum. His left eye was swollen and tumid. He wore the skin-tight orange singlet for the most successful team in collegiate sports history. His name was Zack Esposito. He was a son of New Jersey. He was about to wrestle for the national championship.

Esposito glanced at the cluster of 2,000 fans, clad in orange and cheering his name, but their noise was swamped by the roar of 20,000 partisans who chanted in unison "Army – Army – Army." The public address announcer let loose an emotional kerosene that spurred the anti-Oklahoma State crowd even more when he declared Esposito's opponent, a West Point cadet who would soon be deployed for Iraq to serve out his military commitment.

On the elevated platform sat the Cowboy coaches, flanked by team trainer Chris Pickering and longtime team physician Dr. Tom Allen. Over the past 16 weeks the robust Dr. Allen, a former varsity pole vaulter and past dean of the OSU medical school, had treated virtually every team member for various broken noses, fractured ribs, chipped teeth, twisted knees, torn ligaments, jammed vertebrae, poked-eyes, bit tongues, and elbows grotesquely bent against the joint. Now their eyes were on the Cowboy 149 pounder.

While Esposito warmed up during the ESPN commercial timeout, teammates waited below in a dank dressing room crammed in the innards of the arena. They grew up in farming hamlets, bedroom communities, urban sprawl, and county seats from the wine country of northern California and the outskirts of New York City to the wheat fields of Oklahoma and the craggy mountains of Idaho.

As small boys, they began wrestling and roughhousing with older brothers, good friends, or fathers in living rooms and graveled playgrounds. Many were natural athletes who excelled in other sports year round. Others were too small to stand out in games that required bulk and height; all they could offer was boundless energy and a will beyond their years.

Along the way they found wrestling, and the sport became their home. As they grew older and taller, they discovered a special talent to always end up on top. As defeats became more and more uncommon, recruiting calls became more and more recurrent, and dreams of glory took hold. In the end, they longed to wrestle for Oklahoma State University under the guidance of their hero, Olympic champion John Smith.

Oklahoma State is college sport's rendition of the New York Yankees, except the Cowboys have won with greater frequency. *Sports Illustrated* referred to the land-grant university located an hour north of Oklahoma City as "the Juilliard School of wrestling." Since 1928, when the NCAA began sponsoring a wrestling championship, OSU has carried away 34 national championships, more titles in one sport than any other school, and more than all of the Notre Dame football and UCLA basketball championships combined. During that span, 80 Oklahoma State wrestlers won 132 individual NCAA championships, and on six occasions the Cowboys produced four NCAA champions in eight possible weights. OSU recorded unbeaten dual match streaks of 70, 73, and 84, crowned more All-Americans than any school in the nation, and compiled a dual match record of 842-87-20 in 82 years of competition. Since 1924, some 36 OSU wrestlers qualified for the United States Olympic team. Nine Cowboy wrestlers brought home a total of 11 gold medals, a higher medal count than some 35 countries.

On this night, Esposito was wrestling to become the Cowboy's 126th NCAA champion. He was a native of Three Bridges, New Jersey, and had captured three high school state titles while competing for Blair Academy, a private boarding school tucked in northwest New Jersey and known for mass-producing Division I wrestling talent. Three older brothers introduced the social studies education major who aspired one day to be a college

Zack Esposito struggles for position against Army's Phillip Simpson in the NCAA finals. *Courtesy Dr. Jeremy Cook.*

wrestling coach, to the sport. "I grew up around the sport my whole life. I got suckered into it, to tell you the truth."[2]

The olive-skinned, brown-haired Esposito possessed the silhouette of a Roman centurion. According to Coach Smith, he "brings the rest of the team up"[3] with a single-minded passion to become a dominating world-class wrestler on the national and international scene. The diligent student, who each day devised a daily game plan on "how to get better,"[4] chose Oklahoma State even though his three brothers were outstanding wrestlers at other institutions. Highly recruited by Lehigh, Esposito chose "… to take my own path and do something on my own."[5] Although this was his third year removed from New Jersey, the wavy-haired Italian was adapting still to small-town university community life. He occasionally rode horses outside Stillwater with teammates but had not yet developed a deep and abiding love for the quaint charms of rural middle-America. "All we hear in here is country music. I fall asleep listening to that stuff."[6]

Excellent from the standing position, his mode most resembled Coach Smith's protocol of relentless and constant attack. "A lot of the great wrestlers dominate on their feet. You go back and look at Coach John's matches where he just tears guys up on his feet."[7]

Although Esposito was equipped to deliver a barbarous and unyielding torrent of offense, Coach Smith worried that Esposito needed to shore up his defensive skills, and sometimes lost his train of thought during a match. But he recognized Esposito's tapeworm appetite to become an NCAA champion, and according to the Cowboy coach, "...the hungry guys usually win."[8] When asked which of his career victories had been the most gratifying, the Cowboy junior stared straight ahead and turned quiet for more than a moment. "I haven't won the big one yet. That one will be the most satisfying."[9]

Esposito, pulled out of redshirt status during his freshman year, won 25 matches and defeated 13 nationally-ranked opponents that initial campaign. A gritty competitor when facing difficult opposition in pressure situations, he recorded falls over archrivals Iowa and Oklahoma in tight dual matches, defeated a defending national champion on the road, and placed second at the Big 12 Championships. But a devastated Esposito failed to place at the NCAA tournament, and entered his true sophomore year absorbed by his dream to become an NCAA champion. During that second year he racked up 33 victories, went 19-1 against ranked opponents, won the Big 12 Championship, and advanced to the NCAA finals where he faced Jesse Jantzen of Harvard in the NCAA title match. He lost again.

Esposito's journey to the 2005 national finals began 363 days earlier, the Monday after his loss to Jantzen in the national finals. That following summer the determined Esposito served as a camp counselor in wrestling camps across the country and continued to train. In late August, he joined teammates in Stillwater for volunteer preseason workouts in the quixotic Cowboy wrestling room, a process that began just days after the 2004 NCAA Tournament ended.

Coach Smith gave the five returning NCAA qualifiers (Esposito, Hendricks, Pendleton, Blackmon and Rosholt) two weeks off to recover from the physical and mental rigors of the previous season. Each wrestler then met with Assistant Director of Strength and Conditioning Gary Calcagno, who designed a weight-training program for the entire thirty-man roster. "In early April we began Phase One with a three-day per week metabolic circuit. The routine began with a back squat to elevate the testosterone level. Every major body part was covered. Three timed sets of 10 repetitions flushed out lactic acid, and helped the body get ready to make strength and power gains. This phase extended through June."

The muscular, dark-haired Italian son of two college professors, Calcagno approached his task with the intensity and studied fervor of an architect building a high-rise. "[After the NCAA's] I met with Coach Smith to decide who needed to be on a 4-day or 3-day a week training program through the summer. Once that was determined, we developed Phase Two, a 12-week training cycle. [That summer] was special—most of the starters were in Stillwater for the entire three months. Each workout lasted about ninety minutes. Except for [Steve] Mocco—he went about two hours. He and Esposito were the leaders in the weight-room. Coleman Scott, even though he was an incoming freshman, had an impressive work ethic you hoped to see in older guys. Johny [Hendricks] wasn't dialed in yet. But if one guy's intensity stood out, it was [senior-to-be Jake] Rosholt. He was relentless. He had a look in his eyes."

"In September, Phase Three began. That time was devoted to major strength and size gains, and every wrestler was put on a four-day per week lifting cycle. It was a great time for team building. Everyone gathered at the same time each morning to lift. Explosive lifts and mass building was crammed into four weeks.

" In October, we began the In-Season Phase, where the guys reported in the morning, or between classes, to fit in a workout. That phase continued into early November—then the intensity of the workouts was ratcheted up. Until the end of the season [December-March], starters lifted two days per week. One day was a total body, explosive lift. The other day we worked on our Hammer Strength Push-Pull equipment…six specially designed machines that focused on total body, multi-joint movements, and core stabilization. Guys went through three or four sets of ten reps on each machine—followed by a 30-second rest period at the end of each set. This phase lasted until the end of the regular season. And remember—these workouts were in addition to the afternoon wrestling practices that went for a couple of hours—where guys would lose 15 pounds and burn 5,000 calories."

A year-round, sophisticated, weight-training program for a college wrestling team had been unheard of during John Smith's years as a competitor at Oklahoma State. "OSU wrestling had never had a bona fide strength coach before, and Coach Smith was cautious at first." But after seeing the results, according to Calcagno, Smith became a believer. "[American University Head Wrestling Coach] Mark Cody was an assistant at OSU at the time. He had been an assistant at Nebraska earlier, and observed how their football program developed strength in their offensive and defensive lineman. He advocated to Coach Smith the value of a structured strength and conditioning program for wrestling. Coach [Smith] kept his eye on me that first year, but now he cuts me loose and lets me work."

Calcagno recognized early on that wrestlers were unique in their outlook. "They are the hardest working, most disciplined, most intense,

UPPER RIGHT: Cowboy wrestlers train year-round in the 30,000-square foot strength and conditioning facility, under the direction of strength and conditioning coach Gary Calcagno. *Courtesy Kim Parrish.*

RIGHT: Gary Calcagno, Cowboy Strength and Conditioning Coach for wrestling, believes the wrestlers are among the toughest and most dedicated athletes in college athletics.: *Courtesy Oklahoma State University.*

most passionate athletes I have been around. You don't worry about them slacking off like guys sometimes do in other sports." The 15 male and female OSU athletic teams work out year round in the massive weight-training facility, the size of a small department store, located below Gallagher-Iba Arena. Athletes from the various sports often interacted—but not so the wrestlers. "The wrestlers run from exercise to exercise. Not a real sociable bunch when they're lifting." Calcagno's duties didn't include advice on nutrition and diet. "Most of these guys have been pulling weight so long—they have their own system. You don't want to mess up their process."

The wrestling complex is located in the newly-constructed $56 million OSU Athletic Center, a comprehensive superstructure that serves as home to Cowboy sports. Unique in all of college athletics, the architectural magnum opus included an academic counseling center, the 30,000-foot strength and conditioning facility, and sports medicine facility, all built around a 13,611-seat coliseum, called "the best arena in the country."[10] The original "Gallagher Hall" was built in 1938 and dubbed by the college sporting world as "The Madison Square Gardens of the Plains." The 6,381-seat gymnasium, named after Cowboy wrestling coach Ed Gallagher, was the only arena in the nation to bear the name of a college wrestling coach. In 1988 the facility was renamed Gallagher-Iba Arena by former wrestling coach and then-athletic director Myron Roderick. Ironically, Gallagher, while serving as

Coach Smith poses with Hendricks, Roshalt, Mocco and Esposito in the Cowboy wrestling room. Pictures of the eighty Cowboy NCAA champions, the first one crowned in 1928, hang in the background. *Courtesy Dr. Jeremy Cook.*

the Oklahoma A&M athletic director in 1934, hired 30-year old Henry Iba as the schools' head basketball coach. Together their Oklahoma State teams accounted for 905 wins and 13 NCAA titles. Now the Cowboy arena bore their names, and was home to 48 national championship banners, exceeded only by Stanford, USC and UCLA.

Imbedded in the second floor of the massive brick structure was the fabled OSU wrestling room. Half the length of a football field with walls paneled in orange protective padding, the rectangle room was carpeted with three orange wrestling mats. Traumatized freshmen, pinned to their backs for the first time in years by grizzled veterans, read the word "COWBOYS" spelled out in large, black ceiling tiles. Unlike many of the other practice facilities the Cowboys would visit in the upcoming 14 weeks, no inspirational sayings or mission statements adorned the walls. The words "Oklahoma State Wrestling" were imprinted under a line of windows across the west wall. On the south wall a four-foot mural featuring seven horsemen stampeding across the plains was silhouetted in black. Engraved plaques, bearing the names of collegiate and Olympic Cowboy champions through the century, hung on one wall. On the far end of the room a training table sat next to two orange water coolers. The well-lit and ultra-modern facility was a far cry from the windowless dungeon that had served as the Cowboy practice room from 1939 into the 1980s. Wedged in the lower intestine of the old Gallagher Hall, the showers were cramped, ceiling pipes dripped onto the mats, and the same dank, sweat-laced air seemed to circulate season after season.

Ironically, those early baby-boomer days were the golden years of collegiate wrestling, both at Oklahoma State and around the nation. That era predated the popularity of college basketball, which had been considered just another winter sport wedged into the dead zone between football season and spring training. The first NCAA basketball tournament was held in Kansas City in 1937, with a field comprised mostly of teams from the Midwest. New York, with a more substantial fan base from which to draw travel funds, staged the first truly national collegiate competition in 1938 when it sponsored the inaugural National Invitation Tournament.

In contrast, the first NCAA wrestling tournament had been held 10 years earlier. The 1928 wrestling championship was only the third national championship sport established by the NCAA, after track and field and swimming, and featured wrestlers from across the nation, with an emphasis on Eastern and Midwestern schools.

During that popular era of college wrestling, both basketball and wrestling thrived at Oklahoma State. Legendary basketball coach Henry Iba arrived at Oklahoma State, then known as Oklahoma A&M, in 1934 and over the next 36 years won 655 games and two NCAA titles. During the same interval, Cowboy wrestlers assembled a dual meet record of 281-18-13 and stormed to twenty-one NCAA championships. Throughout those decades, Gallagher Hall was routinely sold out for wrestling matches. Fan popularity for wrestling rivaled, and often exceeded, that of basketball. The competition between schools was vigorous and dramatic, and the matches often visited the realm of the bizarre. Students stood in line to fill the 6,381 seats. During epic matches against rivals like Oklahoma and Iowa State, fire marshals looked away as standing-room only crowds exceeded 8,000. Matches against in-state rival Oklahoma, referred to by local media outlets as "The

Bedlam Series" because of its raucous and chaotic nature, were often televised statewide.

The rules of competition during that era contributed to close, low-scoring, competitive contests that were personalized and dramatic. The boisterous, emotional crowds that shook the floor gave the event a special flair and drama. In terms of fan popularity, those were the glory years of collegiate wrestling. But two separate, unrelated events made their way into the collegiate sports environment and chilled the popularity of college wrestling in the late '70s.

The first was the rise in popularity of televised college basketball. John Wooden's UCLA teams ushered in the classic 1979 NCAA finals match-up between Michigan and Indiana State that featured Magic Johnson and Larry Bird. CBS's coverage of college basketball subsequently exploded, resulting in a windfall of cash that flowed into athletic departments' coffers. College basketball coaches began doubling and tripling the salaries of their university presidents. Network announcers became more popular and well known than Nobel Prize winners. The funding for other secondary sports such as wrestling, even at schools like Oklahoma State, became marginalized. Media coverage of basketball mushroomed at the expense of low-revenue secondary sports.

To keep up with other schools in this arms race for college basketball prominence, OSU upgraded its arena and hired OSU alumnus Eddie Sutton as head basketball coach in 1990. Sutton quickly built the program into one of the elite teams in big-time college basketball, but the poularity of college basketball, spurred on by ESPN's heavy coverage, came at the expense of wrestling in terms of fan support, student backing, and media attention. Fans spent finite recreational resources on basketball instead of wrestling. Water-cooler chat revolved around office brackets. News entities reported on college basketball instead of the NCAA wrestling tournament, which was inconspicuously wedged in the middle of the three-week period in early spring known as March Madness.

The second factor which led to the depression of college wrestling's popularity was the advent of Title IX legislation—the collection of federal laws passed in 1972 which shifted monetary resources in athletic departments from secondary sports such as wrestling, swimming, and gymnastics to women's basketball, softball, and volleyball. As a result, scores of universities eliminated numerous wrestling programs around the country, and the popularity of college wrestling began to decline.

During that interval the Cowboys were perennial top-10 finishers in the NCAA tournament. Still they could not pierce the competitive veil Iowa coach and legendary wrestler Dan Gable held over the college wrestling world from 1978 to 1997, when his teams won 15 NCAA team titles.

On April 4, 1983, everything changed.

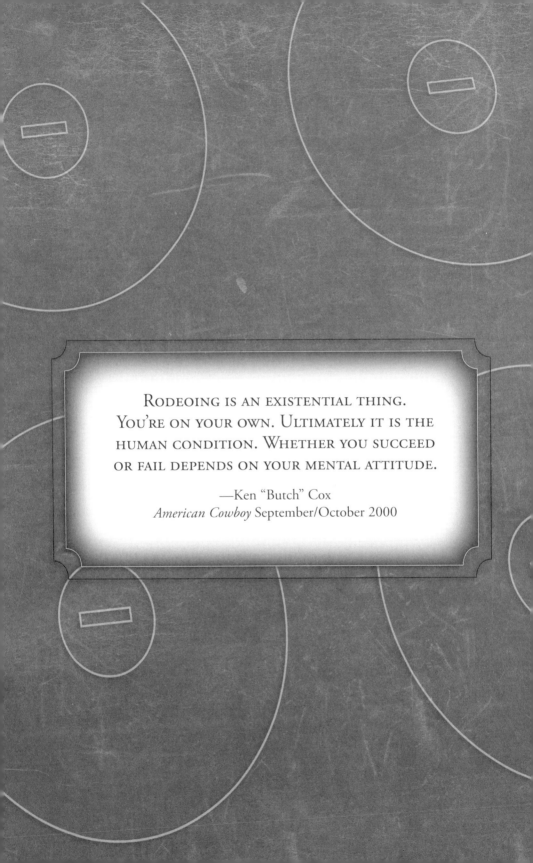

Rodeoing is an existential thing.
You're on your own. Ultimately it is the
human condition. Whether you succeed
or fail depends on your mental attitude.

—Ken "Butch" Cox
American Cowboy September/October 2000

two

john w. smith

THE CROWD NOISE caused round light bulbs in the ceiling to burst, sending a mist of shattered and powered white glass to float onto the arena floor. A 13-year-old boy with olive skin and dark, wavy hair sat on the edge of the orange mat and crouched down, gripping a white towel wrapped tightly in white trainer's tape. As the seconds on the digital clock wound down, the boy's eyes were fixed on the scorer's table as he walked onto the mat behind the trembling official like a boy sneaking up on a feeding frenzy. At the scorer's signal, he tapped the official's shoulder with the towel. The hand of the wrestler wearing the orange singlet was raised in victory, and the boy stepped quickly off the mat and resumed his crouch, waiting for the next match to commence. The slightly built boy's name was John Smith, and although he could hardly defend himself against the onslaught of his six sisters, he liked wrestling. He was the younger brother of Cowboy wrestler Lee Roy Smith, who an hour earlier had won the 1978 Big 8 wrestling championship as Oklahoma State captured its twenty-fourth conference title.

Twelve years earlier Lee Roy Smith, III, a fourth grader at Epperly Elementary in Del City, Oklahoma, returned from school with what seemed to be innocuous news. A teacher, who doubled as the school's wrestling coach, noticed the young Smith boy's playground agility and urged him to try out for the wrestling team. Lee Roy joined the squad, and in doing so set in motion a chain of events and accomplishments that realigned the wrestling world for the next three decades.

The Inner Rage. John William Smith, the seventh child of 10, was born on August 9, 1965, to Lee Roy and Madalene Smith. On a bus late one night in 2005, as headlights bore into the night and his wrestling team rested behind him, John quietly and respectfully observed that as he grew into being a man, he never thought much about becoming a spitting image of his mother. "But I have," he said.[1] Perhaps he caught the physical resemblance as he glanced in a mirror. Maybe he thought of other qualities that prompt a man to stand up and be counted.

Madalene, a registered labor and delivery nurse, worked the same shift in the Mercy Hospital pediatric ward in Oklahoma City for more than 40 years. She assisted in the delivery of thousands of babies, but could not bear to watch her four sons wrestle. Husband Lee Roy understood, "She just doesn't like to go, she gets nervous. She follows them very close, she's very knowledgeable about the sport. She attends a lot of the events, but when it comes their time to get on the mat, if she's in the gym you can't find her."[2] John's mother passed on olive skin, deep brown eyes, dark hair, raging devotion, and a measure of athletic ability to her son. Lee Roy recognized Madalene's athletic bearing soon after they met. "Their mother was a good athlete, too, an excellent basketball player. The Little Dixie Queens down at Ada tried to get Madalene to go to Central State University, and they'd pay her way and she could play for their team, but she chose not to and went into nursing instead."[3] On that bus ride John reflected, "I am in awe of what my mother accomplished. I didn't appreciate it at the time but what she did was unbelievable."[4] A devoted Catholic, the deeply religious matriarch of the Smith clan routinely slipped Bible verses into John's workout bag before matches. "It's part of his motivation. He's got his tricky ways."[5] In partnership with husband Lee Roy, the Smiths raised and educated 10 accomplished children.

John's father, Lee Roy Smith, Jr., was a star athlete in football, basketball, and baseball at Southeast High School in Oklahoma City. After completing his schooling, the young father interviewed for an entry-level computer programmer position at the Oklahoma Department of Transportation. Computer science courses were as rare as wrestling programs in the age of Dwight D. Eisenhower and John F. Kennedy, but the intelligent and resourceful Smith learned the trade and programmed computers until his retirement. Wrestling programs were sparse during the 1950s, so when his namesake Lee Roy came home from school and announced he was joining the wrestling team, his father inquired, "What's that?"

Strong helpings of family, church, education, and wrestling sustained the Smith household. Said father Lee Roy, a former member of the Del City School Board and parish council at St. Paul Roman Catholic Church, "We're blessed by God, and we have a very tight-knit family, we care for each other, we support each other. The first thing is our church, being able to be a part of and have that large of a support group. And wrestling. I don't mean the success in wrestling, the whole family has participated in the sport of wrestling in some way."[6] He described the raising of his family as "an enjoyable struggle."[7] He recalled with a rueful grin, "We wanted a large family. Madalene always said we were going to have a big family. I just wish she had told me a number."[8]

John recalled the realities of sharing space with nine siblings. "It seemed like there was a wrestling tournament in the living room every night. Sometimes it was more important to win that tournament than the real tournament you did on Saturday. There were several tough matches and it wasn't always with your brother. There was a little hair pullin' and scratchin' and probably some biting going on. It was intense. A lot of furniture got broke[n]."[9] Summers were spent swimming at the public pool, water skiing at the nearby lake, and skateboarding with buddies on the streets of blue-collar Del City, Oklahoma, a suburb of Oklahoma City. A running back in football and outfielder in baseball, young John participated in several sports in elementary school. When Lee Roy was named Oklahoma's top high school wrestler in the spring of 1976, the nine-year-old John had been wrestling with his older brother for five years. Madalene Smith witnessed from her kitchen window an "inner rage"[10] in the soft-spoken, gentle, and slightly built John, who gave up fifty pounds and seven years to his older brother in merciless backyard brawls that involved bloody noses and swollen lips. "They were fist-fighting. And you could see the hatred, the hostility in their eyes. You know what I think it was? Lee Roy was a little bit better than John. John couldn't take that. The fight started over Lee Roy taking John down. But really, it was the fact that John couldn't dominate over Lee Roy."[11]

ABOVE: John Smith captured two Oklahoma high school state titles and was named a high school All-American while wrestling for the Del City, Oklahoma Eagles. *Courtesy Del City High School*

Lee Roy remembered his second son's emulative spirit was elevated at a young age. "All of the boys were successful from the start. They all had the God-given ability to be wrestlers. John was always very competitive. I don't care if it was tiddly-winks."[12]

The Defeats. Smith survived living room beatings at the hands of his older brother and sisters, won 105 of his 110 high school matches, and became a high-school All-American and two-time state champion at Del City High School. According to Smith, he was not a "blue chip recruit" and no one was taken by surprise when on April 14, 1983 John announced his decision to follow Lee Roy to Stillwater.

Weeks before reporting to OSU, Smith initiated his freestyle wrestling career by losing in the finals of the junior freestyle championships to Mikolai Garkine of Russia 9-6 and later finishing fourth in the national junior tournament, losing to fellow OSU recruit Tim Balzeski.

At the beginning of his freshman season, Smith, who competed at 136 pounds in high school and who weighed in the low 150s during the off-season, was expected to drop a weight class to 126 in order to accommodate OSU coach Tommy Chesbro's lineup plans. But first he had to make a team whose starting lineup included six Oklahoma recruits, and standing in his way was former freestyle opponent Balzeski. Demonstrating an uncanny ability to learn from losses, Smith drummed the Michigan prep star 16-5 in a ranking match, prompting the demoralized Balzeski to leave the team. According to Cowboy coaches, John Smith had "All-American potential."[13]

Smith joined a talented Cowboy squad that had finished a distant second to Iowa the preceding year but believed it possessed the necessary talent to overtake Gable's squad, which had won the previous five NCAA titles.

The Cowboy coaches gave Smith the option to sit out his freshman year and retain four years of eligibility, but the impatient Smith was ready to compete. Out of the gate the young and promising Smith won eight of his first nine matches, including a 10-6 victory over third-ranked Scott Lynch of Penn State and fifth-ranked senior Mark Zimmer from Oklahoma. But his first taste of elite NCAA competition took place at an early-season tournament when former NCAA runner-up Kevin Darkus drummed the freshman 19-2. Smith acknowledged he was somewhat intimidated by his opponent's credentials and overtaken by the stronger Iowa State senior. "If I had gone out there and not known it was Kevin Darkus, it might have been a different match. It was mostly his strength that beat me. I couldn't really get anything going because he tied me up so much. I never really exploded like I should

BELOW: High school junior John Smith (far right) and his Del City teammates pose for a team picture. *Courtesy Del City High School.*

have, but I'll be coming back at him. I've got two or three more shots at him and next time it'll be better. It can't get any worse."[14]

Days later, in his first dual match against in-state rival Oklahoma, Smith survived two first-period takedowns and rallied back to tie Mark Zimmer 6-6. Smith met Darkus once again in the finals of the Midwest Championships in January, where he lost again but narrowed the margin to 9-4. Days later he met the No. 1-ranked Darkus for a third time in a dual match in Ames, and managed a 7-7 tie. In the Big 8 finals the two wrestled again, with Darkus hitting a first period five-point move in galloping to an 8-1 victory. Again, Smith noted how his opponent's superior strength seemed to make the difference. "He's enormously strong. The five-point cradle cost me the match. I stepped up and he caught my legs and I couldn't break it. At the end, when I had to bridge for so long, it took a lot out of me. I could feel myself getting closer to the mat."[15] The freshman Smith, on the strength of 28 wins in 32 matches, entered his first national tournament seeded number three in his weight. "Both of my losses were against the number one seed. I had high expectations."[16]

In the opening round Smith pinned John Aumiller of North Carolina in 1:03 but was stunned in the second round by 10th-seed Dan Foldesy of Cleveland State 6-2. When Foldesy lost in the next round, Smith was eliminated from competition and went home without a medal, his dream of becoming a four-time All-American vanquished. His nemesis Darkus won the title, and in-state rival Zimmer of Oklahoma placed seventh. Lynch, whom Smith had defeated earlier in the season in an open tournament, won the championship at 134. But Smith found no solace in these comparisons. "It was the most devastating defeat of my life. I sat on the top row of the Meadowlands [arena] in New Jersey and cried for what seemed like hours. My dreams were shattered."[17] The memory of that defeat seared into Smith, and would provide the impetus for future developments, but the motivation was not quick to settle in.

Weeks later the exhausted and discouraged Smith could not muster the desire to enter the National Open Freestyle Tournament, hosted that year in Stillwater and a precursor for qualifying for the Olympic team. "About an hour before the weigh-ins [my roommate] hit me on the head and said, 'Let's go weigh in.' I said, 'Hey, I'll get killed at 136.' But he dragged me up

Late Cowboy wrestling coach Tommy Chesboro offers John Smith instruction before one of his 154 collegiate victories. Smith considered Chesboro, whom he referred to as "my coach," to be one of the finest wrestling tacticians in the sport. *Courtesy Oklahoma State University.*

here, and here I am. And I'm glad I am."[18] Smith, who had not trained since the NCAA tournament two weeks prior, won four straight matches before falling to Iowa's Barry Davis 13-0 in the finals.

In the spring of 1984 Smith was competing in the shadow of older brother Lee Roy, the country's top-ranked 136.5-pound freestyle wrestler. "...Lee Roy can chew me up and spit me out as much as he wants. But he has taught me a lot. He's showed me a lot of stuff that's really helped in this tournament."[19] Smith's surprising performance that weekend boosted his confidence and provided the first installation in what would later become a trademark Smith training tool—vigorous training balanced with restorative rest. "To tell you the truth, I thought I'd be out of this tournament by this time. I really, honestly, did think that. I haven't worked out in two weeks, since the nationals [NCAA tournament]. I don't know what it is, it's really weird, because I feel like I'm in as good a shape now as I have been all year long."[20] Weeks later, the renewed Smith was the only United States winner in the 18 to 20-year-old-group competing in the Espoirs World Cup matches in Canada. In August he returned to Stillwater to train and prepare for his second season of collegiate wrestling, but this time under the guidance of a new head coach.

During the off-season, long-time Cowboy coach Tommy Chesboro had been fired by the athletic director who hired him fourteen years earlier, former OSU wrestling coach Myron Roderick. Joey Seay, the head coach of Division II powerhouse Cal-State Bakersfield, was chosen as Chesboro's successor. Roderick was clear in expressing the expectations imposed on the OSU wrestling coach. "I've talked to Joe and explained to him very plainly what the pleasures are and the responsibilities are at Oklahoma State University. Wrestling is a very unusual sport from the standpoint that you've only got two or three teams in the United States that have any capabilities at all in the NCAA [tournament]. Of course here at Oklahoma State we feel the capabilities we have are to be an NCAA champion. Of course, that doesn't mean we are going to be one every year, but we're going to do everything possible. We're fighting an uphill battle, there's no doubt about that, because of Dan Gable."[21]

Seay's strategy to challenge Gable's seven straight NCAA titles was to bring to OSU a style grounded in motion and conditioning as well as the traditional Cowboy virtues of strength and technique. The style was beneficial for

Smith's development, for it provided a framework for the lanky Smith, constructed more like a college golfer or an aspiring accountant than a square-jawed, thick-necked wrestler, to take advantage of his quickness and flexibility in order to neutralize stronger and more physical opponents.

By January 6, 1985, he was 27-1 and ranked third in the country at 134 pounds, with his only loss coming to No.1-ranked Jim Jordan of Wisconsin. A week later he moved up to second behind Jordan, but the Cowboy coaches still considered placing Smith at 126 to make room for another talented Cowboy to take over 134 and further solidify the lineup. But Smith, who weighed in the mid-140s during the days leading up to a weigh-in, was reluctant. "I'm scared that when I get down there [126] I'm not going to be strong enough to compete. I think it's going to change my wrestling, it's going to make me a different wrestler and I'm going to try a different technique because my strength won't be there. I'm not a real strong wrestler now, I rely on my slickness. In some situations I use my strength, but down there, most of my strength will be gone and I'll have to rely all on slickness. And that scares me. I don't know if my legs will hold up."[22]

Seay was concerned that Smith, who had added almost two inches in height as well as more muscle mass since the previous NCAA tournament, was simply too big to drop down a weight class. So he arranged for what at the time seemed to be an exotic testing process where "...Smith's body fat [would be] measured by a method in which he is immersed in water, as well as have him tested for hydration and dehydration potential. Those results should indicate Smith's physical capabilities at 126 pounds."[23]

The test results were not in the Cowboy coaches' hands when Wisconsin visited Stillwater on February 3, so Smith remained at 134 and faced No. 1- ranked Jim Jordan that same evening. In a match punctuated by defense and counter-wrestling, Jordan released Smith with twenty-two seconds remaining in a 0-0 third period, and attempted a match-winning last second takedown. Smith defended the last second shot, and won 1-0. He was pleased with the victory, which elevated him to the number one spot in *Amateur Wrestling News'* collegiate ratings, but was dispirited about his capacity to score takedowns. "I feel like I'm kind of in a slump right now on my feet, not much is happening with me on my feet, I can't get much going."[24]

Days later the Cowboys suffered their worst loss in school history, a 40-6 shellacking at the hands of Gable's Iowa squad. The Cowboys scored only three takedowns as a team, and Smith separated his shoulder in the first period of his match against third-ranked Greg Randall. Unable to continue wrestling, Smith was forced to default the match and saw his record drop to 28-2. Seay predicted the injury would keep Smith out of the lineup "...from a few days to the rest of the season,"[25] but Smith won the Big 8 tournament the following weekend with a sore shoulder taped to his side and only two days of practice under his belt.

Two weeks later the Cowboys traveled to Oklahoma City for the NCAA tournament. In the seeding meeting, where coaches decide on the tournament brackets, Smith relinquished his number one seed to Wisconsin's Jordan in a split vote, due in part to Smith's injury default against Iowa three weeks earlier. While the debate raged behind closed doors, Smith was philosophical about the process. "It's not important to me, you've got to beat them all. They're fighting it out right now between me and Jordan, but it doesn't matter."[26]

But his stunning and premature exit in the previous year's NCAA tournament still haunted him. "I was beaten by a senior who had a pretty good year but who was nowhere near my talent. I think the mistake freshmen make is overlooking their opponents. I was looking toward the semi-finals with [Michigan's Joe] McFarland, I already had my eyes on the semi-finals. And I got hit hard, but I learned, it was an experience."[27]

The seeded wrestlers won as predicted, and Smith advanced to the NCAA finals to meet Jordan for the third time of the season. The shoulder separation restricted his on-the-mat training, and much of his conditioning took the form of running stadium steps and performing half-speed drills. But Smith also was depleted emotionally from his semi-final win against Randall from Iowa the previous evening. "I gave it all I had in that [Randall] match. I was drained afterward. That was the toughest match I'd gone through in a long time."[28]

Jordan's motion style and superior strength leveraged a 7-4 win over Smith, who after the match attributed the loss to a deficit in conditioning. "He just gassed me out. That's all there was to it. I knew I wasn't in the best of shape but I had to take care of my shoulder [during the lost workout time] or I wouldn't even have been here. I'm not pleased with second but..."[29] The loss to Jordan forced Smith to interrogate reality and face his shortcomings. "I was never in the match. He out-skilled me, out-techniqued me, and out-powered me the entire match. My favorite moves were the high-crotch and duck under, but there was no way I could beat him with those moves."[30]

Even though Smith lost in the NCAA finals, he could look back on the first half of his college career with satisfaction. He had won sixty-five of his seventy-three matches, was ranked number one in the country for a portion of his sophomore season, captured a Big 8 individual title, and earned a runner-up finish at the NCAA tournament. "My emotional state after the loss to Jordan in the finals was not remotely close to my attitude after losing during my freshman year. Even though I lost to Jordan, I still finished second in the nation. I'm not sure there wasn't a little sense of satisfaction that I did place, after the devastation of not being able to come back and wrestle the previous year. There was a little part of me that accepted that second place finish. But as I went through the summer, the loss became as painful as a toothache. Here I am. I have two years left in college. I want to be the best wrestler in the world, and I haven't even won the NCAA tournament!"[31]

Such an aspiration seemed rather far-fetched and naive. "I came to OSU when I was 18. I had just turned 20, and if I didn't redshirt I would be 21 without any real focus on freestyle. With the '88 Games coming up, I sensed a real urgency in terms of time. I knew I was not going to win with power, but rather with skill. I accepted that responsibility and went forward."[32]

Age of Discovery. He informed the coaches of his desire to take a redshirt year and work on the deficiencies he perceived in his style. "Coach Seay was willing to give me a year off. During that season OSU was struggling, and at various times the coaches were ready to pull me out of my redshirt status. I went through three or four different meetings [with the coaches] and I fought it all the way. I was just making too much progress both technically and mentally to slow down. In the end Coach Seay supported what I was trying to accomplish. He allowed me to progress. He saw what I was trying to do, stepped aside, and didn't get in my way. It turned out to be the most important decision a coach ever made for me."[33]

Smith began his technical makeover by reflecting on the physical, strong styles employed by Darkus and Jordan, and the problems those styles had presented. "I knew I didn't have the power to stand still and muscle people. I understood I was going to have to move my feet to offset the power of my opponents. So I started to develop the low single."[34]

The low, single-leg takedown required Smith to attack his opponent's leg in the area between the upper ankle and lower knee with the speed of a hydraulic nail-gun piercing one's shin. Just as it is easier to leverage a heavy log from one end as opposed to lifting the middle, Smith attacked the opponent's ankle as opposed to the hips and upper leg. "I was not the first guy to work on a low shot, but mine was very different. Very technical, with numerous finishes and ways to score back points. Going to the ankle and knee all stemmed from using motion to attack from a lower level."[35] Smith, an education major, was diligent and meticulous. "I made written notes after all of my practices. I documented in my notes what had worked during practice. After I started moving my feet, I just began to feel it. I also paid attention to the European stance, which had been very successful internationally. It was different from the American stance where you're bent over at the waist. When I began working these moves it opened up other ways to score. I started scoring back points off takedowns."[36]

Soon Smith began to develop a sixth sense for applying his discovery. "The move was so much instinct. Knowing when an opponent is going to step forward. Knowing what he's going to do when you move him."[37]

As the technique began to develop, workouts took on a new tempo and urgency. He toiled with the focus and enthusiasm of an inventor in the laboratory on the brink of a new discovery, often losing track of time as he tried out new ideas and nuances. "Physically it was tough, but mentally it was almost effortless. I wanted to do it. I knew it would work. I could not wait to get to the wrestling room every day. I could not wait to compete with what I had developed."[38]

He worked out several times a day, regularly breaking into the wrestling room at midnight to ingrain and tweak his new discovery. So focused was Smith with his new findings that he went months without calling his parents. He punched a workout partner for slacking up during a practice, resulting in a broken hand that took Smith 18 months to heal. "I can remember a particular time in the workout room where me and this guy spent 15 minutes working out and an hour and a half fighting. One would sit on the other until one cooled off. Things would be all right, but then, before you knew it, we were back at it again. There have been a lot of battles in that room."[39]

He trained with a desperation fueled by the pain of a prior loss and the hope of future success. "The disappointment of finishing second [in the NCAA finals] gave me a completely new attitude. I began to develop a sense of urgency, and began to think, 'This is how I'm going to win. This is how I can do it.'"[40] The time of discovery also left a sense of isolation as he watched his teammates travel and compete. "It was a lonely time. I had been wrestling since I was five years old. I had always had a team. I had always been a starter. I had always been the center of attention in some ways. But [during the redshirt year] I was not a part of the team. All of a sudden I was not starting. Suddenly I was not stepping out on the mat. I didn't feel as if I was needed. The pain and loneliness that flowed from that experience ignited the hunger I had been looking for."[41]

Smith's inner world was lit by fire as he continued to focus with the obsession of Michelangelo painting the ceiling of the Sistine chapel. It was his personal Age of Discovery. "There was always an end to what I was working for. And it was not for money or fame. You want to climb mountains that have never been climbed. I'm not sure you could go as deep into the process if it was just for money or fame. To try to become the best at something is one of the most fulfilling experiences you can have. After you see results, it drives you even deeper. I developed a hunger and an excitement as I felt myself making progress. In one day a person can become totally different when you're as intense as I was that year. But you have to see results on the way. A little bit of success along the way is very important."[42] Taking a year-long sabbatical was transformational. "Because of the redshirt year I became double the wrestler I had been."[43] He spent the summer of 1986 unveiling the transformation. After winning the National Open, Smith traveled to Russia and captured a gold medal at the Goodwill Games, a precursor to the 1988 Olympics, and featuring many of the top freestyle wrestlers in the world. "I was beating everyone badly. I was beating national champions. The guy I beat in the finals of the Goodwill Games went on to win the World Championships weeks later."[44] Smith chose not to compete in the World Championships. "I wanted to be an NCAA champion before I won the World Championships, so I passed on the World Championships. Otherwise, I'm not sure I would have stayed in school."[45]

He returned to Stillwater in August ranked as the No.1 collegiate wrestler in the nation at 134, and continued to compete in freestyle meets in preparation for the Olympic trials coming up the following summer. In early November, at the Hall of Fame Wrestling Classic held in Stillwater, he destroyed two opponents. But days later the Cowboys traveled to Lincoln, where Smith was upset by Nebraska's Gil Sanchez in the Cowboy dual opener after being tilted to his back in the final period. Smith perceived the loss as a personal insult. The Cowboy squad returned to Stillwater, but an assistant coach rented a car the following day and drove an outraged Smith to nearby Omaha, where Sanchez was scheduled to compete in an open tournament. He crushed the stunned Sanchez 6-2.

Evidence of the transformation continued. In December, Smith trounced an Arizona State opponent 16-4. Days later he scored seven takedowns in two minutes in racking up 24 points against an Oklahoma rival. At the Virginia Duals in January he registered two pins and a technical fall. He won the Big 8 title by defeating Sanchez again 14-3, and entered the NCAA tournament in College Park, Maryland with 38 wins against a single loss. To reach the finals he pinned his first opponent, then won his next three matches by scores of 23-8, 22-7, and 20-9.

In the finals he drilled Sanchez 18-4 for his first NCAA title, and was named the tournament's outstanding wrestler. After the victory he attributed some of his motivation to revamp his style to the stabbing pain to the soul he experienced after his previous two losses in his previous NCAA tournaments. "That really hurt bad and I haven't lived it down since. I take it to the workout room every day with me. When I get tired I look back at that day at the Myriad [the site of his loss to Jordan in the 1985 NCAA finals] and I work a little harder."[46] The losses allowed Smith to retool the psychological aspects of his game as well. "That layoff traveling through the Soviet Union helped me a lot. I was able to pick up a little experience as far as the mental aspects of the game, how to control your emotions on the mat, and when you get behind how to come back like a champion."[47]

Later in the summer Smith entered the U.S. Wrestling Festival in Durham, North Carolina. With one hand bandaged to protect broken bones and ribs taped to support torn cartilage, he won eight matches in three days to capture the 136.5-pound championship. Noticing that his cartilage "...was sticking out so far I thought I had broken a rib,"[48] Smith made his way about the arena with a large bag of ice taped to his side. "After about 30 minutes you can't feel anything. But it thaws out after the first period, and I can feel it then."[49] Smith continued to compete. "I'm going to have to be hurting awfully bad not to wrestle. I can wrestle with pain. It's a part of the sport."[50] The resilient senior-to-be then proceeded to win the Pan American Games in Indiana and the World Championships in France just days before his final year at OSU began in the summer of 1987.

As his senior year gained steam, Smith continued to complete his academic responsibilities, attend freestyle tournaments around the world, and compete for the Cowboys. During the first week in November he was virtually unstoppable in a pre-Olympic tournament in Seoul, South Korea. Three weeks later he traded red, white, and blue for an orange singlet and won five matches at a one-day tournament in Norman, Oklahoma. Two weeks later he pinned a Fresno State competitor in the remodeled Gallagher-Iba Arena in Stillwater to claim his 123rd victory to become the winningest Cowboy wrestler in history.

As Smith reflected on those times years later, he noted how the metamorphosis permeated his attitude as well as physical style. "Often wrestlers have to reinvent themselves when they reach this level. The gift to change one's mindset and think differently about oneself is a great challenge from which great rewards can be reaped. But it requires that one consider no option other than winning. Even now as a coach I see young guys negotiate with themselves as they are sorting out their expectations, sometimes just moments before a match, or even during competition! 'Well, maybe just wrestling for Oklahoma State is enough. Maybe being a conference champion is enough. Or becoming an All-American is enough.' But the ones that climb that final mountain are the competitors that seal off any options other than success. But for some, there's only one option, and that's getting your hand raised. It can be scary."[51]

Weeks later Smith traveled to Ames, Iowa, to defend his national title. As he entered the Big 8 tournament two weeks earlier, Smith had amassed 10 major decisions, 7 technical falls, and 15 pins while winning 40 matches against no losses. He held margins of 248-6 in takedowns, 29-1 in near falls, and 11-0 in reversals. He trailed 29-191 in escapes, only because of his propensity to take opponents down and then release them so the takedown slaughter could begin again.[52]

At the NCAA tournament he stormed to three pins and a 21-8 decision, then defeated Iowa's Joe Melchiore 9-2 for his second consecutive national title. The victory placed Smith in second place behind Dan Gable on the NCAA's consecutive winning list with 90 straight victories, and 112 consecutive wins, counting freestyle competition. The next day he returned to Stillwater, celebrated his NCAA title for 24 hours, then squeezed in four days of training before winning the World Cup competition in Toledo, Ohio. He continued to train for the Olympic trials to be held in Pensacola, Florida in June. Two opponents stood in Smith's path of making the Olympic team—nemesis Jim Jordan, the Wisconsin wrestler who had physically dominated Smith in the 1985 NCAA finals, and Randy Lewis, the tournament's No.1-seed who had defeated Smith in a qualifying tournament the previous month, ending Smith's collegiate/freestyle winning streak at 131 straight matches.

During the 1984 Olympic trials held four years earlier, an arbitrator's ruling had given Lewis a paper victory over Smith's older brother Lee Roy in a controversial bout. Olympic coach Dan Gable testified on behalf of his former Iowa wrestler against the elder Smith during an arbitration proceeding.

Smith defeated Jordan 10-2 and 5-2 to set up the grudge match against Lewis, where he exacted family vengeance by winning 8-4, and then captured the deciding match when Lewis defaulted with an injured right knee. Smith claimed no hard feelings and acknowledged Lewis' skills. "Wrestling him the last two months made me a better wrestler. I couldn't force the pace against him. He made me slow down because he's so fast. That's the first time I've wrestled like that in 10 years."[53]

The World. Remarkably, the 22 year-old college senior from Del City, Oklahoma arrived in Seoul for the XXIV Olympics as the gold-medal favorite. He set up camp in the Olympic Village two weeks before his competition was to begin and spent most of his time focusing on conditioning. "I'm anxious to get started. Seeing other Americans win gold medals motivates me. I haven't been out to one event. I'm concentrating on what I'm here for. I know right now I can go the whole six minutes without stopping. I'm mentally and physically prepared."[54] He would need to be sharp, for his weight was bulging with many of the world's greatest wrestlers, including Russian Stepan Sarkissian, who dropped down from 149.5 to challenge Smith, who had earlier in the year defeated the two top Russians in the weight class in freestyle competition. Smith knew what was in store. "Every tough wrestler in the tourney is in my half of the draw except the Russian."[55]

Smith began the competition at Sangmu Gymnasium in the early morning hours of September 28 by defeating Hungarian Jozsef Orban 11-4. In the early evening he defeated 1982 world champion Simeon Chterev of Bulgaria, who broke Smith's nose in the process. The match was stopped three times for Smith to wipe blood from his face. "That's the first time I ever had trouble with blood on the mat,"[56] said a detached Smith shortly after the match. Later the same evening he beat Marian Skubacz of Poland. The heavy bleeding had stopped, "…but it hurts after everything is over and I settle down."[57] After that match the dehydrated and weakened Smith walked a half-mile to a training area where he toiled to make weight later that evening. "I was the last one to make weight. After I took my rubber sweats off I still was a pound over. It took me 25 minutes to get that pound off in the sauna."[58] The last bus back to the Olympic Village, located several miles away, had departed minutes earlier, so Smith and a Finnish wrestler, the last two competitors in the gym, hitchhiked a ride to the nearest busy street. They could not locate a taxi, so they hitchhiked with a Korean official. "He couldn't speak English, but I showed him the ID card we wear around our neck, and he took us right to the village,"[59] said Smith. By this time it was 11:00 p.m. The exhausted Smith found something to eat and watched films of his day's matches for two hours. "I noticed that I'd been forcing things a little, and I decided to make them come to me."[60] He located a trainer for the daily drainage of blood from his ruptured and abscessed cauliflower ear, then called it a night. It was 1:00 a.m.

The following evening Smith faced Avirmed Enhe of Mongolia, needing only to avoid a lopsided loss to advance to the gold medal match. Smith employed a conservative strategy in the opening frame. But trailing 4-2 after one period, he became the aggressor, and turned the Mongolian star to his back to gain a 4-4 tie, then hit a series of takedowns to win his sixth consecutive match 12-7, setting up a Thursday evening gold-medal confrontation with European champion Stepan Sarkissian, the Russian star who was moved down from the 149 weight class to challenge Smith.

The Cold War had yet to thaw, and Russia was stung by Smith's earlier dominance of their No.1-ranked 136-pounder Khaser Issaev three straight times. So they sent Sarkissian, who had been the No. 2-ranked Russian behind their international star Arsen Faedzaev, down a weight class in an attempt to establish Soviet dominance. Smith's plan was not to go toe-to-toe with the stronger Russian, but to keep him off balance with a constant threat of attack. "He's very talented, but he explodes in flurries and then lays back for a while. I'm going to try to put the pressure on him the whole six minutes."[61] Smith's vigorous conditioning program had paid off, for he was the only undefeated wrestler in his pool. "That's by far the toughest six matches I ever wrestled in one tourney. I feel like I've got a lot of momentum because I've beaten a great field of wrestlers."[62]

With his father watching from the stands, Smith countered two early leg shots launched by the muscular Sarkissian, scored a takedown of his own, and felt the Russian's determination gradually melt away. "When I defended [Sarkissian's leg shots] and he couldn't get a takedown, I could see a change in his attitude."[63] Smith continued to lay down the law, and when the seconds clicked down on his 4-0 lead, a smile creased his sweaty and bruised face. When the match ended, Smith ran across the arena and waved to his father, and later thought of his older brother and life-long mentor who had written his younger brother letters in preparation for the match against Sarkissian, who had beaten the older Smith earlier in the decade. "Lee Roy has always been my hero. I wanted the gold medal for myself and Lee Roy,"[64] Smith said.

As Smith stood on the medal platform with his abscessed ear, jammed thumb, and broken nose, he became the 11th native Oklahoman to win a wrestling gold medal at the Olympics. Opposing coaches stood perplexed at their own athletes' inability to control the willowy and slender Smith, who seemed almost Houdini-like in his ability to extricate himself from vulnerable situations. His future coaching rival Dan Gable offered one explanation after observing Smith's virtuoso performance, "He's almost like air and it's kinda difficult to take air down."[65]

The gold medal concluded the first phase of a startling turn-around for Smith, who beginning in 1983, had been beaten 19-2 by Kevin Darkus, 13-0 by Barry Davis, ousted in the second round of the NCAA tournament, and had been dominated by Jim Jordan in the NCAA finals. Beginning in 1987 he won an NCAA title, the U.S. Olympic Festival, the Pan American Games, the world championships in Clermont-Ferrand, France, a second NCAA title, the U.S. Olympic trials, and now the Olympic gold medal.

The following months were a whirlwind as Smith crisscrossed the nation giving speeches, promoting wrestling, and appearing at clinics, camps, and autograph sessions. Though he considered retiring after the 1988 Olympic Games, USA Wrestling, the governing body for the United States amateur wrestling efforts, had begun providing financial support for successful competitors who wished to continue their training and competition. Smith negotiated endorsement deals that afforded him more financial freedom to continue his disciplines. In the meantime he became known for his financial acumen as well as wrestling competence. "Wrestlers tend to be good businessmen, and John's one of the best. People really have an interest in John Smith, and by being the best [wrestler] we have he's able to reach out to people."[66]

In the intervening years between 1988 and 1992 Smith continued his assault on the freestyle wrestling world. He won three World Championships (1989-91), the Pan American Games Championship (1991), the World Cup championship (1991), and the Goodwill Games (1990). At the 1990 World Championships he outscored his opponents 58-4 and defeated a Bulgarian 10-0 in the gold medal match. He was named the U.S. Olympic Committee's Sportsman of the Year in 1991, becoming the first U.S. wrestler ever to receive the award. In March, 1991, he beat out Notre Dame football star Raghib "Rocket" Ismail and won the James E. Sullivan Award as the nation's outstanding amateur athlete for 1990, becoming the first American wrestler to receive the prestigious award that usually went to swimmers and track and field athletes. Tim Panaccio of Knight-Ridder Newspapers placed the award in perspective, "He may be unknown in most circles, but Smith is the Muhammad Ali of wrestling.

Smith, the only wrestler to win four consecutive world titles, is considered America's greatest wrestler ever. Ever."[67]

During this interval Smith's training went on almost non-stop. After winning the 1990 World Championships in Tokyo, he took a well-deserved week off in Cancun, Mexico. "It was the most miserable week I ever spent. I couldn't even lay on the beach. I'd be on the beach and all of the sudden I'd be running in the sand, go a mile down. I was running. I was in the weight room every day. I was doing my stance and my motion out on the sand. I was trying to get someone to wrestle Greco-Roman with me in the water."[68]

Distraction. By 1991, Smith's success in freestyle wrestling progressed in tandem with OSU's return to dominance in the college wrestling world. Head coach Joe Seay was named *Amateur Wrestling News'* 1990 Man of the Year, and had led the Cowboys to two consecutive national titles and five Big 8 championships. Acting on a tip from an anonymous phone call alleging improprieties in the program, the NCAA began an investigation of OSU wrestling in March of 1990, resulting in Seay's suspension in May of 1991, followed by the NCAA's 39-page letter of inquiry tendered to the school in November. OSU Associate Athletic Director for internal affairs and 1970 NCAA champion Dave Martin, along with former head coach Tommy Chesboro, gave the program guidance through that summer. Smith and fellow Cowboy and Olympic gold medal winner Kenny Monday agreed to coach the 1991-1992 team on an interim basis upon their return from the World Freestyle Championship in Bulgaria in early October. Other former Cowboys helped conduct workouts when Smith and Monday's freestyle commitments took them away.

As Christmas approached, the NCAA letter of official inquiry had not arrived, and Smith was growing impatient. "Right now I'm just looking for some direction from someone so I can tell the kids where we're going. I'm tired of being in limbo and not knowing anything. I can only tell the kids to be patient for so long before they start being frustrated and getting scared."[69] The Cowboys finished second to Iowa in the NCAA tournament, but in light of the pending NCAA investigation, declined to accept the runner-up trophy.

A distracted Smith continued to train for the 1992 Olympic games while serving as the Cowboy's co-interim coach, but wearing the dual hats of an

Olympic athlete-in-training and the head coach of a Division I athletic program took its toll. "I realize that it's impossible to do them both...I was trying to train with athletes in between workouts, and I was kind of putting 50 percent into both. I was cheating both sides."[70] A disconcerted Smith granted only one interview during the summer, and his frustration with the dual role was revealed. "[I'm] disappointed with the situation that's taken place, with the investigation and the NCAA, with the way it's been handled. It's been frustrating for me to be put in a situation and not really feel that there's been a lot of support there. It's been tough, and it's been a frustrating year for me."[71] As much as he tried to focus on training, the issue remained a distraction. "When I was at [the Olympic] training camp in Pennsylvania in July, I was told the verdict would be out before I left [for Barcelona]. Then I was calling home from the Olympics, asking if anybody had heard anything, and nobody would say anything. I just figured, 'Oh, nobody wants me to know because of the Olympics.'"[72]

The distractions carried over into Smith's on-the-mat performance. At the Olympic trials on June 6 Smith, in what was called "one of the biggest upsets in American wrestling history,"[73] lost 4-2 to John Fisher, formerly of the University of Michigan, in the first match of a best-of-three series to determine who would represent the U.S. at the Barcelona Olympics. It was Smith's first loss to an American in four years, and it came the day after he was awarded the International Wrestler of the Year Award, becoming the first American to capture the award, with the previous six being awarded to Russian wrestlers. In previous bouts against the same opponent Smith had won by a cumulative score of 38-1. "Just sitting here thinking about that loss...Here's a guy, Fisher—he's a respectable wrestler. He trains hard; he deserves good things in the sport. He's wrestled for a long time. But he really hasn't done much internationally, never placed in a world event. And yet, he beat me. It's like, he doesn't deserve to beat me."[74] But Fisher did beat Smith, snapping a 56-match winning streak and forcing an evening rematch which pushed Olympic champion Smith to the brink of elimination. Brother Lee Roy witnessed his younger sibling's loss, and provided his teary-eyed brother a five-word message that would become the Cowboy Wrestling Mantra – "Find a way to win."[75] Smith returned later in the evening and struggled to defeat Fisher in two tight matches. A close call in the final match prompted the crowd of 4,542 to jeer an official's decision, the first time an American crowd had ever booed Smith, but the upset was averted and Smith qualified for the Olympic team for the second time.

Days later Smith went into seclusion and began training for what he sensed might be his final competition. The eyes of the wrestling world followed America's greatest wrestler in his efforts to gain a second Olympic gold medal. To suggest that Smith downplayed his international fame is an understatement of Olympian proportions. During the six years they dated, Smith told his future wife Toni little of his Olympic achievements. He was so opaque in his description of his accomplishments that Toni thought John was helping out with the Special Olympics event held in Stillwater annually to benefit children with developmental disabilities.

He was searching for the magic level to win championships, and as always in his career, the quest was one of attitude and perspective more than conditioning and technique. "Right now I'm not where I need to be. I'm having a tough time right now finding myself—finding myself mentally. But it's early enough where I think I can work through it. It's just a battle, an everyday battle, to find what I'm looking for."[76] Brother Lee Roy recognized the look in his little brother's eyes. "Starting July 2, he'll have no distractions. No interviews. No phone calls."[77] As the final competition drew near, brother Lee Roy reflected on John's stunning loss to Fisher. "When all is said and done, when the Olympics are over and John has to point to the turning point of his career, yes, it might be that match."[78] Smith's focus was now on Barcelona; but the checkmate at the hands of the unheralded Fisher was an eye-opener. "I didn't think I had to compete. I thought I could turn it on, turn it off, go out and destroy when I wanted to. I've lost a lot because of that. Right now, my biggest fear is that I've lost something going into the Olympics. But I'm trying to do what it takes to win."[79]

Smith wore the scars of an experienced international wrestler. "Cold gyms where you could see your breath as you warmed up. No hot water in the hotels. KGB agents following us around. Hard mats. Sparse eating that was native to the country in which we were traveling. I thought I had seen it all."[80]

But in Barcelona, his personal struggle continued. Smith scraped through tight matches in the opening round, and lost an overtime match in the final preliminary bout round to nemesis Lazaro Reinoso of Cuba, who had defeated Smith 56 matches earlier. "This is the worst match I've wrestled in five years. I'll be lucky to get through three rounds of the Olympics if I wrestle like this. My confidence was shot from the start of the match. The last three times I wrestled him, I scored 38 points. I can't remember the last time I scored two points in a match. I don't think I ever have."[81] That loss, his first and only blemish in what had been otherwise a perfect world and Olympic record, would haunt Smith long after his competitive career ended, but he qualified for the finals on the strength of points accumulated in earlier matches. Friends and family members gathered around televisions across Oklahoma to watch Smith defeat Iran's Asgari Mohammadian 6-0 to win the gold medal, making him the first American wrestler since George Mehnert in 1904 and 1908 to capture gold medals in two consecutive Olympics. His mother Madalene followed her routine of attending Mass during her son's match. "This was a hard tournament for John. But I thought he'd pull through, and he did."[82]

American wrestling devotees were not the only fans watching the match with keen interest. Kami Barcini, a former wrestling champion from Iran, was 14 years old during the Olympic games, and remembers the match well. "I met John in 2004 while helping coach United States wrestlers during the 2004 Olympic trials in Indianapolis. I was wearing an orange OSU wrestling shirt, and John approached me and struck up a conversation. That was a great moment in my life."[83] By this time, Smith's reputation in the worldwide wrestling community was significant, even halfway across the world. "You have to understand—wrestling and soccer are the most popular sports in Iran. Wrestling champions in Iran are national heroes, and the benefits of winning a world or Olympic title are enormous. Our fans are wonderful. The wrestling community is very close, almost like a family. Our great amateur athletes are like NBA stars or major league ballplayers in the United States."

Reminiscent of Americans watching a Super Bowl, Barcini recalled his homeland's passion for the sport. "When John Smith wrestled Asgari Mohammadian for the Olympic gold medal in 1992, it was a national event. Television didn't broadcast the match, but Iranian radio stations carried it live. Young people, grandmothers, and grandfathers were all gathered around a table listening. Our nation was going through tough times during that period. Supporting an Olympic athlete from our country brought our nation together."

"John was a national hero in Iran. I had his posters on my wall when I was a kid. I had many of his Olympic matches on videotape, and I watched them over and over. All of my buddies tried to copy his style. Quick like a panther. He was from the United States, but my country felt a special kinship with John. He was the greatest wrestler in the world. Of course, we pulled for [Mohammadian], but we were satisfied to see John win."

The stocky, well-spoken Cowboy wrestling fan, born some 7,000 miles from Stillwater, marvels not only of Smith's accomplishments, but also at the his relative standing in sporting history. "Many people don't understand what [Smith] accomplished on the world stage. He went around the world whipping the toughest guys in the most demanding sport in the world, in the toughest weight class (62 kilograms/136.5 pounds). Doing that once would be a tremendous accomplishment, but John did it six times." Barcini then pushes back from an empty plate of pizza and smiles. "I wanted to be like John."[84]

Smith's second gold medal allowed him to reflect years later on the distinction between being a first-time champion and a defending champion. "Winning the first national championship or the first gold medal or the first world championship was like when we had our first child. There is a newness and exhilaration that comes from experiencing something for the first time. But as we had more children, the feeling was more of a mature sense of confidence and accomplishment for the inner self. It reminded me of the difference between holding our first child for the first time as compared to our looking out over our family when they grow and become older. It brings a feeling of calm reassurance that you did make the right decisions and that you did go down the right path."[85]

Smith's decision to revamp his style seemed to provide the impetus to conquer the collegiate and freestyle wrestling world. But in retrospect, America's greatest wrestler credits a renovated frame of mind over a refined technique. "In the final analysis, I'm not sure style really matters. We can talk about the low single leg and how effective it was for me, but what changed in me was my passion, drive, and commitment to develop into the athlete I wanted to become. If it had not been the low single, it would have been something else. My passion and commitment

John Smith, with his left hand bandaged, overcame injury, mental fatigue and distraction to win his second Olympic gold medal and complete his career as a competitor. *Courtesy Jeffrey G. Nolan.*

developed to the level that I was going to find a way to win my matches. In the 1992 Olympic Games, I was really banged up and had an extremely tough tournament. I won the tournament, but didn't hit one low single during the entire competition. What got me through was the same element that helped me win over the years. My frame of mind. Losing was not an option. Somehow, find a way to win. One cannot underestimate the importance of frame of mind in tough one-on-one competition. There is nothing tougher. It exposes every weakness. The level of fight is exposed for everyone. My freshman year I didn't have that level of fight. My insecurity and lack of confidence were exposed. The highest levels of character are required to excel in sports involving one-on-one competition due to the demands of the sport. I can teach the low single leg all over the country, but that's not what makes national champions. It's the frame of mind. When people see talented athletes in action, they don't understand the frame of mind world-class athletes have. That is what makes them great. Tiger hits the ball wonderfully, but ultimately his confidence and frame of mind wins major championships. Tell him he could only hit a three wood off the tee, he would find a way to win."[86]

The 27-year-old Smith also recognized that the effects of time were tilting against him, even though several international champions had extended their careers well into their thirties. "I won some tight matches that I felt a year ago I would have dominated. I think as I get older, my style of wrestling is becoming a little tougher for me to wrestle – the quick, explosive movements I like to use. I feel like I might have lost a step as far as that style of wrestling. If I continue, I'm going to have to change my style of wrestling."[87] But issues reached beyond the physical limitations of aging. "Right now, I'm about 60 percent of what I'm capable of. My body is at 100 percent, but my mind is not. I've been questioning myself throughout this last six months of training, questioning why I did some of the things I did during the year."[88]

After the Olympics, Smith returned to Oklahoma, where 3,000 fans and well-wishers lined the streets of Del City, Oklahoma to pay tribute to their favorite son. Later he would take time to view the unveiling of a statute of his likeness, at the recently named John Smith Fieldhouse at Del City High School.

Even though the NCAA had not issued its final report detailing its findings, OSU officials recognized the need to bring the uncertainty to a conclusion and call a coach. Less than one month after capturing his gold medal in Barcelona, Smith was named as the seventh head wrestling coach in Oklahoma State history. His decision was not an easy one. By taking the job Smith essentially ended his competitive career, lost opportunities to cash in on his status as a world-renowned athlete, and took over a program in shambles.

Finally, during the first week in November, the NCAA handed down its verdict. Smith's former coach Joe Seay was found to have improperly compensated wrestlers and recruits participating in camps and open tournaments, and was found to have instructed wrestlers to provide false testimony to NCAA investigators. Coach Smith's Cowboys were placed on three years' probation and banned from NCAA tournament competition for the upcoming season. Initial scholarships were banned through August, 1994, and limits were placed on recruiting visits, and wrestling camp participation. The Cowboy's runner-up finish in the 1992 NCAA tournament was expunged from the record, and Seay was essentially banned from college coaching for five years "unless Seay and the institution appear before the infractions committee."[89] College athletics' most storied program in any sport had survived the death penalty, but its new coach's ability to recruit and attract top-flight wrestlers was decimated.

Reaction from the college wrestling community to OSU's penalties was mixed. Oklahoma coach Stan Able commented on the effect of the rulings on his own program. "The greatest relief we have, and other coaches around the country have, is now you know you're all recruiting with the same ammunition. Their improper recruiting has cost us a lot of athletes, which has suggested we haven't done our job. [But] I knew we were working our butt off. Even though the public wouldn't know it, in my heart I would know it."[90] One high school wrestling coach described OSU's plight as "kind of like a death in the family."[91] Myron Roderick, the OSU athletic director who hired Seay, commented, "No doubt about as stiff as you can get without eliminating the program completely."[92] Lee Roy Smith, then the head coach at Arizona State, called it "…a sad day for wrestling."[93] When asked about the possibility of younger brother Pat Smith transferring from Oklahoma State to Arizona State to pursue his record-setting fourth NCAA title, the Sun Devil coach demurred. "I would rather leave that to Oklahoma State, to John and Pat. I'm not preying around, looking for leftovers."[94] But the perceptive older brother and former Cowboy great balanced reality with optimism. "I would hope they could start looking toward a new future and building a new era as soon as possible. Obviously, without aid [OSU received a two-year ban on new scholarships], it's going to be difficult."[95]

With a lineup populated by walk-ons and second-tier talent, the Cowboys struggled during Smith's inaugural season as head coach. Every team member with remaining eligibility took a redshirt year, including Smith's younger brother and three-time national champion Pat. The season was marked by historic losses. Nebraska broke a 13-year, 15-match losing streak to OSU, posted the most points ever scored by a visitor in Gallagher-Iba Arena, and crushed the Cowboys 39-12. Days later Minnesota won in Stillwater, followed by a 27-19 drubbing at the hands of Oklahoma in the Cowboy home arena. In February the Cowboys fell to Arizona State, coached by Lee Roy Smith, who after the dual commented on the peculiar nature of the match. "It's kind of difficult to get real competitive, to put yourself in a real competitive state of mind, when [you] look over there and see your brother, who as an older brother you've tried to nurture and help and give direction to. From that standpoint it was a little awkward, but nevertheless I think it's something that will be a very competitive rivalry that will be fun also."[96]

The 1992-1993 Cowboys finished their dual season 4-7, compiling the worst record in OSU wrestling history since their inaugural 1914 team went 0-1, but Coach Smith made no excuses. "That's not putting faith in my athletes, and my athletes are getting better. Even if I've got four or five walk-ons, I see them getting better and I'm going to go with those guys. As a team, we're going to keep taking lumps. This is the first of many firsts; first time OU's beaten us [since 1985] and there probably will be more firsts this year. Sanctions are obviously designed to hurt you, but if we have a good recruiting year we'll bounce back."[97]

Rebound they did. The 1993-1994 recruiting class was ranked fourth in the nation, including two first-team high school All-Americans. A substantial herd of redshirt talent that had stood behind the bench a year earlier in street clothes, was reactivated, and the revamped OSU squad opened the season ranked No. 2 in the country behind Penn State. Days later the reinvigorated

Cowboys polished off the Nittany Lions and stormed through pre-season tournaments to claim the No.1 ranking. They handed Oklahoma's new coach Jack Spates his first Bedlam loss 28-9, racking up 40 takedowns in the win. Days later Lee Roy's Arizona State team fell in Stillwater, with Pat Smith piling up 14 takedowns in 2:39 for a technical fall. John Smith cracked after the match, "At least I've got bragging rights for the year. I told Lee Roy this was for breaking my toe when I was 10."[98] After a week of practice in which they "worked on pinning people,"[99] OSU flattened Northern Iowa 41-16, setting up the dual match with Dan Gable's Iowa Hawkeyes, who had refused to wrestle OSU the year before because of the NCAA sanctions. Even though OSU's 118 pounder failed to show up for the weigh-in, the Cowboys slipped past Iowa 23-16 before a full house in Gallagher-Iba Arena. A week later they handled 14th-ranked OU 25-18, with Pat Smith surviving an upset bid by winning in overtime, and capturing his 91st straight win. They prepared for the NCAA tournament by winning their 24th Big 8 championship, and on the strength of Pat Smith's fourth and freshman Mark Branch's first NCAA titles, the Comeback Cowboys captured their 30th national title.

Few would have believed it would be the last national team title OSU would win for almost a decade.

The Drought. The freshman-laden squad of 1994-1995, with the fourth Smith brother Mark in the lineup, lost twice to Iowa and finished second to Nebraska in the Big 8 tournament and seventh in the NCAA tournament, the lowest finish for an OSU squad since their first team of 1915. The 1995-1996 team won 15 of 19 duals, but lost the season opener to Oklahoma and finished a distant sixth in the NCAA tournament behind Iowa. "This team has got some holes right now. We didn't look aggressive at very many weights…We did a lot of pushin' and shovin'. This team, right now, is not that good. I've got some young kids. Either some of these guys are going to step up and 'wrestle'—go out and just wrestle—or they're coming out [of the lineup]."[100] After the season's end Coach Smith was optimistic but realistic. "I'm not sure at this point if we can challenge Iowa next year either, but the good thing at this point is we have 10 returning."[101] In 1996-1997 an older and more experienced OSU team, led by NCAA champion and three-time finalist Mark Branch, went undefeated during the regular season, was ranked No.1 much of the year, and entered the NCAA tournament as the pre-tournament favorite, but finished a distant second behind Dan Gable's final Iowa team. Smith was mentioned as Gable's possible successor to the nation's elite program, but he chose to stay in Stillwater. "If you start lining things up with the No. 1 program in the country [Iowa], you'd say that we're way far behind. It's tough at times here financially. We don't do without, but at the same time we could do with more. You need the little extras to help you prepare, to help you feel like you're at one of the best programs in the nation. I don't know if anyone's going to dominate again. I've got to get this program to the quality the University of Iowa has had. Ultimately, the wrestlers decide things on the mat, but it certainly helps to have 14,000 or 15,000 fans cheering you on. That's something I've focused on…bringing our fans back and getting involved with the program again."[102]

The 1997-1998 team, with five All-Americans and national champion Eric Guerrero returning, again went undefeated during the dual season and defeated Iowa and first-year head coach Jim Zalesky in a road dual match, but finished third in the NCAA tournament. The 1998-1999 team again won all of its dual matches, extending OSU's consecutive dual winning streak to 68, but again placed third at the NCAA tournament, this time behind Iowa and Minnesota. Minnesota snapped the school's 73 match dual win streak in 1999-2000, as the Cowboys lost four dual matches for the first time since 1985-1986. A loss to Michigan State was referred to by one wrestling writer as "the most shocking defeat of a Cowboy team since a 1991 loss at Northern Iowa."[103] After storming out to an early lead in the NCAA tournament, they won only three matches in the quarterfinals and semi-final rounds, finished fifth behind fourth-place Oklahoma, and did not send a wrestler to the NCAA finals for the first time in 28 years. Six Cowboys did not live up to their pre-tournament seedings. "I knew coming in we had a chance to finish right where we did. I think I could accept it a little more if we'd done it on our own terms. We didn't finish the way I wanted."[104]

The "gritty" 2000-2001 team upset top-ranked Iowa early in the season, and then downed No.1-ranked Minnesota on the road, drawing Coach Smith's compliments. "That may not mean technique. That may not mean skill. It may mean, like in the back yard, whatever it takes. The bottom line is when you're down by one and there's one minute to go you find out a

John Smith and an official discuss a call.
Courtesy Mika Matzen.

lot. Give me a kid that's going to fight hard and execute when he needs to execute. I'm not talking about going through the motions of fightin', I'm talking about fightin'."[105]

The team was rocked mid-season when 10 members of the Cowboy basketball team and staff were killed in a plane crash while returning from a game in Boulder, Colorado. Said then-freshman Chris Pendleton, "Not a lot of people know how close the basketball team and the wrestling team were, but we were very close."[106]

The squad wore a black patch on their uniforms to honor the 10 who died. "That '10' just reminds us of them and ourselves and our mortality.

You just have to think about your family and your friends, and it's a good reminder."[107]

The 2000-2001 Cowboys went on to register 115 ½ points at the NCAA tournament, but finished third to Minnesota, who claimed the title without a finalist but with 10 All-Americans.

The next year Smith had low expectations for his 2001-2002 team. "A realistic goal for this team going in is probably finishing in the top five. It would be hard to see us compete at this time for a national title. I think it's the first time in my 10 years that I've ever said that, but I've got to be realistic and understand what I have right now."[108] Smith was prophetic, as the Cowboys did take fifth place behind eventual winner Minnesota.

The Cowboys had not won an NCAA title for eight years, and the OSU wrestling community searched for answers. Some attributed the drought to the Gable stranglehold, but the Iowa coach had departed two years earlier, and the void had been filled by Iowa State and Minnesota, not OSU. There was talk of staff discord that adversely affected recruiting efforts, and Smith worried that he placed too much burden on assistants in the recruiting process. But the most piercing criticism came in assertions that Smith, who considered the takedown "the art of the sport," placed too much reliance on designer moves and slick technique and too little focus on brute force and "toughness." Moreover, college wrestling coaches around the nation had developed defenses to effectively counter the low single-leg take down, referred to by Dan Gable in the Iowa coach's 1999 instructional video as "the John Smith technique."[109] More strident critics called Smith's teams "Chokelahoma State" for a perceived inability to finish strong at the NCAA tournament after issuing dominating performances during the regular season. These assertions were unfair, but Smith understood they contained a grain of truth.

Since he began coaching, Smith had been frustrated at his wrestlers' unwillingness to employ his uncompromising devotion to winning and unwavering commitment to training he had employed during his career. Similarly, his wrestlers were discouraged they could not meet their legendary coach's expectations. But just as Smith had adapted to his environment a decade earlier in developing a new way to wrestle, the Cowboy coach gradually revamped his coaching and teaching methods during the late 1990s. It began in the head and worked down.

He recognized that elite athletes could often not replicate their success in the role of coaches because of their impatience with students who did not possess the same talent level or internal drive as the elite athlete did during their heyday. "I began to understand that athletes had to be brought along at the right pace. Instruction had to be tailored differently to each athlete."[110] In that vein, he relinquished the assumption that his wrestlers had to build their offensive arsenal around the low single-leg attack. "I came to realize not everyone had the aptitude to wrestle that style, nor is everyone committed to train at the required pace. It's a much harder style of wrestling. No circling and looking at each other. The whistle blows and you're on the attack. It's not a defensive or mistake-sensitive style of wrestling. You're not concerned about mistakes. You'll make mistakes and you'll be overly aggressive at times. It's the total opposite of conservative wrestling."[111]

He also focused on constructing self-reliance and maturity in his wrestlers so they could diagnose their own mistakes and find their own voice on the mat. "Actually, coaches need to criticize technique and not courage. But that's more difficult because it takes thinking and patience. It takes moving the wrestler to the point where he thinks for himself. He understands I can't feel what he feels out there. I can only see it. I cannot solve his problems as a coach. In those critical moments he has to think for himself. But I can't force that mindset on these young men. They have to come to that point on their own. To have wrestlers who have no option other than winning is a great thing for a coach. Wrestlers like Pendleton, Esposito, and Steve Mocco draw the others up with them. They motivate their teammates in ways that I can't as a coach. But I can't force them into the mindset of a Pendleton, who is ready to come in each day and pound it out. That would do them more harm than good. I have to hope they come in here ready to make mistakes and learn on their own and be patient when they're not. Patience is one of the most important components of my job description."[112]

From an operational standpoint, he began to recognize the value of inserting the head coach's presence into the recruiting process. "When I first began coaching, I didn't understand how important it was to the recruits and parents for the head coach to make a visit. We probably lost some guys because of that. Now I get in those living rooms."[113]

But the ultimate component of the coaching makeover was an inner transformation. "Coaches have to learn to give and give and give and not expect anything in return in the short term. It's similar to the dynamic we face in parenting. We are such an instant-gratification society. We expect for our efforts to reap instant rewards. It's not like that."[114]

Along the way, the evolution of John Smith as coach took hold. Like several of his earlier squads, the 2002-2003 team was ranked No. 1 early in the season on the strength of seven returning starters and seven redshirt freshman, including Kevin Ward, Chris Pendleton, Jake Rosholt, and Rusty

John Smith's development as a coach included sorting out disappointment when his wrestlers failed to meet his own personal standards. *Courtesy Mika Matzen*

Blackmon, along with the addition of true freshman Zack Esposito. In years past the Cowboys would seldom lose a regular season dual, storm through the Thursday afternoon and evening rounds of competition at the NCAA tournament, only to falter in the crucial quarterfinal and semifinal bouts Friday afternoon and evening.

But the afternoon hours of March 21, 2003 set in motion a trend that would define the Cowboy program for the ensuing years. On that Friday the Cowboys managed to win five of seven quarterfinal matches. While they won only two of five ensuing semi-final matches that evening, those who had lost in the winner's bracket responded by winning twelve of fourteen consolation bouts late Friday evening and Saturday morning. OSU went on that weekend to crown two national champions and seven All-Americans, and capped off an undefeated dual season by winning the NCAA tournament by a team record 143 points. In the tunnel area of Kansas City's Kemper Arena, away from the crowd, Smith wept tears of relief. "Sometimes, because of who we are, we put ourselves at the top and we didn't belong there. But we earned this and are back on top right now."[115]

The 2003-2004 team regrouped after an early-season loss to Missouri, maintained its No. 1 ranking all season, and won its second consecutive NCAA title by outscoring Iowa by 41.5 points. The Cowboys seemed to be back.

A Place to Stand. In a *Los Angeles Times* article published days before the beginning of the 1992 Olympics, Smith was portrayed as a selfish and isolated soul "obsessed with three things: himself, wrestling and winning. Anything or anybody else had better get out of the way."[116] He took losing as a personal insult. "I've probably hurt a lot of people because of this. But you gotta' do what you gotta' do if this is what you want. I didn't get to be a five-time World Champion giving people time. I did it by being selfish and sometimes probably rude."[117] The zealous commitment to training and winning overshadowed everything. "Anything that gets in my way, I pretty much eliminate. I don't have too many close friends. I don't have too many close relationships. I just can't afford to have them to go where I want to go, to do what I want to do. I really focus on myself. I really figure out and find a way how I can win, how I can beat everybody, I'll do whatever it takes."[118]

After 1992, the transition from elite athlete to coach was occasionally soul-searching. "Being a world-class athlete is about being selfish. You have to. But being a coach is about giving and giving and giving, but I am at peace with that. It was difficult to make that transition when I retired at 26, giving up that pretense that it is all about me. My first couple of years in coaching were as much about myself as they were the wrestlers. I am now at peace with the stance of being a giving person and not a taking person. Not that I'm like that all of the time, but that is the dynamic I strive for."[119]

Change forced Smith to come face-to-face with his own self- perceived inadequacies, and sometimes the process was arduous. "…I identified those weaknesses and went to work on them. Whether that would be my personality, working in recruiting or work in the administration. When you work on weaknesses it's very rewarding to make changes and for me the changes I have made as a coach have enhanced my life in general, it has made me a better father and a better husband."[120] He tries to spend his evenings on his farm outside Stillwater where he and his family tend horses and raise sheep and goats. He shuns attention, smiles softly and often, and relishes time with family. After the lights go out and the house is quiet, he sometimes tinkers with his fishing equipment and reflects on his good fortune. Still usually a one-meal-a-day man, he arises early to help his older son Joseph feed their animals. "It builds discipline and makes my son realize that nothing just happens. Growth takes patience and change."[121]

Smith's popularity results in a constant flow of invitations to give speeches, dine with some form of royalty, and attend endless ceremonial events. But beyond nurturing his family, the Cowboy coach's appetites are simple and direct.

"Winning is enough."

* * *

Smith retired in 1992 as arguably the greatest American athlete of the 20th century.[122] He had captured six consecutive international titles, an accomplishment unparalleled in American wrestling history. He captured all of the major titles in amateur wrestling, including the Olympics, the Goodwill Games, the Pan American Games, and the World Cup. He became the first American wrestler in 80 years to win two Olympic gold medals. His victories included six consecutive world-class championships, two gold medals in the Pan American Games in two attempts, two gold medals in the Goodwill Games in two attempts, five freestyle national championships in five attempts, two NCAA crowns, and 90 consecutive collegiate victories. He was the first wrestler to win the James E. Sullivan Award as America's outstanding athlete, became the first American to win the Master of Technique and Wrestler of the Year by the International Wrestling Federation, and the first wrestler ever nominated for the World Trophy, honoring the most outstanding athlete on six continents, which he won in 1992.

Beginning with his first high school match for the Del City Eagles in December 1979, Smith compiled a high school mark of 105-5. He went 154-7-2 at Oklahoma State on his way to two NCAA titles. His international record was 100-5, and his domestic freestyle record was 77-3. During

John Smith chair-wrestles in Gallagher-Iba Arena. *Courtesy Jim Bowen.*

those dozen years he competed 458 times and had his hand raised on 436 occasions, for a success rate in excess of 95 percent.[123]

* * *

Enigmatic and inquisitive Barry Zito, the former Oakland A's major league pitcher who changed teams and signed a $126 million contract with the neighboring San Francisco Giants in 2007, was always seeking a competitive edge. He read extensively, Ernest Holmes' 1919 book *Creative Mind* was an early favorite, dabbled in spirituality, and practiced yoga.

He had heard rumors about a special brand of mental toughness standard in collegiate wrestling, a sport he was patently unfamiliar with. So the California surfer, the son of a musician-father and an ordained minister-mom, drove through an Iowa blizzard, before spring training began, and tracked down John Smith and the Oklahoma State Cowboys at a tournament.

At the end of an extensive brain-pick, the proud Zito told Smith of his own .618 winning percentage, 13th best in the major leagues. Baseball writers had been impressed with Zito in 2002, awarding him the Cy Young Award as baseball's best pitcher. But the curious Smith was puzzled—how could someone who won only a little better than 6 out of ten games be paid $126 million? "How come [your winning percentage] is not in the 90's?"

Zito was impressed. "It's that wrestling mentality. It's raising the bar." After a long talk with Smith, the Giants ace pitcher left the dank arena and walked into the cold Iowa air wearing a Cowboy Wrestling sweatshirt. [124]

* * *

Three-peat. John Smith's large office windows face the western horizon and overlook the deep green turf of Boone Pickens Stadium. Adorned with mementos of past victories and family memories, the office provides a way station for the constant flow of wrestlers and visitors who happen by, often unannounced. The Monday following OSU's NCAA victory in March of 2004, newly-crowned national champion and team leader Chris Pendleton sat across from Smith. "Chris and I visited this morning, talking about doing something as a program we haven't done in a long time. Chris wanted to talk about us winning three straight NCAA titles. That's something we haven't done here since Art Griffith's teams did it in 1954-1955-1956. Chris came in on his own and wanted to get the process started, talking about three-peating."[125]

Smith had been thinking that very thing months before, while on the bus ride from St. Louis, where the Cowboys had captured their second straight NCAA title and 32nd in school history. It would not be easy. He already was in the process of assembling one of the most grueling schedules in Division I wrestling history. By chance, OSU was on the visitor's end of nine away matches against eight top 20 teams to be wrestled in six different states and three time zones.

The ten-man OSU lineup was juiced with four returning All-Americans: the moody and idiosyncratic junior and returning NCAA runner-up Zack Esposito at 149; the free-spirited and loquacious sophomore and fifth-place medalist Johny Hendricks at 165; the sensitive and expressive senior team captain and returning NCAA champion Chris Pendleton at 174; and the taciturn, cantankerous junior and returning NCAA champion Jake Rosholt at 197. This Murderer's Row accounted for two national championships and a combined career record of 220-37, and gave the Cowboys the strongest middle and upper weight punch in the nation. But questions loomed in the remaining six weights, where 10 candidates carried a respectable combined record of 175-61, but only one of the 10 had qualified for the NCAA tournament, and none were named in pre-season rankings as potential All-Americans. Unless the Cowboys could stock those six weights with NCAA-level performances, the probability of injuries, the inherent difficulty of repeating a championship performance from the previous year, and the potential of upsets to Murderer's Row made the margin of error small and unpredictable. Smith had entered campaigns with top-ranked teams and high expectations before, only to be disappointed at year's end. "In college wrestling today the high school talent level is greater than ever before. With limitations in scholarships [9.9 scholarships distributed among some 30 wrestlers], the days are gone when a small number of schools can monopolize talent. Add to that the upgrading of facilities across the nation, and it is more difficult to win the national championship now than ever."[126] On that sunny March afternoon OSU appeared to occupy a post position among several major programs hungry to compete for a national title.

But a roommate, a phone call, and a runaway freight train in search of the Holy Grail shifted the force of gravity in college athletics' toughest sport. One-hundred twenty days later, nothing would ever be the same.

IT TOOK A FIGHT
TO BRING OUT THE FIGHTER IN HIM,
AND A FIGHTER WAS WHAT HE MOSTLY WAS.

—Larry McMurtry, *Lonesome Dove* (1985)

three

The Orange & Black Match

11.07.04

THE CIVIL WAR was the strangest war of all. West Point class-mates who drilled together and wore the same dress blues became blood-enemies. When they harmed the enemy, they also harmed one of their own. The soldiers wore different colors but were aware of an ugly reciprocity. It looked right but felt misplaced. There was no joy in victory, for family fights always touch that nerve which is the most quick and tender. The most severe beatings can be dealt at the hands of brothers and older cousins. They know our vulnerabilities. They know what to say and how to make us cry. The same raw nerve is scraped and bruised when collegiate wrestlers face off in "ranking matches."

A ranking match is the standard seven-minute bout staged between two teammates in real-time conditions, and utilized by coaches as a compass to determine who will occupy the starting slot in a weight class not occupied by tested and battle-hardened talent. Not unlike violin prodigies competing for the first chair at Juilliard, these auscultations are family struggles, raw and blatant in their vulnerability. They carry the cold objectivity of an audi-tion and the sublime subtlety of a dogfight. Not for public viewing, they are a wrestling team's version of an in-house corporate takeover.

In those weight classes dominated by returning starters, grizzled veterans routinely massacre heralded, fuzz-faced freshmen. Upsets seldom take place, but lightning can strike as the hierarchy of expectations is capsized. The previ-ous year, in a routine ranking match that now occupies a chapter in Cowboy

LEFT: Senior Clark Shouse, an Academic All-American from Morrison, Oklahoma, was one of 18 wrestlers to win four Oklahoma state high school titles. *Courtesy Oklahoma State University.*

wrestling lore, supremely confident and talented true freshman Daniel Frishkorn pinned two-time national champion senior Johnny Thompson, who went on that season to become a four-time All-American, with Frishkorn iced away in redshirt status. But in the OSU wrestling room, where 28 of the 32 squad members were high school state champions, young talent constantly struggled to catch a coach's eye and bubble to the top. There was no better way to gain notice than by winning a ranking match against a teammate. In those weights where dominance had not been established by a veteran chieftain with proven abilities, two to three unproven wrestlers per weight competed behind closed doors, in the seclusion of the wrestling room, out of public view, and at the mercy of their own abilities.

While winning a ranking match was an important milestone in a young wrestler's maturing process, it did not guarantee a spot in the lineup, but rather provided an opportunity for the yearling to showcase his talents against outside competition during the first stages of the season. If the "first chair" wrestler did not continue his winning ways in those early dual meets, he could expect to "rank" later in the season, or be replaced by a teammate who might have impressed the coaches during workouts or performances in early-season open tournaments. In the end, performance trumped sentimentality and seniority. According to Smith, "We are always evaluating. The goal is to assemble the lineup that has the best chance to score points in March [at the NCAA tournament]."[1]

Smith likened the process to his own experiences in qualifying for two United States Olympic teams in 1988 and 1992. "You're wrestling guys who you train with every day and who know your style. It makes for anxious times, and can cause a wrestler to tighten up. Someone always walks away disappointed. But the season is a marathon."[2]

The first lap of the five-month seasonal marathon for the 2004-2005 squad took place on a crisp, cold mid-November evening in the Cowboy wrestling room with a cluster of ranking matches held in the five weights in question. Winners of those matches would face the top-seeded wrestler in that weight the following evening in the Orange & Black intersquad match held in Gallagher-Iba. On the day of the ranking matches, to simulate live conditions each wrestler was required to make weight one hour before match-time. The matches were held in the wrestling room on the center of three orange mats. Teammates surrounded the mat in small clusters. To avoid the appearance of partiality in the event of a close ruling, the matches often were officiated by an outside referee brought in for the event. Smith placed the struggle in perspective several days earlier. "Guys will use the

BELOW: Redshirt freshman Ryan Freeman, one of two Cowboys from Missouri, amassed a 129-31 high school record. *Courtesy Oklahoma State University.*

ranking matches to identify areas where they need improvement, and will make adjustments that will benefit them later in the upcoming matches."[3]

The matches began at the 125 pound weight class, where four-time Oklahoma high school champion Derrick Fleenor faced high-school phenom and true freshman Coleman Scott, whose parents had traveled from their home in Pennsylvania to see their 18-year-old son compete the following evening in the Orange & Black dual. But Fleenor rallied from a 2-0 deficit and edged Scott 3-2. Ethan Kyle, a three-time state champion from Missouri, broke open a close match and pinned Oklahoma state champion Justin Porter in 6:56 as teammates winced as if viewing the autopsy of a friend. Former state titleist B. J. Jackson defeated four-time state champion Clark Shouse at 149. Tennessee state champion Kevin Ward and state champion Eric Dabbs won their respective matches, setting up a rematch the next evening of their regular practice-room battles at 157. Afterwards, Coach Smith placed the week's competition in perspective. "I love ranking matches. It gives you a chance to see where you are and a chance to look at the areas you haven't worked on enough. After [Wednesday] I know we haven't worked on chain-wrestling enough. Getting off the bottom is always a tough transition for freshmen, because they are used to taking a guy down and pinning him. We also have some guys here who have been in the program who aren't ready to just give spots away to freshmen."[4]

The next evening, the Orange & Black dual was designed to test the rookies in a public environment, unveil new faces to the fans, and give the established starters a chance to bring their game into season-level quality. The coaches divided the team into two squads, proportioned equally with veterans and rookies, and a live dual match was held before fans in Gallagher-Iba Arena. The annual contest broke the monotony of training, provided fans an opportunity to become acquainted with new faces, and gave the coaches a forum to evaluate new-fledged talent.

On the day of the inter-squad dual match the non-qualifiers held a light workout, and as afternoon turned to early evening, an awkward silence permeated the locker room as the 20 teammates separated into two opposing tribes of 10. The 20 were clad in black sweat pants and sweat tops, all except Clay Kehrer. The tall Texas freshman wore a different style of sweatshirt than the rest of the team and did not seem embarrassed when assistant head coach

Sophomore Ethan Kyle, a three-time state champion from Missouri, served as a training partner for Eric Guerrero during the Athens Olympic games. *Courtesy Oklahoma State University.*

Mark Branch directed him to change. Teammates avoided eye contact as an awkward silence permeated the room. Earlier in the week Coach Smith noticed the heightened pressure. "As we're getting closer to challenge matches next week, people get a little more tense and uptight; they want the best out of themselves. If they're not performing up to their expectations, just like anyone, they get a little bit concerned . . . maybe second guessing themselves."[5]

At 7:28 p.m., responding to Coach Smith's prompting, the wrestlers entered the arena, jogged a circle around the bright orange mat, acknowledged the appreciative cheer of the crowd and took their respective places in two opposite rows of folding chairs: 10 facing 10. The lineups were sprinkled with nervous freshmen that only months ago were wide-eyed recruits, flattered that they were being recruited by Oklahoma State. The team was a national collection of small-town wrestling prodigies. The 33 team members came from 14 different states. Twenty-nine hailed from small communities of less than 100,000 people. Twenty-eight were state high school wrestling champions. They all took different journeys to Stillwater, but most of the sojourns began with an early-evening phone call placed after their high school wrestling practice. A soft, earnest voice laced with a slow and courteous Midwest-southern twang spoke to each wrestler by first name. "This is John Smith from Oklahoma State. We're interested in you becoming a Cowboy."

* * *

Malcolm Gladwell suggests in his book *Blink-The Power Of Thinking Without Thinking* that decisions made "in the blink of an eye" can be more accurate than those drawn from laborious and methodical analysis.[6] Gladwell described the psychologist who learned to predict the durability of a marriage just after a few minutes of observation. He discussed Vic Braden, the well-known tennis teacher who can predict a double-fault before the racket makes contact with the ball. Gladwell tracked the story of an antiques dealer who almost instantly recognized that a marble statue on display at a famous museum was not a priceless sixth century relic, as had been asserted by experts. "They simply took a look at that statue and some part of their brain did a series of instant calculations, and before any kind of conscious thought took place, they felt something."[7] The statue turned out to be a fraud.

Similar discernment is required for college wrestling coaches who comb the nation each year in search of high school talent. Smith makes it his business to prospect those high school wrestlers with the ideal combination of talent, work ethic, citizenship, academic promise, and mental toughness necessary to excel in the dominant program in college athletics' most demanding sport. His recruiting net reaches from coast to coast, relying on his own trained eye as well as tips from former OSU wrestlers and the dozens of contacts he has accumulated in the wrestling community spanning the past 25 years. "We are a national program. We look at kids from Oklahoma as well as from across the nation. The local guys grew up watching OSU wrestling. They have seen high quality wrestling and have experienced high quality competition at a very early age. If they take advantage of it, they can be assets to our program. They know the tradition, and they have the spark. They have waited a long time to put on the orange singlet."[8] But only 12 of the 31-member OSU roster were from Oklahoma, and just six of the 300 qualifiers at the upcoming NCAA tournament would be products of Oklahoma high school wrestling.

Smith assembled a melting pot of talent from across the country, and the diversity keeps the coaches on their toes. "Bringing in a national class creates interesting challenges, because geography often dictates behavior. My guys from the West coast are laid back. Instead of punching you in the nose, they will high-five you. My guys from the East coast grew up in concrete jungles, and they need to be stimulated all of the time. Headphones. Video games. Television. You name it. But Stillwater is a good melting pot where guys from across the nation can meld their cultural differences into a single mission. But believe me, my job is never boring."[9]

Educational psychologists write that by the time children reach their 12th birthday, strong beliefs have been formed about the academic subjects in which they will succeed or fail.[10] The same is true in wrestling. "Most of my wrestlers, not all but most, have been competing since they were five or six years old. By the time they reach high school, they are the stars at their respective levels. The skill level of high school wrestlers is getting better and better. They become more and more positioned to make a significant impact in their freshman and sophomore years."[11]

Mastering the art of recruiting is a never-ending learning process. "There are no set formulas, and you never know when you'll hit a gusher or a dry hole. Kids will surprise you. Sometimes a highly-recruited young man from a well-coached program will have already bumped up against his potential. Other times we discover 'works in progress' who did not have advanced high school coaching, but still possess that special something that transcends just a won-loss record, and it's our job to develop that intangible championship quality. Surprises are always around the bend. You just never know."[12] But while Smith factors in the unexpected as he scours the nation for potential talent, he knows that no shortcuts exist in wrestling and recruiting. After a lifetime of being around the sport, Smith developed that trained eye Gladwell discusses in *Blink*, but he understands the end product is up to the competitor. "I usually cannot give them pride or make them tough. They are tough when they get here. What we can do is create an environment where they can figure things out for themselves. About life and wrestling."[13]

Through trial and error, experimentation and grinding perseverance, the 39-year-old Smith learned that mastering the art of recruiting also is a work in progress. "I have learned a lot on the way. For example, when I first began coaching, I didn't understand how important it was to recruits and parents for the head coach to personally visit recruits. We probably lost some guys because of that. Now I get in those living rooms so I can evaluate them and they can evaluate me. I also need to be there to dispel rumors. With the advent of message boards on the Internet, misleading information is often passed around on the availability of scholarships, who will wrestle, and who's being recruited. It helps to be there to clear the air and set the record straight. Also, it legitimizes the wrestler in his own eyes if the head coach is there. That is important. And being face-to-face helps in my final evaluation, because shortly after I enter the living room, I can usually tell what I'm getting. The way the recruit interacts with his parents and siblings. The way the parents interact with each other and with me. I gain a first impression, and I'm right much of the time."[14]

In a family sport like wrestling, parental involvement is the rule. "I don't necessarily shy away from demanding parents, but you can sometimes see immediately that there could be problems. But you never can be sure. Sometimes loud parents produce quiet kids. Sometimes quiet parents

The Cowboy locker room—cleaner than a college student's dorm room!
Courtesy Kim Parrish.

produce loud kids."[15] Smith recognized when you sign the athlete, you often sign the dad and mom as well. "If parents think they are giving me their son to raise, I tell them they are wrong. They have to remain involved as much or more than ever."[16]

Smith understands the influence he and the other coaches have on a recruit is significant, but not as strong as the parental relationship. "Occasionally I will have a favorable impression from a recruit, but after I meet the parents, I know it won't work out. Parents talk with their child 150 times a year, and have more influence than I do."

In Division I programs, football and basketball programs offer full scholarships to individual athletes, but wrestling is considered an "equivalency sport," coaches are required to divide 9.9 scholarships among an entire team, and virtually no one athlete is awarded a full scholarship. Some receive only textbooks for their classes. Others, who could be full scholarship athletes at other schools, receive only the status of being a member of the Cowboy wrestling squad. Smith has to turn away countless wrestlers each year who only want to participate in team workouts for that outside shot at somehow making the team, and for the status conferred within the wrestling community when one states, "I wrestled for Oklahoma State."

The recruiting process is time consuming, expensive, and emotionally exhausting for coaches who invest years and resources into the fortunes of a teenager whose mind changes daily. Moreover, when the recruit finally chooses a school and comes on campus, the work does not end, it expands. "My assistants and I wear lots of different hats every day. Teacher. Counselor. Coach. Confessor. Encourager. Disciplinarian. The list is long, but we enjoy what we do."[17] While the same personal issues facing the wrestlers seem to cycle in year after year, the culture through which those issues are played out is in constant flux. "College kids these days have more opportunities for distractions. For example, when I was in school 20 years ago, not everyone had cars. Now it seems like everyone does. Instead of one bar, now there are 50 bars. Kids want to go to the city for the weekend. Temptations are greater. It's more of a struggle for the student athlete. There are so many things out there they could have a heck of a lot more fun doing than coming in here every day and wrestling. They sacrifice a good portion of their college life to be a wrestler."[18]

Smith navigates through ever-changing waters. "My teams are inevitably a reflection of contemporary youth culture. Remember when Kurt Cobain [lead singer and guitarist for the rock band Nirvana] committed suicide in the mid-90s, and his death spawned the grunge movement? That movement reached its peak in the late 90s, and I observed it among my student-athletes in the way they dressed and acted and talked. Now I deal with distractions caused by communication technology. I collect cell phones from my wrestlers every time we check into hotels. Otherwise, they're talking to their girlfriends day and night and I would never get a word in. But ironically, I send text messages to recruits now. They don't count as phone contacts by NCAA rules, and it's the way kids communicate these days. I have to adapt, or I'm sunk. "The NCAA outlawed text messaging effective August 2007.

When a college athletic program has a coach with star quality like Smith, the school can have more access to recruits, and that notoriety can perhaps break the tie in close recruiting battles, for aspiring champions can project their aspirations through the coach's success. But Smith believes the recruits must ultimately find their own way. "One of the joys of teaching is discovering the mystery of every recruit. Sometimes you take on a guy with character flaws that stand in the way of his being a champion, and you work with him as he matures. Self-centered kids become team-oriented. Very often guys come in that are very low-maintenance. They train diligently, study hard, and are exemplary citizens. In fact, that's the rule rather than the exception in our program. One or two bad apples can suck you dry and destroy what you've worked for. I've seen it happen. Internal weaknesses stand in the way more than physical limitations. In the end, the outstanding student athlete realizes our program can help them optimize their talent and live out their dreams both on the mat and in the classroom. Those are the ones we look for. Those are the ones who wear the orange singlet and become champions."[19]

———————————

Eighteen-hundred fans, the marrow of the OSU wrestling fan base, crowded close to the floor as the 20 teammates clad in black sweats jogged around the mat and took their seats in the brightly lit arena. Coach Smith, dressed in dark slacks and a light orange dress shirt, sat passively at the scorer's table in order not to show favoritism, then moved moments later into the stands. The Orange & Black dual had the festive, non-partisan feel of a family reunion. Pre-match introductions were dispensed with, as most fans knew the wrestlers by first name. Rock music from the 80s blared from the public address system as the matches progressed. The fans relaxed, for they knew a Cowboy would win every match.

Lanky, blond-haired pre-med major Derek Stevens opened with a 5-2 win over Derrick Fleenor. Redshirt freshman Daniel Frishkorn pinned Ethan Kyle in 46 seconds. At 141, Senior Ronnie Delk faced freshman Ryan Davis. Delk, the only member of the team who was married, hoped one day to become a school administrator and wrestling coach. The polite, well-spoken education major had rotated in and out of the Cowboy lineup since his freshman year. A natural athlete who excelled in football and baseball in high school, Delk aspired to the threshold standard in the OSU wrestling culture: "…to make the team, maintain a winning record all year long, do whatever it takes to help my team win a national title, and become a national champion."[20] A potential bout against Davis had simmered in Delk's consciousness throughout the scorching Oklahoma summer. After losing two close matches in the 2003-2004 Big 12 tournament and being denied an at-large bid from the coaches to advance to the NCAA tournament, the two-time high school champion painfully tolerated the whispers that the highly-touted Davis might replace him. "I've kind of had that fueling my fire all summer. I have a little newspaper clipping that talks about 141 not being a solid weight and I look at that every day."[21]

Ryan Davis, one of the most naturally-gifted athletes on the squad, attended high school powerhouse Blair Academy in New Jersey, where he racked up a career record of 155-8 and three national prep titles. Days earlier, the homesick Davis had been on a pay phone at an out-of-town tournament, trying to buy a bus ticket home, when his match was announced. Urged on by a frantic assistant coach, the Cowboy freshman slid off his clothing down to his singlet, walked out without warming up, and registered a technical fall. For the past 18 months he had only sparred with teammates due to a severe knee injury that threatened his competitive career. The theme from the 1980's film *Top Gun* played in the background as Coach Smith watched Delk score takedowns in each of the three periods to earn an impressive 8-3 victory over a heaving and visibly fatigued Davis.

ABOVE: Backups Eric Dabbs (sophomore) and Ryan Davis (freshman) won 299 high school matches, two state championships and two national high school titles between them, but neither could break into the Cowboy lineup. *Courtesy Oklahoma State University.*

At 157, junior Kevin Ward, who began the previous season as the starter before losing his slot to freshman Johny Hendricks, defeated sophomore Eric Dabbs 3-2, which prompted Coach Smith to take notice. "Dabbs is a tough cookie. He is a good kid and he trains hard. The good thing is we've got [two] fine young men that have an opportunity to wrestle there this year."[22] The core of the Cowboy lineup, All-Americans Esposito, Hendricks, Pendleton, and Rosholt cruised to victories. Pendleton, a defending national champion who won by fall in 59 seconds, wore the only solid black singlet of the evening. Coach Smith seldom named a team captain. "I don't want one individual to feel like he is responsible for the team. Everyone has to take care of himself when it comes to competition."[23] But the squad looked to Pendleton for leadership, and the mature and seasoned Cowboy senior accepted the role. "The leaders I want are guys like Pendleton who will lead by example. Guys who train hard and go to class. Guys who can say things to their teammates that I or the other coaches can't say or do. For this team, Pendleton is the guy."[24]

Junior Rusty Blackmon, the 2003-2004 starter at 197 and an NCAA qualifier, had dropped down to 184 during the summer to face Texan Clay Kehrer, the winner of the previous day's challenge match against Jack Jensen. Kehrer scored a second period takedown, earned 1:31 of riding time, and held on to win 3-1, even after curiously releasing Blackmon from the down position with 30 seconds left, a move that drew the ire of Coach Smith later in the week. Kehrer was the only wrestler of the evening to exhibit any emotion after his match, clapping his hands after the final buzzer. "I had a hard time making him wrestle. I knew if I could take him down, I could beat him."[25]

BELOW: Jack Jensen, a history major from Sheboygan, Wisconsin, was embroiled in a dogfight all season at 184 pounds with fellow redshirt freshman Clay Kehrer. *Courtesy Mika Matzen.*

LEFT: Redshirt freshman Brent Parkey won three state titles at Madill, Oklahoma high school. *Courtesy Oklahoma State University.*

BELOW: Freshman Jake Duke, a history major from Stillwater High School, was a standout in wrestling and football in high school. He battled Rosholt day in and day out in the wrestling room. *Courtesy Oklahoma State University.*

As national champion Jake Rosholt worked toward a second period fall over tough freshman Jake Duke from Stillwater, Steve Mocco, the acclaimed transfer from archrival Iowa, was nowhere to be found. Finally his name was announced, and the Cowboy heavyweight ran into the arena like his hair was afire, wearing an orange singlet for the first time in public, and seemingly oblivious to the largest cheer of the evening. He shook the hand of workout partner Mike Christian, a senior pre-law/economics major with a bandaged nose, who battled Mocco before being pinned at the 1:57 mark.

After the match, fans, girlfriends of wrestlers, students, faculty, and family members milled about onto the hardwood maple floor as arena workers rolled the mat into three large cylinders and placed them aside. Autograph seekers gathered around the wrestlers, who heeded Coach Smith's pre-match direction to remain after the match and chat with fans and students. Pendleton and Mocco drew the largest crowds.

Coach Smith stood patiently near the edge of the chairs as a flock of journalists held microphones near his mouth. "Probably one of our better ranking matches as a team. I was encouraged by some things...Clay Kehrer in particular. He deserves the spot and he wrestled like he was determined to make it. The things that some of the guys did wrong, mainly as far as weight, is hitting them in the face with neon lights right now. It's hard to be tough on a guy like Ryan Davis [an 8-3 loser to Delk at 141]. People need to realize that this kid, a year ago, couldn't move his foot and there was a chance he would never wrestle again. That was his first match he's had in over two years."[26]

At practice the following day, Coach Smith scrolled down his two-page hand-written list of notes written in small, delicate print resembling an architect's scribe, and offered snippets of critique and encouragement from the previous evening's performances as the wrestlers, dressed in workout gear, sat on the orange practice mat. The wrestlers who had lost their ranking

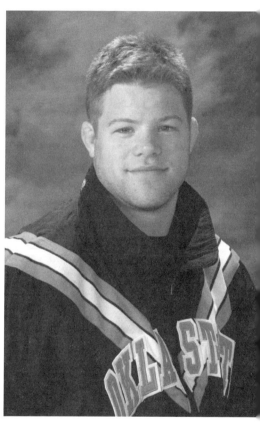

ABOVE: High school All-American Mike Christian tested Steve Mocco in the wrestling room at virtually every practice. The pre-law/economics major from Lynnwood, Washington, who posted a 30-16 career record for the Cowboys, is a banker in Tulsa. *Courtesy Oklahoma State University.*

matches would receive attention from the coaches in managing their disappointment, a process that would likewise contribute to team unity. "Fleenor, I liked how you won your match without getting a takedown. You found a way to win. Davis, great effort to even be out there after a two-year break. But the bottom line, you made a tactical error in managing your weight and you gassed out. Esposito, think beyond the takedown…think about rolling him to his back. Also, you grabbed your eye and didn't call time out. B.J. should have taken you out. He felt sorry for you. Hendricks, tying up is a comfort zone you need to get out of. Pendleton, good effort. Blackmon, you didn't seem to be interested in your match. Clay, you're up 2-0 with thirty seconds left and you let him up? Ride him out. Don't put him in a position where he's one takedown away from winning. Mocco, good intensity. But be aware on driving the arm bar too far."[27] A wrestler can be disqualified from a match and consequently eliminated from the NCAA tournament if a potentially dangerous maneuver such as an arm bar is applied improperly in the eyes of the official, and Coach Smith cautioned against that possibility. "I worry about the guy who screams and hollers in the national finals and our wrestler gets eliminated."[28]

He then called out the four Cowboys who suffered wrestling's most glaring indignity and were pinned the previous evening. "You never know when you might be thrown to your back. I don't care who I'm wrestling, when I get taken to my back, I get up. I don't care if I have to choke myself out." To "choke out" is wrestling parlance for a competitor who loses consciousness while straining to move from his back onto his side or stomach. "If I'm in that position, I get up. It's an issue of personal pride, and it starts in this wrestling room. I take pride in this room. That's where it begins."[29]

Glancing at the black leather notebook that contained notes penned in small, careful script, Smith stepped back and placed his hands on his hips. "Our conditioning looked solid. But some of you didn't cut weight properly, and it showed in your endurance. Bottom line, I'm giving you the freedom to manage your weight on your own. But if you don't manage it properly, then you're mine. You can't train while several pounds over your competitive weight. It won't work. Some of you sacrificed performance because of how you cut weight. That won't happen under my guidance."[30]

Smith then stepped back, glanced at the final item on his list, and spoke softly. The Oklahoma State football team was practicing outside the west

A scrupulous note-taker, Coach Smith records his thoughts during a Cowboy practice. His notes reach back 20 years. *Courtesy Kim Parrish.*

window of the wrestling room, and the padded walls and heavy heaters created made the wrestling room feel like a stuffy cocoon. "Be aware of the guy who gets hyper-intense during the first few seconds of your match. You may assume you will work your way into the match at your own pace, but occasionally you run into a guy who starts banging you around right off the whistle and you find yourself in trouble. Most of the time it happens at the very beginning of the match. Bring your intensity up to meet him. It won't last. Believe me."[31]

At 4:20 p.m. the team trudged upstairs to an indoor concourse area one-half mile in circumference, which circled the basketball arena. Off Smith's whistle they ran sprints in half-mile ovals. Afterwards they paired up on the cold, gray concrete and struggled for control over their opponent's hands and arms through constant grasping and tugging. "Three periods of hand fighting. Keep your head up and hands inside."[32] During the drill, Mocco tripped redshirt freshman Jack Jensen to the concrete floor and the exercise almost elevated into fisticuffs. "Later in the season there will be fights every time we do this drill."[33] Before blows were landed, Smith intervened and the drill resumed.

With the completion of the Orange & Black dual, the first stage of qualifying for a coveted spot in the starting lineup was complete. Younger wrestlers staked their claim in the lighter weights. As the season progressed some would tighten their grip, while others' hands would be pried loose in the heat of competition. The first shots were fired and the battle was joined. The campaign of 2004-2005 was underway.

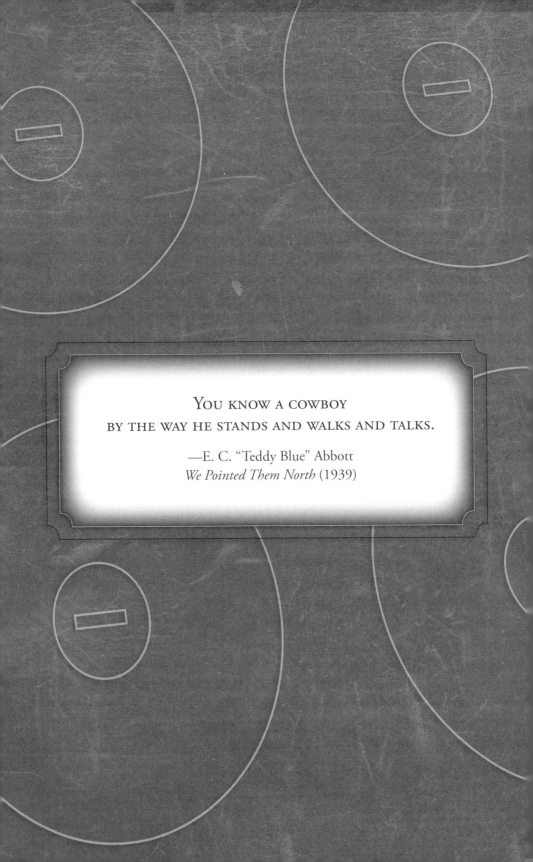

YOU KNOW A COWBOY
BY THE WAY HE STANDS AND WALKS AND TALKS.

—E. C. "Teddy Blue" Abbott
We Pointed Them North (1939)

four

the university of tennessee at chattanooga/ boise state

11.14.04

TENNESSEE CHATTANOOGA (UTC), the Cowboy's opening dual opponent for the third consecutive year, was coached by Iowa star Terry Brands. The former Olympian hoped to restore a winning tradition in the wrestling-starved border state. UTC had captured 19 conference championships since 1978 and hired Brands in hopes of restoring credibility to a program that had fallen on lean years. The 36-year old Brands, a two-time NCAA champion for Iowa in the early 90s, competed against the Cowboys in his collegiate days and coached against OSU during his tenure as an assistant coach at Nebraska and Iowa. He scheduled the Cowboys in hopes of providing a benchmark upon which his team could measure their progress. "We believe that in order to be the best, we have to wrestle the best."[19]

The first match of the evening matched OSU redshirt junior 125-pounder Derek Stevens against UTC's Matt Pitts. Stevens, a pre-med major who aspired to be an orthopedic surgeon, admitted that thirst, rather than nerves, usually kept him up the evening before a match. Stevens was a two-time state champion at nearby Norman High School, and had accumulated 49 victories for the Cowboys in various open tournaments over the previous three seasons. He wrestled in two varsity duals the previous year, where he lost a 4-2 heartbreaker to then-fifth ranked Sam Hazewinkel of Oklahoma, and defeated Lehigh All-American Mario Stuart 3-2. The current semester, along with his wrestling duties, Stevens was enrolled in the deadly trinity of pre-med courses that often sent aspiring doctors scurrying to other majors—Fundamentals of Organic Chemistry, Immunology and Advanced Physics.

Most of Stevens' matches resembled pitchers' duals between Cy Young winners. Low scoring, meticulous, and cautious, the cerebral Stevens, who was prone to read John Irving novels during long bus rides, relied on strategy and timing and sought to convert the pace and flow of the match from an alley brawl to a chess match. The book on the brown-haired, lanky Stevens was clear—if he scored one takedown per match, he would probably win. If he could muster two takedowns, he was most certain to win. Three takedowns and he was a world-beater. Possessing excellent defensive skills, Stevens was difficult to ride for a full period and seldom gave up back points, wrestling's proverbial long ball. He knew how to use the out of bounds line as an extra defender and seldom initiated high-risk moves that could result in disaster. A cross-country runner in high school, he possessed the lungs necessary to wrestle seven tough, intelligent minutes. If left in the lineup all season, Stevens would stay in all of his matches and win more than his share. But could he grind out those close encounters necessary to be an All-American at the end of the year against opponents of superior athletic ability? Oklahoma State had produced so many All-American wrestlers in their storied history that in Stillwater the term "All-American" had been transfigured from an adjective to a verb. 206 wrestlers "All-Americaned" 401 times.

Stevens' encounter with Pitts followed the prototypical pattern of many of his matches. After a scoreless first period, Stevens chose the down position and escaped in seconds. Neither wrestler managed a takedown in the second period, and entered the final frame with Stevens leading 1-0. Pitts escaped in nine seconds into the final period to tie the score 1-1. Stevens was in a familiar situation—no first period takedown, with both wrestlers trading escapes in the second and third periods, leaving the match tied 1-1 in the third and final frame. The first wrestler to score a takedown would probably checkmate. Pitts scored a takedown just 17 seconds after his escape to lead 3-1. Stevens escaped 6 seconds later. Trailing 3-2, he could win the match with points in the final 1:28. While the wrestlers stalked one another with cautious aggression, both Frishkorn and Delk warmed up behind the bench with coaches Branch and Guerrero flanking them, expressionless, arms folded. Seeing time running out, Coach Smith stood up, took one step toward the mat, and with hands cupped, barked, "No half shots,"[20] imploring Stevens to move his feet and generate offense. But Pitts controlled Stevens' head and arms the final 90 seconds, and Stevens could not score the needed takedown. So the opening match of the opening dual of the season for the top-ranked and defending national champions was a 3-2 loss.

As the final buzzer sounded, Coach Smith tossed his scorecard down and turned away as Stevens, shoulders heaving with exhaustion and body covered with a film of sweat, picked up his warm-up gear, walked away from the mat, and disappeared under the bleachers, making no eye contact with any coach or teammate. The Cowboy wrestlers are seldom congratulated immediately after a victory, much less consoled after a loss. Winning is expected, and those who lose are avoided as if they carried a contagious, deadly virus.

One afternoon after a long and brutal practice, Stevens leaned against the wall of the wrestling room, holding a backpack crammed full of textbooks, his hair wet from a locker room shower. He almost smiled as he spoke of "the dark side" of competitive, big-time college wrestling. "It's the heartbreak and broken dreams. You taste a measure of success yourself, you see others succeed on a higher level, and you want to be like them. You want to have that experience, so you keep coming back. Maybe it will happen."[21]

That afternoon Stevens could not achieve a necessary last-period takedown, but in the upcoming weeks he did master Organic Chemistry, scoring an A in a course that sends lesser men scurrying away. They wanted to have that experience of academic success, so they kept coming back. Maybe it would happen for them. It certainly did for Derek Stevens.

The Cowboys went on to win eight of the remaining nine matches, but potential weaknesses were exposed early. Ronnie Delk was taken down three times but held on to win 12-8 after jumping out to a 7-1 second period lead. Top-ranked Zack Esposito was thrown to his back and came from behind to earn a 15-10 victory over an unranked freshman. As he sat on the bench, the discouraged junior informed assistant coach Pat Smith he was quitting the sport and going home. The less than sympathetic Smith was non-plussed, "If you're going to quit, go clean out your locker. But

Daniel Frishkorn establishes position against Boise State's Scott Jorgenson. *Courtesy Jim Bowen.*

don't take your wrestling shoes with you. Leave those here for someone else."[22] Esposito stayed.

Second-ranked Johny Hendricks gave up two final-period takedowns and lost 5-3. An unranked wrestler took down Jake Rosholt twice before the Cowboy national champion achieved a third-period pin. Mocco, competing in a college match for the first time in 18 months, faced UTC heavyweight Diaz Edwards, who stood on the edge of the mat slapping himself in the face as if to say, "What am I doing here?" With the orange singlet reflected against his skin like translucent neon, Mocco flattened Edwards in 14 seconds, and sprinted off the mat to the crowd's wild delight.

OSU flattened Boise State in the afternoon dual 38-0, highlighted by Mocco's 12 takedowns en route to a 26-11 technical fall. Smith was realistic in his post-match comments, "There was some good, some not-so-good and there was some bad."[23]

The Cowboys were given Monday off to rest and catch up on studies, then gathered at 3:00 on Tuesday for practice. There was a time in the recent past, during Cowboy practices, when John Smith would engage in live wrestling with his team, starting on the north side of the wrestling with the lighter weights and working his way south across the room through the middle and heavy weights, whipping them all. These days Smith seldom went full speed. But even though 12 years had elapsed since he last competed, at his unalloyed core he was still a wrestler. One Cowboy wrestler recalled months earlier seeing Smith wrestling with Jamill Kelly, a silver medalist in the 2004 Olympic games in Athens and former Cowboy, who

Ronnie Delk unleashes an explosion against Jacob Scoles of Boise State. Delk got the fall at 6:27. *Courtesy Jim Bowen.*

was riding Smith in the center of the middle mat in the wrestling room. Smith noticed his young wrestler watching, caught his eye and subtly gave a "watch this" wink. Moments later Kelly was reversed and plastered to his back.[24] Occasionally wrestlers would come to the wrestling room after lunch and before afternoon practice to wrestle Smith, who would occasionally leave his office early to dress out for practice. He still seldom ate more than one or two meals in a day, and appeared he could make weight again if called upon by his country. Today Smith, dressed in black sweat pants and orange t-shirt, stood and spoke in a conversational tone as he paced in a small circle, gesturing with his hands as he held a whistle on a string. "We're expected to win 20 matches out of 20 matches and dominate everyone, but we're just at this point in the season. It's very difficult to wrestle your best early in the year. We are not there yet."[25] The Cowboys had won 18 of the 20 pairings during the two duals, but Smith knew whenever Oklahoma State lost even one match it provided the opposition a measure of hope. "We didn't wrestle complete matches. We stopped moving, got out of our stance, lost focus, and gave up some third-period takedowns."[26] Several wrestlers did not meet Smith's gaze, but the agitated Cowboy coach spoke of a theme that would punctuate much of his teaching emphasis throughout the season, the process of chain wrestling. Not just hitting one move, but igniting a series of consecutive attacks, like standing dominos falling one upon the other. The execution of a sequence of moves that progressed seamlessly, structured like a chain, one after the other. "We did not chain wrestle. We made one attempt and stopped. We will drill on that today."[27]

He glanced at freshman Daniel Frishkorn, who wore a long-sleeve sweatshirt taped tightly at the wrist. Frishkorn won by injury default at an open tournament on the previous Sunday after driving his opponent to the mat in the first minute of his first match. "This weekend two guys went down with serious injuries. That comes from a lack of intensity and it only takes one time. You seldom see guys wrestling with intensity who get injured."[28]

Smith then passionately discussed "scrambling," where wrestlers frantically battle in a tangled, dirty, disarray until one ends up on top. "We win scrambles. In a scramble someone's going to quit. We don't quit unless we die. We don't quit scrambling. I can't teach you that. Winning a scramble comes from a desire to put points on the board. Anytime you get in a scramble, do not quit until you end up on top. Win or die."[29]

He walked away and glanced at a black leather notebook containing meticulous notes that mapped out the day's workout. "Spend 25 minutes going through set-ups to shots. Chain wrestling. Let's go."[30]

A moment after the drilling began, someone screamed from the south side of the wrestling room where the upper weights worked out. A wrestler had been poked in the eye, according to the deliverer, "up to the first knuckle."[31] No one stopped wrestling. A trainer slipped on rubber gloves, walked over and applied eye drops and a wet pack. The white-shirted trainer dropped to his knee, applied an antibiotic to the redden eye, and softly whispered, "You should be all right in a few minutes."[32]

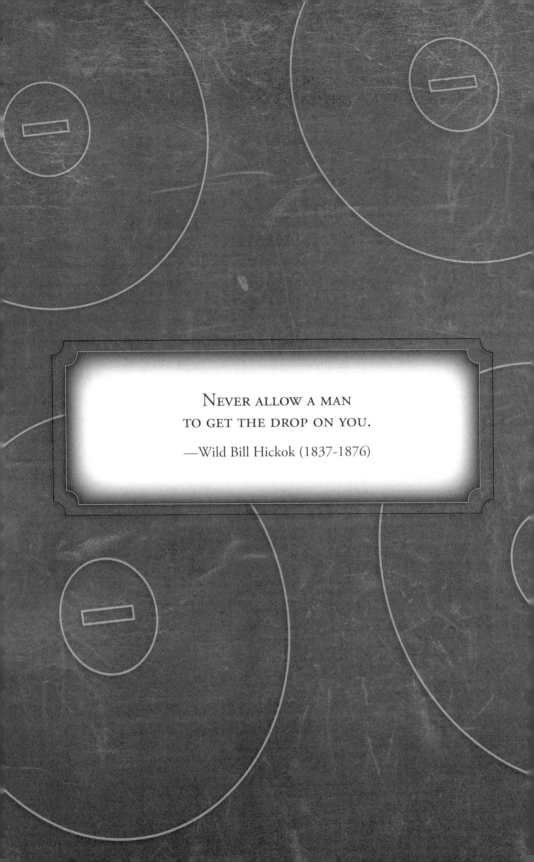

Never allow a man
to get the drop on you.

—Wild Bill Hickok (1837-1876)

five

12.05.04

DURING COACH SMITH'S TENURE at OSU his teams held a winning record against all opposition. That is, everyone, except the Minnesota Golden Gophers.

In their 14 meetings during Smith's 12-year tenure as Cowboy head coach, OSU and Minnesota stood 7-7. The previous season the Golden Gophers visited Stillwater and upended the No. 1-ranked Cowboys, on Senior Day, 17-16. But the unlikely defeat seemed to goad the Cowboys, as they regrouped three weeks later to capture the NCAA Championship over second place Iowa.

Minnesota coach "J" Robinson was a 1969 OSU graduate and a top assistant to Dan Gable in the forging of the Iowa wrestling juggernaut during the '70s and '80s. He became the Golden Gopher head coach in 1985, and through exceptional recruiting and coaching, Minnesota replaced Iowa as the Big Ten's dominant program, capturing consecutive NCAA titles in 2001 and 2002. Robinson's entire 2002 squad won individual All-American honors, a feat even Oklahoma State never had accomplished. Within weeks of this OSU dual match, Robinson had been elected a Distinguished Member of the National Wrestling Hall of Fame for his efforts in the promotion and coaching of wrestling.

But success had not come quickly, for building a Division I championship squad is a long and tedious process. The task requires a coach to generate fan support, find allies within an athletic department that traditionally fawns over lucrative sports such as football and basketball, and establish the credibility necessary to attract a perpetual flow of blue-chip recruits, all on a limited budget.

It took Robinson 15 years to win his first NCAA title at Minnesota. But while climbing to the top was slow and laborious, sliding back down the slippery slope could be headlong and ruthless. Two seasons earlier, Robinson's team finished a strong second at the NCAA's, but the following year's troupe had fallen to eighth. A sympathetic John Smith understood "everything can come apart at any moment."[1] His first Cowboy squad won the 1993-1994 NCAA title, but finished seventh the following year, the lowest finish for an OSU squad since the NCAA first sponsored the tournament in 1928. The Cowboys then experienced a nine-year drought, before winning their next championship. The vagaries of cut-throat recruiting and budget limitations in an era of heightened competition, along with the challenge of guiding college students through the unpredictable and sometimes eccentric travails of homesickness, girlfriends, making weight, academic responsibilities, meeting parental expectations, and not being a starter for perhaps the first time in their wrestling lives, presented perpetual challenges. Yet despite these demands, Minnesota wrestling remained near the top. In 2004 Robinson gathered a top-flight recruiting class, and with plans to insert several redshirt freshmen into his 2005 lineup, he hoped to ripen his team into national contenders.

On Tuesday before the Minnesota match, with his team dressed in workout gear and seated in the wrestling room, Coach Smith delivered a short scouting report on Minnesota's tendencies. His voice was firm and clipped. "Minnesota will take repeated knee shots and then back out, trying to draw stalling calls. They'll have a good crowd in their small arena, hoping they can intimidate an official. Some stalls will be called against us. Expect it. We can't do anything about it."[2]

The stalling penalty, college wrestling's version of college basketball's 35-second clock, was designed to speed up action and generate more scoring. NCAA rules require a wrestler to stay near the center of the mat when possible, and to initiate offensive moves. If, in the judgment of the official, a wrestler is not adequately aggressive, penalty points are assessed after one warning. "In response to their knee shots, we should counter with re-shots all day long. We'll drill for 20 minutes and wrestle two matches. Let's go."[3]

For the next two days the team drilled, conditioned, and wrestled live matches, but on Friday the intensity was reigned in. They drilled and wrestled one live match but suspended the customary sprinting drill after practice to allow wrestlers to regain leg strength after the trauma of workouts the previous three days. After practice concluded, Coach Smith set out the weekend travel plans. "Vans will leave from Gallagher-Iba tomorrow morning at 5:30 a.m. Randy [equipment manager Randy Pogue] will have your equipment cleaned, so be ready to go. I want everyone who is staying in a house tonight to make sure someone wakes you up. We will arrive in Minneapolis at 10:00, check in, and take a nap...and work out at 3:00."[4] Every year since 1988, Coach Smith had conducted a summer wrestling clinic for colleagues on the coaching staff at Augsburg College. The private Lutheran university, located in the heart of the Twin Cities, is a Division III wrestling powerhouse. Later in the year it would capture its ninth national title, crowning 10 All-Americans and four national champions. "If anyone needs to work out Sunday morning we'll go back to Augsburg. Weigh-in is at 1:00. The match is at 2:00. We'll fly back to Tulsa that night immediately after the match."[5]

The next morning at 4:40 a.m. Coach Smith was on his cell phone waking up wrestlers. The squad boarded the vans on schedule, made the 75-minute drive to the Tulsa airport and touched down in Minneapolis at 9:20 a.m. The wrestlers gathered their black nylon bags containing gear, books, and a change of clothes, climbed into two white rental vans commandeered by assistant coaches Mark Branch and Eric Guerrero, and drove to their hotel to rest and study.

The Sunday afternoon dual match was held on the Minnesota campus in the university's Sports Pavilion, a small auxiliary gym attached to the primary arena. Smith walked to morning mass near campus with members of the wrestling staff, and returned to the hotel for a weight-check of his wrestlers.

A bitterly cold, sun-drenched afternoon greeted the Cowboys as the vans carried the team one-half mile from the hotel to the arena. Weigh-in took place in a small 10'x 30' dressing room, bordered by lockers and located off a downstairs catacomb of hallways built in cinder block and painted white. After the 1:00 p.m. weigh-in, the wrestlers hurried 30 paces down the hallway to their small locker room and began their pre-match routine of eating snacks—bagels and cream cheese, fruit, deli meat, Gatorade, and Power Bars.

At 1:10 p.m. Steve Mocco slept face up, stretched across the locker room floor with a white towel draped over his face. His trademark blue bathroom slippers were pulled over white socks, and he drew long, gentle breaths as he dozed. Walking out of the locker room, Smith looked down at his heavy-weight. "He probably couldn't sleep last night…now he has weighed in and finds himself relaxed for the first time in 24 hours."[6]

Smith left the locker room and stood inside a door that led into the arena. Fans filed in as giant video screens, suspended above the mats by thick cables, reflected video highlights of landmark Minnesota victories over Oklahoma State, including footage from Minnesota's stunning defeat of the Cowboys in Stillwater the previous year.

Smith stood alone, dressed in a conservative dark suit and orange print tie, with hands in pockets. Seeing his image flash on the giant video screen, he turned away and began walking back to the visitor's locker room. As he entered the locker room, Smith slipped by Jake Rosholt. The taciturn Cowboy sat motionless next to the door, eyes closed, knees pulled under his chin. In a small bathroom area that adjoined the dressing facility, Ronnie Delk held his stomach and grimaced, cramping from the recent and sud-den influx of food and drink into his previously empty stomach. Coach Branch pounded Hendricks' side with his fist, trying to force the bloated 165-pounder's food to settle. After the wrestlers consumed their post weigh-in snack, nervous stomachs stuffed with food mixed with adrenalin caused the two bathroom stalls to flush continually.

Earlier that morning, Randy Pogue, working from a list of specific requests submitted by the wrestlers, made a grocery run for items the wrestlers would consume after the one o'clock weigh-in. For an hour before each road match, Pogue was the most important individual in each wrestler's life, for he carried with him their list of requested pre-match snacks. One hungry and parched wrestler wanted blue Gatorade while another required bottled Sprite. Some requested cinnamon-raisin bagels, while others insisted upon whole wheat. The no-nonsense Pogue, a psychology major who sought a career in sports management, used his degree regularly in negotiating with the wrestlers' eccentric eating habits. Returning from the local market, he placed the groceries on a masseurs' table located in the shower area. Within minutes, the table resembled the aftermath of a Red Cross food-drop in an undernourished country, littered with empty wrappers, hollow Gatorade bottles, orange peels, candy wrappers, plastic bags, half-used mustard bottles, scraped-out cream cheese containers, seedless and gnawed-down watermelon rinds, and opened tuna cans so sparkling clean they appeared to have been washed in a dishwasher.

Manager Randy Pogue's considerable skills at behind-the-scenes problem solving set the stage for the Cowboy's championship season. *Courtesy Oklahoma State University.*

Over the next few minutes, the wrestlers pulled on their orange singlets and black warm-ups, laced on their shoes, and sat in meditative silence. The room smelled of sweat, tuna fish, and pine-scented air freshener. At 1:45 p.m. the match referee walked into the locker room for his pre-match comments. The official wore a black windbreaker over a stocky frame, with his hair styled in the most primitive form of crew cut. "I know many of you. I called last year's dual with Iowa. If you keep banging and going forward you'll have no problems with me today. If we get to the edge of the mat, listen up. Be cautious about doing something goofy like launching your opponent off the stage. Good luck on last year's success. Let's have a good match."[7]

The official slipped around Coach Smith and left the tiny locker room while Smith stepped to the center of the room. "All right guys, bring it

in."[8] On cue, the wrestlers gathered in a tight circle around unofficial team captain Chris Pendleton, who whispered unknown remarks to his team-mates before voicing a personal prayer on behalf of his team. The ten wres-tlers turned to Coach Smith, who spoke with a sharpened urgency. "Leave nothing out there. If you have a chance to get majors, then get majors.

The Cowboys traveled to the Twin Cities to take on Minnesota on the Golden Gophers' raised stage. *Courtesy University of Minnesota Intercollegiate Athletics.*

Put 'em away. Let's go." He glanced at Pendleton. "Lead 'em out. Lead 'em out."9

The team filed out, marching through the maze of hallways and up a flight of stairs before trotting into the darkened arena to a light crackling of applause from the Minnesota fans.

Consistent with his penchant for marketing and promotions, combined with an innate understanding that he must not only win matches but also entertain fans, Coach Robinson and the Minnesota athletic department took advantage of the No. 1-ranked Cowboys' visit. They had prepared a minute-by-minute extravaganza, choreographed to the last detail and designed to entertain the announced crowd of 3,058 by showcasing Robinson's young but talented squad. The event had the feel of a college concert, a darkened arena with a giant structure suspended from the ceiling that poured light on the maroon mat. The mat itself was rolled out on a waist-high stage elevated like a boxing rink without the protective ropes. The Minnesota mascot, clad in a yellow Gopher costume, rappelled from the one-hundred fifty foot ceiling via thick, yellow ropes. He flashed by two of the giant screens before touching down, all to the delight of the fans. Earlier in the morning, a typed schedule that controlled, in detail, everything but the outcome of the matches, was handed to the OSU staff:

12:39	Highlight tape of 2002 season
1:03	Live interview with Gopher Assistant Coach
1:06	Highlight tape of 2003 season
1:27	Live interview with OSU Coach John Smith
1:31	Pre-game interview with Gophers
1:37	Pre-produced "rivalry video"
1:45	Introduction of public address announcer
1:49	Introduction of OSU team
1:49:30	Minnesota Mascot repels from rafters to the tune of "Mission Impossible"
1:51:30	Introduction of Minnesota team
1:52	Wrestlers introduced…alternating
1:54	Full Color Guard/National Anthem
1:58	Welcome/Clear Floor
2:00	Match #1 begins

Minnesota took an early lead with 10th-ranked senior Bobbe Lowe's 12-3 thrashing of Derrick Fleenor. Walking off the mat after the match, Fleenor seemed to grimace as he passed by Smith, who avoided eye contact. Fleenor almost collided with Esposito, who was up from the bench and leaning over trainer Chris Pickering. "Do we have any Pepto-Bismol?"[10]

Next up for the Cowboys was 133-pounder Daniel Frishkorn, who shook Smith's hand and bounded up the three steps leading onto the elevated mat. Frishkorn was the top-ranked high school recruit in the nation in 2002. His 182-11 record still stood as the winningest in Virginia prep history. The 20-year-old redshirt freshman won four state titles at Great Bridge High School, Virginia, and the previous season had stunned defending two-time national champion Johnny Thompson with a defiant first period pin during the Orange & Black dual. Wearing black shoes with yellow trim, the sharp-featured redshirt freshman began to wrestle his first road match as a member of the Cowboy varsity. The journey to this spot was long and winding.

While recovering from a serious childhood illness, Frishkorn spent long hours watching professional wrestling on television. His uncle, an amateur wrestling fan, asked the precocious boy if he were interested in becoming a wrestler. Frishkorn said sure, and during the first few weeks of junior wrestling he imagined himself to be in training to be a professional wrestling superhero himself. But he soon learned this sport boasted no predetermined winners and losers. Victories had to be earned. Participating in one of the many youth wrestling clubs in the area, he realized wrestling was fun, and winning was gratifying. When he reached the eighth grade, his mother Karen recognized her son's special aptitude for the sport and moved the family to nearby Great Bridge High School in Chesapeake, Virginia, known for its high academic standards and accomplished wrestling program. The move was a windfall for Frishkorn's development. His high school coach was Steve Martin of the legendary Martin clan of Virginia, the Commonwealth's first family of wrestling and inventor of the fabled wrestling maneuver the Granby Roll.

Steve's older brother Billy was an All-American at Oklahoma State in the '70s under Tommy Chesboro, but Steve wrestled at Iowa under Dan Gable, and had come to Great Bridge, according to Frishkorn, "like a bat outa' hell,"[11] drilling and training the Wildcats to a level of technique and mastery that had bordered on college-level precision. The diligence paid off. Frishkorn, with the assistance of his grandfather, whose generosity and support allowed him to showcase his talents in various high school open tournaments across

Virginia high school star Daniel Frishkorn, who struggled with his weight throughout the season, possessed an explosive offensive arsenal. *Courtesy Mika Matzen.*

the nation and won everything in sight. He captured four state titles and became the number one high school recruit in the country. Schools like Cornell, Penn State, Arizona State, and Nebraska had called for his services.

But Frishkorn had decided on Oklahoma State. "I sensed the guys at OSU were a tight-knit group...a real positive environment. No cliques. No trash talking. The guys hung out together. They supported one another. I liked that. When it comes down to the end of the year and the going gets tough, and you need every edge, a close team can sometimes provide that winning edge. I saw that in Coach Smith and the OSU program."[12]

He arrived at OSU brimming with confidence. Only once in high school had he experienced the ultimate form of competitive humiliation shared by all wrestlers at every level: getting pinned—a stinger he experienced his senior year in high school. "I was beating my guy by three or four points. I was on bottom about to hit a Granby when he locked up a cradle.

He had these long arms and I felt him lock it up. That was the first loss of my senior year. I wanted to go undefeated and be a four-time state champ. It was pretty tragic."[13]

Constantly fighting his weight, Frishkorn developed an understanding of his own metabolism and how he needed to fine tune the weight loss process to be at maximum strength. "I want to come in from six to nine pounds over about five days before competition. I'll bring it down to within two to three [pounds] a day out. The key is watching what you eat and drink those last couple of days. I try to eat lots of carbs and really watch what I drink. You want to have those carbs running through your system the last twenty-four hours so you don't step on the mat and hit a wall. But it's the liquids that will bring you down. Gotta' watch those."[14] Recognizing that the physical and mental stress of conditioning and managing his weight could make it difficult to maintain proper focus on his studies, [the biology major took pre-organic chemistry in the fall], Frishkorn completed summer classes to help relieve the academic pressure when wrestling season began. "It works out best when you're pulling weight."[15]

An East Coast native who enjoyed fishing and crabbing, Frishkorn had to adjust to land-locked Stillwater. "It was a big culture shock coming from the beaches of Virginia out here with the cows and the farmland and the crops. I saw a cow at a petting zoo once when I was young…now they're everywhere."[16] He even admitted to spells of homesickness. "But my teammates and I do everything together. On Friday we'll go to someone's house and then go out as a team."[17] The common bond he shared with his teammates was the collective desire to maximize their wrestling potential. "Around here you don't hear guys come in and say 'Man, another practice. I can't wait to get this over with.' Rather, it's like, 'Do you want to drill? Let's work on something.' Guys are here to get better and to win."[18] Frishkorn understood his sights were set high. "My expectations this year are to go undefeated and win a national championship. I believe I can if I keep my weight down. There's no doubt in my mind."[19]

The scoreboard registered a 4-0 Minnesota lead as Frishkorn climbed up the three steps onto the elevated mat. He stood atop an island of brightness, illuminated by a cluster of shining stage lights raised against a dark sea of Minnesota fans dressed in flannel shirts and jeans with snow gear piled at their feet. The rowdy fans, pleased to be inside the toasty gym and protected from the artic front which had slipped in the day before, greeted Frishkorn with catcalls as he jogged to center stage to face freshman Mack Reiter. Reiter was the first blue chip recruit from Iowa ever to sign with Minnesota, and he was off to a blazing 12-1 start, leading the team in pins. His only loss had come at the hands of Cowboy true freshman Nathan Morgan, at the Omaha open tournament days before. Frishkhorn had been dominating Morgan in the Cowboy wrestling room, and although Reiter was ranked 12th in the country, the Cowboy coaches thought Frishkorn had the fire-power to post a win.

Their hopes were confirmed when the aggressive Frishkorn hit a spectac-ular throw 1:30 into the first period, giving him a 2-1 lead. He started the second period in the down position, immediately bracing against an inside cradle attempt which Reiter initiated off the whistle. Frishkorn then came to his feet and escaped in fifteen seconds.

During his senior year in high school the top-ranked Frishkorn had been cradled and pinned by an inferior opponent, for the only fall he suffered in his entire high school career. He realized his short frame, coupled with an occasional tendency to place his head on the mat while maneuvering for a single-leg takedown, made him vulnerable to an inside cradle, a move in which the offensive wrestler locked his hands around the opponent's head and leg and tilted him to his back in a cradle-like motion.

Frishkorn and Reiter circled for another minute before Frishkorn snapped an off-balance Reiter to the mat, causing teammate Chris Pendleton to drop his jaw in awe. Reiter managed another escape before the second period ended, giving Frishkorn a solid 4-2 lead with 1:22 in riding time.

The third period began with both wrestlers in the neutral position. Frishkorn could score a much-needed four-point major decision for the team with a combination of two takedowns and back points during the final two minutes.

Just 33 seconds into the final period, Frishkorn shot a single leg and felt Reiter sprawl back, which forced Frishkorn's head to flatten to the mat. Realizing he did not have the proper angle to finish the move, he momentarily stopped his motion and rested his head on the mat as he clung to Reiter's leg. In that instant, Frishkorn weighed the need to rack up more points against the urge to eat up time and claim the victory. At that moment Reiter felt his opportunity, with his eyes narrowed like a sniper in the grass. Dropping to Frishkorn's side, he vice-gripped his hands around the head and inside leg, and while pressuring his own head into Frishkorn's inside hip for leverage, Reiter cranked Frishkorn clockwise toward his back in a circling motion—a textbook inside cradle. Frishkorn's vantage point prevented him from seeing Reiter's hands, but the moment they locked Frishkorn sensed danger. He momentarily gained stability as he posted an arm to halt Reiter's pressure. But the Minnesota freshman knew he was in the proper position to finish the move if he only could complete the turn. With the adrenalin that springs from revived hope, he drove Frishkorn to his back at the 1:27 mark, as the Minnesota fans erupted in joyous glee.

To score a fall, a wrestler must force his opponent's shoulders into contact with the mat for a full second. Frishkorn's inside shoulder touched the mat, and he strained to keep his outside shoulder, then less than one inch from the mat's surface, from touching. Frishkorn's face remained expressionless, almost stoic and understanding, while his body strained and barely shook, as if Reiter was attempting to force Frishkorn's shoulder to touch the top of a red-hot oven.

Frishkorn finally struggled to his stomach but was unable to break Reiter's grasp. The buzzer sounded and Reiter was awarded two points for a takedown and three points for a near fall. The Minnesota crowd roared with delirium as the referee raised Reiter's hand for a 7-4 win, giving Minnesota a 7-0 lead in this dual against the top-ranked Cowboys. The panting Frishkorn walked behind the bench, grabbed his warm-up bag, and trudged to the back wall, sitting underneath a basketball goal as assistant coach Eric Guerrero spoke to him in the patient tone of a knowing teacher. "In work-outs you've resisted making rapid transitions between moves and you got cradled. You've got to be more open-minded. You're five points better than that guy."[20]

At intermission, while the team rested in the locker room, Smith cornered Frishkorn at the end of the hall. "You let him stay in the match. You gave him an opening in the end and he took advantage of it. You better learn a lesson from this loss." [21]

Smith stepped back and let silence wash over the dejected Frishkorn. "You shot and you sat there, and it cost you a match. But you're still my 133 pounder."[22] He would not be for long.

The Cowboys went on to win seven out of the eight remaining matches. Johny Hendricks, exhausted after pulling out an inspiring 5-3 sudden victory, threw off his headgear and rested on all fours behind the bench, his chest heaving like a heavy John Deere engine at idle. Ronnie Delk, talking around a piece of rock candy he had drawn from the pocket of his warm-up to celebrate his victory, looked admiringly at Hendricks. "That's gutsy", he said, exuding that sweet euphoria of a winner's recovery after his dominating 8-1 decision over Quincy Osborn at 141. "That's gutsy."[23]

Coach Smith swung around, took in the condition of his exhausted 165 pounder, and motioned to his brother, Pat. "Get him off his knees and against the wall." Smith walked behind the Cowboy bench and joined Coach Branch as they admonished Hendricks for allowing Nagel to stay in the match. "That's going to come back and bite you this year."[24] Indeed, it would.

Frishkorn, soothed by Smith's intermission lecture, rejoined the bench sporting a baseball cap tilted to the side as he sat like a boy watching televised wrestling.

Clay Kehrer, the only other Cowboy to lose, dropped a 5-4 cliffhanger to the previous year's number one high school recruit, Roger Kish. Mocco won a sudden-victory decision over nemesis Cole Konrad. Afterwards he sprinted downstairs to a locker room where he climbed on a stationary bicycle and pumped his legs furiously for 30 minutes as his older brother, Joe, exhorted him on with a rhythmic chant. "Faster. Faster. Faster."[25]

Agreeing to be interviewed by the Minnesota media during intermission, Coach Smith still felt the sting of Frishkorn's loss as he spoke to the crowd. "It can be a long afternoon, especially the way we lost the second one."[26] But the Cowboys captured seven of the afternoon's 10 matches, and left town with a 28-10 victory. The match alternates between Stillwater and Minneapolis almost every year, and the Cowboy victory gave a visiting team the victory for the sixth consecutive year. So much for home field advantage.

At the airport, Steve Mocco's father Joe gave Coach Smith a token of congratulations—a chunk of venison wrapped in foil and left over from the weekend's rations. The size of a large dictionary, one wrestler wondered if it would pass through airport security. When the team arrived in Tulsa, they loaded their gear from baggage claim and gathered around Coach Smith. "Turn in your singlets to Randy. We'll work out at 3:00 tomorrow."[27]

The Cowboys returned from Minneapolis to Stillwater victorious from their first road match of the year. The most grueling and competitive coast-to-coast national tour ever undertaken by a college wrestling team had commenced. In the evening's five close matches, the Cowboys had lost three, with victories coming against lower-ranked individuals. A road dual against in-state rival Oklahoma awaited the following Sunday. Plenty of challenges lay ahead.

The next afternoon the team gathered around Smith as he summarized the weekend, gesturing as he spoke. "After the 125 match, we outscored them in takedowns 19-2. This reinforces what we have worked on all year. If we hand-fight hard and take advantage of our skills, we will kick their butt on our feet. This is still a sport that will be won or lost on our feet, for the most part. I see some of you becoming total wrestlers on your feet. If you stay in your stance and stay in their face, you can be devastating. But that takes much greater intensity, and it starts in this room. Drilling and hard wrestling. Let's go."[28]

Smith then went down the lineup without notes giving a detailed, move-by-move critique of each wrestlers' performance. The Cowboy head coach took no notes during the previous day's match, but in the wrestling room this day described fine points and minutiae as if the action was playing on a video screen rather than in his memory. The urgency in his tone and manner caused the words to tumble out, and the theme remained the same for each wrestler. "We're not where we need to be. We have to raise the bar. We're a better team than what we showed yesterday. There are triers and doers. You can't try to get the big takedown or the big escape. Around here you have to do it."[29]

Before the season began, Coach Smith sat in his office, holding his right forefinger just barely an inch away from his thumb, staring through that small space, reflecting on the small difference between trying and doing. "A wrestling program is always this far from coming apart at all times."[30]

The following week he was to discover this week just how prophetic his words could be.

TAKE ME TO BOOT HILL AND
COVER ME WITH ROSES, I'M JUST A
YOUNG COWBOY AND I KNOW I DONE WRONG.

—Old Cowboy Song

six

12.12.04

THE COWBOYS WOULD TRAVEL TO NORMAN to face archrival Oklahoma on the Sunday afternoon before final examinations. At practice the previous Thursday, Smith's focus was on academics. "For those of you with finals on Monday, I'm giving you time off between now and Sunday, so you better be banging away at the books. Take advantage of the time. Don't leave anything undone. If you can turn a B into an A, get it done. Make sure you've given me your correct exam times so we can schedule practices around your tests. We've had a good semester academically, and we want to finish it off on a good note."[1]

The OSU "Academic Services for Student-Athletes" component of the athletic department is led by Assistant Athletic Director Dr. Marilyn Middlebrook, and provides counselors, tutors, and mentors to the university's student-athlete community. Cowboy academic counselor for wrestling, Dr. Jeremy Cook, coordinated the OSU wrestlers' scholastic efforts, and possessed a technician's knowledge of degree requirements and NCAA academic rules. The 6'2" goateed Ph.D. spoke with the quiet precision and passion of one who has mastered his craft. "I have an extensive file on every wrestler. OSU, the [Big 12] Conference, and the NCAA all have different academic standards that must be met. We're on top of it every day. No basket weaving…everyone's on a degree track, and must take at least 12 hours. I scout professors to see how they teach. Who gives essays and who gives multiple-choice tests. I send out grade-checks to professors. Some respond

Dr. Jeremy Cook, an expert photographer, snaps thousands of pictures of Cowboy wrestlers each season. Dr. Cook and Alan Good, Academic Counselors for the wrestling team, helped the Cowboys lead the nation with four academic All-Americans during the 2004-05 season. Since 2000, OSU wrestling has lead the Big 12 in Academic All-Big 12 selections and is tied for second with Michigan for the second most Academic All-Americans.

and some don't. Like all students at OSU, the student-athlete has an academic advisor provided by the university, and I don't intervene there unless I'm asked." [2] Dr. Cook is in constant motion, but with 32 wrestlers to monitor, extra eyes are always needed. His own eyes gleamed as he described his methodology. "Our guys are real good about taking care of their academic responsibilities. Going to class is a key component to their success. I have an extensive and somewhat subversive network of teachers, teammates, and students that help me monitor that issue."

As the sun began to drop out of the west window of the wrestling room, the Sunday afternoon starters lined up before Smith after practice giving him their exam times, then slipped on workout gear so they could drop some weight in anticipation of the OU match.

The University of Oklahoma, OSU's in-state rival located south of Stillwater some 80 miles, had historically been one of the top wrestling programs in the nation. Sooner wrestlers had won 64 individual national championships since 1929. Sooner teams had captured 21 conference championships and seven NCAA titles. Seven times an OU wrestler had been named Outstanding Wrestler at the NCAA championships. The program had supplied qualifiers to the U.S. Olympic Team in 10 of the last 14 Olympic Games. These accomplishments elevated the Sooner wrestling program to virtual elite status, but OU's standing had long been overshadowed by two other raging beasts—OSU wrestling and Oklahoma football. OU led the nation in NCAA football championships with eight, and routinely drew more fans to its spring football game than the wrestling team attracted during an entire home season. The OSU wrestling team was arguably the most successful collegiate program in the history of any American sport.

Entering this dual match with Oklahoma, in 84 years of head-to-head competition, the Cowboys held a series lead of 114-24-9 over OU. Jack Spates, the gregarious Oklahoma coach who came to OU from Cornell in 1994, had managed one victory and two ties in 22 dual matches against the Cowboys. Since becoming head coach, John Smith was 19-3-2 against the Sooners, with two losses coming his first year as the Cowboy chieftain. Smith never lost to Oklahoma while wrestling for the Cowboys, and over the past 11 years had endured only one loss to Oklahoma in a dual meet.

This one-sided domination by OSU over OU in wrestling almost mirrored the relationship between the team's football programs—the Sooners owned a 75-16-7 dominance over the Cowboys on the gridiron. With OU football fans requiring systemic wins over their in-state rival, five losses over the past nine years to OSU contributed to the dismissal of two OU head football coaches, and the public reproach of another. The Sooners expected to beat OSU in football, and the Cowboy fans expected wins over OU in wrestling.

Talk-radio junkies speculated on the question during the week leading up to the match—whether the Sooners would trade a dual match victory against the Cowboys for a top 10 finish at the NCAA tournament later in March. Many argued that most OU fans gladly would accept that indenture with the wrestling devils. A dual victory over OSU would signal that the Sooners were closing the gap in securing a sacred birthright, one that had been clenched to the Cowboy bosom for ages like a jealous and possessive proprietor.

While OSU held a dominating series edge, recent duals had been competitive. In this Sunday afternoon match, Cowboys Frishkorn, Ward, Hendricks, and Mocco would be heavy favorites. Esposito, Pendleton, and Rosholt would be solid favorites, but would face nationally ranked, proven, and highly-motivated opponents. Fleenor and Delk would be underdogs, although Delk always wrestled tough with former national titlist Teyon Ware.

If the Sooners could pull off just two upsets before their home crowd, the upset was possible.

While fans and coaches from both schools were emotionally invested in the outcome as only devoted partisans can be, the Cowboys had only three native Oklahomans in their line-up. Could the remaining seven members of the team, who hailed from six different states stretching from California to New Jersey, convert the intensity of this intra-state rivalry, long called the "Bedlam Series" by media and fans, into a Cowboy victory? When John Smith awakened Saturday morning before the match, he was cautiously confident of victory. But before the day would end he was not so sure.

No practice was scheduled on Saturday. As a rule, Smith gave little time to pre-match analysis and strategy, particularly early in the season. "If we wrestle our way, we will be fine."[3]

Most of the team came to the wrestling room that afternoon to check their weight or drill with a workout partner. The day before, Frishkorn had considered the importance of the OU match to his team and the university, "This means a little bit more than a regular meet. This is about representing your school."[4] As the time for practice approached, the usually punctual Smith was nowhere to be found, and the door to the wrestlers' lounge was ominously closed. After a torturous half hour, Frishkorn walked out of the lounge and failed to make eye contact with his teammates as he walked along the edge of the practice mats to his locker. A grim Smith made no eye contact as he entered the wrestling room and asked about the whereabouts of backup 133-pounder Justin Porter.

Like a priest receiving confession for which he was not prepared to offer absolution, Smith had learned that Frishkorn, while studying for a chemistry exam the evening before, had succumbed to that seductive enchantress who haunts and plagues all wrestlers from Halloween to the Eyes of March—the desire for food and drink. Weigh-in was less than twenty-four hours away, and Frishkorn was seventeen pounds over his appointed weight of 133.

An experienced upper classman leaned against the wall with arms crossed, shaking his head from side to side as he held back a rueful grin. "I think he broke."[5] In the wrestling world, to "break" is to separate that physic cord that tethers the wrestler's will to his preordained purpose. Sometimes that cord breaks suddenly, in the heat of battle. Other times it frays gradually, in the silence and aloneness of desperation, when dreams of glory begin to fade under the mist of reality. All wrestlers break. For the fortunate soul, the severing is only temporary, like a bad, foul dream. Cowboy assistant coach Pat Smith related how, while on a road trip his junior year, he gave in to the allures of a water fountain that beckoned him in a hotel lobby and held him hostage. Fifty ounces later, he shook the grasp, donned his sweats and melted the water off.

Other times, the break is permanent and ultimately beyond reattachment, like years ago when Coach Smith found a note posted on the hotel door of a highly-ranked Cowboy wrestler struggling to make weight, the day before a dual meet at the University of Minnesota. The note was short and direct. "It's over. I quit. Don't try to find me."[6] The coaches and staff fanned out in the artic-like Minneapolis winter and searched for their comrade for 36 hours. After forfeiting the weight class to Minnesota the next day, the Cowboy team, who went on to lose to Minnesota, found their lost soul waiting at the airport gate. He flew home alone and never wrestled again.

By now virtually the entire team gathered in the wrestling room as Frishkorn walked out of the lounge and into the locker room. Some drilled with their workout partner, while others sat around the room in tense silence.

With Frishkorn out of the lineup, Smith turned to redshirt freshman Justin Porter to fill the vacancy at 133. The two-time state champion from Vinita, Oklahoma, unaware he would be called upon to make weight on Sunday, weighed 143 before practice, but lost five pounds during one hour of drilling. "I'll float off a couple tonight, work out in the morning, and I'll be fine. It's not the first time I've made weight at the last minute."[7]

As the team concluded the workout, Coach Smith sat on a chair reviewing notes from his black leather folder, and looked up as Steve Mocco approached. Smith stared up at his heavyweight, and for a moment the OSU coach appeared stricken.

Giant blisters, caused by the scraping abrasions, irritated by sweat and friction of daily workouts, had developed on Mocco's forehead. If it appeared to the OU team physician that any of Mocco's skin irritation might be contagious, the match official could prevent him from wrestling.

Rumors flew that same physician had pulled the Sooner squad off their practice mat several weeks ago to prevent the spreading of a rash. Cowboy athletic trainer Chris Pickering treated the irritated area with a medicated cream, and Mocco was sent home with directions from Smith. "Be back at 10 in the morning. You need to wrestle tomorrow."

Mocco's face reddened. "I want to wrestle."

Smith heard the defensiveness in his undefeated heavyweight's voice and smiled. "You need to wrestle."

Mocco's hands slid away from his side like he was drawing a pair of revolvers. "You think I don't want to wrestle?"

Smith laughed. "I know you want to wrestle."

"I'll wrestle."[8]

So, in the course of a day Smith faced the prospect of replacing two almost-certain wins with two foreseeable losses. A small group of underclassmen, sitting near the orange Gatorade coolers at the end of the room, conducted a weight-by-weight analysis of the next day's dual. Worse-case scenario, with Frishkorn and Mocco out, the Cowboys would be favored at five weights, the Sooners at four, with one toss-up. Finally, someone dared to whisper the unthinkable. "We could lose tomorrow."[9]

A beleaguered Smith, up the night before with an abscessed tooth, walked slowly from the wrestling area to the coach's dressing room. He carried the black notebook. "I'm going home."[10] An Oklahoma win could have a slight impact on in-state recruiting, afford OU temporary bragging rights over the Cowboys in their dominant sport, give Spates his first win over the Cowboys in more than a decade, and provide a glimmer of hope to hungry teams who were lying in wait to challenge the Cowboys.

The team vans departed Stillwater the next morning under cold and clear skies, and arrived at OU's Lloyd Noble Center at 11:00 a.m. The wrestlers found the tiny red and white visitors' locker room, where they deposited their equipment bags emblazoned with the "OSU Wrestling" logo. They tracked down the scales, located in the official's locker room, across the hall from their dressing room. One Cowboy stepped on the scales holding an eight-ounce plastic cup of tap water filled to the brim. If they made weight with the cup, they stepped off the scales and drank the cool liquid, then walked to a trashcan to spit their mouths dry.

They returned to their locker room where Randy Pogue distributed their post-weigh in snack. After taking their share of food-stuff and arranging it before their lockers, the wrestlers sat staring at the cups of yogurt, bagels, and candy-wraps with the longing of Buddhist monks resting before a sacred shrine.

When one o'clock finally arrived, the wrestlers trudged across the hall for the official weigh-in. Doc Allen had examined Mocco and informed Coach Smith the troubling abrasions were dry. The medication and ointment had worked.

As the wrestlers were called to the scales weight by weight, they presented to the opposing team's doctor their fingernails for examination, placed their arms above their heads and turned around to reveal

Dr. Tom Allen, retired Dean and nation-ally prominent Professor of Medicine at the Oklahoma State medical school, has served as the physician for the OSU wrestling team for over a decade. A former college pole-vaulter, Doc Allen "...treated virtually every team member for various broken noses, fractured ribs, chipped teeth, twisted knees, torn ligaments, jammed vertebrae, poked-eyes, bit tongues and elbows grotesquely bent against the joint." *Courtesy Oklahoma State University.*

any contagious skin rashes, then stepped on the electronic scales. Doc Allen would threaten to take the team home if Mocco were not allowed to wrestle. "If they give us trouble, I'll bow up."[11]

Mocco, a Stillwater resident transplanted from New Jersey, via Iowa City, was still learning the vagaries of the Midwestern dialect. "What does 'bow up' mean?"

All the competitors cleared the pre-match tests. They hurried away to scarf down their carefully-selected fast foods in the small and dimly-lit locker room. While they ate, Coach Smith and his assistants stood in the hallway where Johny Hendricks paced from room to room. "I'm just wandering around. I can't sit still." [12]

Coach Smith suppressed a grin, glanced at his watch, and turned to freestyle wrestler and former Cowboy Muhammad Lawal, a transfer to the OSU program who had placed third in the NCAA championships the year before. "You're the best dresser on the team, Mo. Are my pointed shoes out of style?"[13] The polite and diplomatic Lawal grinned and walked away.

The wrestlers finished their food and rested. At 1:30 p.m. some pulled on their warm-ups and haphazardly walked down a long and ramped tunnel into the arena. They ran laps around the mat and began their pre-match rituals of ghost-wrestling, drilling, and calisthenics, occasionally sneaking a glance into the stands, feeling the eyes of the crowd. Coach Smith walked to the OSU bench, sat alone, and watched his wrestlers like a father watching sons romp in a playground.

At 1:45 p.m. the team and coaches walked back to their locker room as the fans, mostly OSU supporters, filled in the section of the arena cordoned off for the match. Arena seating was first-come first-serve.

Minutes later head trainer Chris Pickering gave the team the 10-minute signal, prompting those who had not done so to slip on their orange singlets under their warm-ups. While Rosholt finished shaving in the locker room, outside the door assistant trainer Sarah Tackett, a master's degree candidate at OSU in sports psychology, applied her makeup before taking the floor with her team. When asked if the excitement of the matches was a payoff for thankless hard work caring for the athletes in the wrestling room, she replied with no hesitation. "I like the matches, but I like practice just as much. It gives me the chance to apply what I'm learning in my program."[14] Sarah worked with several OSU teams, and witnessed the intensity of college athletics from an interesting perspective. "The best fights during practice take place in the wrestling room between the wrestlers, and in the football stadium between the offensive and defensive lines. The meanest fights take place between the girl athletes, who fight with their words."[15]

At regular practices, Coach Smith stationed at least three trainers in the wrestling room for each OSU workout. During warm-up and drills, they gathered on a bench near the north end, next to the two orange Gatorade coolers, which they filled with ice and drink before each work out. They pull on rubber gloves when live wrestling began. Sarah slung a black nylon medicine bag full of tape, medicines, scissors, and gauze across her shoulder and the trainers scattered across the wrestling room. They plugged bloody noses, cleaned and wrapped scrapes and gashes, iced bruises, wiped up blood spilled on the mat, and disinfected affected areas. Often they evaluated more serious injuries to determine if additional medical attention is required from the physician on call in the Athletic Center downstairs in Gallagher-Iba Arena.

At 1:58 p.m. Smith caught Pendleton's eye, prompting his team's leader to begin the pre-match ritual. "Bring it in." The team gathered around. Pendleton looked down at Esposito and waited as the junior perfectionist sat on the floor, tying and retying his wrestling shoe. Pendleton counted him down. "4-3-2-1."[16]

Esposito completed the final tie at the count of 1, and looked triumphantly up at his teammates. "I nailed it."[17]

Pendleton led the team in the traditional pre-match, wrestlers-only prayer. On his 1-2-3 count, the team chanted "Cowboys."

They then looked to Coach Smith. A long pre-match speech was unnecessary. The wrestlers knew the importance of this match to their program, fans, and coaches. Many had seen or wrestled against today's opponent for years, they knew what to expect, and Smith's comments were to the point. "Seven minutes, men. Leave nothing out there."[18]

The Cowboys walked through the tunnel toward their bench, to the applause of the orange-clad OSU faithful. Cowboy fans held a solid majority in support this sunny, early winter afternoon in Norman.

Coach Smith followed behind his team. He walked quietly, with his hands in the pockets of his conservative blue suit. Moments later, the arena darkened and the Sooner wrestlers made a dramatic entrance. They received high-fives from their coach as they moved quickly into the darkness and music.

Oklahoma took command early, winning the first three matches and posting a 10-0 lead. The Cowboys roared back, capturing the next three matches and taking a 13-10 edge on the strength of Johny Hendricks' first-period cradle and pin.

The Cowboy fans breathed easier as O-State, now with a three point lead, would begin to roll out Murderers' Row...three national champions in the final four weights, beginning with team captain and defending national champion, the senior considered by some as the best pound for pound wrestler in the country, the soul of the Cowboys—Chris Pendleton.

ABOVE: Justin Porter, unexpectedly called into action when a teammate failed to make weight, fights off Oklahoma's Joe Comparin. *Courtesy Stillwater News Press.*

UPPER RIGHT: A four-time high school state champion at El Reno, Oklahoma High School, Derrick Fleenor struggles for position against Oklahoma's Sam Hazewinkel at 125. *Courtesy Stillwater News Press.*

RIGHT: Ronnie Delk fires out a "snake" against Teyon Ware of Oklahoma. Delk hit the devastating move often during his career. *Courtesy Stillwater News Press.*

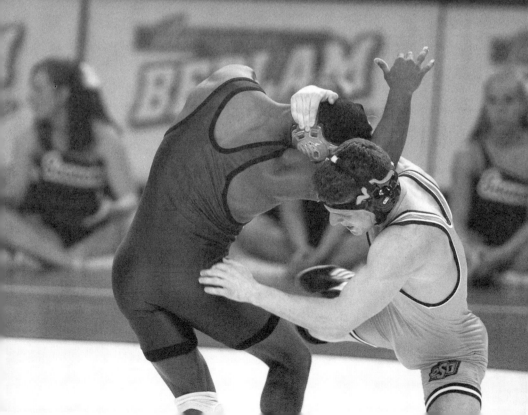

Born in California, the round-faced, strong-browed Pendleton came to OSU as a skinny 150-pounder with limited skills, striking athletic ability, and a prodigious will to succeed. He was inserted in the starting lineup to replace an injured starter his freshman year, but failed to place in the NCAA tournament. He redshirted the following year, put on 15 pounds of muscle, and developed his skills in the richly competitive wrestling room, always pushing against an apprehension that he faced since childhood. "I don't like to fail. I don't like knowing someone else is better than me. I think that definitely is my biggest fear. Failing at anything."[19] After a richly-competitive and successful redshirt year, Pendleton stormed to a 30-2 record his sophomore year, losing a heartbreaker in the NCAA quarterfinals, which to date he called his most disappointing moment in wrestling. "In reviewing the videotape of my loss, I could tell why Coach Smith was not happy with me. I was not in the match. I looked half awake. I didn't do the right warm-up and didn't get my mind set, and it came back and bit me."[20]

As a 12-year-old he began his wrestling career in the seventh grade when his father, a former high school wrestler, noticed Chris' school had added the sport and encouraged his son to give it a try. But many of his serious competitors were grizzled, seasoned veterans who had been wrestling since the age of five. "I was not very successful. Really pretty average."[21] Chris pursued the sport until, "I lost my focus"[22] when he entered high school, and found himself dismissed from the squad. "I was lost as to what I wanted to be or do with my life. I was going through a really tough time. I was involved with the wrong crowd and it showed. I didn't do well athletically or academically, and my life was going downhill real quickly."[23]

But an accidental meeting with his high school coach would prove fateful. "I happened to run into my coach after my freshman year and he said 'We're going to this tournament…why don't you come on the trip?'"[24] Chris rejoined the team and rediscovered his passion for the sport. "The more I put into the sport, the more I got out of it. I started being successful on the mat and also started being successful in the classroom. It's funny how the two go hand in hand. Wrestling gives you focus, priorities, and a set schedule. It's such a discipline, and the discipline rubs off into other areas of your life. Academics started filling in all of the areas that previously had sidetracked me."[25]

Soon the hard work began to pay dividends. "I didn't turn the corner until my junior year in high school, when I decided to give all my time to wrestling. I had been a swimmer up to that point. Then I had a growth spurt and my weight jumped from 103 to 140. My senior year I won the state championship and went 52 and 0, and won the Reno Tournament of Champions. That's where the OSU coaches noticed me."[26]

A late bloomer not heavily recruited out of high school, Pendleton became interested in OSU through his admiration for John Smith's accomplishments, but came to appreciate the entire coaching staff. "I came to OSU because of the coaches. Coach Smith is the greatest American wrestler ever. The coaches are very approachable and they give you honest answers. Even when I was just a camper, and had not developed into a recruit, they spent time answering my questions. I would ask them about technique, what it was like to wrestle at OSU, how did they get so good."[27]

Pendleton went on the win the NCAA title his junior year, and had his sights set on finishing strong. "My goals for this year are to repeat as national champion, and do it in a way I'll be remembered at OSU. There [are] many great wrestlers here… you have to do something so special to stand out. I want to do something special to always be remembered; I want to be outstanding wrestler in the NCAA Tournament this year. We haven't had that in almost a decade."[28]

When reflecting on his career, Pendleton thinks back to his early days of wrestling, and considers how the sport has provided focus and structure at a critical time. Surprisingly, the 2004 NCAA champion still considers the bronze medal he won at the state tournament during his junior year in high school as "by far" his most gratifying moment in wrestling, even more so than his 2004 NCAA title. "My freshman and sophomore years I was lost as far as what I wanted to be or do. That accomplishment gave me direction and purpose."[29]

Pendleton faced seventh-ranked E.K Waldhaus, a senior transfer from the University of Wyoming who came to OU after his freshman year, and was coming off his most successful year as a collegiate, posting a 28-10 record for the Sooners and placing third in the conference meet the year before. The Colorado prep wrestling standout and football walk-on possessed superior leg strength and had led the Sooners the previous season in takedowns.

A 22-year-old math education major, who qualified for the NCAA tournament only once in his three attempts, Waldhaus was 0-3 against the defending national champion Pendleton, but had experienced success with his double-leg in those matches. His game plan was to control Pendleton's head from the neutral position and score from his feet with leg shots.

At the opening whistle Pendleton, bobbing in and out like a deadly moth, danced toward and around Waldhaus with mercurial foot-speed. His white wrestling shoes seemed to be dusted with quicksilver, as the Cowboy captain snapped a leaning Waldhaus by him into a briny deep single leg takedown in just 23 seconds for a 2-0 lead. Waldhaus made it 2-1 with a quick escape as the twenty-two wrestlers, coaches, doctors and support personnel on the OU bench passively sat back in their chairs, grimacing as if watching their teammate receive a bad haircut. But the usually relentless Pendleton, whose takedown repertoire resembled a Sunday afternoon smorgasbord, curiously failed to register a serious takedown attempt for the next minute, finally replicating his earlier takedown against Waldhaus, hitting another snap-down into a single leg for a 4-1 lead.

Waldhaus escaped to trail 4-2, and with 2:14 left in the period the Sooner bore deep on a single leg, but could not finish the move, for Pendleton sprawled, impelled Waldhaus' head to the mat, and circled around for his third takedown of the period and a 6-2 lead. But 20 seconds later, and with only seconds left in the first period, the inexplicable happened. Pendleton gave up the wrestling equivalent of a turnover deep in his opponent's territory. In an attempt to come to his feet, Waldhaus braced his legs and arms up to a tripod position and turned toward Pendleton, where to his delight, he found Pendleton's inside leg there for the taking. The Cowboy had inexplicably moved from a leveraged and controlling position behind Waldhaus over to his opponent's side, where Chris' leg was served up in sitting duck form. Waldhaus snatched in the leg and drove Pendleton to the mat for a reverse with just 20 seconds left in the first. Slowly rising up from the mat like a coal-miner finishing a double-shift, an exasperated Pendleton gingerly banged the mat in frustration. While he escaped just before the period ended for a 7-4 lead, the number one ranked Pendleton, finding himself in a battle he did not expect, seemed to hit a panic button that brought about certain recklessness and fatigue, resulting in defensiveness and a surreal sense

Cowboy captain Chris Pendleton gives up a rare takedown on the mat's edge during a 11-10 loss to E. K. Waldhaus from Oklahoma. The defeat was Pendleton's first and only of the season, and left a "scar on his heart." *Courtesy Stillwater News Press*

of a comb being caught in a snarl that thwarted his natural grace and relentless aggression.

The Cowboy assistants recalled their own common experiences— Olympian and three-time national champion Eric Guerrero entered the final period leading an Iowa opponent, only to lose. Pat Smith getting pinned in his first collegiate match, still recalls the experience. "You can't execute. You get defensive and freeze. It happens to all wrestlers at some point in their career. Your opponent will see you panic; he will get an adrenalin-rush and you'll experience an energy drain…the net effect is significant."[30]

Trailing 9-6 entering the third period, Waldhaus made it 9-7 with a quick escape. Waiting for the strategic moment, seconds later he fired the first of two deadly double leg takedowns, the elementary maneuver taught to all junior wrestlers across the world, a move which seldom works against championship-caliber wrestlers.

The second manslayer came with just 18 seconds left in the match, a takedown which allowed E.K. Waldhaus, to the delight of the enraptured OU bench, to post a shocking 11-10 upset over the previously undefeated and

RIGHT: Jake Rosholt receives medical treatment from Cowboy trainer Sarah Tackett during his 14-4 victory over Joel Flaggert of Oklahoma. *Courtesy Stillwater News Press*

Coach Smith and Jake Rosholt confer during an injury time-out. The Idaho native's practice habits and ability to deliver during high-stake matches earned Smith's respect. *Courtesy Mika Matzen*

seemingly unstoppable Chris Pendleton, who now sat behind the OSU bench alone for the remainder of the afternoon, occasionally shaking his head in disbelief as if he had been dropped onto an alien planet without explanation.

Waldhaus had scored his first victory over a higher-ranked opponent, propelling the Sooners to a 16-13 dual match lead with two matches left. If OU sophomore Joel Flaggert, ranked 11th in the nation, could achieve the upset against Jake Rosholt, the Sooners would enter the heavyweight match leading 19-13 and would win the dual if heavyweight Jake Hager could avoid being pinned by Mocco. OSU had waged a spirited recruiting battle for both Flaggert and Hager's services. Oklahoma was so gratified Flaggert had chosen the Sooners over the Cowboys, they mentioned the recruiting victory inside the Sooner media guide. Flaggert's choice was motivated by his life-long affection for OU football, much to the incredulity of Cowboy assistant Pat Smith, who reminded the high school senior, "You're going to wrestle and not play football."[31]

John Smith found the rationale peculiar. "OSU was beating them in football too during that time. But that's recruiting. You never know what might motivate a guy."[32]

But the rugged Cowboy Jake Rosholt posted a workmanlike 14-4 victory over Flaggert. When Mocco wrapped up Jake Hager 13-2, the Cowboys slipped the collar with a 21-16 victory.

Spates was beaming and giddy in defeat during the post-match press conference. "If you had said to me before the match that going into the 197 match we'd be up by three, I would have told you we were going to win the match."[33] He attributed Rosholt's gutsy victory to Cowboy's ripened maturity. "The difference was experience. Rosholt has been in a lot of great matches and Joel has been in one Bedlam and a total of two duals in his career."[34]

BELOW: Steve Mocco, nursing a scary scab on his forehead which was superbly finessed by Doc Allen, looks for an opening against Oklahoma's Jake Hager. *Courtesy Mika Matzen*

Oklahoma City sportscaster Mark Rodgers interviews Coach Smith. College wrestling received as much local media coverage as college basketball before the ascent of March Madness in the 70's and 80's. *Courtesy Dr. Jeremy Cook*

But if Coach Spates was positive after the defeat, Coach Smith was solemn and forewarning in victory. "I felt like we did the minimum. We were fortunate to come out of here with a win. There are a couple of issues within the program that we have to get ironed out. Some things can happen that take the focus off what your team is trying to accomplish"[35] Looking across the faces in the press room, Smith then sent an undisguised message to his squad, who read the newspaper reports with more regularity than did the OSU coach. "We can't allow the media to tell us that we're national champions. Those titles are earned and this one will be earned."[36] Smith thanked the media as he got up and headed down the hall to the Cowboy locker room, which was quiet as a study hall as the team sat on benches, staring at the cold, concrete floor.

Smith's discontent was evident as he began to speak in a tone meant to chasten and encourage, progressing down the lineup weight by weight. "Porter, the guy's worn out in overtime and you give him a takedown. You're wearing an orange singlet, son. You give nothing up. You go to the death."

He spoke to each wrestler, echoing common themes. Apply pressure from the first whistle. Establish your dominance early. Snuff out any hope they may have. Don't wait till the third period."[37]

His most passionate words were for team captain Pendleton, who lost for just the second time in two years to a wrestler he had earlier controlled. "I don't know what happened to you mentally today. This has happened before but you've been able to come back. To break down mentally is the only way you can ever lose. This match should remind you every day that if you give guys hope, they will challenge you. You gave up the easy reverse in the second period and the challenge started right there. You gave him hope right there. When he shot at you there was no reaction. You didn't feel at your best and you made mistakes. One more takedown and this guy breaks, no matter how you felt."[38]

Pendleton stared ahead as Smith's voice dropped to almost a whisper. "That match needs to burn in you all season. That's the match you take into the room every day to make sure it doesn't happen again. That match is a burn on your heart, Chris. *A burn on your heart.*"[39] There was speculation in the Cowboy locker room that due to the day off Smith gave the team on Monday, Pendleton was as much as sixteen pounds over early in the week, and that the last-minute effort to make weight reduced his voltage. But whatever the reason, the talented Pendleton had mysteriously lost to a highly-motivated opponent.

The Cowboy coach slipped on his blue suit jacket and made his way to the door, turning around to face his squad, which remained motionless as if disoriented by the percussion of Smith's admonition.

"The disappointing thing to me is that we did the minimum today…the bare minimum. I feel as if we were defeated out there today. We have to make the commitment to start wrestling from the start. Once that whistle blows, you're in a fight. Today in seven matches we did not make that commitment. Collegiate wrestling is tough…we have to be up for every match."[40]

* * *

Before practice the following Monday, Smith called Frishkorn into his office for the better part of an hour, explaining the ramifications of his failure to make weight against Oklahoma the preceding day, but being careful not to send the uncertain freshman in a walking coma of devastation and insecurity.

Smith had spent hours on the telephone, talking to parents about ripple effects if Smith allowed Frishkorn to move up a weight, an alternative Smith might consider if it was determined the freshman's academic pressures and physical growth and development made 141 a better fit. But first he had to deal with Frishkorn's failure to make weight. "You put yourself ahead of the team. You made it easier for guys in the future to do what you did. Now is not the time to decide where you want to wrestle."[41] Over the ensuing months Smith would consider how to handle Frishkorn's transgression. "He may lose some scholarship money. He will have to build bridges with his teammates. Someone will say something to him in the locker room today. This team is self-policing."[42] Smith looked across his desk at the penitent freshman, glancing at his watch before heading to practice. "Let me warn you. The older guys on this team will confront you today. Watch your mouth or you might get smacked."[43]

At practice Smith stood before the team in gray sweatpants and a gray OSU wrestling sweatshirt. As he reviewed his notes for practice, backup 157-pounder Eric Dabbs, the son of a wrestling coach from Anadarko, Oklahoma, tightened a face-mask designed to protect his lacerated nose. The injury was received at a recent weekend tournament in which several Cowboy underclassmen participated. After receiving the injury, during his 15-minute "blood time-out" Dabbs filled his cupped hands twice with blood. Under the rules, a wrestler has 90 seconds from which to recover from a "non-bleeding injury." If blood is involved, the match is governed by the "bleeding timeout" provision of Rule 7.44 In that circumstance, the wrestler has unlimited time to stop the bleeding subject to the official's discretion. Blood on a singlet does not necessarily result in a change of uniform…only if the clothing is "saturated with blood" does the official required a change of uniform. Teammates giggled as Dabbs clamped the mask on. Smith walked to the edge of the mat, placed his notebook on a window ledge, and turned to his team. After reminding them to turn in their text books by the following Friday, "otherwise we'll get a bill from the Bursar's Office," and going over the holiday practice schedule, his attention reflected back on the dual with archrival Oklahoma. "Their strategy is to go zero-zero in the first period, and then take the match to the mat in periods two and three and see what happens. We have to make these guys wrestle us off the whistle. They know if they get in a wrestling match with us we're going to kick their ass because we know how to wrestle. Don't get me wrong. I don't want us charging in and making lots of mistakes. But there's nothing more devastating to an underdog than pressure. First of all, you intimidate them because of who you wrestle for. Add pressure to that and that's what makes you great. It's your commitment to wrestle hard from the first period."[45]

After practice Smith sat on a chair adjacent to the middle mat, almost whispering as he watched the wrestling room empty at the end of the evening. "We really didn't wrestle badly against OU Sunday. With this lineup we'll struggle at 125, 141 and 184."[46] He paused as Steve Mocco fired off pushups between fits of ghost wrestling on the heavyweight end of the mat. "I am considering bringing Nathan out of redshirt for the Michigan State match [in January]."[47] Freshman Nathan Morgan, a multiple-state champion from California, had paper-sliced his way to an undefeated record in open tournament competition during the first month of the season by spraying a gentle mist of takedowns on virtually every opponent. But his raw toughness was still in question. "Right now he's not close to being tournament-ready, either physically or mentally. But he is very talented, and has the capability of winning some matches down the road if we bring him along patiently. It's tough on the team to fall behind early in every dual. Morgan could prove to be an equalizing force, and could contribute to building team chemistry on down the road."[48]

As Mocco walked to the water station, Smith stood to his feet. "Whenever OSU comes to town, many of our opponents consider our match their national championship. It's not the highlight of their week…it's the highlight of their year. They see OSU on their schedule and they circle it on their calendar. Parents, aunts, uncles, girlfriends, and girlfriends' parents all come in to see little Johnny have his shot against Oklahoma State. For that reason I have to remind our team this is a long season, and if we are going to achieve our goal of winning every match, I can't let them get too high or too low on a week-to-week basis. Stabilizing the lighter weights might help do that."[49]

As Smith and Mocco walked out and into the night, a solitary Chris Pendleton sat against the wall on the center mat, soaked in sweat and holding his headgear with his left hand…his right hand folded on his chest. Perhaps he was feeling along the edges of the crevices and fault-lines of a burned heart, as sweat dripped from the end of his nose and cold rain fell against the window of the Cowboy wrestling room.

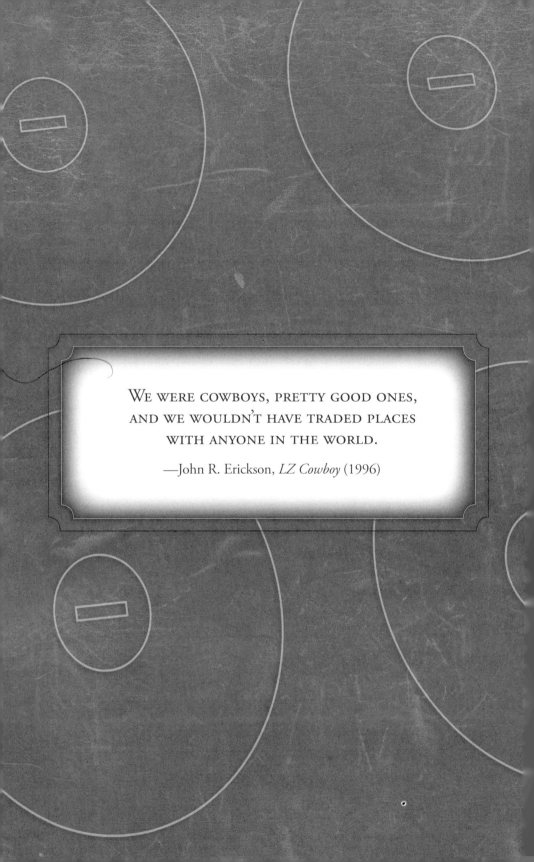

WE WERE COWBOYS, PRETTY GOOD ONES,
AND WE WOULDN'T HAVE TRADED PLACES
WITH ANYONE IN THE WORLD.

—John R. Erickson, *LZ Cowboy* (1996)

seven

the western invasion

12.22.04

IT WAS A SUN-DRENCHED and cool Saturday morning, the day before the great invasion of the West, and the OSU wrestling squad inched through the security checkpoint at the Oklahoma City airport, one wrestler at a time, trudging wearily toward the gate that would take them on the next leg of the toughest schedule in recent college wrestling memory.

Carrying no snacks, they were attired in Cowboy casual…some boys wore Levis, others donned sweat pants, but all were dressed in the standard-issue nylon orange and black OSU wrestling travel top that identified them as members of the Cowboy wrestling team. All except Frishkorn, who wore no orange. Oblivious to the gaze of curious onlookers, they made their way through the maze of security and shuffled down the airport mezzanine toward their gate, walking alone, one after the other. Esposito was first, 100 feet ahead of Kehrer, who carried a metallic backpack that seemed ready to blast forward at any moment in time. As the others passed through the security area, some carried cell phones, while several walked alone in a music-induced cocoon, ears plugged and mouths unsmiling, ill-equipped to respond to the security officer who asked "What's it like to be number one forever?"[1] They walked on without speaking, their gaunt and scraped faces contained an element of weariness that belied the holiday season. Many had traveled to wrestling tournaments since ages that can be counted on one hand. They knew the drudgery of travel, the gnawing discomfort of making weight, and the exhilaration of competition. But here the road forked. Some would return as conquerors while others would face an opponent and lose. But they knew through experience the grade and elevation of both ways home.

As they gathered to board their flight, another team assembled at the gate. Geared out in the formal costume of war, a detachment of soldiers from nearby Fort Sill Army Base waited to board the same flight and head west for the holiday into the warm and safe embrace of content fathers and worried mothers. The shaven-headed soldiers, wearing polished boots and overstuffed duffel bags, gathered in small groups and exuded an aura of virtuous joy as they spoke the language of war and gorged on hot cinnamon rolls. Some paced through the corridor of the airport, others sat and stared. Cell phones were not abundant…most stood in lines to use pay telephones as they struggled to make themselves clear to parents and girlfriends who seemed to be talking to strangers, not the sons or daughters or boyfriends or girlfriends whom they knew only months ago and now whose voices had changed and were off to war. This assembled group also faced a fork in their road, a journey not yet taken, whose sequel was not assured.

Coach Smith boarded the plane with his team where he recognized and spoke briefly with coaching colleague Mike Stoops, the younger patriarch of the football-coaching Stoops brothers, who recently had been named head football coach at the University of Arizona. Stoops, who played college football at Iowa, asked about his alma mater's wrestling coach's fortunes, appreciating the tenuous and fickle footing upon which all in the brotherhood of college coaching stand, regardless the sport.

As the aircraft crept from the gate, a flight attendant announced the presence of the Fort Sill soldiers and the Oklahoma State wrestling team. Both groups received a hearty applause from the passengers on the flight, with one partisan in a red OU sweatshirt whispering "boo" as the Cowboy team was acknowledged.

The Oklahoma State wrestling schedule was national in scope, extending coast to coast, designed to mold, pour, and set a team prepared to enter the NCAA tournament three months later battle-tested and ready. No team in the country would travel so far, with such frequency, and against such difficult opposition, as the Cowboys of 2004-2005. This schedule was designed to seek out the toughest competition in the country, under the most difficult of circumstances, brought about by long and arduous travel made more wearisome by the discipline of continuous weight-control, all so individual and team weakness could be exposed and strength identified. This early portion of the schedule would take the Cowboys west. During a five-day period they would compete in a tournament in Reno, Nevada on Sunday, then travel to California for two dual meets on Wednesday before returning to Stillwater two days before Christmas. The team would then disperse for a short holiday break before resuming training.

The western tour began at the Reno Tournament of Champions, a one-day 16-team event held each December—well-stocked with top-ranked wrestlers—which often served as a prelude to the vicious NCAA match-ups in March. The tournament featured the best officials from across the nation, rewarded wrestlers with handsome mementos and carried with it the feel of a legitimate national testing ground for the year's individual and team competition.

The Cowboys, Reno tournament champion the previous two years, brought 15 wrestlers to the annual event. Thirteen would compete on Sunday. Several tournament weights included highly-ranked athletes, most notably at 197, where Jake Rosholt could face any combination of six nationally-ranked opponents as the day progressed. After competing on Sunday, the Cowboys would rest and train on Monday, travel by bus through the California wine country for two matches in two cities on Tuesday, then bus all night back to Reno where they would catch a return flight to Oklahoma City on Wednesday, December 23.

The Cowboys arrived in Reno on Saturday afternoon and lounged in the hotel lobby for forty-five minutes as the coaches negotiated with hotel officials on room details and assignments. Coach Branch handed out room keys to the tired and hungry wrestlers, who carried their bags to rooms shared with team members. He then rushed to locate The Black Box, a small black suitcase which contained electronic scales the size of a small pizza container wired to a digital readout box calibrated to the nearest 10th of one pound. The scales, which were hurriedly plugged in on the tiled bathroom floor in Randy Pogue's room, were afforded the sanctity and care given to the black box carried by Secret Service agents who travel with United States Presidents, with controls necessary to launch bombs and destroy planets.

Coach Smith, who witnessed the weight check before gaining the necessary peace of mind with which to enjoy dinner, and who possessed an uncanny ability to know how much a wrestler would weigh by glancing at his face, said to one wrestler, "How could you be three over?"[2]

After the weight check Smith took the elevator to the thirty-fourth floor of the hotel for the ritualistic "seeding meeting" which involved some forty coaches, assistant coaches, and tournament officials who met for drinks and snacks before they would deliberate and vote on tournament pairings. This meeting consisted of the core members of the wrestling culture…men and women of the wrestling community who remained involved in the sport through competing, coaching, officiating, and administering wrestling events. As the aroma of hotel egg rolls and chicken wings wafted through the corner suite, the coaches, all outstanding former college wrestlers in their own right, carried on the oral tradition of the wrestling tribe, telling and retelling stories of events gone past. Ricky Stewart, a former OSU national champion and then assistant coach at Oregon, sat and listened while a fellow coach told a group, through words and a swirling of arms, of Stewart's legendary first period pin, off a fireman's carry, of wrestling great and future Olympic champion David Schultz, a match John Smith heard on the radio at the age of 12. While the story was being told, a group of coaches picked over the remains of the ravaged food table.

When the meeting began, the coaches poured over computer-generated brackets, arguing how contestants in each weight should be seeded. Theoretically, the better wrestlers are paired against the second tier of talent so the superior wrestlers in each weight would meet later during the competition.

Like timing in love and politics, seeding in tournament wrestling is everything, because whom one is paired against makes all the difference. In addition, head-to-head match-ups are an important objective criteria used in evaluating wrestling during post-season competition. A good seed can result in a coach's wrestler advancing farther in the tournament, which means a higher finish for his team, and equates to a better record for his athletic director to consider at the end of each year as that coach and his program are evaluated. Thus, coaches take the seeding process very seriously. While some coaches argued with a vociferous, red-faced aggression, others subtly negotiated and formed unspoken coalitions with the panache of a matchmaker.

Coach Smith's status in the wrestling community and the standing of his team usually make the Cowboys the 800-pound gorilla in the room, as well as the unspoken fulcrum against which other seeds are placed. For example, a wrestler seeded number three would avoid meeting Steve Mocco, while a number four seed would likely face the Cowboy heavyweight in the semifinals. Seldom are the Cowboys ever the intended beneficiary of any coalitions or tacit agreements.

Smith, sitting in the corner of the suite next to Doc Allen, spoke only after the other coaches had advanced their case, but when he did speak the group usually deferred to his understated, but principled, advocacy. When overruled, he deferred to the other coaches, with the secure knowledge that good wrestlers and not coaches in hotel suites usually determine the winner.

In the end, the Cowboys earned six number one seeds—five going to Murderer's Row and one to defending champion and fifth year senior Ronnie Delk, who through Smith's machinations at the seeding meeting, was scheduled to wrestle Frishkorn in the semi-finals if the wrestlers performed according to expectations. A Delk vs. Frishkorn match-up in live tournament conditions, and not in the familiar confines of the wrestling room, would help the coaches choose their starter.

No one deserved to be in the lineup more than Delk, but the decision called for the strongest collection of first-tier wrestlers…one that would stand the best chance of scoring points in the crucible of post-season competition.

* * *

Ronnie Delk had been a forty-two pound third grader from Collinsville, Oklahoma, when his hero John Smith signed a pair of his tiny wrestling shoes. "My cousin won a trophy wrestling. I told my dad I wanted a trophy too. He said you're going to have to start wrestling."[3] And wrestle he did, compiling a 133-19 high school career record and winning two state wrestling titles. "I had three or four Division I schools looking at me, but my life dream was to wrestle for Coach Smith. I wanted to be a Cowboy."[4] An all-around athlete who excelled in football and baseball in high school, Delk likes to fish and hunt during his down time.

Delk entered his senior year at OSU with a 48-37 record. His goals were lofty, but accepted as the norm, "To help my team win the national championship, and to be a national champion myself."[5] He believed in the Cowboy Way. Train hard every day. Put the team before yourself. Do what the coaches say. Remember those who have gone before you. Carry the burden of winning like a proud yoke. Be a good example to the younger guys. Fight like hell every day.

The previous year Delk had lost two matches by razor-thin margins to highly-ranked wrestlers in the Big 12 Tournament and failed to receive an at-large bid from the coaches to the NCAA tournament, an event he never qualified for. This was his last chance.

The physical education major who aspired to be a wrestling coach and school administrator was the only married member of the Cowboy squad. He and his wife Stacy, an elementary education major, were married in the spring of 2003. They approached the challenges of college wrestling as a team, and much of their emphasis revolved around food and diet. For like most of the Cowboy squad, Delk struggled to balance the demands brought about by studies, training, and a constant and gnawing hunger known only to college wrestlers.

The thick-necked, wavy-haired senior was not expected to vie for a starting position when he entered the Cowboy program. "It was kind of intimidating at first, but you get in there and get a couple of takedowns and things start to click. I had Johnny Thompson [two-time national champion] in front of me, and Eric Guerrero, [three time national champion and Olympic team member in the 2004 Athens games] was training for the world championships. They were beating me up, but it eventually paid off."[6]

Nor was the freshman Delk expected to prevail in 2002 against highly-ranked Luke Moffitt when the Cowboys wrestled their archrival Iowa, in Iowa City, in the cold winter of Delk's sophomore season. "With 30 seconds left I took him down and put him on his back…then I put him on his back again and won the match. It pushed us in front, and we ended up winning the dual. I was supposed to lose but I was not going to lose."[7]

Going into this season Delk's offensive limitations from the neutral position were a major cause of concern to the Cowboy coaches. His favorite move was a high-risk "throw" he performed from the neutral position. "I like to execute some type of upper body throwing position, straight to the back."[8] While some takedowns start at the leg and take several seconds to progress to a position of advantage, Delk's throws, when executed, resemble a cowboy throwing a steer into clod-dirt and are nuclear in their suddenness and devastation, as he flings his unsuspecting opponent from the neutral position to his back, resulting in takedown and back points, and often a fall. Like a "Hail Mary" pass in football, it is devastating. But if an opponent expects the throw, it is easier to defend. If a throw is the primary weapon in the wrestler's arsenal, it becomes even easier to defend and more difficult to execute. Thus, Coach Smith and the assistant coaches worked with Delk extensively on penetration to his opponent's legs.

At the team meeting on Saturday evening at the casino hotel, the wrestlers sat in the hallway of the eighth floor. Smith spoke as an occasional hotel guest stepped off the elevator and waded through wrestlers sitting with backs against the hallway in shorts, sweats, and underpants. "Tomorrow weigh-in at seven. Come back to the hotel for breakfast at 7:15. Tell Chris [Pickering] what you want for breakfast."[9]

Smith talked extensively about pre-match preparation. "Warm up well, especially in the morning. Prepare yourself to wrestle five matches tomorrow. Drink plenty of fluids. Get something in your stomach early."[10]

The next morning Smith stayed at the hotel, ensuring that the kitchen was equipped to feed his wrestlers at 7:15 a.m. sharp with adequate supplies of pancakes and eggs, while his assistants escorted the team to the weigh-in.

The team ate breakfast on schedule, piled back into the four white vans, and made the twelve-minute drive through fog and 28 degrees to the Reno Livestock Center, where they crawled out of the vans, into the arena and onto one of the 15 mats laid out like giant tiles over the blue tarp which covered the dirt-clod floor. The support staff carried in medical supplies, liquids, equipment, and gear, while Smith toted one end of the giant orange Gatorade cooler, waving with the other hand to the OSU fans who made the trip to Reno for wrestling and gambling before Christmas Day arrived.

Groups of wrestlers scattered across the mats, jogging, stretching, drilling, or lying motionless in colored clusters. The arena also hosted rodeos, and the uneven surface of the arena, torn to clods by horses and bulls, was covered with a giant blue tarp. A ring of red-brown dirt lay exposed on the outside of the arena surface, like sidewalls over the ears of a burr haircut, where the tarp did not quite cover the surface. Doc Allen walked among the mats, chatting up officials whom he had befriended through the years, communicating with Coach Smith through unspoken glance and gesture. The Cowboy wrestlers and fans occupied a section in the end zone of the arena, with wrestlers sitting among fans and equipment as they endured the long, timeless delays waiting to wrestle. Esposito's two brothers, in from out of town for the match, watched their younger brother as he slapped his thighs and ghost-wrestled. Steve Mocco's older brother Joe barked a cadence as he helped the Cowboy heavyweight warm up. Between matches a cadre of five officials lounged on a starter's table, exchanging pointers on how they train their sons in the sport. Moments later one stood up, stretched and walked to an adjoining mat where he greeted two wrestlers, both warming up, and both wearing the same color uniform. He chuckled at the timekeeper, "Looks like another ranking match."[11]

Both Delk and Frishkorn, who lunched together the day before in a sandwich shop next to the hotel, advanced through the brackets and met in a semi-final match early in the afternoon. With both wrestlers wearing the sacred orange singlet of a Cowboy starter, the usually aggressive Frishkorn was cautious against Delk, and the first period ended scoreless, with Delk making the only serious takedown attempt. The scoring drought continued as they traded escapes in periods two and three. Branch and Guerrero sat stoically on coaching chairs, offering neither wrestler any encouragement or instruction. Smith, coaching another match on an adjacent mat, swiveled his head back and forth like a spectator at a Wimbledon match. Eight seconds into the overtime period Delk scored the only offensive points of the match with a quick takedown. After the match both wrestlers walked off the mat expressionless and with no emotion. There is satisfaction but no joy in beating a brother.

In the casinos of Reno the House usually wins, and in the Reno wrestling tournament, OSU was the House. The Cowboys romped, claiming 11 top-six finishes, including five champions, and won the team title for the third consecutive year. For a team to crown five champions in any tournament is a rare accomplishment.

Pendleton bounced back from his loss at Oklahoma with two technical falls and a pin, winning the tournament's Outstanding Wrestler Award after receiving an injury default from his opponent in the finals with only 30 seconds left in the match. That a coach would wave the white flag and declare his wrestler injured with only seconds left in a match, and then seeing that wrestler walk off the mat under his own power, Smith shook his head with incredulity.

Rosholt smashed the field with three technical falls and a 6-0 win in the semi-finals, all topped off with a pin of Scott Barker of Oregon, a transfer from Missouri whom Rosholt defeated in the 2003 NCAA finals. During the match Smith ran onto the mat, protesting Barker's use of a "key lock" maneuver, an illegal and dangerous hold that forces the wrist against its joint and can result in the snapping of a bone. Smith was livid at the sight, "I would have pulled him off the mat if necessary."[12]

But the official intervened before Rosholt was injured, and he proceeded to stump-grind Barker into submission with a fall.

The team returned to the hotel after the finals and immediately began to think about food. Smith, who had not eaten since the evening before, chose not to attend a crowded reception and dinner provided for coaches, but chose to dine with Doc Allen, as they fretted about injuries. Stevens had a concussion. Ward injured his ribs and could be out indefinitely.

The wrestlers rested and studied most of the following day, allowing their bodies to recover from the grueling 14-hour tournament in which the 13 Cowboys wrestled 66 matches in one day. Several had black eyes. Others had some form of bruise, scrape, or abrasion on the knee, elbow or face.

The next morning the chartered bus departed Reno at 8:45. The wrestlers, coaches and staff sat comfortably, and others slept or read, while most watched movies on the DVD screens positioned throughout the bus. *Dodge Ball* and *The Big Lebowski* led off…HBO's *Band of Brothers* was deemed too slow-paced. The coaches and support staff sat toward the front of the bus; upperclassmen sat in the middle seats, while the freshmen and sophomores rested near the back. Chris Pickering, trainer and liaison to Coach Smith on issues like injuries and rehabilitation, sat symbolically between the

Treating and rehabilitating injuries was a constant challenge throughout the season. Head trainer Chris Pickering and team physician Dr. Tom Allen flank Coach Smith during the Oklahoma match. *Courtesy Mika Matzen.*

wrestlers and the head coach, enjoying a John Grisham novel his mother had given him as a gift. A former accomplished high school wrestler from Iowa, Pickering became interested in the sport at the urging of his three uncles.

The wrestlers leaned their heads against the cold glass windows, watching the rows and rows of grapevines speed by as the bus charged through the California wine country. Rosholt, a ranch management major, surveyed large sections of isolated and rich farm land cascading by through the bus windows.

The bus stopped at noon near an isolated service station. The team climbed off the bus and walked with urgency into the fast food section, where they each chose, with care, their afternoon snack. Smith perused each bag as they climbed back on the bus. "The guys not having to make weight always have the heaviest bag."[13] A careful headcount was done. Two years earlier in Oregon the team bus, traveling between Corvallis and Eugene, left then-freshman Jake Rosholt behind.

As the bus plowed across central California, thundering down a winding incline, swaying, passing cars and changing lanes, it reached speeds that made Delk proclaim solemnly, "Give me some water from that bottle. I don't want to die thirsty."[14] But the bus arrived safely at a picturesque oceanside hotel at 2:45 p.m., where keys were distributed and bags unloaded. "Be back in the lobby at five," Smith said. "We'll go to Cal Poly to work out."[15]

Most of the team tossed their bags into their room and hurriedly climbed down a steep row of steps leading to the clean, white Pacific beach. A chilly eastern breeze blew in across the waves, but many went shirtless, walking as a group by two mouth-gaping female sunbathers who awakened to see boys walking toward the setting sun, some seeing an ocean for the first time. One wrote "OSU Wrestling" in the sand and had a friend snap a picture as he knelt down by it. Hendricks snacked on corn nuts as he explored the rocks. Many took pictures. One called home.

An hour later the bus departed for California Polytechnic State University. Nestled in the foothills of San Luis Obispo, Cal Poly is the second largest land-holding university in California, located midway between Los Angeles and San Francisco. Recognized as "the best largely undergraduate university in the West" by *U.S. News and World Report* for 12 consecutive years, its 18,000 students study engineering and architecture as well as agriculture, but unlike OSU's excellent agriculture programs, Cal Poly is 10 miles from the Pacific Ocean. Wrestling coach John Azevedo acknowledges the special challenges the idyllic oceanfront environment poses. "It's a challenge. They see all of their friends going to school and not having to worry about going to practice or about what they're eating. But if you have that desire to be a national champ you're willing to make the sacrifices."[16] A native Californian, Azevedo attended Oklahoma State before transferring to Cal State Bakersfield, where he captured an NCAA title. Reflecting on his decision to leave his native California out of high school to attend OSU, he took a pragmatic approach, "I was a California boy but I wanted to be a national champion…they [the Cowboys] produce national champions and national championship teams. I don't see them slowing down any time soon. "[17]

The coaches from both squads arranged earlier for the Cowboys to work out in the Cal Poly wrestling room after the Mustangs concluded their workout the Tuesday evening before the Wednesday match. Walking into the cramped, well-worn dressing room occupied by the Cal Poly squad, Smith looked around at the small locker rooms and worn carpet. "I hope our guys notice how nice our facilities are."[18]

Smiling proudly, Pendleton replied, "I signed, didn't I?"[19]

Several fans asked to observe the Cowboys practice, but the coaches declined, using the time for extensive personal instruction, going from wrestler to wrestler to offer direction and critique—to Mocco's leg attacks, Frishkorn's sprawl and defense, Hendrick's completion of single legs, and Esposito's defensive technique.

Wearing workout clothing that had begun to reek from three straight days of sweating and travel, the wrestlers burned off weight and honed their technique. Their concentration was snapped when a scream pierced the quiet wrestling room.

Assistant Head Coach Mark Branch, working out with Mocco, suffered a separated shoulder when he fell to the mat at the hands of the OSU heavyweight. Doc Allen applied an ice bag, mentioning to no one in particular, "He's going to have some tough nights ahead,"[20] referring to Branch's anticipated pain and discomfort. After the ice pack was applied, Branch, using his good shoulder, began demonstrating a technique with Rosholt. Mocco, without a workout partner, began running sprints, ghost wrestling, and hitting pushups.

As the team showered after practice, Smith spoke with a Cal Poly wrestler who lingered in the dressing room. The tanned wrestler sat on a wooden bench by the locker room and bemoaned his fate. "Surfing makes it difficult for me to be the best I can be."[21]

Coach Smith, buttoning his shirt, looked at him without expression or comment. Many prospective NCAA champions have been lured away from their best wrestling performances by the siren call of the California waves. Such would not be the temptation for the wrestlers from Stillwater, Oklahoma.

Minutes later the team gathered around Smith. "Tomorrow morning we weigh in at 10 o'clock. The match is at 11. Right after the match we shower up and drive to Fresno. We should get there two to three hours before we wrestle."[22] Because the team would make weight that morning for the Cal Poly match, they would not weigh in again upon arriving in Fresno. The Fresno State wrestlers would weigh in that same morning with the Cowboys in abstentia, but Smith asked Coach Guerrero's uncle, a former wrestler who lived near Fresno, to witness the Fresno State weigh-in. "After the match at Fresno, we'll shower up, go eat, and head back to Reno to catch our flight home."[23]

As the bus pulled out of the parking lot, someone inquired about meal money. Catcalls from the wrestlers erupted when Smith began with… "When I was in Russia…" The athletes and support staff are provided a per diem for food, the amount depending upon in what part of the country they are competing. While doling out those funds, Smith is prone to talk about the "old days" when wrestlers weren't so "pampered," sometimes referring to his days on the international amateur circuit when he would compete in Russian gyms so cold "you could see your breath" and stay in Soviet lodging not yet graced with hot water.[24]

With the age-old response of one generation responding to another's version of "when I was a boy," in good-hearted humor the team wailed in unison, "Here we go again, more about the Russians."[25]

Wednesday morning Coach Smith awakened early, climbed down the steep stairs to the beach, and watched as a group of dolphins slid past before turning west, churning away from the rising sun. The team bus pulled out at 8:45 a.m. and made the 10-minute drive along the Pacific coast to the Cal Poly campus, the large bus weaving through the adobe-glazed campus buildings to Mott Gymnasium. Built in 1960 and shaped like a giant Quonset hut with a capacity of 3,032, young children in wrestling tights, escorted by coaches and parents, were entering the gym an hour before match-time for a scheduled clinic by Coach Smith.

Smith, the sport's most revered icon of his generation, regularly conducted clinics in the gymnasiums of opposing teams before matches, encouraging wrestlers and exhorting coaches with his coaching and teaching philosophies. These teaching sessions, where Smith offered practical instruction and advice on improving technique and solving problems, were done at the request of the opposing team's coach to help promote youth and high school wrestling in the area. Olympian Eric Guerrero recalls when he was a nine-year-old boy his father took him to a tournament where OSU wrestler and Olympic gold-medal winner Kendall Cross spent several minutes talking to the young wrestler, encouraging him in his athletic pursuits, even recalling his name when seeing him in an elevator later in the day.

Some one-hundred coaches and almost as many junior wrestlers attended the clinic, including a small group of eager girls. They gathered in the stands and sat around the mat as Smith stood in the mat's center in pressed slacks and knit shirt, speaking and taking questions in a relaxed and informal manner as the wrestlers and coaches looked on with rapt attention. Several small boys in the audience wore Oklahoma State Wrestling t-shirts.

One coach asked about the tedious work required in developing Olympic-level skills. Smith warmed up to the topic. "Developing good technique takes more work than you can imagine. Science tells us a move has to be repeated some 20,000 times before it becomes instinctive to the point we can rely upon it while under pressure."[26]

A high school coach asked about the balance between conditioning and teaching skills. "It's tempting to concentrate on conditioning too early in the year. It's easy for a coach to lean against the wall and blow a whistle while guys run sprints. If you want to be that coach, then be that coach, but you'll lose a lot of matches. Teaching skills is tougher. But remember, your wrestlers will come to the point later in the year where rest is as important as conditioning. You have to walk that fine line."[27] Smith gently mussed the hair of one small wrestler as the children gradually moved in toward him as he spoke. "I have my wrestlers almost all year. You only get them for four months. You have to use your time wisely."[28]

More wrestlers and coaches drifted in as Smith discussed how wrestling technique had evolved over the decades. "The most important moves are still the basic moves—sit out turn in, stand up, single leg, double leg. They haven't changed in 50 years, and long after I'm gone they will still make up wrestling's fundamental skills. Wrestlers have to know all components of the sport. Otherwise you will be exposed. In order of importance—takedowns, getting away, and riding. I also emphasize the importance of both offensive and defensive scoring. A sprawl counts as much as a low single leg. My guys go 50% on their feet, 30% on bottom and 20% on top."[29]

As the clinic ended, fathers took the mat with sons and began practicing the pointers Smith had demonstrated. Small boys came up from behind the Cowboy coach, wrapped their arms around his legs and toppled him to the mat. One small boy stood up, flexed his muscles at his father, and boasted, "I pinned John Smith."[30]

As the clinic ended Smith made his way back to his team, signing programs, shirts, shoes, wrestling uniforms, and posters and the back of men's shirts along the way. Now 30 minutes before match-time, the Cowboy wrestlers sat in the tiny locker room and quietly consumed sandwiches, bagels and cream cheese, fruit, Gatorade, and water. Rosholt commented on the flavor of the Power Bar he preferred while Kevin Ward relaxed reading an Ann Rule novel given to him by Pendleton, who 10 minutes later called the team together for its pre-match prayer. "Protect our opponent and us from injury. Help us to wrestle to the best of our ability. Our Lord who art in heaven…"

Coach Smith then stood next to his wrestlers as they crowded together in the small locker room, 1,546 miles from Stillwater, Oklahoma, three days before Christmas. "This is one of those days where we have to ask a little bit more of ourselves. Go through your routine and be ready to go. We have some matches where we can pull some upsets. Let's go."[31]

The Cowboys walked down a small hallway, through two white swinging doors, and into the gymnasium, where they ran laps and rolled on the mat. Loud rap music, with the questionable words bleeped out, blared from the sound system.

On a curious morning where the crowd seemed more interested than partisan, OSU radio announcer J. Carl Guymon's voice seemed to drown out the silence in the arena—Oklahoma State defeated Cal Poly 32-9, winning 7 of 10 matches. The referee and match announcer repeatedly referred to the Cowboys as "Oklahoma." During one match the scorekeeper failed to turn on the riding time clock, and was diplomatically asked to do so by Coach Branch. Before defending national champion Pendleton's match, a fan on the front row loudly encouraged Pendleton's freshman opponent with the words "Show him the lights. He's ain't got nothing."[32] The crowd giggled, and Pendleton scored a 19-4 technical fall.

Coach Smith protested a close call during a Justin Porter takedown attempt, and received his first bench penalty of the year for telling the official in a conversational and straightforward tone, "Those are not the rules." Under the rules of college wrestling, a coach can be penalized for "questioning the referee."

The official replied, "Don't talk to me like that, John."

"But I'm just saying those are not the rules."

The official walked to the Cowboy bench, looked to the official scorekeeper, and misidentified the name of Smith's employer. "Bench penalty. Oklahoma."

Smith smiled, "Give me another one."[33] But the match continued.

Cal Poly marketed its university as providing a "learn by doing" educational experience. Perhaps it was this spirit that prompted the Mustangs to invite the top-ranked Cowboys to sunny San Luis Obispo on this sunny late-December morning. They learned how they stood relative to the nation's top ranked team; but the Cowboys learned some lessons as well.

The Murderer's Row went 5-0 with two falls and two technical falls, but the Cowboys actually trailed 6-3 after three matches, with Fleenor and Delk dropping decisions in the lighter weights.

The Cowboys were developing a consistent and troubling pattern...falling behind in the early matches, relying on their five All-Americans in the heavier weights to make up the deficit. But as the Oklahoma match had shown the week before, if only one of the Cowboy stalwarts stumbled, duals against better competition would come down to the wire.

With its current lineup, OSU could send as few as six wrestlers to the NCAA tournament. One upset would drop the Cowboys back into the middle of a pack.

After the match, the wrestlers filed back into the locker room. Coach Smith stood at the door speaking to a man wearing a blue windbreaker and an OSU baseball cap. He was presumably a Cowboy graduate living on the west coast, taking a rare opportunity for him and his children, who played by his side, to see his alma mater perform. Coach Smith escorted the slim, brown-haired man into the locker room, where he was introduced to the team as former OSU baseball great and major league star Robin Ventura. Coach Smith told the team that Ventura's consecutive-game hitting streak of 58 consecutive games had been honored by *Sports Illustrated* as one of the top 10 feats in the history of college sports. Ventura congratulated the Cowboy wrestlers, who momentarily stopped ripping open food wrappers and guzzling Gatorade, and reminded Smith, "You did OK too." Esposito, from New Jersey, informed his teammates "He played for the Yankees."[34]

As Ventura slipped from the locker room, Cowboy freshman and 133-pounder Nathan Morgan, from nearby Bakersfield, California and home for the holidays, made his way into the locker room. Wearing a gold cross under a sweatshirt "I bought for 10 bucks,"[35] the blond 133 pounder, called "Sunshine" by his teammates, was teased about a new short haircut. Smith spent several minutes talking to Morgan and his father as the team loaded onto the bus for the three-hour trip to Fresno. Something appeared to be up.

As the bus driver plotted the 145-mile trip inland to Fresno, post match comments filled the air. Mocco inquired, "When will we eat?"[36]

Esposito observed, "My guy had sweet hair. Hair goes far down here."[37]

Those sitting in the back begged for movies as the Cowboy bus rolled through miles and miles of farmland and vineyards. A freshman solemnly whispered from the back of the bus, "We're getting further and further away from food."[38]

At 5:40 p.m. the chartered bus completed the three-hour drive from Cal Poly to Fresno and pulled into a nearby Denny's Restaurant for a short meal before the 7 o'clock match. The team filled four booths and four tables. Studying the menus like Talmudic scholars pouring over holy and ancient parchments, they flipped the laminated likenesses of desserts placed on the tables over and over, back and forth, as they talked and laughed.

Fresno State University, a public university resting against the majestic Sierra Nevada mountain range, was surrounded by the fertile San Joaquin Valley. Even though university officials would close the program in the summer of 2006 for "cost-reduction" reasons, the Bulldogs enjoyed a solid wrestling history. Veteran coach Dennis DeLiddo compiled a 244-125-5 dual record over 18 seasons, dominating the Western Athletic Conference since their induction in 1992. The Bulldogs had crowned no national champions, but achieved 12 top 25 finishes at the NCAA tournament. Smith eyed the expansive campus as the bus rolled toward the arena. "This could be a national power year-in and year-out. A state university with good recruiting potential."[39]

The bus stopped. The wrestlers unloaded their gear and headed for the front door of the gym. The flamboyant DeLiddo, known for his exquisitely colored pullover sweaters and fiery demeanor, pulled Coach Smith aside as the Cowboys walked into the gym, expressing his displeasure to the Cowboy coach for sending an emissary to witness the Fresno State wrestlers weigh in. Smith listened patiently, smiled, and patted DeLiddo on the shoulder as he went to find his team.

The Cowboy match would be wrestled in the North Gym, the smaller of two arenas that featured Bulldog wrestling. A candid FSU official explained before the match that a dual meet later in the season with the lower-ranked and perhaps vulnerable Iowa Hawkeyes was being heavily promoted and held in a larger downtown arena. The event was being billed as possibly the largest crowd in Fresno State history, but the official confessed the match with OSU had not been heavily promoted. "We don't want to wrestle OSU during the holiday season in a larger arena because they will probably kill us."[40]

Before an enthusiastic, hostile, and well-informed wrestling crowd, the Cowboys continued their disturbing trend of falling behind early, but won eight of the next nine matches to flatten Fresno State 34-6. Backup Justin Porter won his second consecutive match. Pendleton, with friends and relatives from his nearby hometown of Lemoore, California, cheering, slipped off a Leemore High t-shirt and proceeded to take opponent Chris Gifford down 10 times before pinning him at the 5:52 mark. Rosholt and Mocco defeated ranked opponents. Coach Smith, making his way back to the locker room amidst autograph seekers after the match, remarked, "We need to get better."

After the match, the team quickly showered, loaded onto the bus, and headed for Reno with the insouciant anticipation of a meal soon to come. Tonight was the first evening since the beginning of the season, now six weeks old, where an impending weigh-in did not loom directly ahead. As the bus traveled down a busy street made bright by the neon, the giddy and relaxed wrestlers gave a running critique of the chain of restaurants which lined the boulevard, and offered thoughts on other basic appetites they had been deprived of as the season began to compress on their hearts and souls.

Finally the bus pulled up in front of a hamburger restaurant that featured freshly fried burgers, fries, and its specialty—thick ice cream shakes. The wrestlers filed out, lined up, and began placing orders. Soon Esposito was wearing a cook's paper hat given to him by a kindred restaurant employee who sensed these young customers' desperate holiday glee. The wrestlers sat at tables together and enjoyed their first meal eaten with abandon and without guilt for days. By the time the bus rolled away everyone would be at least 10 pounds over their competitive weight.

As the bus left Fresno, almost as if a switch had been pulled, the bus full of wrestlers and coaches fell asleep, stretched across aisles and on floors, with stomachs full and souls at rest. As they breathed quietly and deeply, Coach Smith checked phone messages, made notes in the black folder, and looked out the front window as the bus charged forward in the darkness and the cold toward home.

The Cowboys arrived in Reno at 4:15 a.m. to a virtually empty airport. Some wrestlers raced airport wheelchairs up and down the deserted corridors of the airport… others found secluded benches where they continued to sleep. Finally, at seven, the airport opened and wrestlers passed through security to an empty row of chairs that overlooked the gray and gloomy airport tarmac. Gradually each wrestler found a spot on the hard airport floor. Early morning passengers walked by with curious expressions, some grinning and others scowling, as the team spread on the floor in an area half the size of a wrestling mat and lay motionless, exhausted by the exertion, competition, starvation, and travel of the past four days.

The western invasion was complete.

I LEARNED A BUNCH FROM THE OLD GUYS.

—Mike Miller, *American Cowboy* July/August 2000

eight

michigan state

01.06.05

THE COWBOYS RETURNED from the western campaign on a cold, sunny afternoon of December 23, 2004. Over the previous five days the team barnstormed over two thousand miles by plane and almost eight hundred miles by bus. Cowboy trainers had treated a concussion, separated ribs, scraped knees, blackened eyes, and busted lips. The wrestlers won a tournament and two dual matches, made weight twice, kept possession of their number one national ranking, and looked forward to a delicious, restful three-day holiday before a series of practices would resume on the morning of December 27 at a pace and frequency that would make the swing through California look carefree and mild.

During the break between the Fresno State match on December 23rd and the Michigan State dual scheduled for January 6, the Cowboys held a flurry of workouts, giving the coaches their last good moment for a prolonged time of intense teaching and conditioning without the preoccupation of travel plans, making weight, meeting academic obligations, and preparing for outside competition. During this interlude the wrestlers worked out 20 times. The practice of December 28 was typical: strength and conditioning coach Gary Calcagno oversaw a hellish early morning of weight training, followed by a morning drill in the wrestling room. The afternoon practice called for lecture and more drilling, followed by the 30 wrestlers in groups of two scattered throughout the wrestling room, an archipelago of 15 dogfights resembling

Freshmen Jake Duke and Taylor Hosick drill in the wrestling room. *Courtesy Kim Parrish.*

wrestling matches, ending with an interval of marble-hearted conditioning drills.

After Smith's comments the team "drilled" for an hour. Drilling involved one wrestler repeatedly rehearsing a maneuver at full speed, with the defensive wrestler pushing back and resisting, but allowing his counterpart to complete the move. Each wrestler was expected to accomplish four to five moves per minute. The defender held a fine line between resisting too much and not resisting at all, and Smith could sense a letup across the wrestling room. "If I see one more guy spin someone down from a double leg, the team will put on tennis shoes and run stadium steps tonight. Coaches, kick them in the ass if you see them do it. That kind of effort does not put points on the board in live competition."[1] After Smith urged the wrestlers to drill with more vigor and speed, the volume in the room increased as the decibel of grunts amplified and the thud of wrestlers landing on the mats became louder and more frequent.

The sounds of a wrestling room are unique – the muffled thump of feet, knees and shoulders being thrown onto the mat or into the wall. Belching, labored breathing, painful screams, and the squeak of shoes on the mat. Muted sounds of execution—the blood, bone and salt of the soul – as men struggled for position against foes both real and imagined. The silence of quickness, the scream of gravity, the sweet and ruthless, and deafening deficit of balance, as the mat absorbed the knees and elbows and faces and hips as the hopes of the tireless drowned out the sound and fury of broken dreams.

An hour of drilling left the offensive wrestlers at the point of controlled exhaustion, as they continued to work through different scenarios they could face in a match. Smith often stopped the drilling to demonstrate on the nearest wrestler the finer points of a maneuver. To be the guinea pig during a John Smith demonstration is to know the meaning of the life of a double-tied shoelace—a leather lace hitched tight and frozen—as one's face is implanted deep into the core of the mat, driven by Smith's hips that bear against the shoulders with the weight of a double anvil. He lifts the wrestler's ankle high in the air, leveraging the face deeper into the mat, while lecturing the team for 45 seconds on how to properly break an opponent's death grip around the legs through the black art of leverage and weight. The wrestler was finally released. Disoriented, he climbed to his feet as his flattened cheek found air and life, and blood returned to the face as a friend.

Smith then paired up the wrestlers and they began straining through live matches. Occasionally starters were paired up with other starters. Smith explained, "It gives the first-line guys a level of appreciation of how good their teammates are. It gives them confidence."[2] Other times a starter was paired with an assistant coach, a workout opportunity which usually provided the varsity wrestler tougher competition than he would find in any dual or tournament during the season. But tonight, in a scheme known as "bait and shark," two backups alternated on one starter for periods of three minutes, one after the other.

Moods were sour, and the matches bordered on dogfights. Scheduled to last seven minutes, Smith prolonged them to 10 after barking at Hendricks, sitting against the wall in a black t-shirt and shorts with sweat flooding his unshaven and darkened cheeks. "You had no emotion in your workout tonight."[3]

Delk slammed Frishkorn into a concrete wall, and quickly asked, "Are you ok?"[4] Eric Dabbs took an unprovoked swing at freshman Ryan Freeman, which landed against the side of the unsuspecting freshman's headgear.

Smith moved to the north end of the room, the domain of the lighter weights, and kneeled on one knee, whistle in hand, as he watched deposed junior Derek Stevens wrestle with new fervor against Coleman Scott. As this white-hot interval of training dropped into the cold and dark Stillwater holiday mornings and nights, the Cowboys caught a stride. Smith stood and leaned against the orange padded wall. "I'm pushing these guys as hard as I've ever pushed a group."[5] Smith was fond of his team. "I would place the welfare of any of my children in the hands of any of my wrestlers."[6] In decades past, on some campuses, wrestlers were often considered the bad boys of college sports. Wrestling room aggression often morphed into bar fights and campus rumbles. But in the current era, with fewer scholarships and higher academic requirements in place, college wrestlers represented a higher echelon of student athletes. "I trust these guys. They are good people and good citizens."[7] But new challenges waited around the corner.

The holiday break gave Smith and his brain-trust, assistant coaches Branch, Pat Smith and Guerrero, more time to reflect on the biggest coaching dilemma facing them so far in the young season—how to avert the beating they were taking in the lighter weights. So far, 125 pounders Stevens and Fleenor had won only one dual match between them, and both failed to place at the Reno tournament. Like a poker player holding the winning card, the staff suspected true freshmen Scott and Morgan might be projected as potential All-Americans. For now, they waited in the wings. The coaches debated whether they should insert the teen-aged, true freshmen into the lineup mid-season. To be successful on the college level, the coaches strove to help each wrestler find his own voice consistent with his own abilities, skills, values, temperament, and personal mission. For a freshman, stepping into a lineup for the first time was a daunting prospect with potential for great payoff. "It gives our young guys a challenge to be on a national championship team. That has value. These next 10 weeks of competition are equal to three years of training. Even moderate success will catapult them into next season with tremendous momentum, and their teammates want them in the lineup. They want the best chance to win matches. They want the best team out there."[8]

But Coach Smith, who had only placed four freshmen into the starting lineup during his 13 seasons as head coach, also knew the risks. "They will wrestle guys bigger and stronger, both mentally and physically. They will get popped somewhere down the line, probably more than once, and it could take a big toll on their confidence…and faith is everything at this level. If you don't think you're going to win, you rarely surprise yourself. And that could carry into next year. You just don't know."[9]

While Murderer's Row amassed a 73-2 record leading up to the holiday break, the lower weights were thin on projected blue-chip talent. Stevens and Fleenor were a combined 9-10 at 125, and with Frishkorn moving up to 141, a slot opened at 133. In a close dual match, coming out of the gate with two losses, and depending too often on the middle and heavier weights to consistently pull the team out of early deficits was a trend the coaches wanted to change, especially by national tournament time, when upsets lay hidden around every corner.

So while the Cowboys appeared to the media and the wrestling community to be the prohibitive favorite to capture their third consecutive national title, the Cowboy coaches worried the team was vulnerable to a squad more balanced from top to bottom. The upcoming match with unranked Michigan State illustrated the point. While the Spartans were unranked as a team, they had five wrestlers individually ranked in the nation's top 20 weights, the same number as the Cowboys. Granted, their ranked wrestlers were not placed as high in the rankings as the Cowboys, but the point was made—OSU might be vulnerable to a team capable of producing seven or eight All-Americans against the five Cowboy superstars. At the national tournament, a wrestler who is defeated in the early rounds and has to wrestle consolation matches to place third or fourth can score for his team as many or more points than a national champion produces, by racking up major decisions and falls as he grinds his way across the bracket.

So Coach Smith made his decision. He would bring true freshmen Coleman Scott and Nathan Morgan out of redshirt status, and insert them into the starting lineup against Michigan State. The idea had been percolating in the Cowboy coach's planning since before Christmas. He had discussed the possibility with Morgan's father in December after the Cal Poly match while standing outside the team bus, and now was the time to pull the trigger.

Smith was hesitant to place true freshmen into his lineup, and had done so only four times in his thirteen years at the OSU helm. Pendleton and Esposito were the last to receive the baptism by fire. Esposito still remembers the process. "I wanted to wrestle from the very beginning," he said, "I didn't see myself sitting out. I didn't want to watch the team win the national title and not be a part of it. I definitely think Nathan and Coleman are ready."[10] He echoed the coaches' desire to put the best team on the mat. "Our best guys should be out there."[11] Smith said it this way, "We're just in a position where we feel we have to put our best team on the mat. This is playing out to be a very competitive year and we want to have our best team out there."[12] Pendleton, who was pulled out of redshirt for his first match as a Cowboy, remembers. "I got pulled out against Joe Heskett from Iowa State. He was ranked No. 1 in the nation, undefeated at Iowa State, and I got whipped pretty bad."[13] The Cowboy team leader empathized with their challenge but did not lower his expectations for the beardless and fresh-faced youngsters. "We expect them to win, and they expect themselves to win."[14]

This untested lineup would be unveiled against Michigan State. The Spartans, slowed by weather and bottom-heavy with spotty talent, were coached by 14-year-veteran Tom Minkel, who brought his team to Stillwater a week late off the heels of a snowstorm and a 25-10 loss to in-state rival Central Michigan. Michigan State was scheduled to wrestle Oklahoma State on January 6, but inclement weather postponed the match for one week. To the Cowboy's relief, Michigan State arrived on the 13th, allowing the Cowboys to break the monotony of practice.

Travel grinds down college athletes, even the young and physically trained. On the way to the Detroit airport the day before, Michigan State drove through a snowstorm, avoided by minutes a tragic 200-car pileup outside Detroit, boarded their flight one seat short, a benevolent passenger relinquished her seat, and tended to a sick wrestler on the airplane—only to arrive in Tulsa at midnight the night before the match with the top-ranked Cowboys.

The Spartans' five ranked wrestlers were led by undefeated 125-pounder Nick Simmons, an All-American two seasons ago who finished fifth in last summer's U.S. Olympic freestyle trials. Simmons' brother Andy, ranked third in the country at 141, carried a 21-1 record. OSU had won 23 of the past 24 duals against the Spartans, but was upset in 1999 in East Lansing. Coach Smith said "This is a team that has tested us whenever we have wrestled them. It gives us good, hard looks at some things we have to do differently because of their physical style of wrestling. We have to be ready to wrestle for seven minutes."[15]

In the wrestling room minutes before the match began, freshmen Morgan and Scott warmed up with the same pace and movement they had employed hundreds of times before, over years and years, since they were small boys wrestling in junior matches and tournaments all across America. But tonight they were wide-eyed and dreamlike, for they were dressing out for the first time in the black warm-ups and orange singlet reserved for the Oklahoma State varsity. After Pendleton led the team in its customary pre-match prayer on the south mat, Smith's pre-match speech was short and pointed, as the Cowboys prepared to wrestle at home for the first time in 60 days, "Let's put some of this hard work to use."[16]

The Cowboys jogged into the arena, made the customary circle around the orange mat, and lined facing their opponents for introductions. A crowd of less than 2,000 filled the bottom sections from baseline to baseline.

According to a college rule ostensibly designed to make matches more pleasing and interesting to the crowd, coaches may by a random draw determine which weight class will be wrestled first. Coaches hope the draw will allow them to send out one of their better wrestlers early in the dual, perhaps setting the tone and establishing momentum for the rest of the matches. For the only time the entire season, Smith utilized the random draw, hoping to avoid starting off the evening by putting Coleman Scott out against heavily favored Nick Simmons. The strategy worked, as the drawing dictated action to begin at 165, with favored Johny Hendricks taking on an unranked Spartan.

Hendricks and Pendleton led off the evening with wins. Freshman Clay Kehrer lost. But the Cowboys led 13-3 after four matches when Mocco scored a fall in 1:03. Now it was time for 18 year-old freshman Coleman Scott's first match as an OSU starter.

Ideally coaches hope to bring a young freshman wrestler out for the first time in the most favorable of conditions, perhaps against another younger, less experienced opponent whose experience and attitude will not fracture a wrestler's confidence, and whose style matches up well against the fledging, so that the initial match will prove to be a positive learning experience. In that regard, the circumstances could not have been worse for Coleman Scott's first match as an OSU starter. He would face the undefeated Simmons, an All-American two seasons earlier who redshirted the previous year to compete for a spot on the United States Olympic team. His hard-boiled style

ABOVE: Always on the attack, Zack Esposito applies a punishing leg-ride to Darren McNight of Michigan State. Esposito defeated the Spartan 14-4. *Courtesy Mika Matzen*

LEFT: Michigan State's R. J. Boudro tries to fight off Chris Pendleton's textbook cradle during a dual in Stillwater. Pendleton won the match 11-4. *Courtesy Mika Matzen*

and lanky build provided the absolute worst trap the wide-eyed Coleman Scott could wander into before a home crowd at Gallagher-Iba Arena. To make matters worse, Coleman had spent a good part of the day pulling weight, and he appeared drained and shrunken at the weigh-in. Moments before the match was to begin a radio commentator expressed his hope that "it doesn't get ugly"[17] in the young Cowboy's first varsity match before the home crowd.

Smith gave Scott a short pep talk before his match, shaking his hand as the true freshman stepped out dressed in orange. Simmons paced to the center circle with a look of impatient contempt, wearing a green singlet trimmed in white. The official whistled the match to begin. Within seconds Simmons was in deep on a leg. Scott seemed to give the takedown up, bracing not to relinquish back points early in the first period; but suddenly he fortified his back leg against Simmon's forward pressure, regained his balance, and began to

Coleman Scott, pulled out of red-shirt status after the holiday break to shore up a slow-starting lineup, struggles for control against Michigan State's Nick Simmons during his first varsity match for the Cowboys. *Courtesy Mika Matzen*

scramble near the edge of the mat as legendary OSU head coaches Eddie Sutton (basketball) and Mike Holder (golf) looked on, offering support to the only Cowboy team attempting to defend a national title for the season. Then lightening struck.

Scott, not understanding he was a wide-eyed freshman wrestling in his first varsity match against an All-American senior, gained his balance, took aim, and with audacious purpose stuck Simmons to his back, bringing the Cowboy bench and the Gallagher-Iba crowd of 2,567 to its feet, and going up 5-0 just one minute into the match. As he held Simmons to his back, Scott's face held the expression of a weathered and hardened veteran.

* * *

Coleman Scott was an 18-year-old, brown-eyed freshman from Waynesburg, Pennsylvania who began wrestling in first grade. He was a serious student, a business major and the son of restaurateurs. He aspired to open an eatery with his sister after graduation. Like most of his teammates, he was a high-school superstar and a three-time state champion with a career record of 156-12. An outstanding soccer player and center fielder with a rifle arm, he was graced with narrow hips and broad shoulders, with the flexibility of a ballet dancer and the balance of an acrobat. He was courteous, polite, and capable of crying when happy or sad. He was close to his parents and two sisters, and found an extended family among his wrestling companions at OSU. One could find him hanging out with Mocco or his roommate Nathan Morgan, or any number of Cowboy teammates. His mother Mary believed wrestling helped young men learn to interact with others. Her only son had the natural gift of ease and comfort in his bearing, making new friends easily, and cherishing friendships from his young past, particularly those forged through the crucible of competitive wrestling. That was why the phone call Scott received recently, just days before Thanksgiving, hurt so badly. He learned two of his best friends, one a fellow wrestler from high school, were killed in an automobile crash. Coleman competed with the team in an open tournament the following Saturday and on Monday flew home to say goodbye to his friends for the final time. Coach Smith held him upright through his grief, and he rejoined the team the following week. One of his friends was buried in wrestling warm-ups and headgear. Bearing that special form of grief only the young can tolerate, Coleman Scott returned to Stillwater.

Coach Smith watched Coleman daily at practice and knew he possessed special talents. He wrestled Fleenor and Stevens tough in practice, and seemed to be "foaming at the mouth" to break into the Cowboy lineup. He won tough scrambles in workouts, and responded well to pressure weeks earlier in registering back-to-back victories over both Stevens and Fleenor during ranking matches just before the Minnesota match. Watching Coleman progress, Smith commented, "I'm learning something about that young man."[18]

Excellent lower-body strength and flexibility made him a tough rider, and he was skilled in turning opponents over. He also possessed uncanny defensive skills, able to transform what appeared to be vulnerable positions into points. But Coach Smith also discerned the freshman's liabilities. "He has a tendency to be too patient, and needs to learn to pull the trigger, especially early in the match. Sometimes he gets out of his stance, and is prone to lean forward with his arms outstretched. He also struggles with his weight. But he is a battler. He wants to compete."[19]

* * *

Michigan State's Simmons battled back in the final period with a three point near fall and a riding time point to win 6-5. Coach Smith was pleased

ABOVE: Daniel Frishkorn fights from the bottom position against Andy Simmons of Michigan State. *Courtesy Mika Matzen.*

BELOW: Sporting a mask to protect a broken nose sustained during practice, Nathan Morgan controls Ryan Froese of Michigan State in his inaugural varsity match as a Cowboy. *Courtesy Mika Matzen.*

BELOW: Coach Smith congratulates Nathan Morgan after his first varsity win, while coaches Eric Guerro and Pat Smith look on while stylish Jamill Kelly, a 2004 Olympian, stands behind the bench. *Courtesy Mika Matzen.*

with the Waynesville, Pennsylvania native's debut. "Coleman had a good effort. He put up five points and didn't score again. You have to keep scoring against older guys, but he can take some positives out of the match."[20]

As a disgusted but exhilarated Coleman Scott trotted off the mat to the locker room, Nathan Morgan stood on the edge of the orange mat and listened as Coach Guerrero softly spoke instructions through the holes in his headgear. Wearing a padded mask to protect a broken nose sustained during the holiday practices, the Californian slashed unranked Ryan Froese for seven takedowns for a 20-5 technical fall in his first match as a Cowboy starter. "It's a lot different when you put that orange singlet on. We wear black singlets in open tournaments, but the orange one is the official OSU singlet. All the OSU champions have worn it in the past, and a lot of responsibility goes with wearing it."[21]

Smith said of Morgan's performance, "Nathan looked very strong, very dominating on his feet. It makes you look like a smart coach, pulling somebody out and having him wrestle like that the first time out."[22] Morgan reflected on wrestling for the OSU varsity for the first time, "It was a little different putting on that orange singlet for the first time, it was once-in-a-lifetime. The coaches knew how to get me ready, and I felt really good out there. I'm glad we had this one before the Iowa dual."[23]

Pendleton was excited about his young mentorees. "I never doubted Nathan. From the moment he stepped into the room he has done nothing but try to improve. And Coleman…he almost got a pin against a very good wrestler. I know after [Coleman] cools down and comes in [today] and he understands that he just went with one of the best guys in the country that his confidence will be back."[24]

The Spartan coach recognized the lighter-weight ballast the line-up change brought about, and gave a prediction on the OSU's upcoming match against sister-Big 10 school Iowa. "OSU's two young kids were very competitive right out of the chute. Iowa has a pretty good team in places, but OSU has more balance and a lot of talent."[25]

Coach Smith had served up a beginning course of veteran gristle followed by a side of tender, snarling lamb in the form of Scott and Morgan. Kevin Ward posted a solid decision at 157, solidifying his position as the starter. But 141 still remained a puzzle. Frishkorn got the nod against Andy Simmons (younger brother to Nick Simmons) but fell 5-2. In total, three of the four Cowboy freshmen lost. Coach Smith was understated in his analysis. "I'm glad they got to come out and wrestle. The experience will do them good."[26]

At practice the following day Smith reflected on Coleman Scott's tough loss, and dwelled on the danger to a wrestler who jumps out to an early lead. "When you wrestle the better guys in the country, if you score on them early, they're coming right back at you. You have to keep wrestling! You can't wait for them to come to you. You go after them!"[27] His voice quickened as he bore in on Hendricks, who was taken down early in his match. "During the first minute everyone will be competitive and will come out hard and be ready for the upset. Sometimes you don't have the luxury of working into a match at your own pace. If they pick up the velocity, you have to match it.

Steve Mocco pinned Michigan State's Max Lossen in sixty-three seconds.
Courtesy Jim Bowen.

Who cares if he takes you down. Go kick his ass! Go pound him! Go pin him! Go grab a hold of him! Step out to the center of the mat, put your foot out, and be ready to go!"[28]

* * *

Long-time professional football coach Bill Parcells is a boxing fan. He often mentions in conversation a fight that took place thirty years ago between heavy-hitting Cyclone Hart and underdog Vito Antuofermo. In the first few rounds Hart pummeled his challenger unmercifully, but in the

Big 12 Champion Kevin Ward applies an arm-bar during his 6-2 victory over Matt McCarty of Michigan State. Ward's stunning victory over fifth-ranked Trent Paulson weeks later led to his Big 12 conference individual title. *Courtesy Mika Matzen.*

fifth round he began to tire. Antuofermo noticed his opponent's fatigue, and delivered a series of vicious blows that knocked the heavily-favored Hart out cold.

In the locker room after the fight, the boxers were separated in their small dressing room by a flimsy curtain. The dejected Hart could hear his opponent's cornermen planning to take their boxer to the hospital.

Hart then heard Antuofermo's own voice through the curtain. " Every time he hit me with that left hook to the body, I was sure I was going to quit. After the second round, I thought if he hit me in there again, I'd quit. I thought in the same thing after the fourth round. He didn't hit me no more."

After hearing his opponent's confession, Hart then began to weep, softly at first. Parcells sums it up. "He was crying because for the first time he understood that Antuofermo had felt the same way he had and worse. The only thing that separated the guy talking from the guy crying was what they had done. The coward and the hero feel the same emotions. They're both human."

The unsparing Parcells lumped Hart into a category he called "game quitters." They seem "…as if they are trying to win, but really they have given up. They've just chosen a way out that's not apparent to the naked eye. They are more concerned with public opinion than the end result."[29]

During OSU's NCAA tournament drought throughout the nineties, some in the wrestling community might have called the once-proud Cowboys some form of game quitters. When the tough matches rolled around, they found ways to lose, while archrival Iowa pounded and bullied their way to victory when the chips were on the table.

In ten days that hypothesis would be tested, at least for a few weeks, for the Iowa Hawkeyes were coming to Stillwater.

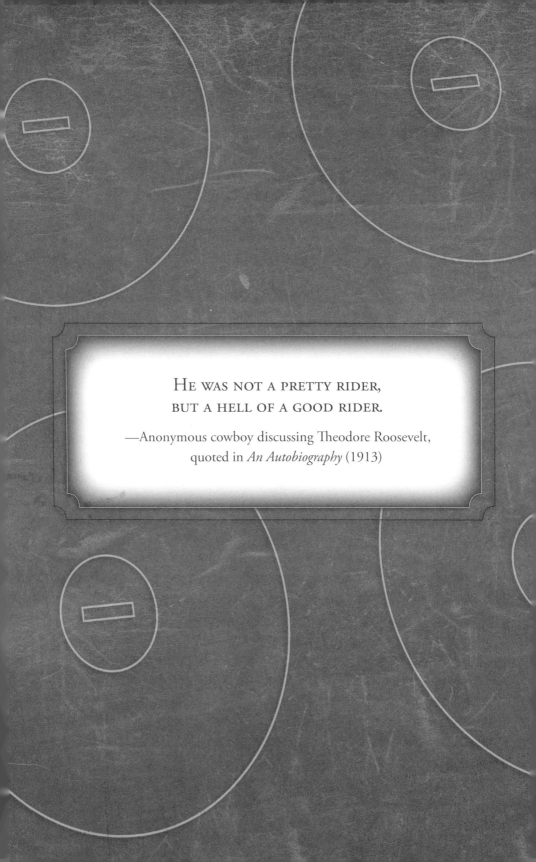

HE WAS NOT A PRETTY RIDER,
BUT A HELL OF A GOOD RIDER.

—Anonymous cowboy discussing Theodore Roosevelt,
quoted in *An Autobiography* (1913)

nine

01.16.05

IOWA'S DOMINANCE of the college wrestling world began during the Gerald Ford presidency and extended for more than two decades. During this time the Hawkeyes, with their relentless, pounding, aggressive style, captured 20 NCAA titles, produced 196 All-Americans, and crowned 58 individual champions. The lion's share of those victories came under the reign of legendary coach Dan Gable, who inherited an Iowa program that had captured national titles the previous two seasons. Gable built on that success, and proceeded to capture 15 NCAA titles during his 21 years at the Iowa helm.

The only team to consistently threaten Gable's chokehold was Oklahoma State. During Gable's tenure Iowa dominated OSU at the NCAA tournament, winning 15 titles to OSU's three. Gable's dual meet record against OSU was a solid 12-5, but he was only 4-3 against OSU teams coached by Smith, with all three Cowboy wins coming against favored Hawkeye teams. Since Jim Zalesky took over the Iowa juggernaught in 1997, Iowa was 1-5 against the Cowboys. The Hawkeyes had not won an NCAA title since 2000 and finished eighth during the 2003 tournament, the school's lowest finish in 29 years.

In the meantime, with two consecutive national titles under their belts, the Cowboys were climbing back to national prominence and enjoyed a streak of four consecutive dual victories against Iowa.

Iowa's four-year NCAA title drought, coupled with the emergence of their chief rival Oklahoma State, caused the Iowa wrestling nation to grumble.

The chief recipient of the criticism was head coach Zalesky, a former Iowa wrestling great who captured three national titles and finished his career on an 89-match winning streak. He was named the Outstanding Wrestler at the 1984 NCAA tournament and was designated *Amateur Wrestling News'* Wrestler of the Decade during the 1980s. He served as assistant coach and head recruiter under Dan Gable for seven seasons and was considered the natural and unenviable heir apparent to the Iowa head coaching position when Gable retired. His first three Iowa teams, benefiting from the gravitas and talent of the Gable years, won three national titles. The respected husband and father of four personified Iowa wrestling values of dedication and aggressiveness, and seemed a sure bet to continue Iowa wrestling dominance. It seemed a certainty when his 2000-2001 recruiting class, which included high school heavyweight phenom Steve Mocco, was ranked as the top group of incoming freshmen in the nation.

But since Iowa's NCAA title in 2000, the Hawkeyes finished second, fourth, eighth, and second respectively at the national tournament. To make matters worse, Zalesky's teams had won only one of seven duals with OSU and Mocco had transferred from Iowa to OSU. Even though Zalesky had been given a contract extension, the Hawkeye fans were grumbling.

So on this day in Stillwater, the stage was set for college wrestling's two most storied programs to clash in a mid-season dual. A *Sports Illustrated* writer roamed the campus, and national amateur wrestling publications set up camp. More media credentials were issued to national media than for any match in recent memory, even though this Iowa team was ranked ninth in the nation, and posed no serious threat to upend the Cowboys on the bright and sunny Sunday afternoon in Stillwater. But the media was in Stillwater not to just cover a wrestling match. They were there to report a story of betrayal, revenge, and the shifting of college wrestling's balance of power.

After a long absence, a new world order in college wrestling seemed to be reestablishing its capitol city in Stillwater. Beginning his twelfth season as Cowboy head coach, Smith became the fifth Cowboy coach to lead his team to consecutive national titles. With an infrastructure of excellent facilities, adequate budget, excellent assistant coaches, and a place for graduates to foster their Olympic dreams, a stable of deep and talented recruiting classes was gradually being amassed. Even during Iowa's years of dominance, the

OSU program had been flavored with national championship talent, but now those numbers were growing in depth and breadth. Oklahoma State was gradually returning to its reputation as the place to be if a young and talented wrestler aspired to Olympic glory.

The media also belabored a story of betrayal. Months earlier in a move that stunned the wrestling community, devastated the Smith family, and ran contrary to wrestling's cultural norms, John Smith's nephew, Mark Perry, spurned the Cowboys' scholarship offer and decided to take his talents to Iowa. Mark's OSU wrestling pedigree was deep. Mark's mother was John's sister Cathy. Mark's father was Coach Smith's former teammate, fellow All-American at OSU, current and longtime business partner in a lucrative wrestling camp enterprise, and Coach Smith's former assistant head wrestling coach, Mark Perry, Sr.

Chris Matthews, the OSU Athletic Department's coordinator for media relations for wrestling, arranges interviews, maintains the wrestling web site, prepares press-releases, and assembles the Cowboy wrestling media guide. *Courtesy Oklahoma State University.*

Mark Perry going to Iowa would be likened to the Pope denouncing his Catholic loyalties and joining a neighborhood Baptist church, or a lifetime Red Sox fan trading his season tickets behind the dugout at Fenway Park for two in Yankee Stadium. It simply was not possible. It made no sense. How could it happen?

The 20-year-old dark-haired redshirt freshman bore the facial resemblance of a Smith, but his lanky frame stood taller than his uncles Lee Roy, John, and Pat, and his Smith-like independent spirit captured this intelligent, sensitive, articulate young man who longed to forge his own identity away from the shadows of his legendary uncles. "Growing up I was a real big Oklahoma State fan. I definitely thought I would go to school there. It was really a tough choice to rule out Oklahoma State, when you grow up [there] like that, and this year they were the best. It was between them and Iowa at the end."[1]

Stillwater is an intimate community, and some speculated that Mark Perry's resignation as John Smith's assistant coach in August of 2000, young Mark's freshman year in high school, had strained family ties, and Mark's decision to choose Iowa over OSU was influenced by that turn of events. But the younger Perry, named the nation's top high school wrestler in 2003, already had demonstrated a capacity to take a road less traveled when he left his hometown of Stillwater after his freshman year to attend the prestigious Blair Academy in New Jersey, a private New Jersey high school known for tough academics and excellent wrestling teams. "I knew if I went to Blair I'd have more options. Blair is at a different level both wrestling and academically from [Stillwater] High School. Our high school wasn't known for either, really. I had never taken a test that wasn't multiple choice before. I haven't taken one since I got here. The kids here [at Blair] are all at a completely different level. They're preparing you to succeed in college, where in a lot of schools they're just trying to get kids through. We have study hall every night, and the workload here is tremendous."[2]

Perry's high school coach at Blair Academy seemed to understand the context of Mark's decision. "That was probably the most difficult decision he's ever had to make. It went against family, it went against everything he's been brought up with. Oklahoma State and Iowa, they just don't like each other. Crossing over that line was a difficult thing to do. I mean, who wouldn't want to wrestle for John Smith? This is a guy that he idolizes. The fact that he grew up in Stillwater, and coming back to a place like that, it still doesn't sit well with him or his family."[3]

Mark's decision not to attend Oklahoma State traveled like an electric shock through the Smith family, and that he chose archrival Iowa made the cut deep and painful. Smith recalls the day with chagrin. "I was very disappointed. Up until the last day I thought Mark was attending Oklahoma State. It hurt my family and me and was a blow to our program. It still hurts. I don't understand it completely to this day. I truly believe he would have been better off as a Cowboy. But he is my nephew and the son of my sister, and I love him. I hope he wins every match he competes in, except when he wrestles a man in an orange singlet."[4]

If anything, wrestling is a family sport, often handed down by fathers to their sons with the passion of a craftsman passing down the family business. It is also an experience shared deeply by siblings. At the NCAA tournament later in the season, seven sets of brothers and three sets of twins would compete. The wrestling community was replete with sets of brothers who grew up in the sport. Among the OSU starters for the Iowa match, all but one had a brother or father who had wrestled or who had been intimately involved in his career. Of the 19 teams OSU competed against during the year, more than half were flavored by some combination of fathers, sons, brothers, or cousins. Conversely, at Parent's Day for the Oklahoma State football team just weeks earlier, of the 17 graduating seniors, only nine fathers or stepfathers attended the special pre-game ceremony. At the NCAA wrestling tournament weeks later, all of the nine OSU qualifiers had a contingent of parents, siblings, relatives, and friends who traveled from across the United States for the event. It was a family reunion.

But if Smith lost a nephew to Iowa, he gained the services of a heavyweight from the Hawkeyes when national champion Steve Mocco stunned the college wrestling world the previous summer and announced his intention to transfer from Iowa to Oklahoma State. This story line also attracted endless attention from the local and national media. *Sports Illustrated* even referenced Mocco's decision in the lead paragraph of its match coverage with "Witness the shock waves the two-time All-American and 2003 NCAA champion sent through college wrestling last summer when he transferred from Iowa to rival Oklahoma State."[5]

Mocco won an NCAA title in 2003 while a sophomore at Iowa, then took off a year to train for the 2004 Olympic team. After failing to make the squad, he concluded a change was necessary.

With a sensitivity that belied his scary persona, the new Cowboy heavyweight was clear in expressing his affection for the Iowa coaching family. "I want to thank the University of Iowa for helping me progress not only as a wrestler but as a student and a person as well. Coach Zalesky and Coach Brands have been strong influences on me."[6]

So Perry chose Iowa over OSU and Mocco picked the Cowboys over the Hawkeyes—both giving up a love they knew for a love they had never known,[7] and in the meantime, broke with the past and dealt with historic losses and feelings of disloyalty to the sources of values that had made them what they were this Sunday afternoon in Stillwater. Change is painful, particularly that form of change that demands one to adapt to a new and strange environment "…because it challenges people's habits, beliefs, and values. It asks them to take a loss, experience uncertainty, and even express disloyalty to people and cultures."[8] But the change was made and the journey was underway. At pre-match introductions Mocco stood in orange and black by his coach John Smith, and Perry stood in gold and black by his coach Jim Zalesky. They both seemed at home.

Now it was time to wrestle.

With the Michigan State match postponed to the Thursday before the Iowa dual on Sunday, the Cowboys weighed in twice in four days, an inconvenience that Coach Smith welcomed. "Competing twice in four days at a high level will give our team, especially the younger guys, an idea of what the national tournament is like. The hours are crowded, the body adjusts, and we become a little more battle-tested. As a coach you can't replicate that pattern with one dual per week. Regardless of how hard we go in practice, there is nothing better than live wrestling against outside competition."[9]

The team assembled by late morning and checked their weight before the 1:00 p.m. weigh-in. Some sat in the locker room. Others lay across the mats in street cloths, dancing in that dream world between sleep and anxiety, as the backups and redshirts filtered in and took places away from the starters who would soon be on public display.

At 12:25 p.m. the Iowa team entered the wrestling room to stretch and pre-weigh before the 1:00 p.m. weigh-in. Mark Perry, wearing bright gold sweats with his head raised defiantly and lips tightly pursed, was the first wrestler through the door. His teammates followed and sat silently against the south wall, near Mocco's practice area and waited for the coaches' prompting to enter the locker room where the scales rested in judgment on the floor. Minutes later, as the wrestlers gathered in the crowded locker, the coaches took their positions near the scales and wrestlers were called to weigh in one by one, small weights first, working up to the heavier wrestlers. At most weigh-ins there is a palatable, growling hunger in the air, but today there was that unmistakable tension that flows when broken relationships occur simultaneously and bridge the past with the present. Mocco made swift eye contact and nodded toward his former teammates, while Perry and the Hawkeye team grimly and with purpose stepped on the scales and filed out to their locker room where they would eat their snack and dress out.

For days the Cowboy coaches had been considering that one spot in the lineup that was still a matter of debate—the mature and dependable senior Ronnie Delk, who desperately wanted one last shot at making the team for the national tournament, or the talented freshman Frishkorn, still struggling from the equilibrium of not making weight for the Oklahoma match and being moved up a weight by the coaching staff for the duration of the season. Both wrestlers were 3-2 in dual matches. Delk won the headup match against Frishkorn in the Reno tournament, but Frishkorn held a slight upper hand in recent workouts. Both weighed in for this match, and both dressed out and warmed up in the wrestling room, but neither knew who would compete later in the day.

With minutes to go before match time Johny Hendricks, who would face Mark Perry at 165, patted Mocco on the shoulder as they both sat on the center chairs. "Are you ready?" Mocco nodded his head and softly replied, "Yes."[10]

Coach Smith, dressed in blue slacks and white shirt which blended well with an orange tie with black trim, stood on the north mat and watched Scott and Morgan drill on their feet. "Take good hard shots. Takedowns to their back. We want back points today."[11]

Both young Cowboys had seen the Iowa-OSU match on television as boys. Now they were grizzled veterans of one varsity match, and they wore the orange singlet.

Smith, never fond of the inspirational pre-match speech, walked toward the north window, paused and turned back, "Alright, let's get ready to wrestle. About fifteen minutes out."[12]

RIGHT: Coach Smith urges a wrestler on during the Iowa match. During Dan Gable's tenure, Smith held a 4-3 dual record against Iowa, but his Cowboys could not match Gable's Hawkeyes at the NCAA tournament. *Courtesy Mika Matzen.*

LOWER RIGHT: Nathan Morgan takes down Iowa's Mario Galanakis on his way to a 12-3 major decision. *Courtesy Dr. Jeremy Cook.*

He leaned against the window perch and looked to the north as fans walked to the arena through an unseasonably warm January afternoon. Since Smith had been the OSU head coach, he had won 8 of 11 dual matches against Iowa. But as he told a reporter only days before, "You're only as good as your last match or your last tournament."[13] Smith then glanced at his watch, and walked to Ronnie Delk, who was ghost wrestling near the center of the wrestling room. He touched Delk's elbow and whispered into the senior's left ear. Delk nodded his head. As Smith walked away, Delk began running sprints up and down the room like a blowtorch had been gas-fired and placed against his gaunt rear end. Smith had given Delk the nod...he would be wrestling today.

While Coach Smith checked with his assistants to make sure there were adequate chairs on the bench for the entire staff to sit, Pendleton brought the team to the center of the south mat four minutes before the hour. He prayed, and the circle tightened as he whispered, "Let's show them who is best. Cowboys on 3. 1-2-3." Then they were out.[14]

A crowd of almost 8,000 looked on as Coleman Scott relinquished a lead in the last period for the second straight match and lost 5-3. After the match Smith stood over and admonished Scott, who sat quietly against the Gatorade cooler behind the bench.

Morgan, struggling to keep his face protector on to shield his newly cracked nose, scored near falls in the first and second periods in a 12-3 major decision to give the Cowboys a 4-3 dual match lead.

Then came Delk, who brought the Cowboy crowd to its feet when he nailed a takedown with eight seconds left to upset No. 7 ranked Alex Tsirtsis 3-2 at the buzzer. "As soon as I locked up that cradle, I knew it was over with," said a happy Delk, who flashed a shark-like smile to the Cowboy bench as the referee counted off the match's final seconds.[15]

A satisfied Ronnie Delk smiles after edging Iowa's Alex Tsirtsis 3-2 on a last-second near-fall. *Courtesy Dr. Jeremy Cook*

With the dramatic victory Delk seemed to regain the lead in his race with Frishkorn for the nod at 141, but both wrestlers knew grueling road trips lay ahead. The tide could turn.

Esposito fought off a late takedown effort by Iowa's Ty Eustice to send their match into overtime, where the top-ranked Cowboy rode out the Hawkeye and won 2-1.

Kevin Ward was man-handled and finally pinned with three seconds left in his match by Joe Johnston as Smith slammed his hand on a nearby chair.

Then the fans moved forward in their seats, the lights seemed to brighten slightly as Johny Hendricks, in his neon-orange singlet, walked to the center circle to face Mark Perry, while John Smith turned his back to the mat and walked to his chair.

* * *

Johny Hendricks was a 21-year-old redshirt sophomore from Edmond, Oklahoma, and one of two native Oklahomans in the Cowboy lineup. He possessed coal-dark hair and eyes, a dark stubble that grew like prairie grass, the strength of a forklift, and the light heart of a playful lion about to consume its prey. He began wrestling at the age of five, and until he reached high school, his father Keven, who recognized his son's single-mindedness early on, was his only coach. "I had given him $20 to go out with his friends but he gave it back. He told me, 'I'm going to the gym.'"[16] The enigmatic Hendricks, whose playful demeanor belies the heart of a medieval executioner, likes wrestling because it is a sport with no excuses. "When I get on the mat with my opponent, it's just him and me. The wrestler who wants it more will win. Nothing outside the circle counts. Other athletes don't understand why we come in here day in and day out and push ourselves to the absolute limit. But winning a wrestling match is a great feeling of personal accomplishment that no one can take away from you."[17]

His older brother, a helicopter mechanic for the 101st Airborne Division, was on call to be deployed to Iraq at any moment. He had one uncle who was a helicopter pilot, and another who was a chopper mechanic as well. His mom and dad watched from the stands.

Hendricks was reputed to be, pound-for-pound, the strongest wrestler on the squad. Referred to as "freaky-strong," strength that defies the laws of physics, by his incredulous teammates, he frustrated Smith by turning on his uncanny power at will, usually late in a match. Bemoaned Smith, "He does it when he gets mad. I wish he would get mad earlier."[18] Johny wrestled with the innocent abandon and expressiveness of a schoolboy at recess. Quick to smile, he drew Pendleton's ire one day during practice by laughing while Pendleton held him to his back. Through gestures, shrugs, quizzical expressions, waves of the hand, and occasional questions, his matches were more like theater than skirmish. While in the standing position, he constantly adjusted the rubber pads on the headgear that covered his ears, almost as if he was trying to hear more clearly a far-off beat to a different drummer.

Always the winner in post-practice wind sprints, Hendricks' blue-collar training habits wore his opponents down, and his substantial "gas tank" allowed him to carry on a running dialogue with his opponent, officials, coaches, and the crowd throughout a match. While Esposito before him and Pendleton after him struck like screaming eagles descending on a helpless turtle resting on a rock, Hendricks moved in like a bulldozer breaking up a concrete floor—steady, relentless and hydraulic in pace and distance—grunting and screaming in exertion as power trumped form. His disarming innocence permitted the sophomore to be one of the only wrestlers who

Smith allowed to question his authority. When told by Smith, during the end of a brutal practice session, to achieve five escapes within the next five minutes, the sweat-drenched Hendricks shook his head like his coach had gone mad. "What do you think I'm doing? Sitting on my ass?"[19] His technique was sometimes less than textbook, and Coach Smith fretted over his limited offensive repertoire. He had the propensity to finish moves in ways that defied the laws of physics, and the previous year he had been vulnerable to being ridden. But he had the tendency to win virtually all of his matches, especially the big ones, against the toughest opponents, when the stakes were the greatest. In short, he was a big-game wrestler who reveled in pressure. Coach Smith reflected on Hendricks' growth both on and off the mat, "What helped him more than anything is once he became a better student academically it helped him athletically. His freshman year he wasn't responsible. He learned some hard lessons."[20]

He felt the pressure of wrestling John Smith's nephew today, but it was not a new phenomenon, for the two had met weeks earlier in Omaha at a pre-season tournament. In that match, with Coach Smith standing 100 feet away and barely able to watch, Hendricks won 7-5 in overtime. "I don't want to lose to that guy. I know how important it is to our program for me to win that match. Last summer he said he was going to ride me out and beat me."[21] Hendricks, excellent at scouting past opponents for rematches, filed the victory away for the next time he faced his Iowa nemesis, and that time was now.

The expectant crowd came to its feet as third ranked Johny Hendricks shook Mark Perry's hand in the middle of the circle to begin the match at 165. The lanky Perry, wearing the black Hawkeye singlet trimmed in gold, was an accomplished mat wrestler, while Hendricks was better on his feet. Perry opponents were cautious of his unconventional "scrambling" style, while Hendricks' attack, which featured a warehouse of orthodox single leg and double leg takedowns, was more conventional. These styles took effect within seconds, as Hendricks struck deep on a single leg, only to be stymied by a Perry scramble. Hendricks took two more deep shots in the initial period but failed to convert. Perry took no serious shots and the period ended scoreless. So in the opening frame Perry avoided being taken down by Hendricks and entered the final two periods – the time when mat wrestlers can often claim an advantage—in a scoreless tie. But in staying away from Hendricks he initiated no serious offensive moves, and therefore risked a stalling call.

The second period began with Hendricks in the down position. He scored an escape within 30 seconds to take a 1-0 lead, and extended his lead to 2-0 five seconds later when Perry was called for stalling. Hendricks, who continued to move forward against the backpedaling Perry, was energized by the crowd's lusty boo when Perry took an injury timeout to rest while the Iowa bench tended to a purported right shoulder injury. During the timeout Hendricks walked back and forth along the edge of the mat while John and Pat Smith walked beside their 165-pounder, matching his stride and shouting instructions through Hendricks' headgear over the roar of the crowd.

As the official began the final period, Hendricks faced a strategic decision. He could let Perry up, make the score 2-1, and work toward a last period takedown to secure the victory, or try to ride Perry out, perhaps risking a reversal which would tie the score, but also adding to a riding time advantage. The bold Hendricks chose to attack Perry at his opponent's point of strength, and began a tough final period ride. The crowd erupted when Perry was again penalized for stalling, resulting in a one point penalty point for Hendricks and making the score 3-0. Seconds later Hendricks drove Perry off the mat, and as the wrestlers turned to return to the circle, Perry shoved Hendricks. This escalated the crowd into an even higher level of frenzy as both coaches approached the mat to calm their wrestlers down. But Hendricks, playing to the moment like an experienced Shakespearean actor, drew more noise from the crowd as he pumped his outstretched arms up and down with his palms facing up and stalked about the mat while Perry kneeled and waited in the center circle.

Hendricks was resolute in continuing to ride out his opponent – he wanted to beat Perry at his own game. But when action began again, in his desire to sustain his ride, Hendricks illegally locked his hands around Perry's waist, resulting in a one-point penalty and a 3-1 score with some 45 seconds left. With John and Pat Smith rising and sitting in their chairs like twin pistons firing in a road race, Hendricks continued his relentless pressure from the top position, exhorting the crowd as time ticked down, and claimed

Johny Hendricks exhorts the home crowd after his 3-1 decision over Iowa's Mark Perry. *Courtesy Jim Bowen*

a 4-1 victory. Perry walked off the mat without acknowledging the OSU bench. The Cowboy coaches embraced their 165 pounder and led him to the chairs where he was greeted by his teammates.

The Cowboys won three of the next four matches, highlighted by Pendleton's first period pin and Mocco's workmanlike 4-0 decision over his replacement in the Iowa lineup, Matt Fields. As Mocco wrestled, the Iowa bench looked on with the longing expression of a jilted lover watching a forlorn lover dance with a new suitor. The Cowboys prevailed 26-12. Mocco downplayed his 17th straight victory as a Cowboy, this one against his former coaches and teammates. "I saw a lot of my old teammates and the coach, and it wasn't that bad. We are all professionals."[22]

At the post-match press conference Mark Perry attributed his loss to Hendricks' superior effort and the passion of the moment, "I was emotionally drained. I don't wrestle that way. I took bad shots and didn't do much. I didn't deserve to win. He wrestled harder and he won."[23] But on an important level everyone gained standing, even Perry, who came to Stillwater for the first time as a foreigner in a familiar land to face the bloodlust of the Cowboy faithful, as well as the broken hearts of his ancestral line. Certainly Johny Hendricks was a winner, as was John Smith, who clarified any ambiguity anyone might have suspected in sending out one of his wrestlers to face family. "Don't get me wrong, he is still a nephew, but I am coaching the guy in orange. I have a 165 pounder named Johny Hendricks that is wrestling to win."[24]

In the locker room the next day Coach Smith's voice went up an octave as he addressed his squad and reflected on the match. "You have to remember, we're going to get everyone's best effort every time they face you. The teams we wrestle now will not be as tough in the NCAA tournament. I see it every year. They measure their progress on how they do against us. Iowa had been gearing up for this match for a month. Some of your toughest matches all year will be during this stretch of the season. That's a great situation for us, because it prepares us for the end of the year. But you must take responsibility as a person and prepare for that."[25]

Prepare they would; for in the next 34 days the Cowboys would defend their number one ranking in 12 dual matches located in seven different cities against the toughest competition in the college wrestling world. Heroes would be fashioned in unexpected corners, and defeat would visit in uncommon ways.

The final push was about to begin.

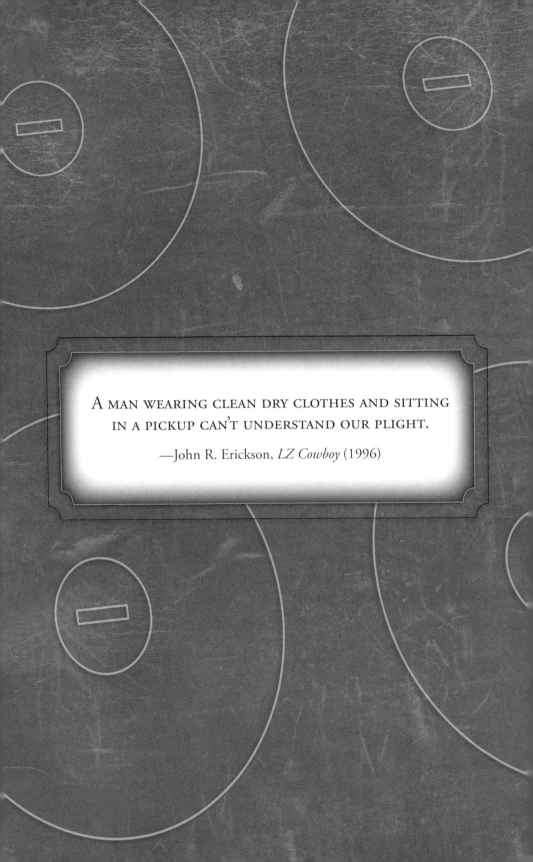

A MAN WEARING CLEAN DRY CLOTHES AND SITTING
IN A PICKUP CAN'T UNDERSTAND OUR PLIGHT.

—John R. Erickson, *LZ Cowboy* (1996)

ten

the national dual championships

01.22-23.05

IT IS A CLICHÉ WORN BARE to say "wrestling is an individual sport," but it is an unalterable reality. Wrestling is lonely. When those who call themselves wrestlers step out wearing the colors of their school and absorbing the scrutiny of their peers, there are no huddles like in football where giants hold hands like elephants walking single-file hooked up by trunk and tail. When a wrestler makes a mistake he does not step to the free-throw lane and receive a forgiving hand from a supporting teammate. He cannot toss a ball around the horn between innings, nor can he secretly blame a doubles partner when spirits sink and shots soar long.

Wrestlers stand alone, with no opportunities to hide their inadequacy and failings behind a pungent mist or film of excuse. There is no amnesty, only judgment. Vindication comes through the cruel and perfect calculus of performance, absent any innuendo. Even though culture gives homage to the strong and silent, the heart and soul needs company. After a match, when wrestlers take that solitary walk off the mat—discrete and isolated— they walk to a bench defined by social networks where their joys and disappointments gain clarity and meaning in the context of a community.

Wrestling is a brotherhood of one contained in a cauldron of a few like-minded and lonely hearts. But a part of Coach Smith's job is to balance the individual with the team. To join the lonely soul with a heaven of maligned angels; not to blend the parts into one mixture, but to create a sturdy wall of separate bricks held up by one another.

The National Dual Championships, a three-day tournament sponsored by the National Wrestling Coaches Association, had provided Smith that opportunity in the past. "The more I can keep 'I' out of the program, the better we will be. But that takes time. It takes spending time with the established starters. It requires spending time with guys who will never make the team, but who want to get better for no other reason than to have better practices. That was one of my shortcomings as a coach early in my career…integrating the entire group into a team. The National Duals helps me do that team-building."[1] Unlike conventional tournaments where wrestlers advance through their brackets based on their individual performances, teams instead of individuals advance forward. If a wrestler loses his individual match, but his team wins, he lives to fight again.

In 2004, 14 of the 16 invited teams were ranked in the top 20 in the nation, although second-ranked Iowa State, fourth-ranked Nebraska, and ninth-ranked Iowa were conspicuously absent. Iowa State and Nebraska, who would meet the Cowboys head-on in duals on their home mats within the next few days, wished to unveil their best efforts against the Cowboys in their home arenas, and Iowa could ill afford another loss at the hands of the Cowboys in the space of one week.

During Smith's tenure, the Cowboys had a measure of success in the event, capturing the title five of eight times. As Coach Smith told his team in the wrestling room before a weight-lifting session on a sun-drenched Monday after the Iowa match, the National Duals was an event he valued. "We have had success in this event because we take it seriously. Some teams don't take it seriously and it ends up biting them down the road. The format will give us great individual match-ups, and that's invaluable in helping us come together as a team. Picking up major decisions and pins is important. Not getting majored is important, but I don't expect any of you to find yourselves in that situation."[2]

As he spoke, Johny Hendricks wrapped tape around the wrists of his sweatshirt to keep in body heat during the impending workout. "If your parents or girlfriends need tickets, have them call the wrestling office and the support staff will help them. You won't have time to do any entertaining. You will have wrestling matches to prepare for."[3]

Members of the varsity gazed ahead without expression, but several younger wrestlers looked up at Smith, their smooth, lineless, scabbed and bruised faces reflected anticipation and anxiety. "We can only take 15 wrestlers. We have to make strategic decisions on who will go so don't take it personal if you have to stay in Stillwater. We have to position ourselves for one guy to cover two weights in case of injuries."[4]

On the flight to Cleveland the following morning, the *Sports Illustrated* article that featured the OSU-Iowa match was passed among the wrestlers and staff. The story included a two-page close-up color photo of Nathan Morgan's California-blond head as the protective mask slid down his face while battling from the bottom position in the Iowa match the previous Sunday. Smith, who denied *Sports Illustrated* access to the team the previous year for fear of distraction, smiled as he read the story. "Nathan might still be on bottom if the official had not called a stalemate."[5]

The Cowboys arrived in Cleveland at 12:58 p.m. under clear, frigid skies, traveled to their hotel in one of three white vans rented for the weekend, and rested until their departure downtown to the Cleveland State University Convocation Center. At 4:30 p.m. the team boarded the vans for the 10-minute drive to the Cleveland State University Convocation Center. As Coaches Branch and Guerrero counted heads to make sure all 15 wrestlers and seven support staff were on board, soft snow began to gently touch down. By the time the vans arrived at the arena the snow had intensified as the temperature began dropping drastically. The team unloaded its gear and trudged in a jagged line through the snow and down into the lower bowels of the 12,000-seat arena. Division II teams were competing in the main arena, so the Division I squads were directed through a maze of hallways and a network of interconnected stairwells, down to an auxiliary gym the size of three basketball courts. The energy and noise and movement in the crowded, dank, brightly-lit auxiliary gym brought the travel-weary Cowboys into the moment. They claimed an area against the wall opposite the Oklahoma University team, whose coach Jack Spates was weaving briskly through the groups of wrestlers shaking hands and waving to fellow coaches. The Cowboy coaches sat quietly in folding chairs against the wall. Steve Mocco sat among them.

Back at the team hotel Steve Mocco's father Joe was in the process of loading a small microwave oven along with ice chests, boxes of foodstuffs,

Steve Mocco's assimilation into the team was a critical factor in the Cowboy's success. Here, he and Jake Rosholt take a moment to strategize before their matches. *Courtesy Jim Bowen.*

plastic bags full of utensils, pies, cakes, and platters of homemade chicken parmesan into his hotel room. To assure Steve was properly nourished on long road trips, members of the Mocco family routinely traveled the country in a white van equipped for sleeping and cooking sumptuous meals. Starving team members often slipped clandestinely into Mr. Mocco's room, outside the watchful eye of Coach Smith, searching for a glorious bowl of pasta and a slice of cake.

After a workout in the small gym, the team returned to the hotel and received instructions for the next morning. Weigh-in would begin at 9:00 a.m., two hours before the beginning of the first round of matches. The Cowboy wrestlers went to bed and hoped a heavy sleep would override their hunger pains—all but Mocco's roommate, Clay Kehrer, who walked into his room and faced plates of lasagna and slices of cake passed around the small, crowded, and aromatic room. He was pulling weight, so he rushed away to sleep in his dad's room one floor above, away from the smells and foodstuffs.

At the weigh-in the next morning, held under the seats and bleachers of the vast concrete bowels of the arena, 15 narrow columns had been cordoned off by waist-high scaffolding that lined the teams up in single-file colonades. At the end of each line a business-like rules officials stood. Electronic scales rested at his feet. Thirty minutes before weigh-in the Cowboy wrestlers stripped down and checked their weight. Some had ounces to spare, so they poured water in a paper cup and drank the equivalency of their wiggle room. They then stepped back on the scales to ensure they had not crossed into that terrifying militarized zone of being over their assigned weight. Every three or four minutes a wrestler asked an assistant coach for the time, for at straight-up nine they would weigh and be free to feel cool water or Gatorade in their parched mouths and bagels in their empty stomach for the first time in several hours.

The rules officials who stood guard by the scales seemed to enjoy marking time with sharp barks. "Thirty minutes to weigh in." "Twenty minutes to weigh in." "Ten minutes to weigh in." As time counted down other teams discretely glanced at the top ranked Cowboys as they stood, joked, paced, and gazed at the boxes of candy bars sponsors cruelly placed by the scales, unaware of the presence they created and the attention they attracted.[6]

Finally the appointed moment came about, and the Cowboys stepped to the scales, starting with Coleman Scott at 125, while the official read the red digital readout. "Scott two-tenths under. Morgan two-tenths under. Delk four-tenths under. Frishkorn even. Esposito two-tenths under. Ward even. Jackson two and two-tenths under. Pendleton two-tenths under. Hendricks two-tenths under. Rosholt two-tenths under. Jensen two-tenths under. Kehrer two-tenths under. Mocco even."[7]

Hendricks stepped off the scales with an expression of disgust and hurt. "I thought I was even. I could have eaten two more ounces." He then unwrapped one of the free candy bars. "This is the ultimate exercise in test marketing. If wrestlers won't eat them, no one will."[8]

The team then traveled back to the hotel for breakfast. The morning snow was now blowing in sheets and steam bellowed up from manholes, but the wrestlers were in the warm vans, and looked forward to a hot breakfast of eggs and pancakes washed down by glasses and glasses of cool water.

The Cowboys' first round opponent was The Citadel. The state-supported military college located in Charleston, South Carolina and made infamous by Pat Conroy's novel *The Lords of Discipline*, was known for its high academic standards and strict military discipline. Citadel's Bulldogs had captured its conference tournament the previous year, sending five qualifiers to the NCAA tournament. Coach Rob Hjerling had been named coach of the year in the fledging Southern Conference. Citadel assistant Jeff Ragan, a former OSU All-American, Big 12 champion, and Academic All-American, offered greetings to his former coach, John Smith, before the match began. The Citadel lineup featured hard-nosed, disciplined, technically-sound athletes who reflected the school's commitment to "duty and honor." Their wrestlers were students and soldiers first. While most of their team enjoyed solid high school careers, OSU would have recruited none of them to its program.

In the first five matches the Cowboys racked up a fall, two major decisions, and a technical fall in storming out to a 20-3 lead, with Coleman Scott firing the first shot with his inaugural pin as a Cowboy varsity wrestler.

In the sixth match Johny Hendricks held a comfortable 7-3 lead over Dan Thompson, and was in deep on a single-leg attempt, but his head was outside Thompson's hip, instead of in the conventional inside position-tucked against Thompson's stomach. The Citadel junior, a two-time Michigan state champion who qualified for the NCAA tournament the year before, instantly felt his advantage. With Hendricks' arms locked around Thompson's leg, Hendricks had no means to brace himself as Thompson fell back and drove Hendricks to the mat head first, like a post-hole digger bouncing against hard red clay. The stunned and dazed Hendricks groaned and motioned for a time-out with his hands, then grabbed the back of his neck and fell back to the mat. Doc Allen and trainer Chris Pickering rushed to Hendricks and administered a series of neurological field tests to establish whether spinal cord damage had occurred, while the shaken coaches looked on. After several minutes Hendricks came to his feet, flashed his patented smile, waved the coaches away, and completed the final 30 seconds of the match, securing his 17th victory on the season.

Pendleton, Kehrer, Rosholt, and Mocco won by a technical fall, injury default, and two falls respectively as OSU finished off the Bulldogs 45-3, but Hendricks did not witness those matches. He was taken to a nearby hospital by Doc Allen and the Cowboy staff, where they waited in the triage area for four hours before doctors concluded Hendricks had sustained a severely sprained neck. Hendricks returned to the arena to watch the Cowboys take on Cornell in the afternoon match, but a barking pain severely limited his range of motion. It appeared his wrestling was finished for the weekend. Meanwhile, the team had two hours to burn before meeting Cornell. Choosing not to return to the hotel in the heavy snowstorm, the squad returned to the small gym and rested.

In the afternoon the Cowboys faced tenth-ranked Cornell, who had advanced to the second round by defeating host Cleveland State. Located in west-central New York, Cornell is the only land-grant Ivy League university, and was the nation's first college to award a university degree in veterinary medicine, as well as doctorates in electrical engineering and industrial engineering. Oklahoma State, also a land-grant institution with highly reputed schools of veterinary medicine and engineering, might argue with Cornell over academic supremacy in those programs, but today any ties would be broken on the mat. Cornell, the Ivy League wrestling champions five of the past 10 years, enjoyed a solid reputation in the college wrestling world. The program had to its credit four national champions and 18 All-Americans. Current Oklahoma coach Jake Spates had guided Cornell to five consecutive Ivy League titles beginning in the late '80s. Proud of the accomplishments of its alumni, the Big Red's media guide featured a "Where Are They Now?" section, which listed an array of former wrestlers since the 1950s who had gone on to careers in business, law, medicine, politics, and education.

The match began on time at three in the afternoon. Chairs for the wrestlers and coaches for both squads were stuffed shoulder-to-shoulder on the same side of the large red mat. Cornell seemed to thrive in the intimate atmosphere as they took two of the first three matches against the Cowboy's freshman-laden lineup when both Scott and Morgan fell in tight contests. After their matches, Coach Guerrero pulled the downcast freshmen behind the Cowboy bench and offered up a combination platter of scolding and encouragement. Earlier Smith commented on the delicate job of bringing young wrestlers along. "I back off from some young guys because I know they are too fragile emotionally at that particular moment to withstand the learning process. If I stay on them too much, it could be harmful. In that case I might have a private talk with them to place their efforts in perspective."[9]

The OSU coaches knew that four matches in two days against nationally-ranked competition would be a baptism by fire for the young wrestlers.

Morgan had been 19-0 coming into the Cornell match, and even though many of his victories came in open tournaments against other younger competition, and even though his first loss was administered by a number-one ranked wrestler from Cornell, to lose for the first time could threaten the fragile confidence of any freshman. Coleman Scott had lost four tough matches to date, and needed a victory in a close contest against an older wrestler to buttress his confidence.

After these defeats, number one-ranked Zack Esposito took the mat to face number two-ranked and two-time All-American Dustin Manotti in a much-anticipated match-up between the top two wrestlers in the weight

* * *

Esposito entered the National Duals 17-0 and ranked number one in the country, but Coach Smith, who stayed close to his 149-pounder during the stressful and tenuous times of the season, understood high rankings do not translate into national championships. "When a wrestler is recognized as the best in the weight class, he has a tendency to punish himself through anxiety and pressure, feelings the athlete did not experience as he was striving to reach the top, and as a result he will lose that emotional edge one has to have in order to be at your best."[10] Sometimes Smith grimaced when he read polls and predictions that prematurely lionize a wrestler. "In the end, the only way to feel comfortable on the pedestal is to earn it by winning a championship." But he placed great confidence in Esposito. "The skills and the groundwork are there."[11]

In a rematch of last year's national semi-final which Esposito won 5-2, the pace was measured and the wrestlers were cautious, a strategy which played into Manotti's hand against the usually frenetic Cowboy.

After a scoreless first period, Esposito began the second period with a quick escape, but moments later relinquished a rare takedown. Another quick escape and a penalty point gave him a 3-2 lead going into the final frame. Manotti took the down position and quickly escaped, knotting the score at 3-3. Both wrestlers, sensing that the next wrestler who scored a takedown would likely win the match, abandoned their cautious style of the first period and began a blitzkrieg of mutual thrusts and sorties, each trying desperately to preempt victory with a winning shot. The Cowboy coaches leaned forward in their chairs, hands cupped around their mouths, barking instruction. At the 47- second mark Esposito saw an opportunity when Manotti stepped slightly into Esposito, raising his chest and exposing his trunk. Hoping to land a silver bullet which would extend his undefeated season, with his mouth grimaced and sweat absorbed into his orange singlet, Zack attempted a high-risk/high-reward inside trip move against Manotti. This maneuver required the offensive wrestler to step unguarded and vulnerable into his opponent, expose his own legs, and execute a vicious upper body throw. It was a spectacular gambit that Esposito occasionally used during his freshman and sophomore years, but a high-risk maneuver he had shelved for more conventional and conservative techniques.

He made the rapid step into Manotti's kill-zone, but the Cornell wrestler was ready. He drove into the exposed and off-balance Esposito, drove into him, and ended on top after a frenzied scramble. Esposito escaped seconds later, but as time wound down he could not force the winning takedown, and lost his first match of the season by a 6-4 count.

The Cowboys won four of the next six matches, highlighted by back-up Sam Lewnes' solid 6-0 victory over Drake Hovis at 165. Son of a steak house owner, Lewnes was a redshirt freshman from Baltimore where he captured two state titles. Against Cornell he was called on to wrestle up from his regular competitive weight of 157 for the injured Johny Hendricks. His first period low single-leg takedown and final period near fall over a taller Cornell opponent tied the dual match score at 9-9. The Cowboys never looked back, posting a 22-12 over the twelfth-ranked Big Red of Cornell, and moved onto the semi-finals where they were scheduled to meet east coast wrestling power Lehigh.

The Cornell match ended at 5:10 p.m., and the Cowboys had more than three hours before their next competition. They trudged across the parking lot through the blowing snow, found their vans, cleared off the snow from the frozen windshields, and returned to the hotel, where they slept and rested before meeting back at the lobby at 7:30 the following morning. Steve Mocco walked into the hotel elevator wearing a pair of knee-length black nylon shorts with the letters "Defense" applied across his bottom. Normally worn by OSU basketball coach Eddie Sutton's players during their practices, the message plastered across the backside of the high-scoring Mocco seemed incongruous. But Mocco's defensive moves had accounted for many of his first period points while at Iowa, and one of his goals in coming to Oklahoma State was to develop an offensive repertoire to complement his prodigious defensive skills. Time would tell. In the meantime, the Cowboys rested and turned their attention to Lehigh.

OSU would travel to Lehigh for a dual meet 22 days later. The 12-1 Mountain Hawks were ranked number five in the nation. They had won seven consecutive dual matches, five of which against nationally-ranked foes, and would provide a major test for the weary Cowboys.

Ninety seconds before the match was to begin an intense John Smith, with his voice rasping and index finger jabbing the air, gathered his team in a tight circle on the corner of the mat. "Take the fight to them. We've been in these big matches, and we know how to win them."[12] As Smith squirmed out of the tight circle, the team closed in around Pendleton for their pre-match rituals. Members of the Lehigh team glanced over as they found their chairs next to OSU. Coleman Scott peeled off his black warm-up, adjusted his headgear, and shook out his arms as Coach Guerrero whispered instructions to the wide-eyed freshman.

Scott led off against Lehigh senior and fellow Pennsylvanian Andrew Rizzi. This was a crucial opportunity for Scott to establish his presence in the lead-off spot in the Cowboy lineup. He had lost close last-period decisions in the recent Michigan State and Iowa duals, and was outwrestled earlier in the afternoon by Mormile of Cornell. But this match seemed to have a foreboding start. At the one-minute mark Scott bore in deep on a double-leg attempt, but Rizzi hooked an ankle, initiated a scramble, and turned into Scott to claim the 2-0 lead. Rizzi followed with a tough inside cradle and attempted to finish Scott off. But the lanky freshman maintained his base, pried Rizzi's hands apart at the 2:10 mark, and when the Cornell senior pulled Scott back into his lap in an attempt to hook up a crab ride, Scott reversed Rezzi and held him to his back to take a 5-2 lead. From then on Scott was in control. Hitting two more takedowns which led to near fall points, he applied a throttling ride during the second and third periods to claim a 12-2 major decision. For only the second time in eight matches, OSU began a dual with a victory, a reality that encouraged Smith. "It's tough on the middle and upper weights when they feel like they have to dig us out of a hole. With Coleman and Nathan in the lineup, other wrestlers can gain leverage from their performances."[13]

Morgan came out hoping to build on Scott's stellar performance, and with a first-period takedown jumped out to a 2-0 lead over redshirt sophomore Matt Ciasulli. Only one of two three-time Pennsylvania state high school champions ever to wrestle at Lehigh, the bushy-haired business major, an NCAA qualifier the previous season, enjoyed a reputation as a hard-nosed tough rider. Ciasulli escaped to narrow the margin to 2-1, knotted the score at 2 with a second period escape, and began the third period in the top position, where he applied his own crushing, period-long ride on Morgan,

Backup Sam Lewnes controls Missouri's Tyron Woodley. Lewnes' 6-0 victory over Cornell's Drake Hovis at the National Duals was instrumental in the Cowboy's undefeated season. *Courtesy Dr. Jeremy Cook.*

Zach Esposito struggles for position against Lehigh's David Nakosone in a 14-10 victory at the National Duals Championships in Cleveland. *Courtesy Jeffrey G. Nolan.*

who fought gamely to break free, but was stretched and crushed by Ciasulli's boa-like leg ride, losing 3-2 on riding time.

After his match Morgan sat on a folding chair away from the team, heaving and sweating, with blood oozing from his reddened nose, too exhausted to put on his warm-ups. Smith walked from his chair by the mat back to Morgan. His words were harsh and direct. "You quit wrestling."[14] As tears formed in Morgan's eyes and Smith walked away, Coach Branch knelt eye-level with the previously undefeated whiz-kid who had now lost two matches within a matter of hours. "These losses can make you stronger if you approach them correctly."[15] Morgan's nose continued to bleed as Branch walked away.

Coach Smith sat with Doc Allen that evening at dinner over virtually raw steak and salad and discussed Morgan's plight. "The word will get out all across the country this week about Nathan. How he lost his lead twice. His opponents will start hammering him from the word go. He is a gentle soul with the heart of a lamb. Does he possess the mental toughness to reach his aspirations? Until now he could win with his velvet smooth technique. But that's not enough. Something's missing. He has memorized 950 Bible verses. He's a very smart young man, a civil engineering major. His teammates love him. He has a wonderful family. He has great technique. While not widely recruited, I knew what I had when I signed him. I was concerned when he forfeited a match in the Junior Nationals. That sends a troubling message to me. He seems to be distracted by blood. You wrestle with a bloody nose. He looks over to me for reassurance throughout his matches. I love the kid, but he has to get tougher." As Smith waved away the dessert menu, his eyes softened, "In fairness, not many true freshmen have ever started for me, and he accomplished that. He is a strong young man. He can make the changes."[16]

OSU lost two of the next three matches but still led 7-6 on the strength of Coleman Scott's four-point major decision at 125, setting up the anticipated match-up of Hendricks and Troy Letters, the odds-on favorite to capture the 165 title. Letters had suffered his only defeat the previous year to the Cowboy's Tyrone Lewis in Lehigh's stunning dual meet victory over the Cowboys in Stillwater. Letters was scheduled to face Hendricks three weeks later when OSU would travel to Lehigh for a dual match, but fans anticipated that the collision course might intersect today. The match went to overtime, and Hendricks lost a 4-3 tie-breaker, straining his hamstring as he fought off Letters on the edge of the mat in the final and deciding period.

With the Cowboys now trailing Lehigh 13-7, Pendleton stung Travis Frick 9-1, and Cowboy 184-pounder Jack Jensen, in a battle with Clay Kehrer to earn a spot in the starting lineup, defeated Matt Cassidy 6-3. The Cowboys were up 14-13 when number-one ranked Jake Rosholt faced number-two ranked Jon Trenge in the evening's second feature match. For some 10 minutes before the match Rosholt paced back and forth along the mat's edge as he waited for the officials to announce his

RIGHT: Defending national champion Troy Letters cranks on Johny Hendricks at center-mat during the National Duals. *Courtesy Jeffrey G. Nolan.*

Johny Hendricks, who sustained a hamstring during a 4-3 tiebreaker loss to top-ranked Troy Letters of Lehigh, fights off a takedown attempt with a hip lock at the National Duals. *Courtesy Jeffrey G. Nolan.*

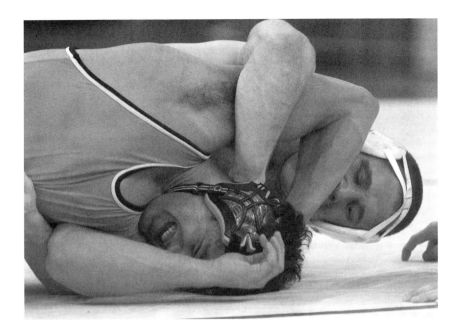

match. Moments before, while warming up, he spat on the cold and gray cement floor next to the mat, and carefully smoothed the spittle out with the bottom of his green wrestling shoes as he waited for the official to announce his match.

Trenge, the brown-haired, granite-jawed Pennsylvanian was the nation's No. 1 recruit in 1999, and battled to runner-up finishes in the 2002 and 2003 NCAA championships. He took an Olympic deferral year off the previous year to train for the United States Olympic Team, where he finished fifth.

Jake Rosholt had never wrestled Trenge. In his relentless, stalking style Rosholt nailed four takedowns over the cautious Lehigh senior. But Rosholt gave up two third-period takedowns to lose 10-8, giving Lehigh a 16-14 lead. Rosholt walked off the mat with a slight, knowing smile, but before he could leave the staging area and pull on his warm-up, Mocco pinned Tom Curl to give the Cowboys a come-from-behind 20-16 victory.

Smith's prescience to pull his young wrestlers out of redshirt was just one more intuitive move that coalesced with the rhythm and flow of the long season. His decision shored up the front end of the Cowboy lineup and gave OSU protection against unforeseen losses by Rosholt and Hendricks,

two stalwarts who had won 33 of 34 matches coming into the National Duals.

Back at the hotel, trainer Chris Pickering examined Johny Hendrick's mauled hamstring and emphatically told Coach Smith, "Hendricks is a wreck."

The unimpressed Smith ordered Hendricks on the scales. "I can name two guys who have won Olympic gold medals with torn hamstrings." He leveled a stare at a grinning Hendricks, who was two and one-half pounds over. "Go to bed."[17]

LEFT: Jake Rosholt braces against Jon Trenge's takedown effort. *Courtesy Jeffrey G. Nolan.*

BELOW: Jon Trenge strains to control Jake Rosholt. *Courtesy Jeffrey G. Nolan.*

The next morning shortly after sunlight, Pickering sat in the lobby detailing on a legal pad treatment plans for the long list of hobbled Cowboys who would face Illinois in the finals later in the afternoon. Morgan and Scott were the first wrestlers in the lobby, some 30 minutes before the appointed departure of 8:00 a.m. Almost a foot of snow had fallen on Cleveland through Saturday night, but on Sunday morning a blinding sun reflected through the bitter, wind-driven cold air as the team's caravan of white vans plowed through slush and into the arena for the 9:30 a.m. weigh-in.

In the first of their two meetings during the season, second-ranked Jon Trenge of Lehigh survived Jake Rosholt's four takedowns in route to a 10-8 victory at the National Duals. *Courtesy Jeffrey G. Nolan.*

Jon Trenge, whose cautious style and final period takedowns trumped Rosholt's aggression, clamps down a bear-hug. *Courtesy Jeffrey G. Nolan.*

The OSU and Illinois wrestlers stood in parallel lines divided by the hip-high metal scaffolding. An official barked "Okie State column, four to five minutes." Over the previous 15 minutes several Cowboy wrestlers had stepped on the scales, read the red digital numbers on the monitor wired to the scaling device, and ambled off. If they were under their required weight they sipped on a cup of water and stepped back on to weigh once again. They had made weight hundreds of times throughout their wrestling lives, and perceived the consequences of a swallow of water like a concert pianist discerned the impact of a slightly loosened piano string. Johny Hendricks stepped in front of Kevin Ward, who held his Gatorade in a brown paper sack, and read the digital readout in disgust, as if the scales had cheated him at cards.

"I'm one [pound] under. I could have eaten more last night." Coach Smith peered down at the scales, "Trust me. You would rather it say one under than one over."[18]

Mocco gently patted Hendricks on the shoulder, and the official called for the second weigh-in in two days to begin. The wrestlers peeled off their shorts, stretched out their arms for a rash check, stepped on the scales, and then rushed off to eat their stash of food.

On the way out of the arena a few members of the squad stopped to gawk at an exhibition match taking place in the main arena between two female high school wrestling teams. Some watched with dropped jaws. Others were expressionless while some looked on with pride and admiration as the female wrestlers battled. After a few moments they drifted to the vans for the short ride back to the hotel where they refreshed the inner abyss with eggs, bacon, and pancakes washed down with pitchers of iced-water.

Coach Smith sat against the wall in the main dining room and attempted to finish his light breakfast while well-wishers dropped by to pay respects. One fellow wrestling coach, a relative stranger who stopped by to speak, suddenly began to demonstrate on Smith an upper-body wrestling maneuver one of his wrestlers had tried with limited success the previous evening. The unfailingly polite Cowboy coach was finally released from the coach's grasp and was allowed to finish his breakfast with his father Lee Roy, the patriarch of the wrestling Smith clan. He often dined with one of his sons while on the road. "Mom called this morning and asked if you had attended morning mass," Lee Roy said. The two-time Olympic champion, known as the best wrestler in the world, suddenly appeared stricken, and nodded gratefully. "She also mentioned the dual last night was too close and you need to work harder."[19]

After breakfast, Coach Smith took the elevator to the seventh floor and came upon Scott, Ward, and Kehrer as they sat in the hallway, backs against the wall, clad only in shorts. Smith checked his watch and mumbled, "Get some clothes on. You're going to catch a cold."[20]

Freshman Scott, who the previous year rode herd over the Pennsylvania high school wrestling world, had shed tears the previous day as he spoke with Coach Smith after his 4-3 tiebreaker loss against Cornell. Coach Smith, who knew he walked the razor's edge by sliding his young freshman into the meat grinder of national competition, calmly told his 125-pounder, "Stop the crying."[21]

The team assembled in the lobby and departed for the arena at 1:40 p.m. Minutes later they filed into the small gymnasium and walked by the Illinois squad, adorned in blue warm-ups with orange trim. The Fighting Illini relaxed across the middle mat and over a maze of folding chairs. No wrestlers or coaches exchanged a comment as the Cowboys made their way toward the far wall and sat under the baseline of a basketball goal. Doc Allen put down a medical journal he was pouring over and tied Eric Guerrero's neon-orange necktie in a tight Windsor Knot.

Illinois, coached by former Iowa assistant Mark Johnson, had been clawing its way into the top tier of college wrestling during Johnson's twelve-year tenure. They were a perennial Top-10 NCAA team and under Johnson had compiled more NCAA Champions, NCAA qualifiers, and All-Americans than at any other time in the school's history. A 127-33-1 record over the past 12 years had supplanted long-time Big Ten rival Iowa as the conference's top team. Before the match, with his wrestlers gathered around in a tight circle, the square-jawed Johnson, dressed in a blue turtleneck, implored his team to "have fun." In contrast, Smith was never heard to tell his wrestlers to "get out there and enjoy yourselves." He urged them to win their matches. Presumably, winning was fun.[22]

Smith predicted the undefeated Cowboys would be underdogs at 125, 133, 157, and 184, and perhaps 165 if Hendricks could not wrestle due to injury. These predictions held true. The Cowboys lost four of the first five matches and trailed 12-4, with Cowboy backup Sam Lewnes scheduled to meet Illinois sophomore Donny Reynolds at 165. An Illinois decision could increase their lead to 15-4 with four matches remaining. Pendleton, Rosholt, and Mocco would be favored to win their matches, but Kehrer would be an underdog to All-American Brian Glynn.

Lewnes stood on the edge of the mat next to his teammate and workout partner Hendricks, who went through the motions of a warm up to create uncertainty among the Illinois team as to who would take the mat for the Cowboys. As time ran down in Kevin Ward's 2-1 loss at 157, Lewnes began to peel off his black t-shirt to take the mat. Smith, standing directly behind Hendricks' ear, remarked to Coach Mark Branch, within earshot, "Look at Hendricks. He's not even taking his shirt off." Smith knew holding a wrestler out because of an injury sometimes pricked that wrestler's conscience "when he sees his teammates sucking it up and they are on the sidelines." Hendricks' ear, always tuned to the frequency of his head coach, immediately peeled off his shirt, stepped in front of his teammate Lewnes, and limped to the center of the mat to wrestle. He grimaced as he bent over to wrap the green identifying band around his ankle.[23]

Seizing the opportunity and smelling blood, Reynolds took the hobbled Hendricks down midway into the first period, rode him with a tough leg ride, twisted Hendricks' injured neck, and applied pressure to his injured hamstring, not illegally, but in a manner that reflected Hendricks' injury-riddled vulnerabilities.

The first wrestler to gain a takedown in a college match will prevail in the match some 80 percent of the time, and to ride out an opponent for the full first period, before he can narrow the gap with an escape, widens the odds against the trailing wrestler even more. Hendricks faced this dilemma at the end of period one, but matters would get worse. He fell behind 3-0 after an early second period escape by Reynolds and forged no serious takedown attempts in the crucial middle period where comebacks are often ignited.

So Hendricks, in the bottom position, trailed 3-0 as the official whistled up the final period. The wounded Cowboy escaped within five seconds, and began to stalk the backtracking Reynolds, who knew he could pull off the stunning upset for the Illinois team if he could frustrate a last-period takedown.

But as often happens, the ebb and flow of the match changed the moment Reynolds began his retreat, for within seconds he was called for two stalling infractions, the second which narrowed the score to 3-2. Knowing another penalty point would tie the score, he went to his knees while attempting an ill-conceived high-inside crotch takedown on the edge of the mat, which allowed Hendricks to score from his knees and not his feet, where the hamstring pain had limited the velocity of his movement. Hendricks bulldozed into Reynolds and gained the takedown to go up 4-3 with seventeen seconds left. He held on, the buzzer sounded and Hendricks limped off victorious. With his hamstring pulled, knee wrenched, neck sprained, and nose bloodied, he smiled at Coach Smith, who said Hendricks' comeback effort "was one of the gutsiest performances I have ever seen on a wrestling mat."[24]

Now the Cowboys trailed Illinois 12-7 as Chris Pendleton took the mat against All-American and fifth-ranked Pete Friedl, whose 55-18 career record included nine wins over ranked opponents. Pendleton gave chase from the opening whistle. Controlling Friedl's head and chain-wrestling through three takedown attempts, just one minute into the match the number-one ranked Cowboy captain bear-hugged his opponent's chest and while standing, wrapped his inside leg around Friedl's front leg and forced his opponent down. Both wrestlers crashed to the mat together, but Pendleton maintained his advantage and ended on top. While Coach Branch admonished Pendleton to "be smart and take your time," the Cowboy captain snaked his arms around the wriggling Friedl and forced the pin at the 1:07 mark, giving the Cowboys their first lead of the night 13-12. Rosholt and Mocco won their bouts and the Cowboys were crowned the National Duals Champions for the third consecutive year.

As fans filed out and wrestlers and coaches milled around the arena floor, the squad gathered for a team photo in the center of the area. Half of the team kneeled on one knee while the heavier weights stood behind their small counterparts and held the championship trophy. The photographer peered into the lens of his camera, raised his head and issued a muffled shout. "Pull a little closer together. A little closer."[25]

Perhaps that is what happened to the Cowboy team on a snowy weekend in Cleveland.

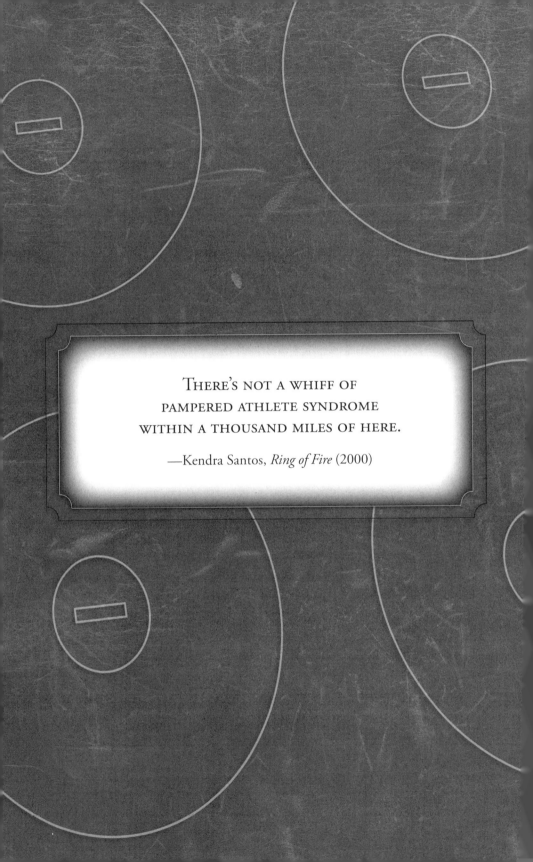

THERE'S NOT A WHIFF OF
PAMPERED ATHLETE SYNDROME
WITHIN A THOUSAND MILES OF HERE.

—Kendra Santos, *Ring of Fire* (2000)

eleven

iowa state & northern iowa

01.27-28.05

THE BREAKNECK PACE CONTINUED.

The Cowboys returned from Cleveland on Monday afternoon and took off Tuesday. Morgan's broken and fragile nose continued to leak blood, while Rosholt nursed a sore knee. Hendricks' strained hamstring and sprained neck were slow to heal. He would not make the critical trip into Iowa later in the week.

Coach Branch placed the upcoming few days in perspective. "It's a tough situation for our guys. We are coming off the emotional high of winning a tough [National Duals] tournament and come home for a couple of days before hitting the road for another couple of duals. Iowa State and Northern Iowa are tough, especially facing them on back-to-back days."[1]

Wednesday morning the Cowboys boarded a chartered bus in Stillwater, crept through Kansas and Missouri, and arrived in Ames, Iowa late Wednesday evening in time for the wrestlers to check their weight and go to bed. On the bus trip down, the small bathroom located in the rear of the bus was not visited a single time by the parched and dehydrated wrestlers.

The next morning, following a quick trip into downtown Ames to purchase some essential clothing items which were left behind in Stillwater the day before, Coach Smith returned to the hotel and lunched with friends Chris Hoffman, a former Stillwater police officer who handled security on road trips, and George Shenold, Coach Smith's neighbor and partner in raising goats and sheep on their adjoining land outside Stillwater. George met John Smith one evening, after observing his new neighbor, raised in the city, clumsily nailing a tin roof on his barn. "It won't stay," said the smiling and knowing Shenold. "That thing will blow off tonight."

Smith, hammer in hand, looked down from the ladder. "No it won't."

Smith had fallen from a tree while checking out a deer stand for his dad, a reality not lost on George, whose outdoor skills were perhaps as highly developed as his new neighbor's penchant for spending time indoors in padded and matted rooms. Smith said, "I will never climb up a tree without a harness again…we have to be reminded we are human"[2]

Indeed, the roof blew off that very evening, and they have been fast friends ever since. "John comes over, he takes his shoes off, and lays on the couch. We don't talk wrestling unless he brings it up. I tell him that I'll take care of the farming and he'll take care of the wrestling." Their only line of contention seems to be in the area of attire. "John occasionally asks me to travel with the team. I told him I would be happy to join him and the boys, but I have to wear my overalls." Apparently, the two struck a compromise for the Cowboy's year-end wrestling banquet. "I wear a suit then."[3] At lunch that day in Ames the friends talked comfortably of pecan farming and police procedures. Wrestling the Cyclones was barely mentioned.

Iowa State's wrestling team was off to its best start since the banner year of 1970-1971, when legendary coach Dr. Harold Nichols led the Cyclones to a second place finish at the NCAA tournament behind Oklahoma State. The Cowboys lost only two duals that entire year, both to Iowa State. This season the respective programs were motoring at their highest levels since that campaign 34 years earlier. This year OSU and Iowa State returned a combined eight All-Americans from last season, nine if Mocco was included. Amateur Wrestling News ranked 16 wrestlers on the two teams in their Top 20.

Former OSU standout Bobby Douglas was named in 1992 as just the fifth wrestling coach in Iowa State wrestling history after 18 seasons at Arizona State University, where his team captured a national title in 1988. Born into poverty in Ohio, he was crowned the first black Ohio high school state champion, captured an NAIA wrestling title, and was an NCAA runner-up at Oklahoma State. The cerebral Douglas, author of several books

Iowa State coach Bobby Douglas wrestled for the Cowboys during the 1964-65 season. He represented the U.S. on two Olympic teams, and captained the 1968 squad. A cerebral coach known for his advocacy of the sport, he was the first African-American athlete to wrestle for the U.S. in the Olympic Games, the first to captain the Olympic team, and the first to coach wrestling at a major university. *Courtesy Mika Matzen*

on wrestling technique, was considered one of the most accomplished and respected coaches in the wrestling community.

After a morning and early afternoon of rest and studying at the hotel, the Cowboys boarded their bus for the 10-minute ride from the hotel to the ISU student athletic facility for weight check and drill. The team filed off the bus and walked across the parking lot to the massive, windowed student workout complex, which housed the ISU wrestling room, a rectangular area which stretches three mats long. Five bulky ropes hang from the ceiling, with thick elastic harnesses bolted to the wall, and a worn, black punching bag swings slowly in the far corner, all watched over by shabby, discolored ceiling tiles.

The Cyclone wrestlers vacated their wrestling room, and the Cowboys drilled, worked out, and burned off weight before the impending weigh-in.

Kevin Ward found a note on the floor which listed tips on defeating the Cowboys. "Stay on their head. Try to ride them. If you can't, cut them."[4] Forty-five minutes later the team loaded back onto the bus for the short drive to Hilton Coliseum, the venue for the evening's match.

In an unspoken rule in all sports at all levels, the head coach sits alone at the front of the team bus, usually on the driver's side. Perhaps he whispers directions to the driver, or wants to symbolically lead his troops into battle from the point position. Maybe he does not want to know what is going on behind him. On this short ride, as was his custom, Jake Rosholt moved up and sat by Smith as the two talked quietly. Rosholt was virtually the only wrestler who ventured to the head of the bus to sit down by the head coach in Smith's customary space.

The team arrived at the coliseum, entered through a side door, and trudged by a guard engrossed in a thick book detailing the Lewis and Clarke expedition. They wove slowly to their dressing room, and were greeted by a king's spread of bagels, sandwich meats, yogurt, and Gatorade purchased and presented the previous hour by the durable and dependable Randy Pogue. But before the Cowboys indulged, they stood for the 6:00 p.m. weigh-in inside the home team locker room. Iowa State assistants joined the OSU coaches at the scales, but Coach Douglas sat in an adjoining anteroom chatting with visitors while he flipped through paperwork.

The Cowboys completed their weigh-in and returned to the intimate visitor's dressing room wedged at the end of a hallway leading into the arena and quietly devoured their pre-match snack. At 6:20 Coach Smith announced "tops and bottoms"[5] and the ritual of dress began. Moments later the match official, clad in striped windbreaker and black stretch pants, entered the tight locker room for the obligatory instructions, "Stay in the center. Show sportsmanship."[6] Matches are controlled mayhem that always begin with a ritualistic handshake. But most twenty-year-old college athletes cannot restrain any opportunity for self-expression. "Shake hands and don't slap hands. I had some of you in the Omaha tournament."[7] He departed the dressing room and the assistant coaches began to hitch up neckties all laced with some tint of Cowboy orange.

In the meantime Coach Smith softly informed Delk and Kehrer they would be wrestling instead of Frishkorn and Jensen, who also made the trip.

When Jensen heard the news he walked to Pat Smith and proclaimed with disappointment, "I should be wrestling tonight,"[8] and proceeded to prepare a gigantic grape jelly sandwich with the leftover foodstuffs that survived the teams' initial onslaught. He devoured it in three massive bites, with his eyes slightly widening as he chewed. While Pat Smith glared at Jensen, Morgan ghost wrestled in the center of the locker room. The coaches had earlier agreed for the match to begin at the 133 weight class, and the Cowboy freshman burned off nervous energy in the guise of pre-match preparation. Because Morgan's match would lead off the evening, Coleman Scott, whose weight class usually lead off a dual, would compete in the final bout of the night. Pendleton urged Morgan to be aggressive and work for the pin, and then called the team in for their prematch huddle.

"These guys are not battle-tested. They haven't faced who we have faced or been through what we've been through. Show 'em we're better. Bring it in…"[9]

The team filed down a narrow, tiled hallway through double doors which led into the arena when Coach Smith heard the National Anthem being played. Several members stopped and bowed their heads as if they were hearing a prayer. After the anthem ended the crowd applauded politely. Coach Smith, wearing a light orange shirt, black sweater vest and khaki pants, and still standing in the shadowy hallway, spoke with urgency and righteous indignation, gesturing with his arms. More than any match this year we're ready to wrestle. Be ready to go."[10]

As the Cowboys jogged into the arena the crowd of 2,635 began to boo through dimmed lights. Steve Mocco, thundering sprints up and down the edge of the mat, spotted one of his former Iowa coaches who had driven to Ames for the match. Mocco jogged over and offered a perfunctory and respectful one-slap man-hug to his former comrade-in-arms. The bright red seats of Hilton Coliseum surrounded the ash-brown basketball court as the Iowa State wrestling mat was centered on the floor like an overgrown red postage stamp. The teams sat in rows of chairs configured like seats at a basketball game, with both teams flanking media row and facing the mat. Four chairs for coaches and staff were lined at each corner of the mat in an angle facing the mat's center, resembling the configuration at the NCAA tournament.

The dual began at 133 with Nathan Morgan's four takedown victory over junior Jesse Sundell. Morgan, not wearing the bothersome protective mask for the first time in several weeks, lost track of the score and failed to wrestle for a major decision in the final period, a tactical error that drew Smith's ire later in the evening. The teams split the next eight matches, and OSU led 18-14 going into the final match with sixteenth-ranked junior Grant Nakamura, a two-time NCAA qualifier, facing Coleman Scott. With Iowa State trailing by only four points in the dual, if Nakamura could achieve a major decision over the Cowboy freshman, the Cyclones earned a tie; if he achieved a five-point technical fall Iowa State would win the match.

The two wrestlers sparred off the whistle for 30 seconds when Nakamura executed a Smithesque low single leg, burst to his feet while elevating his opponent's leg, and lifted Scott's right ankle to eye level as the Cowboy hopped on one leg, walking that razor's edge between control and neutrality. Nakamura glared at Coleman like a banker about to foreclose a mortgage, but Scott's face bore the quiet nonchalance of a gambler who had drawn into an inside straight. As the Cyclone junior lifted the leg even higher and drove Coleman to the mat, the determined Cowboy turned into Nakamura, freed his legs, locked up a textbook double leg takedown, padlocked his arms around Nakamura's waist, and hoisted him into the air like one lifting a cedar post out of a deep and dark hole. At the height of the lift, with Nakamura's feet elevated shoulder high, Scott tightened his grip, wheeled slowly around, walked the Cyclone to the center of the mat and with 1:58 remaining in the first period drove Nakamura into the gold Cyclone logo. At that moment women began rounding up their children and men began to pull on their winter jackets, trying to remember where they parked. Nakamura, wrestling before his home crowd in the biggest match of the season, never initiated another serious offensive move. Coleman Scott, with broad shoulders heaving, walked off a victor. The Cowboys won the dual, but the evening's most intense confrontation had taken place off the mat and outside the view of most of the crowd during the short interval before Coleman Scott's match began. Smith saw it all.

After Mocco's decisive 13-4 victory, the Cowboy heavyweight jogged toward the visitor's dressing room when an Iowa State fan verbally provoked Mocco. The agitated Cowboy tossed his headgear into the stands at the general direction of the fan. A verbal confrontation ensued which involved Mocco, his father, and brother, and several members of the ISU athletic department and fans. Coach Branch, sent by Smith to the corner of the gymnasium where he spotted the episode break out, soothed an overstimulated ISU official who called out, "Do you know who I am?"[11] Assistant Head Coach Branch employed the savvy of a diplomat, neutralized the participants, and directed the OSU wrestler into the locker room to allow cooler heads to prevail.

After the match, the team dressed quickly and hurried to the bus, which waited rumbling in the parking lot outside of the gym. As the wrestlers fell into their seats, Coach Smith paced up and down the narrow aisle of the darkened bus, mindful of a recent brawl involving several NBA basketball athletes and a small group of overreaching fanatics. "The fans that abused you tonight, Steve, no one knows who they are. But the nation knows who you are. You're an athlete and you can't cross that line. It'll bite you in the ass every time. Those guys in the stands who call you a pussy or a weenie or tell you that you suck, they can get away with just about anything they say. But you cannot. You cannot retaliate. You can't do anything about it. Don't even look at them. It's doesn't matter."[12]

The customarily expressive Mocco stood still as he absorbed his coach's scolding.

"I was wrong and I'm sorry."

"You can't do it."

"I was wrong and I'm sorry."

"You can't do it!"

"I was wrong and I'm sorry."

"They were trying to get your goat all night. Every time you walked by them they would say something to you. Let it serve as motivation, but maintain your control. Use your anger to achieve your mission, but don't let them make you look silly."

A small twinkle then fired in Smith's eyes as he looked up and down the bus at his team. He then spoke softly to the bus driver. "You can head out."[13]

The bus absconded the arena parking lot and drove to the hotel. Smith again stood before his squad, this time speaking in the level tone of a college instructor. "No question, we got out of there tonight with a good win. We weren't in the best circumstance to have our best effort, and some guys really came through. We could walk out of there happy with what we did, a win against good competition under adverse circumstances. But we can do better. We had opportunities to get major decisions tonight and we didn't take advantage of it. We must be ready when we see them weaken."[14]

He then began a weight-by-weight analysis of the evening's performances.

Coach Smith, occasionally the master of understatement, started with Esposito, who piled up eight takedowns in blasting his way to a 21-6 technical fall. "Zack, that was a good example of doing what needed to be done out there."[15]

Kevin Ward and Clay Kehrer both lost by decision to ranked Cyclone wrestlers. "Ward and Kehrer, you've gotta give us more out there. You had chances to score points and you didn't get it done. It's like you were afraid to score points. Clay, you hit him with a headlock and you're ready to take him out, and you stop like you're surprised you're there."[16]

He then turned to Ronnie Delk, a 5-1 loser to Nate Gallick. Mindful that the time had come for Delk to make his run at a starting position, Smith spoke with directness. "You're wrestling the better guys in your weight now, and you have to go get takedowns. They're not going to give 'em to you. You've gotta go get 'em, son."[17]

He then looked to the back of the bus, which smelled of cheap shower soap and orange peelings. "There were some individuals tonight who did the job. Coleman Scott, you did the job. You earned that victory."[18]

Sitting by Coleman was Morgan, a 10-5 winner who lost track of the score and failed to wrestle for additional points in the final period to extend his five point margin to a major decision. "Nathan Morgan, you wrestled a good match, but we needed a major decision from you tonight. You're up 8-3 and you lost your place. You say you were tired, but don't you think Mocco was tired to when he made his final push? Don't you think Zack was tired tonight when he got eight takedowns? I don't want you out there *trying*. I want you out there *doing*. Go get it. I don't care you're a true freshman. I'm going to tell you what is expected and I want you to do it. You might not have that opportunity in a different match. When you have the opportunity you have to take it. Your heart won't pop out of your chest. Do it. Get it done."[19]

Jake Rosholt sat alone and stared ahead. "Jake, you get three takedowns the first period and then get blanked? What that tells me is that you're not warming up properly. When I see you run out of energy in the second or third period of a match, you are walking out there without properly warming up and preparing yourself to wrestle. Sure, the gym was cold tonight. But you're in shape to wrestle three periods hard."[20]

A reading light illuminated Smith's face as he turned to his right and glanced at his heavyweight. "Mocco, you did what needed to get done. You jumped out to a comfortable lead, but you knew we needed that major and you went and got it like it was yours."

"I was tired."

Coach Smith grimaced at Mocco's response. "You're going to get tired as hard as you wrestled. It's physically impossible to wrestle as hard as you did tonight and not get tired. It's physically impossible to train yourself to a state of no fatigue during a hard match like that. You guys need to understand. Conditioning does not mean you won't get tired. It means you'll be able to wrestle like a champion and hold up in a three-day tournament when you're fighting for your life, even when you're tired."[21]

Smith stood silently for a moment. "Look at the Russians. At the end of their matches they look completely depleted. Completely worn out. But they find ways to score points at the end of their matches when they have nothing left to give, and they're kicking our asses every year. They find ways to score when they are at the point of complete exhaustion. They get their hands raised and they walk off champions."[22]

Smith checked his watch, rubbed his eyes, and tucked his notebook under his right arm. "One more thought about tonight. Their arena. Their ref. Their crowd. They were fresh. They got every call. This was one of the teams we have to beat for the national championship, and their coach put them in the best possible position they could have been in to beat us. But you took from them any hope they had to beat us in March. After tonight they know they're wrestling for second place."

As Smith spoke the wrestlers seemed bolted to their seats. "We could be satisfied with tonight's effort, but I'm still looking for more out of some of you. What is missing is the drive to beat the people you have to beat to survive. Some of you are not that far away."[23]

Then Smith issued his final warning of the night. "I watched your eating habits closely yesterday and today. Some of you are eating the night before a match but starving yourself the day of competition, and then running out of energy during your match. The food you eat after we weigh in right before we wrestle, it does you no good. Whatever you ate one hour ago is still in your system. It does you no good."[24]

As he spoke, stomachs began to softly rumble. "Some of you don't eat the day of a match so you won't have to drill before weigh in. If you can't drill for forty-five minutes and then wrestle a match, you're in trouble. You've got to be able to drill for forty-five minutes, go wrestle a match, go drill again for forty-five minutes, go wrestle a match, drill for forty-five minutes, and wrestle another match. That's what can happen in the NCAA championships, and that's what we're training for. That's where the champions are crowned, not here in Ames. Whatever you eat in the morning is what you'll be going on that night. So have some foresight and discipline. The night before a match when you have a chance to eat, walk away so you can eat a big meal the next morning. A power bar won't cut it. You don't need protein. You need bread, pasta, a biscuit, or some oatmeal. Don't worry about a big meal the day of a match putting weight on you."[25]

Coach Smith then noticed his chastened heavyweight Steve Mocco still standing in the aisle, and called on him with hopes of making a point. "What puts weight on you, Mocco?"

"Eggs."

Laughter erupted across the darkened bus.

Smith looked puzzled. "Eggs?"

"Fresh eggs."[26]

More laughter cascaded down.

Coach Smith looked out the window into the dark, cold night and grinned. "It's clear you haven't cut much weight. What puts weight on you the day of a match is water. Don't ever starve the day of a match so you can drink a glass or two more of Gatorade or water. Sacrifice a day or two before the match so you'll be in position to eat a good meal the morning of the match. Now go to bed everyone. If you have dirty clothes, then loop 'em up and give them to Randy. Now get some rest."[27]

After making sure the team was settled in their rooms, Smith and his staff sat down at a nearby sports restaurant for a late-night dinner. A group of former Iowa State wrestlers and supporters who attended the dual that evening sat throughout the restaurant. A sense of camaraderie framed the laughter of these middle-aged men, former Cowboy and Cyclone wrestlers, as they related war stories of long ago. The tone seemed one of suppressed joy, and the evening tensed up only once. Pat and John Smith sat at a table enjoying dinner when one of John's former opponents of almost two decades ago, a short and muscled fellow carrying a slight paunch, weaved to the Smith table and slurred a challenge. "You beat me but you didn't out-wrestle me. I was just behind when time ran out."[28] He didn't let up, and continued his rant as customers began to look on in embarrassment.

Finally Coach Smith broke the tension. Speaking to no one in particular, he smiled and spoke. "This guy was one of the toughest I ever wrestled." Appeased and apparently satisfied, Smith's former opponent finally made his way to another table. This encounter demonstrated the intimate and personal nature of the sport. It seems every wrestler carries with him one match that lingers even into adulthood. Of course, it is always a loss, and it always ignites the haunting question of what might have been. For many, it was their first real taste of heartbreak. For others, it would not be their last.

For Smith, the match that haunts him in the night is a narrow 2-1 loss to nemesis Lazaro Reinoso of Cuba in the 1992 Olympics. Smith had served as interim head coach of the OSU wrestling squad for the months leading up to the Olympics. Instead of devoting full time to training, he was forced to deal with an endless stream of time-consuming administrative, personnel, and NCAA problems as he worked to prevent the entire Cowboy wrestling program from unraveling at the seams as a result of the NCAA sanctions. When he finally arrived in Barcelona, Smith was injured, undertrained, and mentally fatigued. Nonetheless, he grinded his way toward the gold medal match, needing only to score one point in the final preliminary match to automatically qualify for the finals.

When he stepped onto the mat with Reinoso, Smith had posted 35 consecutive wins in World and Olympic competition over the previous six years, a win streak unmatched in international wrestling history. He was two wins away from his second Olympic gold medal and a coveted undefeated record in international competition. "I was told by my coaches that I needed to score just one point to advance to the finals. That was the first time in my career I had ever been told before a match that I needed to do something other than just win."

Smith wonders, from a coaching perspective, whether setting the bar at just scoring a single point was a mistake. "Had I been told I had to score ten points and win the match, the result might have been different." Smith dialed in and scored the single point early, but seemed to shut down for the rest of the match, and lost 2-1. It would be his first and only loss in international competition. "In the past I took the mat to score points for my team in a dual, or advance through a bracket by winning matches. I had never been faced with the expectation of scoring a single point. No question, it changed my mindset."

Smith believes that defeat assisted him in his final match, where the following day he went on to capture the Gold medal. "That loss [to Reinoso] helped me wrestle my best match in the finals. I wrestled my toughest opponent in the final match, and wrestled my best match. My loss the day before helped me have that kind of match. But until just before the gold medal match I was in no shape to compete mentally. I was about to wrestle for an Olympic gold medal and I didn't give a damn. Thankfully some coaches helped me get my mind right." But the loss still haunts Smith. "My plan was to go out a winner. It was about more than winning the gold medal. It was the reality that when it was time to be the very best, I gave my best performance. I pride myself on the fact that my opponents got my very best performance during Olympic and World competition. Even today, because of that loss I cannot experience the total enjoyment of being a four-time World Champion and two-time Olympic Champion. In retrospect, being 37-0 in World and Olympic competition would have been more of an accomplishment in my eyes than winning four World Championships and two Olympic gold medals. But I wasn't 37-0. I finished 36-1. History buffs often approach me and ask to know about my loss in the Olympics. As you can tell, that mark on my record still haunts me. Even though I was struggling with injuries and limited training time, that loss never should have happened. When I received my gold medal [in the 1992 Olympic Games], something didn't feel quite right. At the end of your career you want to go out on your own terms."

But if the Reinoso match haunts Smith, his first-round loss in the NCAA tournament his freshman year to 10th seed Dan Foldesy of Cleveland State was the most painful. In that match, Smith was head-locked and thrown to his back for a five-point move, and never recovered, losing 6-2. Foldesy lost his next match, resulting in Smith's elimination from the tournament. His goal to be a four-time All American slipped away. "My loss to Reinoso was due to my mindset, but that match [to Foldesy] was due to errors. I made a couple of immature mistakes, and it cost me. It's painful to lose, but the pain is compounded when you lose to someone whom you know you should beat at the end of the season. That is hard to face, not having your best match at the most important time." When relating the story over twenty years later, the pain is still evident in Smith's softened voice. "I only scored one and one-half points for my team. There was pressure on Coach Chesboro to win an NCAA team championship, and we finished second. Had I performed better, we may have won the team title. We finished second for two consecutive years, and they fired our coach. That was stupid."

The next morning the team rolled out of Ames under a cold, overcast sky. Earlier the coaches planned for the team to remain in Ames and work out in the Iowa State wrestling room during the early afternoon to ensure everyone's weight was down, and then depart for Cedar Rapids in time to weigh in. But on match day, when it comes to making weight, caution usually prevails. Coach Smith decided to confirm the team's weight on the actual scales that would be utilized for the match that evening. A differential of even one-tenth of a pound between scales could prove problematic. So the Cowboys traveled directly to the Northern Iowa campus from their hotel in Ames.

As the chartered bus barreled north along Interstate 35 through rural northern Iowa, several wrestlers slept, some studied, a few sleepily viewed the movie *Dirty Work* which was displayed on the small movie screens scattered around the bus. Others gazed out the windows at tilled fields crusted by ice, as snow hid in furrows and waited patiently for the spring melt. Farmhouses, barns, and grain elevators stood in occasional clumps off the highway, separated from the lazy and sporadic traffic by rows of telephone wires and fence. Iowa is a wrestling state. While young boys in neighboring Indiana play out their dreams with hoops and basketballs, children in Iowa emulate their father's hero Dan Gable and dream of being college wrestlers.

As the bus approached Cedar Falls at 3:25 p.m. a gigantic domed arena, disproportionate to the city's size like a large head balanced on the neck of a small calf, rose above the modest skyline of the snowy and sleepy college village. The chartered bus slipped past large and meaty Lutheran churches, busy diners, car lots, grocery marts, and red brick dorms. It winded and twisted onto campus when it pulled to the curb and asked two hapless students for directions. As the bus pulled away, the students looked at one another, glanced back at the bus, smiled goofy grins and walked toward their dorm, directly toward a window blocked by a white "Sportsmen for Bush" sign.

The bus emptied the wrestlers in a parking lot adjacent to the red brick gymnasium that housed the Northern Iowa wrestling room and hosted the match. Smith remembered four years earlier he stood in the same parking lot while snow fell and stomachs churned as he told his team that an aircraft carrying ten OSU basketball players and staff was missing. That sober recollection, coupled with a mist of fatigue that wafted through the bus, seemed to drag behind the Cowboys as they carried their gear in black nylon bags toward the match scales located in the home dressing room, a white concrete-blocked square, trimmed in purple and circled by wooden lockers which held clean singlets and balls of white, clean, and fresh socks. After the wrestlers checked their weight they drifted into a small anteroom adjoining the locker room and lounged on worn Naugahyde sofas patched by duct tape. After Smith verified the weight of his last wrestler, the team followed him to the Northern Iowa wrestling room for a quick drill and warm-up designed to expel the cobwebs from the mind and muscles and expose the system to the bull-rush that lay ahead.

Northern Iowa was coached by Brad Penrith, a Dan Gable protégé and NCAA champion in 1986, John Smith's redshirt season. A contemporary of Smith, in the 1985 NCAA finals in Oklahoma City, Penrith had wrestled in the match immediately before Smith's fateful defeat at the hands of Jordan of Wisconsin. The New York native had led the Panthers to three top 20 finishes during his five seasons as the Panther's head coach.

The Northern Iowa wrestling room was a shrine to Midwest Lutheran values of snowy fields and seasons of redemption. Standing on one of the two mats and facing east, wrestlers looked out of the well-lighted room into the cold night through one of seven grand French windows, each extending to the top of a fifty-foot ceiling and every one large enough to drive a billowing Iowa farm tractor through untouched. Black rectangular speakers bellowed music from the corners of the room. The noise intersected the hot air blowing from ominous and trembling heaters that swayed four fans hanging from the ceiling. On the far end of the wall, opposite the 20 foot painted mural of a snarling Panther, rested a billboard-size rectangular sign reading, "Northern Iowa's Wrestling Philosophy." The large block letters revealed what could have been the outline of the past Sunday morning's sermon at the University Lutheran Church. It emphasized a theology of personal responsibility, hard work, and disciplined behavior. A small weight room housed with free weights and exercise bikes adjoined the matted area. The wrestling room was a period piece, workmanlike and practical, with the exception of the scripted sign it bore the understated elegance of hard, snow-packed farmland.

After the Cowboys drilled, they crowded into to the home dressing room with the Northern Iowa Panthers for the six o'clock weigh-in. As Clay Kehrer walked into the dressing room Steve Mocco giggled at the cardboard hand-sized "Panthers Forever" placard the Cowboy heavyweight surreptitiously affixed to Kehrer under the disguise of a pat on the back. After weighing in, the Northern Iowa wrestlers rushed one-by-one to a giant orange Gatorade cooler where their Adams-apples pumped like bobbing fruit as they sucked down freezing-cold orange Gatorade. Cowboy Kevin Ward revealed the day before that thirst more than hunger tormented the college wrestler. Ward and his Cowboy teammates strode without a glance past their huddled and bloated opponents toward their own oasis of food and liquid purchased and arranged minutes earlier by Randy Pogue.

Five minutes before match-time, a visibly exhausted John Smith delivered his pre-match remarks. He sensed his tired warriors were beyond a pep talk, so he focused instead on the mundane. "We had several cautions last night against Iowa State for not getting our foot on the starting line at the whistle. We have the same official tonight and he'll be looking for that."[29] He then moved closer to his team and seemed to make eye contact with the entire squad at one glance. "We have some key matches tonight so get yourselves ready. Those of you who know you have a tough battle have to bring your level up. All right, let's bring it in. Dominating win tonight. 1-2-3 Cowboys."[30]

Pendleton spoke barely above a whisper as the team drew in around him. He wore the distinctive black OSU warm-up trimmed in orange and white with the scripted Cowboys sewn on the back of a stand-up collar. "Let's bring our intensity up. Right now. Our Father who are in heaven…"[31]

Northern Iowa's West Gym, host of the 1950 NCAA wrestling tournament, won by Northern Iowa, is tucked in the center of the red brick campus. Constructed in 1925 for some $180,000, it is the home venue for Panther wrestling matches. It seated barely more than 2,000 fans, the bleachers lined the sidelines, and its intimate ambiance placed it into that short list

A sluggish Zack Esposito ties up with Jeff Harrison of Northern Iowa. His methodical 6-2 victory sparked the road-weary Cowboys to a 30-6 road win. *Courtesy Northern Iowa University.*

of Division I facilities Coach Smith fondly refers to as cracker box gyms. As he walked across the gym floor with his hands in his pockets, the Cowboy coach, chagrined by the outrageous growth of college sports budgets and facilities, looked longingly at the low ceilings and compressed seating. "If they modernized this facility with comfortable seating, nice locker rooms, and some fan accouterments, this could be one of the premier wrestling facilities in the country."[32]

Northern Iowa wrestlers had won 21 NCAA individual Division I championships, but Tony Davis' title in 2000 was their only individual champion since 1963. Wrestlers who hailed from Iowa fill 20 of its 31 roster spots, and homegrown Iowans tonight occupied six of the 10 starting positions. Only one Oklahoma high school wrestler wrestled in the Cowboy lineup that night.

Fifth-year head coach Brad Penrith was an NCAA champion under Dan Gable in 1986. His 2003-2004 recruiting class was ranked fourth in the nation, and he aspired to bring back the glory days of Northern Iowa wrestling. He liked his job and reveled in the collegiate wrestling culture, particularly the bond he felt with his staff. "I have one of the best coaching staffs in the country. A lot of head coaches have to micro-manage their assistants and I don't have to do that; I am very fortunate. Each one of these guys has grown and matured and become a better coach since joining UNI's staff. You can't ask for anything more than that."[33]

The match began at 7:00 p.m. sharp. The crowd was vocal and knowledgeable, the Panther wrestlers were game, and the Cowboys were flat. Just plain flat.

At 125 Coleman Scott had ravaged his opponent Chris Helgeson 15-0 in an open tournament only weeks ago. But tonight Scott seemed to walk in his sleep. He traded escapes with Helgeson, which sent the match to overtime tied 1-1. Just seconds into the overtime Scott awakened, reached out like a sleepy teenager slapping a snooze button, and scored a takedown almost at will to win 3-1, making the Cowboy coaches wonder out loud why Scott did not awaken during regulation.

Morgan went through the motions and won 8-2. Esposito scored takedowns in the first and third periods to win 6-2 but received an uncharacteristic stalling penalty, causing partisan hecklers from the stands to shout "who's taking the shots?" Kevin Ward posted a solid 11-5 victory but absorbed Coach Smith's admonitions to "quit standing around." Sam Lewnes, continuing to wrestle for the injured Johny Hendricks, fell to Nick Baima 12-6. Smith slapped him on the back as he left the mat, but the exhausted Cowboy coach failed to stifle a yawn as he sat back down on the folding chairs and leaned forward with his elbows rested on his knees.

Frishkorn edged ahead by a neck in his race with Ronnie Delk for the 141 starting position by scoring three near falls in five minutes in his 17-1 pounding of Justin Swofford. Both Delk and Frishkorn split four matches at the National Duals, and both knew the competition would not be resolved by wrestling each other in the wrestling room. As Coach Branch said, "It comes down to performance in matches."[34]

Team leader Chris Pendleton, sensing his team's uninspired karma, gave up a first-period takedown to Eric Hauan but proceeded to drown the Panther with six takedowns in a 15-6 major decision. As Smith shook Pendleton's hand as he walked off the mat, the coach's body language screamed "that's what I'm talking about" as he paid homage to his senior leader. Jack Jensen, with his mom in the stands, lost 8-3.

Jake Rosholt gave up a first period takedown but strung together six consecutive points for a sluggish 6-2 victory. Steve Mocco disposed of a backup heavyweight in 48 seconds with his 12th pin of the season. The Cowboys posted a 30-6 victory over Northern Iowa, running their dual record to 14-0.

The wrestlers showered and loaded on the chartered bus at 9:45 p.m. for the all-night bus ride home. Before they settled into their seats an irritated Smith ordered the team off the bus and back into the littered visitors' locker room to pick up trash and wrappers left from their post-weigh-in feeding frenzy. During this time Steve Mocco bade farewell to family and friends who drove from Iowa City, the home of Iowa University, to see the former Hawkeye heavyweight perform. Steve's father followed his son to the door of the bus, kissed him lightly on the cheek, and hugged him as his son climbed onto the darkened and quiet bus. Moments later Mr. Mocco handed Coach Smith through the door a chunk of foil-wrapped venison the size of a loaf of bread for the ride back. A wrestler from the back of the bus observed the handoff. "He won't shit for a week."[35]

Smith seemed too tired to offer any post-match comments, and the wrestlers seemed too flattened and numb to listen. Forty minutes out of town Smith directed the bus driver to take an exit into a cluster of fast-food restaurants. Someone farted loudly in the back of the bus, prompting a teammate to awaken from a deep slumber and reflexively bark a common profanity. A disgusted Smith ordered the bus back on the highway. Ninety minutes out of Grand Rapids the bus pulled off the interstate and into a truck stop. The wrestlers ordered and devoured sandwiches and drinks at an adjoining Burger King while teen-aged children approached Mocco for autographs on the bills of caps they bought at the truck stop for the occasion. After the meal the wrestlers hunkered into their seats, but as the bus pulled out of the parking lot the driver applied the loud squealing brakes…Daniel Frishkorn was running across the pavement toward the bus, fearful of being left in the dark Iowa night. Behind him Steve Mocco walked in a leisurely pace.

On the bus, Coach Smith directed Rosholt to locate a seat where he could elevate his injured leg. Smith peered at his watch and picked up his black leather notebook. It was 12:35 a.m. as the bus folded into the cold night. The team would travel all night, 635 miles, and pull into Stillwater nine hours later, greeted by a soft blanket of snow. Outside of Stillwater Coach Smith spoke softly to his wife Toni on his cell phone. With a mixture of curiosity and playfulness she asked what the wrestlers did on long bus rides. John Smith did not break a stride as he whispered back. "We sing songs, and Steve Mocco leads the singing."

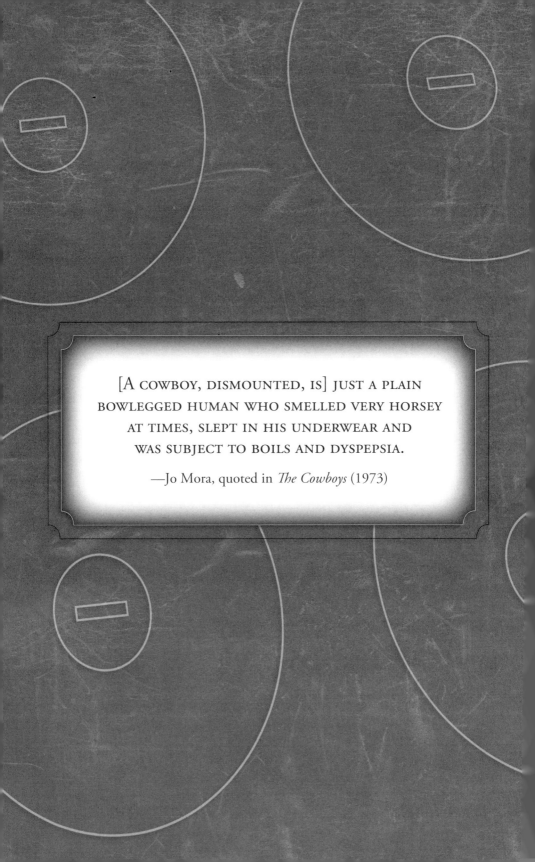

[A COWBOY, DISMOUNTED, IS] JUST A PLAIN
BOWLEGGED HUMAN WHO SMELLED VERY HORSEY
AT TIMES, SLEPT IN HIS UNDERWEAR AND
WAS SUBJECT TO BOILS AND DYSPEPSIA.

—Jo Mora, quoted in *The Cowboys* (1973)

twelve

a mid-season cowboy practice

Early Winter 2005

THREE STUDENT TRAINERS wore rubber gloves and carried a black medical bag equipped with medical supplies fit for a trauma unit and large enough to hold a young bobcat. A physician was on call, just seconds away. The walls were padded, the floor was disinfected, the temperature was regulated, and visitors were often excluded by signs and bolted locks. It was not a triage ward.

It was a mid-season Cowboy wrestling practice.

NCAA rules allow collegiate wrestling teams to conduct organized practices from September to March. Mat-time is regulated by NCAA rule. OSU's workouts are tightly organized and carefully planned. Afternoon practice begins in the early afternoon between 3:00 and 4:00. As the season progressed, that centerpiece workout was preceded alternately by early-morning drill sessions and weight training.

The wrestlers lounged around the mats in small clusters, dressed out in workout gear, and idly chatted while they laced up wrestling shoes. Some had emerged from the 20'x20' lounge adjoining the wrestling room, where wrestlers sat on a thick black sofa watching video on a large-screen television. Pictures of previous Cowboy teams and champions hung from the paneled walls and peered over shoulders. Assistant coaches routinely brought wrestlers into this room to watch film of previous matches. As the wrestlers watched their images and received critique, they grimaced like one listening to his voice on a tape-recorder for the first time.

In the wrestling room each of the 32 wrestlers dressed differently. Gray t-shirts. Black shorts. Skin-tight nylon shirts. Baggy shorts. Tight nylon shorts. White socks. Black socks. No socks. White shoes. Black shoes. Gray shoes. Green shoes. Gray shoes. White headgear. Black headgear. Tape around the wrist. Tape holding on knee braces. White kneepads. Black kneepads.

The team had lifted weights earlier in the day, and brass-nutted boys accustomed to uneasiness moved slowly. Trainer Chris Pickering looked on and instinctively checked for Q-tips and gauze in his shirt pocket. "Everyone is tired and cranky. Pendleton and Hendricks have flu symptoms. We're going to have some dogfights in here today. Everyone is in a bad mood. Can't you feel it?"[1]

* * *

A collegiate wrestling mat is a 42 foot square, assembled by taping together with three-inch mat tape, three 14'x42' strips of polyethylene foam two inches thick covered with non-slip, non-abrasive vinyl. The standard model comes in ten colors, and runs about $9,600. A school logo is stamped dead center, and is surrounded by a 36-foot circle, which represents the boundary within which the wrestlers come to dream. For another $130 you get a 10-foot circle painted concentrically within the larger circle, on which two parallel 12" white starting lines are centered which mark where the down wrestler's hands and knees are placed. The Cowboys have three such mats in their wrestling room laid end-to-end that span half a football field. The mat used for Cowboy home duals, orange with black-trim, high in quality but austere in design, contains no logo or lettering. During a tournament, eight mats cover a standard-sized basketball court.

The uniform of a wrestler is called a singlet, a one-piece skin-tight trunk and chest cover made of spandex or polyester and weighing less than a submarine sandwich. It too comes in all colors, and the designer styles run about $65. In open tournaments, Cowboy backups and redshirts wear black singlets, or some hybrid design of orange. During public matches only the Cowboy starters wear the standard but sanctified orange trimmed in black, with the OSU logo stamped on the left thigh. While the singlets are standard in color and design, participants in this iconoclastic sport are allowed considerable self-expression in the areas of headwear and footwear.

Wrestlers wear ankle-high/lace-up shoes designed for the sport and distributed by major sporting goods companies like Adidas, Nike and ASICS. They come in a rainbow of colors like red, black, white, royal blue, tan, lime-green, and yellow, trimmed in silver, white, and black. The *Black/ Infrared/White Adidas adiStrike John Smith Signature Shoe* runs $117.95. Shoes range in size from 5 to 15, and promise "glove-like fit, breathable tongue, and multi-directional grip." Black and white shoes go well with orange. But often, the more accomplished a wrestler is, the further he will push the fashion frontier in footwear. For example, Rosholt wore green, Mocco wore gray, and Hendricks chose yellow trim.

Wrestlers are required to wear headgears to protect from damage to the ears. Resembling space-age earmuffs kept snug to the head by buttoned straps, they too are available in all colors and designs. They run about $25, and bear names like Brute, Old School, Tornado, and Shockwave.

Socks seemed to be taboo for the 2004-2005 Cowboys. Jockey straps run about $25. Everything else is fluff.

* * *

Smith wore black sweatpants and a gray OSU t-shirt and held a whistle attached to a thick string of orange cord draped around his neck. The subtext of the practice session was technique, but the pretext was a test of will. He made eye contact with team leader Chris Pendleton and mouthed one singular word, "walking,"[2] and the Cowboy warm-up ritual began. The wrestlers climbed to their feet and followed Pendleton, who ran counter-clockwise around the outside portion of the mats at a slow jog. The others fell in behind like a hurricane gathering steam. No one spoke, and after several minutes some began to dogtrot backwards, while others hopped, turned summersaults, or ghost-wrestled as the circle continued to spin, punctuated by forward movements as wrestlers flicked one leg back like a prairie lizard's tongue on a hot rock while they simulated the basic of all defensive maneuvers—the sprawl. Smith pulled a freshman aside, placed his arm on a shoulder and spoke softly as the team continued to circle and gather steam. Without prompting, they gathered again at mid-mat around Smith, who glanced at notes hand-written in small, tight scrawl and bound in a black leather notebook. This was the fourth practice in four days. Scabbed faces and bruised eyes looked up. Before practice Smith lamented that the team seemed confused. "I was not crazy about yesterday's workout. It was clear we are progressing well with our conditioning, but I feel insecure how we are progressing technically."[3]

As wrestlers fanned out across the three mats, Smith struck the point, "Make sure you're communicating with coaches in those areas where you're struggling. I see failed attempts at single legs…guys not pulling them in and finishing. Several of you missed opportunities to score, and it's because you're not paying attention in your drills. It's hard work to focus during drills. There's nothing easy about it. Some say drills are routine. But making your moves instinctive, so you can rely on them in the heat of battle, requires the highest emotion and concentration. Otherwise, it's a waste of time."[4] Smith turned back to the center of the mat and his voice softened. "You have good intentions…don't get me wrong. No one is lazy in here. But sometimes there are days we don't want to be in here. There are days I don't want to be in here. But if you don't pay attention to what you're doing, you'll never get better. If it doesn't take place here, it won't take place out there."[5] His voice

ABOVE: The Cowboy wrestling room, half the length of a football field, sported three Olympians and seven national champions during the 2004-05 season. *Courtesy Kim Parrish.*

LEFT: Coach Smith (far left) looks at a stopwatch and prepares to whistle to begin a full-speed match during practice. *Courtesy Kim Parrish.*

hardened and eyes dropped slightly as he walked away. "There should be no sympathy for anyone here in this room. If you've gotta' pound the hell out of someone here in this room in order to get better, then do it."[6]

The remaining members of the student medical team quietly entered the wrestling room, dressed in matching white polo shirts with an OSU logo on their chests and carrying first-aid gear and an orange Gatorade cooler. Smith noticed them from the corner of his eye and turned back to his team. "We had a couple of fights in here over the last few days. What happens in this room, I want it to stay in this room. I don't want to read about it on the

Internet. If there's an argument or fight or someone's ass got chewed out, it stays in this room. I had two people over the weekend that don't even live in this state, ask me about a fight we had. Don't tell your girlfriend, your mom, your sister or whomever. When you leave this room it stays in this room."[7]

The wrestlers paired up and rehearsed maneuvers for 40 minutes at three-quarter speed, honing their favorite moves, performing up to five repetitions per minute. Much of wrestling involves applying body mass and strength to an opponent's vulnerability, like cutting off the leg of a stern table. The coaches were peppered with a constant flow of questions from veterans. Most of the wide-eyed freshmen remained quiet, while assistant coaches rotated around the groups, talking in conversational tones with selectivity and intention.

Some had talents that rolled in on wheels, while others were wedded to limited abilities. Earlier in the week, freshman Brandon Mason was smacked in the face, resulting in a slight concussion. Mason, a diligent pre-med student, was scheduled to take an examination that evening following practice, but after stopping by the university emergency room for a quick once-over, still felt woozy and disoriented when he arrived at class. He politely asked his professor to postpone his test until later in the week, and when the request was denied, Smith was on the telephone the following day with an academic dean's office and Mason's parent's explaining the circumstances. Smith also made a mental note to deduct the cost of the emergency room visit from the aggressor's scholarship monies the following year.

Finally, with the 30-odd athletes paired up in 15 clusters of controlled mayhem, wrestlers slapped hands and live action began. Upperclassmen began moving about like men stomping out a fire. Smith prowled the room, walking from group to group, watching technique and motion with a trained eye, and making instant diagnoses with the tone and demeanor of a doctor making rounds in a teaching hospital. "We will wrestle two live matches. Don't be afraid to get tired. You've gotta' do it with no fear."[8] The starters and upperclassmen paired up on their selective portion of the mat. Jackhammers versus deep-knife slices. Men in full flight pulled an opponent's leg in like a stoic laundry worker cranking a chamois through a roller. Pendleton took the west half of the middle mat, next to Hendricks and Esposito. Rosholt took the east half of the south mat, adjacent to Mocco. Freshmen and underclassmen slid in the remaining areas, with big guys on the south mat, middle weights on the center mat, and lower weights on the north mat. There was a hard need for points.

When Coleman Scott was poked in the eye and took a knee, holding a hand over his watered red eye, Smith walked away. "Use the other eye and get out there."[9] Two high school students on a recruiting visit sat on folding chairs and observed the Cowboy assistant coaches, who offered encouragement and hands-on instruction when they spotted flaws and dangerous tendencies. Typically, recruits carry the cocky self-assurance of the untested young, but today their mouths were slightly agape, their eyes wide open, and their faces frozen as they watched Pendleton slam a workout partner to his back with the precision of a diamond-cutter,

Taylor Hosick (center), surrounded by teammates, ghost wrestles before practice. "Cowboys" is spelled out in large black letters by the ceiling tiles. *Courtesy Kim Parrish.*

causing a slight flinch as a spray of salty sweat settled over them. The victim offered no resistance, a transgression spotted by Smith, which provoked his only tirade of the evening. "When you go to your back I better see you fighting for position, even if you have to bite his ear off. DO NOT LIE ON YOUR BACK! If I don't see you hitting a bridge and fighting your ass off under there, you're going to stay there 'till you get up. That means if it takes you two days to get off. We'll rotate people in on you. Don't let me see anyone laying on their back. If you have to bite his ear off, you get off your back."[10]

During practice there was seldom any yelling by coaches. Smith's tone resembled a chemistry teacher overlooking a particularly complex lab, watching wrestlers with hearts stretched like thick rope with no give, throwing one another against padded walls. His comments were selective and intentional. "When you continually plow into the wall and walk back to the middle of the mat, it's like taking 15 time-outs. You won't get that during a match. Run back to the middle of the mat. You be the one who hustles. If you're against the wall, keep wrestling."[11] He stared at Frishkorn, who was massaging his own neck after hitting a rolling maneuver against Derek Stevens. ""Rub it after practice."[12]

Smith then marched quietly to the north end of the room and stood by assistant coach Eric Guerrero. They stared at muscled and acrobatic freshmen and sophomores who populated the area utilized by the lower weights. Smith stepped forward and bent down, with his hands on his knees, and spoke to a heaving and sweating freshman in barely a whisper, like a man watching a house burn down, "I know you were trying, but at the end of the day, trying won't get it done. I don't recruit you to *try*. Don't give me 100% and lose. Give me 75% and get the job done. Find a way to win. Sometimes it's not pretty. Sometimes you throw technique out the window and you reach down deep and do what you can to finish on top."[13]

He then walked to the center of the mat and called the team in. No wrestler glanced at a wall clock, for there was none, nor did Smith ever wear a watch during practice. "Keep in mind our mission. The reason we are working so hard right now is because of what faces us over the next few weeks. I know you are tired and sore. You should be. But you can't let fatigue turn practice into a meaningless routine, where you come into the

LEFT: Coach Smith observes his wrestlers honing their technique during a workout. His demeanor during the teaching portion of practice (usually) is that of a chemistry teacher directing a laboratory. *Author photograph*

BELOW: Coleman Scott and Nathan Morgan drill during practice. *Courtesy Kim Parrish.*

room and just go through the motions. Nine out of 10 wrestlers from this point forward in the season will not improve. The five or six guys in your weight who are capable of winning will settle for something less. You would be surprised what they would settle for. Some just want to make it to the NCAA tournament. Others just want to make All-American. Don't settle for less. This is the time we determine that we as a team and individually, we will not settle for less. Why do they lower their expectations? They quit thinking. They lose their edge mentally. You need mental toughness on those days you feel beaten down, but you still walk out and say, 'I had a great practice today.' We develop our mental toughness when we don't feel good. Those are the days we elevate ourselves as wrestlers and as people. If I saw anything over the past few days, I saw a little bit of a letdown. In a three-minute drill, guys being satisfied with 10 escapes instead of 20. Guys laying on their back and not bridging. Guys not pushing through and getting that last takedown. Sure, you're going to have bad days. You're life is spent in this room. But those are the days that will make the difference. You will develop that reservoir of mental toughness now that can be drawn upon when the going gets tough at the end of the year. I don't care how slick your skills are, if you can't develop that mental toughness, you can't win. Remember, the pain of preparation is nothing like the pain of losing."[14]

Live wrestling then resumed as the brightly lit room was punctuated by wincing sounds of bodies slammed to the floor. Knees slid along smooth mat. Men-boys belched, grunted, and screamed. Small movements seemed clogged, like men pulling combs through dirty hair. Forty-gallon trashcans, spaced along the east wall of the wrestling room and lined with huge trash bags, served as spittoons and receptacles for blood, vomit, and sweat. Head trainer Chris Pickering tossed an oozing bandage into one can and tilted his head as he applied a tissue-based cast around the puffy ear of freshman Newly McSpadden and explained the physiology behind a cauliflower ear. "The capillaries in the cartilage under the skin on the ear, when folded, twisted or subject to trauma, rupture and blood collects, like a hematoma or any other bruise. The ear fills up and becomes soft and spongy. I drain the blood with a syringe, and build a cast with a sticky fluid and cotton balls that I then mold around the ear. This has the effect of a compression

Head Trainer Chris Pickering taped, bandaged and braced injured Cowboy wrestlers hundreds of times during practices and matches throughout the year. *Courtesy Kim Parrish.*

device that prevents the ear from swelling and minimizes the puffiness. After years blood will calcify in the ears if the blood is not flushed out. Some guys want cauliflower ears, and they wear them as a badge of honor, emblematic that they have been through the rigors of a Division 1 program. Other guys don't. But in either case, when ears get swollen with fluid, they need immediate attention."[15]

Passing by Pickering, Smith walked to the center of the mat and stopped with hands on hips. "The first 20 minutes brought us to this point. These last five minutes are the most important minutes of practice. Not the first five minutes. Let's go."[16]

A backup looked incredulously at a senior. "He can't make us go three full matches."

"Yes he can."[17]

Several wrestlers staggered around dazed. Two wrestlers exchanged blows and fell over folding chairs. One asked, "Am I bleeding?"[18] Smith told him to not worry and to get back on the mat, and then signaled for trainer Sarah Tackett to clean up and disinfect the blood pool with liquid *Blood Buster* carried in a backpack along with rolls of gauze and tape. Hearing the thud of other bodies against the orange wall padding, her head turned. Frishkorn, wearing skin-tight black long sleeve shirt and black shorts, bulled Morgan into the wall, but opened up a cut over his own right eye. Sarah placed a call to an on-duty physician in case stitches were required, and spoke of the wrestlers' tolerance for pain relative to the other sports. "When a football player goes down, trainers run to his aid. Usually we don't run out to check on the wrestlers. They call us if they need us."[19]

Smith walked around the wrestling room and paired up wrestlers with different partners as they began the third live match of the workout. "There is only one team that will win the national title, and only one guy in your weight who will win the gold medal. Don't let any soreness or tired attitude stand in your way."[20] He glared at Hendricks and Rosholt as they sat against the north wall, chests heaving and sweat pooling about them, and reminded them of their performances in the previous year's NCAA tournament. "It's not worth it. Johny, how did it feel to take fifth? Jake, how did it feel to take third?"[21] The veterans did not return their coach's stare.

After reviewing his notebook and conferring with assistant coaches Branch and Guerrero, Smith turned about the room. "We have to prepare for the worst. What if your nose is broken? What if your knee is torn out? What if your legs are tired and tight? What if you have the flu? We have to be prepared, and now is the time to prepare. Find a way to score points. Find a way to win matches. Find a way to get off bottom. Find a way to hold a guy down. Find a way to put him on his back. Those are the days where you become a different wrestler, because you learn how to find a way that has never occurred to you. Somewhere down the road you will be challenged. You'll be thrown to your back and be down 5-0. You'll give up a takedown. You'll be ridden out. It will be up to you to turn the tide of a match, and only you can figure out how to do it. And we will be the team that does it because of how you're tested in here every day. We train harder than anyone in the country. I promise you that. In a few weeks you will see the rewards."[22]

Smith then pulled back and sat on a folding chair as he watched the heavier weights grunt and tug in full flight. "Some coaches won't test their teams at this point of the season. But if I'm not on their ass this time of year, if I start getting soft, that's a danger sign. It probably means I have slacked off, and they are quitting in practice. They're not giving me and themselves that 100%. They're not coming in on tough days when their body is down and tired and they're not pushing through it."[23]

Smith then moved to a corner and spoke with a coaching colleague who dropped in to observe practice. "I like to concentrate on situations you're likely to be in during a match. If you wrestle thirty to forty matches during a season, you're likely to be in certain situations during many if not most of those matches. All the moves we've covered in those situations are techniques we've broken down and taught over the last few weeks through slow, methodical repetition and analysis. We also use situational drills to reinforce things we have gone over during the past few weeks. Many of our drills begin in situations where guys are in the down position, and are poised to score an escape or a reversal. The toughest position for young wrestlers coming into the program is in the bottom position. It's a tougher area to teach. It's more of an attitude than anything."[24]

Smith then gathered around the center of the mat as he demonstrated the technical fine-print of a Cowboy staple, scoring off the single leg takedown. Morgan served as his guinea pig. "On a single leg when they sprawl and we're against the upper leg, that's wrestling. That's a man's world. If you can't score from this position, you're going to have a hard time winning a lot of matches. We're not going to hit a smooth shot every time. We have to master the scramble position. Who's going to win! I'm going to wrestle until I put the points on the board. A lot of you just settle in and accept a stalemate. The reason...you don't want to wrestle hard. You don't want to wrestle a complete match. A complete match means sometimes we're in a bad position. We get in positions we don't want to be in. You give me a guy who can win those situations and I'll give you a national champion. Bottom line, we've got to win these positions. We can't stop and settle for a stalemate. I can't tell you how many times I saw this in the Olympics. Guys willing to give the second and third effort. Never giving up. Never admitting it's over."[25] He blew his whistle, walked to the wall where his notebook rested, and checked off an item near the bottom of a long list, then announced the final drill of the day—short bursts in which the bottom wrestler exploded from the neutral position. "When you're on bottom, you need to feel like you're under water and you have to come up for air, some way, some how. That's what Mocco does."[26] Smith looked at a certain middleweight not known for his ability to escape, "You've been drowned for two years."[27] Laughter erupted and a smile creased Smith's face.

Smith then announced the pivot point on which all revolved, the "12-minute conditioning drill" lengthened to 13 minutes after the Cowboy coach heard someone voice a complaint. The team gathered around Smith on the middle mat and began, on his whistle, to run in place for 60 seconds. Then they took the standing position and worked on maintaining their wrestling stance, head up and rear down, while hearts thumped and knees buckled. Next they assumed a neutral position with their lead leg in front, again practicing proper form while teetering on exhaustion. Then more running in place as sweaty shirts were peeled off and thrown to the mat. Then more running in place while climbing the ladder as the arms climbed the wrung of an imaginary ladder each time a step was taken, with elbows churning vigorously above the shoulders. Then the stagger and sprawl drill where the wrestlers, on Smith's whistle, simulated 10-15 times per minute the defensive technique of thrusting the legs back from the standing position and turning quickly into the neutral position. Then more running in place while "climbing the ladder." Then the bridging drill, where wrestlers spun their bodies 360 degrees, like a top, with only their head and balls of their feet touching the mat. Then the hip-heist extension, a defensive move that required the wrestler to rotate the hips rapidly into a balanced defensive position. Then the tortuous wall-crawl designed to "build those back muscles," where the wrestler stood three feet away from the wall, faced outward toward the center of the mat, and with his palms placed against the wall behind the head, methodically walked his hands down the wall toward the mat, slowly forming the body into an inverted pretzel. A chorus of grunts and muffled screams filled the room as the steamed and lathered wrestlers then straightened the pretzel by walking their sweaty hands back up the mat to a standing position. This was done 15 times. Then two sets of 20 on the 10-station pull-up bar, as shoulders seemed to burn and smoke like overheated engines. Smith stood among the wrestlers and admonished them to assist their teammates as men dropped to the floor, signaling the end of the workout. The room then grew quiet as most lurched to the locker room. Most had lost between five and 10 pounds of water weight, and had burned up to 5,000 calories over the previous two hours. A few paired up with a teammate or assistant for more work. One performed a continuous stream of pushups as others staggered to the lockers.

Coach Smith roamed the room and approached individual wrestlers or small groups of wrestlers, speaking softly, listening more than talking, sometimes placing a hand on a shoulder and making eye contact. He then sat mat-side in a folding chair as team members filed by, handing over exam times so practices could be scheduled around academic responsibilities. "Prepare for your tests and quizzes. Don't leave anything undone. If you can turn a B into an A, get it done. We've had a good semester academically. Let's don't fall short now."[28] After showering, the younger wrestlers did not walk out of the locker room door that led directly outside, but exited by circling down a hall and passing through the wrestling room so they could file by Coach Smith, who sat on a folding chair reviewing practice notes. On the road Smith is accessible. Kids and adults approach him for autographs and handshakes in gymnasiums and restaurants everywhere his team travels, and his sense of vulnerability and approachability reaches his wrestlers.

At 7:00 p.m. Smith walked across the mat, screwed down the lid on another practice, and tightened it shut. Suddenly he bent over, picked something up, and said softly to no one in particular, "Stop throwing cups on the floor. I have to clean every day."[29] He then whispered to himself, "At the end of the year I want a group of true believers."[30]

Practice was over, but the lights remained on for another two hours as one lonely and desperate wrestler continued to drill and jog around the inside of the wrestling room.

Cowboys call no man master.

—Theodore Roosevelt (1858-1919)

thirteen

missouri, oregon and oregon state

02.05.05

CROWDS AT COLLEGE WRESTLING matches are a different lot.

Most of the fans are graduates of the colleges they support and have been involved in the sport most of their lives. Many are former wrestlers. Perhaps their talents were limited and they did not compete beyond high school but they know their sport and regret misplacing their silver and bronze medals draped with frayed ribbons from seasons long ago. Many of the middle-aged men are flat-bellied, but they move forward with a slight limp. Some have ears filled with gristle that peep from their heads like flesh-bubbles. A small lady, well into retirement, and dressed in pink, with a cane leaning against her orange molded-plastic chair, screams to Rosholt, "Squeeze him till he pops, Jake." They know the names of the holds and maneuvers. They lean and jerk and convulse in their chairs as their heroes strain for position.

Those who are not graduates of the school or former wrestlers them-selves are family members of the competitors, both starters and backups, who drove in from across the nation to watch the rituals of combat and heartbreak. They know the names, records, academic majors, hometowns, and parents of the wrestlers. Mothers and brothers hold hand-held video recorders and sit scattered near the mat. They know which Cowboy has a girlfriend and can recite the current won-loss records of the Cowboys' opponents. Many address the referee by first name and admonish him like

College wrestling fans tend to be knowledgeable and intense. *Courtesy Mika Matzen.*

he was a wayward nephew who spilled grandmother's cherry cobbler at a holiday meal.

There are no hospitality tents where industrialists entertain clients. Politicians and judges do not nonchalantly announce their intention to be present in hopes they might be publicly introduced. Fans often come alone. Few overweight fans are found balancing platters of nachos and waddling to their seats. Young professionals do not come dressed up, they go home first and change into jeans. Middle-age men do not wear baseball hats backwards and talk into cell phones or gaze and wave gleefully into red-lit television cameras. Highway patrolmen do not escort television announcers to their center-court pulpit of wires, laptops and microphones. Students do not paint their faces. Peculiarly, after a home dual match in Stillwater, a large number of the fans make their way down to the floor.

The encounters carry the tone and feel of a family reunion. The seasons fold over, and time is marked. They are glad John Smith is their coach, they like that he dresses and acts like a gentleman, even when admonishing an official, and that he came home to take the torch and carry it forward. Ironically, they seem to be gentle. More than anything, they appear to be at home. They are comfortable being at a wrestling match, and they are here to watch wrestling.

This weekend they came to Stillwater to see two dual matches, for visitors from Missouri and Oregon were in town. The Cowboys had returned from Iowa the previous Saturday morning, took Sunday off, and began workouts again on Monday. The break was a welcomed one-week respite from bus rides, hotel living, and cutting weight in foreign lands. The upcoming weekend featured three home duals in two days. On Friday night Missouri visited Stillwater, while on Saturday the Cowboys played host to Oregon and Oregon State. The days in the wrestling room leading up to those dual meets constituted the first consecutive stretch of tough workouts in several days for the travel-weary Cowboys.

It was a time for intensive teaching and brutal conditioning, with attention given to escaping and riding. Smith strode across the mat in black sweatpants and an orange t-shirt. He stood his ground before his team, which was assembled in a large circle around the center mat. "If a guy knows how to ride me, he can be dangerous. If I give him 40 seconds of riding time, he is controlling the pace of the match. I can't let him control the pace of the match. I must control the pace. More than anything, getting out from the bottom position is a matter *of attitude*. If you don't have this attitude, son, somewhere down the road you'll get ridden out and it will break your heart. *Break your heart.* My fear is that some of you don't understand this attitude. I don't care if you're in a bad position. I don't care if he has an arm bar in, or has a leg or two in. You have to work out of it. If they can't ride you they can't beat you. Getting out is a skill. You know the skill. Go do it! The key is your first move off the whistle. If you make the initial move and transition that into chain wrestling, creating the action and going from one move to the other, you will break their confidence. That's why some of you are building three minutes of riding time in your matches. They make the first move, you stop it, and they quit." Smith points to his stomach. "It's guts under here, guys. It's all about guts."[1]

In several matches thus far a select few of Smith's wrestlers were ridden out in crucial situations, particularly in the final period when offensive points were needed to preserve victories. This rankled Smith. "When I'm on top, from an attitude standpoint it's all about demeanor; from a technical standpoint it's all about stopping their first move. There will be situations where you will be in a match and you will need to hold someone down for 15 seconds or 30 seconds to win. Pendleton and Mocco have mastered this, and it comes from a total commitment to holding your opponent down."[2]

Mocco's eyes brighten as Smith steps toward him. "Steve, is it tougher to hold someone down or to get away?"

"Hold someone down."

"Damn right, it's a lot tougher. You've got to build those forearms and develop that endurance so that when we ride them out for a minute and a half, we are recovered and ready to kick someone's ass on our feet."

"Remember when you rode that guy out, Steve?"

Mocco looked momentarily perplexed. "I've ridden everyone out, Coach." Giggles and gut-laughs floated across the wrestling room.

"No, I mean the Minnesota match where you rode him out to win in overtime. Thirty seconds of hard riding. Changing off. Chain wrestling. Boom, boom, boom." Mocco nodded slightly as if the image came to life.

"Sometimes we intend to bust our opponent down and ride him out, but he makes the first move and we just let him up. Don't sell out! If you decide you want to ride someone out, make him earn the escape. Don't let him walk away like he's taking a stroll. Make him earn the point. If we chose to ride, we should be riding. The only way he comes out is if he earns it with his blood and sweat."[3]

Smith's voice softens. "I don't question our ability to get the tough takedown. I want us to grow to the point that we also dominate on the bottom. We get the escape. We turn 'em. If we do that they know we're going to win, because we're going to beat them on their feet. We know it, and they damn sure know it."[4]

Just as Kareem Abdul Jabbar redefined college basketball strategy in the 1970s by perfecting the dunk, OSU changed college wrestling in the

1950s and 1960s by taking their opponents down without impunity. The Cowboys racked up takedowns in such large numbers that the NCAA rules committee, attempting to neutralize OSU's dominance of the field, altered the rules so that only one point was awarded for a takedown except for the first one, which received the traditional two. The rule quickly reverted back, but the point was made—Oklahoma State teams would take you down. But over the next few years the Cowboys developed a reputation for excellence in mat wrestling as well.

This afternoon the Cowboys spent time drilling on the mat then pushed through three live matches and two sets of grueling sprints the length of the wrestling room. Smith then formed a small circle in the middle of the mat with freshman starters Coleman Scott, Nathan Morgan, and Clay Kehrer while others trudged to the locker room for showers. His tone was not severe, but rather like one offering directions to an uneasy traveler in a strange land on a cold and windy night. "Some will tell you this first year can be a year of getting good experience and getting your feet wet. They will tell you to learn the ropes and learn the system, and chalk your losses up to inexperience. They will tell you next year will be better. But you're not in the lineup to get experience for next year, you're wrestling to get experience for this year. The best experience for next year is to win now. Don't ever let anyone tell you differently. You can tuck these experiences away, think about them over the summer and come back resolved not to do them again. Or you can wrestle like champions today."[5] Smith continued to make eye contact with his young wrestlers as they sat motionless, sweat dripping from their brows and cheeks into soaked sweatshirts. "I'm not griping at you. I just want you to know what it's going to take when March rolls around. That's when the champions are crowned."[6]

After the meeting Kehrer went on to the locker room but Scott and Morgan lingered to talk to Coach Smith. They did that whenever they could. They lingered after practice to talk to their head coach about their lives both on and off the mat. Scott encouraged his coach to watch "ultimate fighting" on Monday evening television. "No gouging. No hitting below the waist. Just lots of fighting. The winner gets a contract."[7] Coach Smith, who seldom watched television, listened patiently, and then gave Coleman pointers on keeping his skin healthy and sanitized.

"Use Ivory. You have oily skin. I had it too. It'll suck all that oil out of your skin. Use it on your body too."

"Not on my body. I use face wash."

"You use face wash on your body?"

"Yea."

"Have you always been that way? Even at home?"

"Yea."

Smith continues his kidding. "Are you ready to wrestle this weekend?"

"Yea."

"I thought about just wrestling you just one match."

Coleman Scott's eyes widened. "Are you kidding? After a week of freaking practice and I wrestle just one day?"

Smith laughed playfully as Nathan Morgan walked up. A lanky blond-haired Californian, a surfboard had more body fat than Morgan, who constantly fretted about his weight.

"What did you eat today?"

"Four egg whites and four English muffins after I lifted weights at seven."

"Why did you have egg whites?"

"They were in the buffet line."

"That's a big breakfast."

Morgan looked guilty. "Yea?"

"You ate every one of them?"

Morgan looked stricken. "Yea."

"That's a big breakfast."

"Yea."

"You don't need eggs. Make sure you get lots of carbs."

"Yea."

"Eat a bowl of chili and beans."

"I had one. It's seven ounces."

"That's a lot."

"Yea."

"It's okay being a pound over eating like that."

"I'm eating more and I'm less thirsty."

"You're eating more?"

"Yea."

Smith wanted Morgan to eat more balanced meals and snack less. "Eat meat twice a week. Maybe three times a week. When I wrestled I was complete carbs. Never ate meat. Ever. Every now and then I would have eggs. Once a week. Scrambled eggs with cheese. Those carbs do miracles. Now that you're weight's under control you can take in twenty-five hundred calories and still be losing weight."

"I've got to go see my tutor in a minute…what should I eat tonight?"

"Go to the cafeteria and eat a big belly full of pasta. They close at 7:30."

Morgan stepped back. "I'll go to Fazolis and have some spaghetti."

"You still have money left?"

"Yea."

"Eat a big plate of spaghetti and some red sauce. When you eat more you work out harder."

"Yea."

As Morgan and Scott walked out, Smith stood up to leave the wrestling after a typical 12-hour day. Before heading home he dropped by the high school gym to watch his son's 50-member youth wrestling team work out. He glared at his two freshmen as they turned the corner, and a sparkle came to his eyes. "Go to little league practice with me, guys. Give something back to the sport."

They both continue to edge toward the door as Coleman looked over his shoulder. "I have to go see my tutor."

Morgan followed behind. "Me too. I'm 15 minutes late."

Smith grinned again. "Give back, son. Give back. Go help the little kids."

"I have to see my tutor."

Smith waved them off and asked Morgan one last time. "What's your weight?"

"One over." They turned and left the room.[8]

Making weight is the wrestler's most feared adversary. Smith spent an inordinate amount of time each day counseling his team about healthy weight management, and constantly monitored their progress. "Managing weight is such a delicate balance. Water levels need to be perfect. The allotment between carbs and proteins has to be maintained. If I were wrestling today I would want to leave practice every day down to weight. Every Day.

I want to work out at the weight I'm going to wrestle. Working out at the weight you're going to compete at is vital."[9]

Nothing distinguished wrestling from other college sports more than the constant burden of weight control. For years, the ravenous athletes spent days melting off body fat and liquid before they weighed in a full 24 hours before competition began. The wrestler then had a full day to replenish his starved and dehydrated system. It was not uncommon for a wrestler to weigh 170 on Monday, make weight at 150 on Thursday, only to see his weight balloon up 20 pounds to 170 again by match-time on Friday. This process played particular havoc on visiting teams, for they were sometimes forced to travel with stationary bikes and workout equipment. If the equipment could not be transported, the team sought out a workout facility at their hotel or at a nearby health club. Carpet floors were preferred, for cheap carpet discreetly absorbed the gallons of sweat generated by a team of 10.

Each wrestler's method of weight management was personal and unique. Johny Hendricks, who believed that fluid-management has cost him at his first NCAA tournament a year earlier, had the process down to an exact science. "I drink three pounds of liquid each workout. I stack six Gatorade cups on the windowsill in the wrestling room. I keep tabs on how many cups I drink during a practice, and how many pounds I work off. Like at today's practice I drank 48 ounces, but I worked off eight pounds, so I drank another two pounds so I would feel better before I went home."[10] The previous year "I was so young and naïve. I drank too many liquids, water, everything, I didn't listen to coach [Smith] and it came back to bite me at nationals."[11]

Wrestlers took these extreme measures for several reasons. To qualify at a lower weight provided a competitive advantage against shorter and smaller wrestlers.[12] Some were unable to defeat a teammate at their optimum weight, so they dropped to a lower weight class in order to break into the lineup. Occasionally, coaches directed a wrestler to move down a weight in order to strengthen the team's effectiveness.

In Smith's day wrestlers used various methods to make weight. They fasted, restricted fluid intake, ran or jogged, utilized exercise devices such as stair climbers and stationery bicycles, wore air-tight rubber suits, sat in saunas and hot boxes, or induced vomiting and utilized diuretics and laxatives.[13] It was common for a wrestler to pull on layers of sweat clothing over an air-tight rubber suit, tape the wrists and ankles tight so hot air would not escape and work out for hours in a heated wrestling room or sauna. After practice, the wrestler removed the tape and watched as warm, salty sweat poured out from the sleeves like a water balloon bursting.

But everything changed in 1997. That season three college wrestlers, attempting to lose an average of eight pounds over a three to 12-hour period, put on rubber suits and exercised vigorously in steam rooms. They had each already lost approximately 20 pounds. Michigan's Jeff Reese, attempting to shed 17 pounds to qualify at 150 pounds, worked out for two hours in a rubber suit in a 92-degree room. He died of kidney failure and heart malfunction. Wisconsin-La Crosse's Joseph La Rosa was wearing a rubber suit and riding a stationary bike when he collapsed and died. Campbell University's Billy Saylor sustained a fatal heart attack while riding a stationary bike during a pre-dawn workout.[14]

The NCAA responded to public outcry and instituted several changes. Weight categories were increased by seven pounds, except for the heavyweight class, which was increased by 10 pounds. Weight allowances during the regular season were no longer permitted. The wrestler's body fat and hydration level were measured early in the season and then factored into a formula which determined how much weight a wrestler would be permitted to drop. This process put an end to the enticement to dump weight at the end of the season. Weigh-ins were moved closer in time to the match, one hour for duals and two hours for tournaments. The use of rubber suits was banned, as well as harmful dehydration practices such as laxatives, emetics, diuretics, self-induced vomiting, hot rooms, hot boxes, saunas and steam rooms.

The changes worked. No fatalities related to weight loss had been reported since their enactment. Coach Smith commented on the effect of the rules the year after they were instituted. "I think it's probably been one of the most enjoyable years for athletes as well as coaches that I've been a part of. You've got athletes enjoying the sport much more because the weight issue has really been eliminated by the new rules."[15] In the years since the rule changes, Smith remained in favor of the renewed emphasis on proper training methods. "The rule changes place a healthy discipline on the wrestler. The focus was no longer on losing weight, but rather on finding a healthy, appropriate weight class and then training in a disciplined and consistent manner. It is a life-long lesson for these young men on weight management rather than weight loss."[16]

But weight control remained the bane of wrestlers' day-to-day lives. From the coaches' perspective, no issue received more attention. It remained one variable where coaches did not hold the cards. They conducted practices, taught technique, lectured on weight management, and established weight-management programs. But on the day before the match, when the parched and hungry wrestler returned to his room after a brutal practice, opened the refrigerator and stared ahead as cold beads of moisture rolled down a chilled bottle of Gatorade, no authority figures were around. The wrestler controlled his own destiny, and the coach was at his mercy.

Thirst and hunger dominated the wrestler's existence. With the practiced touch of a restaurant connoisseur, wrestlers knew, to the half-ounce, the weight of a broiled chicken breast. They understood even the emptiest stomach could not tolerate more than two to three pounds of solid food, but a two-pound liter of water could be quaffed in moments. They believed in urban legends about weighing in—that to curl ones toes, or to stand on one's head before climbing on the scales, or to breathe out as one stood on the scales, would contribute to registering a lower weight. They possessed a sophisticated knowledge of dieting, and favored lean meat, fish, and pasta washed down with small amounts of water. They knew to the minute how many minutes of drilling or live wrestling would burn one pound. Their favorite year in the program was often their redshirt season, where they returned to practice after holiday break with bloated faces and swollen stomachs. They checked their weight with the frequency of adolescent girls glancing at a mirror. They claimed with pure sincerity, "Nothing is better than taking a cold drink right after you pull weight."[17] They knew how many calories one tough workout would burn—as many as 5,000—and they knew to miss one practice could make their weight go sky-high overnight. They constantly worried about their weight, and some had to eat

5,000 calories a day to maintain there weight. They were always hungry. At times they suffered.

Coach John Smith began weighing in as a fourth-grader. In the ensuing 17 years he weighed in hundreds of times, and he never failed to make weight. His last official weigh-in was in Barcelona, Spain, hours before his 1992 gold medal match. He has not stepped on a set of scales since that day. Not once.

* * *

The Cowboys worked hard on Tuesday and Wednesday, then tapered off Thursday in preparation for the Missouri match Friday night. Johny Hendricks, sitting out the evening's match as he recovered from a hamstring injury, battled a migraine headache as he worked out with Ryan Davis.

A carpenter was in the wrestling room calculating where to hang the newly- framed pictures of the 206 Oklahoma State All-American wrestlers. There simply was not enough wall space. Moments later the gravely serious Missouri team filed in and asked for directions to the scales.

The Missouri Tigers, long time mired in the middle tier of Big 8 Conference wrestling ladder, had, through upgrades in coaching, facilities, recruiting, and financial commitment by the university developed into a solid and competitive national wrestling presence since the formation of the Big 12 Conference in 1996. Coached by Brian Smith, a highly successful assistant coach at Cornell, where he regularly attracted top recruiting classes without providing scholarships, for Ivy League schools did not offer athletic scholarships. The Tigers had improved their final NCAA tournament finish for five consecutive years, and had finished 13th the previous year. The previous November the wrestling team accomplished arguably its most significant athletic victory since the Missouri basketball team defeated number one-ranked Kansas in 1997 when they stunned top-ranked Oklahoma State 21-17, handing the defending national champion Cowboys their first loss in 24 duals. Wrestling in a high school gym in St. Louis, the Tigers broke a 29-match losing streak to OSU that dated back to the 1928-1929 season. This year's team, ranked 13th in the nation with a 13-3 dual record, returned four NCAA qualifiers, including two All-Americans, and landed a top-10 recruiting class. Missouri's most accomplished wrestler was Ben Askren, who had defeated Chris Pendleton in the Big 12 finals before meeting Pendleton in the NCAA championship match, which Pendleton won 11-4. This dual in Stillwater would mark the seventh time the two wrestlers had met. Pendleton and Askren were ranked one-two in the nation, and their rivalry was arguably the most durable and highest quality in the country.

As the team warmed up in the wrestling room before the match, Johny Hendricks sat on a folding chair in baggy pants and a t-shirt, still recovering from his headache. Smith was cautious in putting Hendricks back out. "With Hendricks, it's not a question of whether he can go or not. He had a couple of things that needed to get healed up [last week], and we were able to take the time to do it."[18]

Coach Branch barked a warm-up cadence to Pendleton for 10 minutes on the far mat as the Cowboy prepared for his second meeting with Askren this year. "Shoot. Sprawl. Stance." [19]

Pendleton wiped sweat from his brow with a white towel, then tossed it aside when Smith stepped to the center of the mat, a signal that match-time was impending.

"Get your stuff on."[20]

ABOVE: Jake Rosholt works for control against Missouri's Jeff Foust. *Courtesy Mika Matzen.*

LEFT: Headgear askew, Zack Esposito waits for a stalemate call in his 12-2 victory over Orlando Perez of Oregon State. *Courtesy Mika Matzen.*

With this command the Cowboys who were not already dressed dropped their sweats and slipped on their singlets under the black tops and bottoms. Coleman Scott was frowning. After a brutal week of practice he learned today that Missouri would forfeit at 125.

"I was ready to wrestle. I focused all week."[21] Daniel Frishkorn stretched and ran laps after learning he would get the starting nod over Ronnie Delk, who quietly slipped out of the arena and drove home to deal with the heartfelt pain of not being chosen for the evening's dual. Smith then walked over to Morgan and admonished him to be aggressive, and then walked slowly and solemnly to the hallway leading out of the room and methodically but firmly began clapping his hands together as a signal. Pendleton took the cue. After the team prayer the squad filed out without fanfare or speech and into the cheers of 3,000 Cowboy wrestling faithful.

Kevin Ward kicks from the grasp of Missouri's Brad Celeski and gains an escape point. *Courtesy Mika Matzen.*

LEFT: Daniel Frishkorn rings up a technical fall against Missouri's Chris McCormick. *Courtesy Mika Matzen.*

RIGHT: Steve Mocco stomps off the mat after pinning Missouri's Chase Wetenkamp in 32 seconds. *Courtesy Jim Bowen.*

OSU avenged the previous year's defeat by trouncing Missouri 31-9. Murderer's Row, absent Johny Hendricks, racked up two major decisions and a fall, and Chris Pendleton gave up a late reversal, but moving on his feet like a kite blowing in a high wind, posted a methodical 4-3 victory over his nemesis Ben Askren. After the match Smith spoke into a cluster of microphones about Pendleton's victory. He focused on his 174-pounder riding Askren out almost the entire third period. "It was one of those matches where [Pendleton] found himself riding a little longer than usual. You have to go with what's working, and I think he knew where he was at the end. He decided to ride him out and gave up the reversal, which you shouldn't do. I would have liked a 4-1 win instead of 4-3."[22]

Three Cowboys lost. Kevin Ward posted two escapes in losing 5-2. Sam Lewnes earned one reverse in dropping a 7-2 decision. Clay Kehrer, who

ABOVE: Texan Clay Kehrer became only the third starter in Cowboy history to hail from the Lone Star State. *Courtesy Dr. Jeremy Cook*

managed two escapes in a 3-2 squeaker, penetrated deep on a single-leg late in the match, but could not complete the move. Coach Smith recognized Kehrer's effort but measured his compliment with a dose of reality. "Clay Kehrer did a lot in the third period, but we need that in the first."[23] These three Cowboys did not score a single takedown in 21 minutes of wrestling. Their only offensive points came in the form of Lewnes' reversal.

Kehrer's loss dropped his record to 12-12. The redshirt freshman from Texas faced a series of older, stronger, more experienced, nationally ranked opponents over the past several weeks. The noise and fury created by Murderer's Row often had been interrupted by the struggles of only the third Texan ever to break into a Cowboy wrestling lineup.

Texas-bred Clay Kehrer spent his childhood with his brother and sister riding bikes, wakeboards, and jet skis on the lake adjacent to his home. Self-admittedly "too fat for basketball,"[24] Clay related how his mother noticed a flyer at the local YMCA publicizing a junior wrestling clinic. Clay attended and was hooked. In Rockwall, Texas football is king, and when his high school football coach demanded that he give up wrestling to participate in off-season football drills, Kehrer relinquished a promising career as a linebacker for the Yellow Jackets and put all of his chips on wrestling.

Wrestling is the fastest-growing sport in Texas, and good coaching is difficult to find. So Clay bought the John Smith instructional videos, cleared out his family's living room furniture, and went to work. The video tapes were excellent tools in demonstrating technique, but he needed a real-live mentor against whom he could learn and test his burgeoning skills. Clay sought out OSU and Olympic wrestling great Kenny Monday, a freelance wrestling coach working in the Dallas area and a teammate with John Smith on the collegiate and Olympic level. "Coach Monday

BELOW: Clay Kehrer controls Oregon State's Dan Pitsch on his way to a 2-0 victory. One of the winningest high school wrestlers in Texas' young wrestling history, Kehrer sought out former OSU great Kenny Monday for instruction in the Dallas area. *Courtesy Mika Matzen.*

helped me mold myself into what I wanted to become. My development was slow, but by my senior year my growth had progressed exponentially. He helped shape me."[25]

Kehrer went 93-0 over his last two years of high school competition, with 73 wins coming by fall. He was a four-time Texas All-Stater and a high-school All-American.

Because of his success in national tournaments his junior year in a weight where the Cowboys needed an infusion of potential, Kehrer appeared on Smith's highly discriminating recruiting radar. Clay received several division one scholarship offers, but after taking a recruiting visit to Stillwater he decided on OSU, and Smith sealed the deal with a trip to Texas.

Official Pat Fitzgerald looks on as Clay Kehrer struggles to control Oregon State's Dan Pitsch. *Courtesy Mika Matzen.*

ABOVE: Kevin Ward applies an efficient leg-ride. Head-first is Tony Hook of Oregon State. *Courtesy Mika Matzen.*

During his redshirt season Kehrer grew homesick and disillusioned as he was drubbed in the Cowboy's star-studded wrestling room day after day by older and more experienced wrestlers. But opportunity seemed to knock when national champion Jake Rosholt received permission from Coach Smith to move up a weight class, leaving a 184 spot in the lineup up for grabs.

His competition included veteran front-runner Rusty Blackmon, a high school star from Cleveland, Tennessee who placed second at the Big 12 Championships and qualified for the NCAA tournament the previous season, winning three matches, two by fall, before being eliminated. But Blackmon, who had been hobbled by a knee injury in the later portion of the season, had not been able to carry forward his promising 2004 performance from the previous year. Also competing for the spot was Jack Jensen from Sheboygan, Wisconsin, a workout partner turned bitter rival who beat Kehrer in the Omaha Open tournament weeks earlier, but whom Kehrer

LEFT: Kansas high school champion Brett Munson, substituting for an injured Johny Hendricks, works for position against Oregon State's Matt Ellis. *Courtesy Mika Matzen.*

BELOW: Jake Rosholt racks up back points against Oregon State's Gardner. *Courtesy Mika Matzen.*

UPPER RIGHT: Ronnie Delk plants a textbook double leg takedown in his 11-6 victory over Tim Norman of Oregon State. *Courtesy Mika Matzen.*

defeated in ranking matches on two occasions. They also occasionally traded punches in the wrestling room.

Knowing a steadfast spirit is needed as competition heats up both in the wrestling room and against outside competition, Kehrer was gratified he had reached the maturity level to satisfy the high standards his father set for him. "I've gotten to the point [where] I'm setting my own standards. I've gotten to the point where it's not him pushing me but me pushing myself in wrestling, school, and life."[26]

Kehrer entered OSU as a business major with hopes of returning to Texas to join his father in business. He had since switched his major to mechanical engineering, a discipline which suited the lanky, dark-haired, strapping Texan's penchant for working on cars, motorcycles, and all machines that go fast. "Mechanical engineering is a whole new world. I have to prioritize what is important to me. If I have calculus homework due on Friday, and it's Wednesday, I can't devote everything to wrestling because someday it won't be there."[27]

He reflected on a recent turning point in his growth as a person and student-athlete. "This past November and December I had a lot of emotional and mental growth. I know what I want to do in life, and I know what it will take to be successful."[28]

Coach Smith's comments before the Missouri match underscored his intention to keep Kehrer in the lineup as OSU entered the final stretch toward post-season competition. "Clay Kehrer is our starter and always has been. We've chosen to wrestle a couple of guys there for one reason or another, but my mind hasn't changed [on Kehrer] at all."[29] But the Texan's only chance to qualify for the NCAA tournament would be to place at the Big 12 Championships, where four nationally-ranked wrestlers competed in his weight. He had yet to defeat any of them this season. In a few weeks he would have his opportunity. But for now, Oregon and Oregon State waited in the wings.

Oregon State possessed a rich wrestling heritage. Their former coach, Dale Thomas, was the all-time winningest college coach in college wrestling history with 616 dual-match victories between 1957 and 1990. The Beavers had captured 45 conference titles and were twice runner-up in the NCAA tournament. Eight of their wrestlers had captured NCAA titles. They were the westernmost outpost of college wrestling and remained the only school beyond the Rockies to ever have hosted the NCAA championships. Currently coached by Joe Wells, his teams had roller-coasted since he took over in 1993. Their 1995 squad finished second. The 2004 team finished 42nd. This year's team came into the OSU match 9-6-1 in duals. They had never defeated the Cowboys in a dual match, and the Cowboy's performance on Saturday afternoon continued the streak.

The Cowboys won nine of the 10 matches and trounced Oregon State 40-4. The only Beaver to register a win was a former Cowboy wrestler who transferred to Oregon State in 2001. Pendleton and Mocco recorded falls. Scott and Esposito won major decisions. Rosholt earned a technical fall, while Delk, Ward, and Kehrer won by decision.

The Oregon Ducks entered the match with a 5-7 dual record, never having defeated Cowboys in 12 previous dual matches. Their best NCAA finish under coach Chuck Kearney, an Oregon All-American in 1988, was 24th in 2001-2002. They had won 30 All-American honors since 1958. Former Cowboy four-time All-American Ricky Stewart, an assistant coach for the Ducks, received enthusiastic applause when introduced before the match began.

It was virtually the most applause any Duck would receive, as the Cowboys won their 13th straight victory against Oregon, 46-6. Coleman

Scott and Clay Kehrer won by major decision. Frishkorn earned a pin in 46 seconds and ran off the mat under Delk's careful gaze. Backup B.J. Jackson was one of several multiple state champions in the OSU wrestling room who could not break into the starting lineup, but could have started at top programs across the country. Jackson was perhaps the best athlete on the team. The son of a minister, he returned kickoffs and took handoffs

Redshirt freshman B. J. Jackson, the son of a minister and a two-time high school state champion, provided solid backup in the middle weights when starters went down with injuries during the rugged season.
Courtesy Oklahoma State University.

from Heisman Trophy winner Jason White, a high school teammate at Tuttle High School. Having spent much of his life working cattle and ranching, he lived in the dorm for a semester, but plead claustrophobia to Smith, who let him move outside Stillwater, where he lived alone in a mobile home. He enjoyed spending evenings spotting animals with a spotlight. This night he pinned his opponent with one second left in the first period for his first win as a varsity Cowboy. As the official slapped his hand to the mat signaling the fall, Coach Smith raised his hands in the air in triumph, as if he had just witnessed a son ride a bike for the first time. Jackson, hardly the passive sort, was a fire protection major who hunted, fished, rode horses, played golf, snow skied, and water skied in his spare time. After the victory he ran across the mat like a seasoned pro and shook Coach Kearney's hand before he returned to the Cowboy bench. His parents beamed.

Pendleton won by technical fall, and Kehrer cruised to a major decision. Rosholt and Mocco earned pins, but Rosholt's win was the most notable of the night.

Oregon's best wrestler, Scott Barker, a transfer from Missouri, faced Jake Rosholt at 197. Barker had defeated Rosholt in the 2003 Big 12 tournament while wrestling for Missouri, but Rosholt came back to crush Barker in the national finals to claim his first NCAA title. This match was an opportunity for Barker to gain revenge before Rosholt's home crowd, and he started well against the hobbled Rosholt with a first-period take-down. But Rosholt erupted with 16 points in two periods before pinning Barker in the final period. It was red meat wrestling. After the fall was signaled Rosholt rose to his feet, raised his hand in triumph, made the sign of number one, and acknowledged no one he swaggered away from his teammates and coaches to sit in isolation. After recovering he spoke to the media. "I knew I was going to go out and go hard and not make any mistakes," Rosholt said. "Everybody in the country will have a hard time going at my pace."[30]

After the match Coach Kearney offered his respects for the Cowboy squad. "Right now, you've got to think Oklahoma State is the team. Their young guys at 125 and 133 look like seasoned veterans. Both will be big-time players in March."[31]

Johny Hendricks, still recovering from injuries and not wrestling for the fifth consecutive match, took Coach Smith's advice to upgrade his wardrobe while sitting on the Cowboy bench. During this match he was dressed like a young stockbroker in a stylish blue dress shirt and matching blue tie.

Fans gathered on the floor after the match. They lingered, talking until the lights were dimmed. No one wanted to leave.

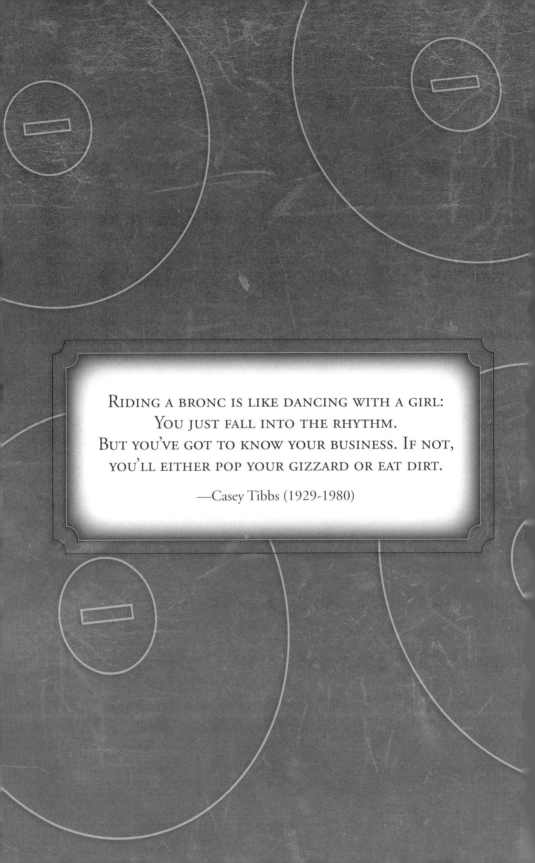

RIDING A BRONC IS LIKE DANCING WITH A GIRL:
YOU JUST FALL INTO THE RHYTHM.
BUT YOU'VE GOT TO KNOW YOUR BUSINESS. IF NOT,
YOU'LL EITHER POP YOUR GIZZARD OR EAT DIRT.

—Casey Tibbs (1929-1980)

fourteen

02.10.05

THE LAST TIME A NEBRASKA WRESTLING TEAM
defeated Oklahoma State in Lincoln, the United States was recovering from
World War I, the Lincoln Memorial was dedicated in Washington, D.C.,
and Walter Hagen captured the British Open. That was 1922.

Since then, the Cowboys had reeled off 44 wins over the Huskers, with
the only defeat coming in Stillwater in 1993 to a team depleted and dispirited by probation.

But as the Cowboys gathered at the Stillwater Municipal Airport on
a cold but sun-drenched Thursday morning for the 75-minute flight to
Lincoln to face the sixth-ranked team for an evening dual meet, the Huskers
thought this might be the year to end all years. They believed they could
beat the Cowboys.

The OSU team woke up early Thursday morning and traveled to the
airport in small clusters, traveling from various dorm rooms and rent houses
around campus where they waited for more than an hour before the chartered aircraft finally arrived. Forty-eight hours later, after returning from
Lincoln, the team would again depart for New York and Pennsylvania for
two grueling dual matches on Sunday. Smith and his staff spent countless
hours throughout the season with travel agents and airlines negotiating the
price of flights, for that line-item on his wrestling budget was significant.
Knowing that lineup changes were inevitable, most of the airlines allowed
Smith to change the name on tickets once per transaction. For the Nebraska

match the coaches decided to charter an aircraft so the wrestlers could return to Stillwater later Thursday night after the match at a reasonable hour, allowing them to rest in their own beds and avoid an all-night bus ride down Interstate 35. Thus, it was necessary to locate an airplane. That was not an easy task. A charter aircraft had been located earlier in the week, but it failed to pass the university travel policy. After the devastating plane crash four years earlier the OSU athletic department promulgated a detailed travel policy designed "…to provide a framework for safe and efficient athletic team travel."[1] The policy required the university's "aviation consultant" to verify that the aircraft and pilots met numerous standards in areas of pilot certification, aircraft maintenance, and operation. When the aircraft they located failed the mandatory inspection process, the coaches were back to the drawing board. If a plane could not be found that conformed to the required policies, a chartered bus would be required.

Coach Smith contacted Mike Holder, the OSU golf coach, whose team flies on time-share jets to its contests and tournaments, for assistance in locating a plane. An aircraft was found, but it too failed to pass inspection. Coach Smith then located, through a chartering service, a 40-seat Boeing turboprop that planned to be flying in the area. The charter company agreed to deliver the wrestlers to Lincoln before traveling on to Illinois State University the following day to pick up a women's basketball team. The aircraft and crew would wait in Lincoln for the match to conclude and return the squad to Stillwater for a full night's rest. The aircraft and pilots met policy requirements, and the bus trip was avoided.

While waiting for the plane to arrive, several wrestlers stretched out across the small chairs in the lobby area while others walked about, occasionally staring into the bright clear sky for the plane to drop down and deliver them to Lincoln. Junior 125-pounder Derek Stevens, inserted in the lineup to replace the injured Coleman Scott, was feverishly studying for an immunology exam while fighting off hunger pains. "I'm two to three hours away from being prepared [for the exam], but I'll be ready."[2] When Coleman Scott strained his elbow during practice earlier in the week, Stevens was given three short days to shed the requisite weight that had accumulated since his last competitive match. Even though the backup wrestlers at each weight stood only a slight chance of competing late in the season, they were required to keep their weight within striking distance in case a starter sustained an injury or could not travel due to academic responsibilities. Stevens looked up from his notes. "Losing the weight has been a distraction, but I can handle it."[3]

While Stevens crammed, pre-med major Daniel Frishkorn walked about the airport lobby and fretted about a physics lab the next morning. This was the seventh out-of-state trip taken so far this season by the Cowboys. Many of the team members, some of whom had never boarded an airplane before coming to college, would be seasoned travelers by the time their careers ended

As the plane appeared as a silver glint in the clear blue sky north of Stillwater, Smith called out seating assignments to the party of 22 scheduled to travel to Lincoln. He reminded everyone they would need a driver's license to board the aircraft, and walked across the tarmac toward the aircraft with his black notebook wedged under one arm. In each hand he carried a paper bag of wrapped gifts given to him by two of his four children, who joined their mother Toni in seeing the team off. Smith sat in his customary port side front, and looked across the aisle at Steve Mocco as the heavyweight conversed with the flight attendant about flight safety, finally asking, "If we crash, do seat belts do any good?"[4] During the flight Smith relaxed, made notes in his black notebook, read a magazine article on financing college education for children, and occasionally looked back at his team while they rested, listened to music, studied, or stared down on flat Kansas prairie, marked by non-linear section lines and patches of snow. Coach Branch walked down the aisle handing out to each wrestler and staff member per diem food money allowed by NCAA regulations.

It was twenty-four degrees and overcast when the aircraft touched down in snow-packed Lincoln seventy-five minutes after takeoff. The Cowboy contingent piled into two white vans and a rented Ford Tarus and headed toward campus for a weight check and drill. The match would be held at the 4,200-seat Nebraska Coliseum located in the center of campus in the shadows of the Nebraska football stadium, but Nebraska's wrestling room and coaches' offices were located in the 13,595-seat Bob Devaney Sports Center situated several miles off campus and named after the legendary Nebraska football coach and athletic director.

This pattern had developed in college wrestling—smaller gymnasiums and field houses, all constructed sometime before the Second World War, were retooled to host sports like wrestling, volleyball, and gymnastics. The arrangement worked out nicely, for the smaller wrestling crowds could be overwhelmed in a gigantic facility, but a rowdy crowd could shake the foundation of a more intimate, albeit antiquated venue and give the home team a distinct home-mat advantage.

After several minutes parking places were located for the vans adjacent to the Devaney Center, and the team walked through brown slush carrying its gear through a maze of tiled and lighted hallways. T-shirt clad Jake Rosholt, carrying a black cowboy hat in one hand and his equipment bag in the other, led the way. Bouncing balls, whistles and the unmistakable squeak of basketball shoes echoed toward the heavy white swinging doors of the Nebraska wrestling room. The wrestling facility was located adjacent to the giant red and white basketball arena, where the Nebraska men's basketball team was holding a closed practice in preparation for a home basketball game days later against the Cowboy basketball squad.

The Cowboys filed into the wrestling room and placed their black nylon bags against the wall while opposing coaches engaged in chitchat, and Randy Pogue slipped out to a local supermarket to purchase the pre-match groceries.

Nebraska was coached by fifth-year coach Mark Manning, a former Division II national champion who came to Nebraska in 2000 from Northern Iowa, where he had sparked a resurgence of that tradition-rich program back to national respectability. Manning's Nebraska teams had been solid competitors in the grueling Big 12 Conference. His squads had accomplished four consecutive top-15 finishes in the NCAA tournament, 13 wrestlers had achieved All-American status, and he had coached a national champion the previous season, one Jason Powell from Choctaw, Oklahoma. He had never defeated an OSU team, even during his stint as an assistant coach at Oklahoma University.

According to the Nebraska media guide, the Huskers seemed pleased with their decision in 2000 to hire Manning to lead their wrestling program. But their short list of potential candidates included at least one other nominee. On that short list in 2000 had been Oklahoma State coach John Smith.

Earlier in the day the *Lincoln Journal Star* posted in bold headlines the provocative question "How Close?" next to a half-page color picture of Smith standing in a blue suit delivering his trademark pumped fist during an OSU match. The story described how Nebraska courted Smith to become its wrestling coach five years earlier, and stated the Cowboy coach "considered becoming the Nebraska wrestling coach in 2000."[5] The Huskers were reeling from an NCAA investigation of their wrestling program when Nebraska associate athletic director Bob Burton, a former OSU athletic department staff member who had developed a friendship with Smith when both were in Stillwater, suggested Nebraska contact the Cowboy coach. "Who wouldn't want John Smith?" said Burton. "Smith was a great wrestler, a great coach, and had the highest international accomplishments in wrestling."[6]

Smith decided to listen. "I came up for an interview and I was impressed. The five things that I saw at Nebraska were great potential, a great administrative staff, a solid recruiting base, and strong conference and schedule to develop and attract top wrestlers and a budget."[7]

Nebraska's interest coincided with an arm-wrestling match between Smith and then-OSU athletic director Terry Don Phillips over the size of the Cowboy recruiting budget. Smith was expected to win national titles at Oklahoma State, and by 2000 the Cowboy title-drought had extended from 1993. Fans were beginning to grumble, but blue-chip wrestlers had to be recruited, and recruiting costs money. Even a tradition-rich program like OSU could no longer cherry-pick the top talent, and the OSU athletic department seemed to take for granted that Smith could gather national titles on a relatively low budget.

When he learned of Nebraska's interest, Smith spelled out his alternatives to Oklahoma State. Essentially, increase the recruiting budget or find another head coach. Phillips, who later became the athletic director at Clemson, found the funds that day to accommodate the wrestling program's needs. Smith withdrew his name from consideration, and expressed no regrets. "Nebraska hired a great coach and he has done a fabulous job. I don't know what would have happened if I left OSU. But I'm happy here and we're doing pretty well."[8]

The weigh-in took place in the Nebraska wrestling room, where plumbing rattled from the ceiling over two red practice mats, and a mural was painted on the far wall citing the top 10 NCAA finishes accomplished by Nebraska. Inside the dressing room next to the scales sat the Husker food table, which featured pears, blueberry muffins, and yogurt carefully arranged like pieces on a chessboard. Minutes before the weigh-in Frishkorn stood on the scales and gently clutched a ripened banana. After verifying he had made weight while holding the fruit, he stepped off the scales and slowly ate the small banana. Morgan stepped on the scales, noted he was a few ounces under, and asked if he could take a swig of water. Coach Smith looked on.

As competitors stepped off the scales, in the background empty cellophane wrappers dropped to the ground as wrestlers held their stomachs and let out loud and crisp belches. Each carried a different tone. All 20 wrestlers made weight without mishap, and the Cowboys loaded their gear to ride vans through slush and road construction to the NU Coliseum, which also served as a workout facility for the general student population. The Cowboys, walking quickly over the cold, concrete floor, dressed out in a giant, shabby basement locker room they shared with Nebraska students who were grabbing an afternoon workout or preparing to compete in an intramural sporting contest.

Minutes before the match began the Cowboys walked up a flight of stairs and down a darkened hallway into the arena. Smith stepped across television cables which lay across the floor and headed toward a media area to conduct an interview while his wrestlers made their way to the mat to begin their warm up. This evening's match would be nationally televised on a cable station that was sampling the college wrestling market in the Midwest.

The coliseum ceiling was rounded and fans sat in bleachers placed close to the mat, giving the brick venue a sense of intimacy and intensity. Former University of Oklahoma head football coach John Blake, then a popular assistant football coach at Nebraska, sat on the edge of the mat with his family, close enough to the action to shake a wrestler's hand.

The crowd of 3,442 took their seats as the Cowboys gathered behind a thick curtain in a public hallway located behind their chairs. Nebraska fans carrying boxes of popcorn and paper cups of soft drinks walked by and looked on curiously. Some offered greetings and disclaimers of good luck while others awkwardly offered hands of welcome as they wished the visiting Cowboys well. Smith gathered his wrestlers around in a tight circle, and his comments were brief. "We're going to have a chance to move forward in a lot of matches tonight. If you're an underdog, find ways to win. I want a lot out of you that first minute."[9] The team slipped through the slit in a tall red curtain and took their seats. Derek Stevens, wrestling in place of the injured Coleman Scott, slipped off his shirt and walked to the mat.

Eighth-ranked Matt Keller edged Derek Stevens 4-2 at 125. Morgan won by major decision at 133, but Frishkorn gave up an early first period lead and lost 9-4. Esposito countered with a 24-9 technical fall, but at 157 Ward was pinned in the final period of a close match. Thus, when Johny Hendricks stepped out for the first time in two weeks, the Cowboys trailed 12-9. The stage was set for Hendricks, coming off injuries and facing the glare of another high-stakes pressure match against a nationally-ranked opponent, to once again get the Cowboys back on track. But he lost, 5-4.

Pendleton, thrown to his back for the first time during the season, pulled the Cowboys to within 15-13 with a hard-earned major decision over Marc Harwood. This set the stage for Clay Kehrer's encounter with Travis Pascoe, the owner of a 20-match winning streak and the second-ranked 184 pounder in the country.

Kehrer ran onto the mat in his orange singlet and gray wrestling shoes trimmed in green. He had split open his chin days earlier during practice, and white trainer's tape framed his face like a frontal halo. Pascoe's takedown 20 seconds into the match gave the Husker a 2-1 first period advantage. When Kehrer locked his hands around Pascoe just seconds into the second period for the first of three technical violations he would commit in the match, the Husker was awarded a penalty point to extend his lead to 3-1. More than a minute later Coach Smith stood up from his seat on the bench and shrugged in disbelief as Kehrer fell behind 4-1 after locking his hands a second time, technical violation number two. But Kehrer hung on and rode Pascoe out for the remainder of the second period, piling up 1:16 in riding time going into the final frame.

Even though Kehrer was trailing, hope remained. If he could escape, earn a takedown, and ride Pascoe out throughout the third period, he would win on riding time. Sensing his opportunity, Kehrer flew out from the bottom position within seconds, cut Pascoe's lead to 4-2, and immediately launched a single leg. But the stronger and more experienced Pascoe stood his ground, stunned Kehrer with a vicious cross face, and scooted behind him for a 6-2 lead.

With just more than a minute left in the match, Pascoe sensed he had absorbed Kehrer's best shot and went to work on building his lead. He let the Cowboy up to take the score back to 6-3, then snapped a winded and grasping Kehrer down for his second takedown of the period and an 8-3 advantage. He then let Kehrer up again and continued his pursuit. As the red digital numbers on the match clock wound down, Kehrer began to back paddle to avoid the major decision, and was hit with a stalling call, technical violation number three, which sent the score to 9-4.

In a final flurry Kehrer attempted a Hail Mary-like ankle pickup, his bread and butter move in high school, but Pascoe countered with a deadly inside cradle, driving Kehrer to his back. The Nebraska bench erupted as its coaching staff, all clad in long sleeve white dress shirts, leaped up in unison. If Pascoe could gain a last-second fall or back points and win by a major decision, more pressure would be heaped on Rosholt and Mocco as they waited in the wings. But Kehrer fought back to his stomach, and the Husker coaches sat back in their folding chairs in disappointment. The final buzzer sounded and Pascoe's hand was raised. According to the scoreboard, which read 11-4, he missed the crucial major decision by one point. The Huskers still led the dual 18-13.

Then came Jake Rosholt.

* * *

During bus trips and plane rides the only wrestler who dared to venture to the front and sit down by Coach Smith was 197-pound junior Jake Rosholt. He did so rarely, and the visits were always short. They spoke softly and sometimes chuckled. After a few moments Rosholt would return to the back of the bus, often sitting near Kevin Ward, his roommate in a rent house located in the middle of campus near several other houses also occupied by wrestlers. The team often congregated at Rosholt and Ward's house in the evenings and played video games to get their minds off food.

Jake Rosholt graduated from Sandpoint High School, tucked in northern Idaho some 60 miles south of the Canadian border on the far shore of Lake Pend Oreille. Though he had never seen a college wrestling match until his junior year in high school, he appeared on Coach Smith's recruiting radar when he captured four state wrestling titles and a high school national championship. The blond-haired and taciturn Rosholt, an education and ranch operations major, sported a Superman tattoo on the outside of his right shoulder and a Byzantine cross on the outside of his left bicep. Before practice he often sat alone and leaned against the wall of the wrestling room, sometimes with his eyes closed. He was not unfriendly, but often spoke only when spoken to. The son of a logger, Rosholt brandished a chainsaw like a sketch artist worked a pencil. His mother loved horses, and Rosholt cherished his time outdoors. When Coach Smith traveled to Idaho to recruit Rosholt, the rawboned recruit took his future coach mountain climbing. According to those who know, Rosholt is freaky strong, a term of endearment that conveys the reality that Rosholt is much stronger than he appears.

Many considered Rosholt the hardest worker in the wrestling room. According to his coaches, "…he kicks ass every day from start to finish. Never lets up."[10] Although not inherently gifted, he "finds ways to have his hand raised in the end."[11] Serious about mastering technique, he listened intently and posed copious questions to coaches. There seemed to be a force field around Rosholt, penetrable only by his teammates, coaches, and family. He was close to his brother Jared, the top-ranked high school wrestler at 215, who signed a letter of intent to attend Oklahoma State the next fall.

Wearing a long sleeve t-shirt and gray wrestling shoes trimmed in green, before his matches Rosholt habitually stalked back and forth along the edge of the mat on the side closest to Coach Smith. In crucial situations he maintained eye contact with his head coach. When Smith barked out an order Rosholt sometimes responded like a sweating and grunting voice-activated robot expeditiously carrying out a spoken command.

In 2002, the quixotic redshirt freshman could post an impressive win against a quality opponent, and then proceed to lose three or four consecutive matches against average competition. According to Coach Smith, Rosholt's talent level was better than average, but not great.

When the 2003 NCAA tournament rolled around at the end of his first varsity season, Rosholt was by all accounts not at that magic level necessary to compete for a national title. According to his coach, he was wishy-washy in performance and attitude. Making weight had been a nightmare. He had sustained nine losses during the regular season and his confidence had not taken root. The tournament seeding had not been kind, for if the 10-seed-ed Rosholt survived his first two matches, he was on a collision course to meet defending national runner-up Greg Parker from Princeton, who had majored Rosholt in a tournament three months before.

Rosholt claimed narrow victories in his first two matches, but when he took the mat against Parker in the pivotal quarter-final round, he was not projected to achieve even All-American status. He was just a 10-seeded fresh-man. If given some experience under his belt and another year under Coach Smith's tutelage, perhaps he could compete at a higher level next year. But coaches Smith and Branch sat with Rosholt in the lonely concrete bowels of Kemper Arena in Kansas City and quietly imprinted upon their temper-mental and brooding redshirt freshman one solitary message over and over again: You are good enough to win. I know what I'm talking about. You can do this. You are good enough to win.

Rosholt took the mat and stormed out to a 5-0 lead before pinning Parker with 40 seconds remaining in the first period. In the semi-finals he easily defeated Oklahoma NCAA runnerup Josh Lambrecht to earn a cov-eted spot in the national finals. There he faced Missouri's Scott Barker, who had days earlier thumped Rosholt 9-1 in the Big 12 Conference champion-ship match.

Before the finals Rosholt sat and listened to his coaches' litany of hope. "You can beat this guy. You can be a national champion." Worked into a quiet, volcanic frenzy, Rosholt's two first-period takedowns established a 4-2 lead. Barker's second-period escape cut the lead to 4-3, but Rosholt erupted for three takedowns and a near fall in the final period en route to his first national title. Freshman Jake Rosholt was a 2003 NCAA champion.

The following year Rosholt racked up 24 wins and a Big 12 conference title, but lost in the fourth round of the NCAA tournament, and finished third. Making weight had taken its toll, so after the season he asked Coach Smith if he could move up a weight class for the 2004-2005 campaign. The previous year Smith had bluntly told Rosholt he did not posses the work ethic necessary to repeat his NCAA run or be an Olympic champion. But after consulting with strength and conditioning coach Gary Calcagno, Smith agreed to consider the move if Rosholt spent the necessary hours in the weight room, building up his already prodigious strength for competition against even bigger and stronger adversaries. Rosholt did the work and was allowed to move up a weight for his junior season.

He came to Lincoln with a 25-1 record and ranked number one in the nation, but Smith was concerned with nagging injuries and inexplicable lapses in technique that plagued Rosholt through the season. Rosholt was scheduled to face Nebraska junior B. J. Padden, a 2004 NCAA qualifier whom Rosholt had defeated in the 2003 Big 12 tournament. Confident and primed for an upset, Padden entered the match with a 22-7 record and was riding a seven-match winning streak.

Nebraska was leading the dual by five points, 18-13. A Padden victory would give the Huskers an eight-point dual match lead going into the final individual match of the night, guaranteeing the first Nebraska win over OSU in Lincoln in 83 years. If Rosholt could claim victory, a Mocco decision would spell victory for the Cowboys.

The match did not begin well for Oklahoma State. Forty-five seconds off the whistle Padden sprawled and moved behind Rosholt for a takedown and then accomplished the highly improbable—he rode Rosholt out for the remaining 2:14 of the first period. Rosholt came to his feet four times in that first frame, but Padden lifted and slammed him back to the mat, head and shoulders first, to the delight of the frenzied crowd. Rosholt finally escaped 30 seconds into the second period, and as the wrestlers battled in the neutral position, Padden led 2-1 with well over two minutes in riding time on deposit.

During each highly competitive wrestling match there are dozens of moves and countermoves that ultimately spell victory. But each encounter usually comes down to one or two maneuvers in crucial times that spell checkmate. With 29 seconds left in the second period and both wrestlers on their feet fighting for position, each had their massive arms locked around the other's chests in a bear-hug pose as they both vied for position. If Padden achieved the takedown he would go up 4-1 with over two and one-half minutes riding time. If he could sustain the top position through the second period, he would simply need to stay off his back during the final period to claim the victory.

The crowd roared as both wrestlers, like two bulldozers pushing against one another while balanced on a circus high wire, strained against the other.

Finally balance gave way as they crashed to the mat, and the Nebraska coaches turned their heads in disappointment when Rosholt won the scramble and avoided the takedown that would have sealed victory for Nebraska. Instead, Rosholt scored the takedown and led 3-2, but Padden still had one minute and three seconds of riding time going into the final period.

Now leading 3-2 as the third and final period began, Rosholt was on the top position. If he could ride Padden out, he would cancel out the riding time advantage and win 3-2. If Padden escaped within the next three seconds, the score would be tied 3-3, but Padden could win with the one point riding time advantage.

Rosholt kept Padden on the mat for a full minute, but with 59 seconds left in the period Padden came to his feet and turned into Rosholt, who reached around Padden's torso and locked his hands by the tips of his fingers as they both walked a death waltz around the mat. If Padden could break Rosholt's slippery and tenuous finger-grip with 21 seconds remaining in the period, he would tie the score at 3-3. But with Nebraska coach Mark Manning standing on the side of the mat screaming on the verge of implosion, Rosholt hung on as the action was forced out of bounds. The wrestlers came back to the center of the mat, and Rosholt rode Padden out the remaining half minute. The buzzer sounded with Rosholt leading 3-2. No riding time was awarded. Once again, the injured Rosholt found a way to win. His victory made the team score 18 –15 in favor of Nebraska with one match remaining.

Next came Mocco, who mounted a quick 5-0 lead and lead 9-2 after the first period, but then seemed to throttle back his aggression after the major decision was secured, and cruised to a 12-2 major decision, giving the Cowboys four team points and locking up what appeared to be a one point 19-18 Cowboy win.

After Mocco's match ended the crowd mingled around the mat while the Cowboys began stuffing their gear into bags for a quick shower and the flight back home. With luck they could be in Stillwater by midnight.

But as the team walked through the crowd toward the locker room they noticed an agitated Coach Smith carefully staring at a monitor on the official's table while Nebraska coach Mark Manning gestured frenetically with his palms facing the ceiling, forcing a smile, and bouncing his head with every declarative sentence as the bright television spotlights bore down. Official Cody Olson was leaning on one knee talking frantically into a telephone.

This was the deal. Under the NCAA rules a wrestler is responsible for maintaining action during a match by staying in the center of the mat and wrestling aggressively. Failure to maintain this required level of action is considered "stalling."[12] If the referee determines the wrestler is violating this standard, the wrestler is first issued a warning. If the stalling occurs again, the offending wrestler's opponent is awarded one point. Stalling is considered a "technical violation."[13]

An unrelated rule provides that a wrestler in the top position may not lock his hands around his opponent's body unless the opponent comes to his feet. If the hands are improperly locked, the offending wrestler is penalized one point. No warnings are issued. This also is considered a technical violation.

The rules further provide in a rather obtuse fashion that technical violations such as stalling and locking hands have a cumulative effect, i.e., the first technical violation results in a one point penalty; the second results in an additional one point penalty; the third results in an additional two penalty points, and a fourth results in disqualification of the offending wrestler.[14]

During Rosholt's match, Nebraska Assistant Coach Mike Greenfield informed Head Coach Mark Manning of a possible scoring issue in the previous match between Kehrer and Pascoe. The Nebraska coaches realized when the official called Kehrer for stalling with 22 seconds remaining in the match, that constituted the third technical violation against Kehrer—two stalling calls and one locked hands call—which under the "cumulative" rule should have resulted in a two point penalty instead of a one point violation. Thus, Pascoe would have prevailed by a score of 12-4 instead of 11-4, equating to a four point major decision for the Huskers instead of a three point conventional decision, resulting in a 19-13 lead going into Rosholt's match at 197. Under this theory when Rosholt won, the Huskers led 19-15, and when Mocco defeated Manstedt 12-2 for a four point major decision, that knotted the score at 19-19.

The Nebraska coaches neither brought the issue to the official's attention before Rosholt's match began, nor did they inform the official before or during the heavyweight match. Accordingly, when Mocco took the mat, he believed the scoreboard when it read 18-15 in favor of Nebraska. According to that official score, posted in lights above the mat, if he could win by eight or more points and earn a major decision, the Cowboys would prevail 19-18.

Veteran official Cody Olson, a former Nebraska wrestler, was on the telephone with his officiating supervisor, whom he had awakened from his evening's sleep. While he deliberated the issue with his boss, the fans and wrestlers milled around the crowded scorer's table and waited for the official's verdict. When it became apparent the official was not sure of the proper call, Coach Smith assembled his team in the parking lot and the vans rushed them away to the airport through the frigid Nebraska darkness with the evening's outcome still pending.

They arrived at the airport at 9:40 p.m., gave their bags to airport personnel, and filed onto the aircraft. There they rested their heads on airplane pillows, pulled blankets under their chins, and looked forward to resting in the warm, dark aircraft as it returned them to their own beds in Stillwater only 90 minutes away. But there was a slight problem, the plane would not start.

A firing pin smaller than a deck of cards had malfunctioned, and the plane's engines would not fire. It was a simple enough problem to fix, but FAA and insurance regulations required that a credentialed mechanic perform the repair, and no one was available at 10:30 p.m. on a cold winter's night in Lincoln, Nebraska.

The team filed off the aircraft and gathered back in the same airport lounge where they had assembled 10 hours earlier. The team scattered out to find a warm sofa, chair, or piece of carpet to find sleep while a mechanic was located and repairs made. They would not sleep long.

Coach Smith sat on a sofa in the lounge area between Rosholt and Mocco, sipping coffee and watching the evening's matches on a hand-held video recorder Randy Pogue had utilized to tape the match. Ten minutes into his viewing, the usually deliberate Smith sat the camera down, bolted from his seat, and ordered the entire squad into the empty pilot's lounge located down a hallway adjacent to a coin-operated food dispenser. The team quietly crowded in together as Smith stood among the 22-member party. He held a cup of coffee in his right hand as he spoke, as a dark stubble began to show through his darkened and drawn face. The clock read 11:45 p.m.

In a voice strained with emotion and exhaustion, Smith laid it out. Regardless of difficult travel conditions, hostile crowds, and tough competition, he urged his wrestlers not to feel the complacency that victory can bring. "We got our asses kicked tonight and we deserved to lose to a team that's not even in our league." He was saddened that some of his wrestlers who lost seemed not to care. He agonized over mental mistakes and lack of focus, even accusing some of his wrestlers of succumbing to the pressure of the moment. "Some of you coughed it up a little bit. I'm not going to be a hypocrite and say it didn't ever happen to me, sure it did. But it only happens once. The second time it could be at Lehigh or the NCAA semi-finals or the NCAA finals."[15]

He then went around the room, and no one was spared from his wrath except Derek Stevens, the 125-pound backup junior pulled into action only days earlier.

"Nathan Morgan, I don't want to see you wrestling scared anymore. You're worrying too much. You fret about every little thing from eating to your warm-up. Just go through a good routine, then get out there and go. You're that good. You can do it."[16]

Frishkorn, who led going into the final period only to get turned to his back twice in the final minutes, sat against the wall and stared at his shoes. "Daniel, suck it up, son. You're out there just begging your nose to bleed. No question… this guy is bigger, but you chose to go up a weight. You've got to hold those big guys down. That's what it's going to take if you're going to be wrestling at the end. You stopped wresting against a national finalist in his home gym his senior year in their biggest match of the year. He's not going to give anything to you. You have to earn it. The first two periods you looked like a guy who could do some damage. In the third period you're one takedown from breaking the guy and then you get turned. You not only got turned you dropped your head. Also, you're the only guy who didn't drill today,"[17] referring to Frishkorn's decision not to drill when the team arrived in Lincoln hours earlier.

Esposito posted 11 takedowns in his 24-9 romp, but because he did not achieve a near fall, the 15-point differential in his match equated to a four-point major decision for the Cowboys and not a five-point technical fall. A 15-point differential in a match without a near fall results in four team points—with the near fall the team is awarded five points. "Zack, you looked good on your feet, and I liked your aggressiveness. But you made a mental error in not taking him to his back. We needed five team points. At least make the attempt."[18]

With wrestlers and staff cramped into the poorly-lit lounge no larger than a modest living room, Smith began to refer to his wrestlers by weight-class instead of name. "One fifty-seven, where are you?"[19] Kevin Ward, who took a tight match into the third period only to be caught on his back with 37 seconds remaining and pinned, sat on a table against the wall. He seemed to brace himself as Smith lowered his gaze. "You're ass is home this weekend. You're not going [to Hofstra and Lehigh]. I'll give you time to think about it and I'll make a decision whether or not you wrestle for me again this year."[20]

The 19th-ranked Ward was now 15-8, and his hopes for a banner season seemed to be slipping away. "You have the guy on the ropes, and you don't finish a shot? You get taken down with a short little fireman's carry and get pinned? What's that about? And where are all of the deep underhooks coming from? Create action and go score!"[21] Smith planted his hands on his hips and glared around the room. It was now past midnight. "We had four matches tonight where we had guys on the ropes and they were ready to quit and we make dumb mistakes. Stick his ass into the mat. Plant his ass into the mat and win the match!"[22]

Earlier in the evening Coach Smith looked on as the playful Johny Hendricks, warming up for his match, gawked as a Husker fan walked by carrying a boxful of refreshments from the concession area. "One sixty-five, you've been off two weeks but you're hot-dogging and having fun before the match talking about eating cheeseburgers and nachos while your opponent is back there getting ready to win a match! He's getting his game face on. His girlfriend's in the stands. His mommy and daddy are here. He's going to win at home! You gave him no respect. Put on your game face and quit jackassing around…understand everyone's coming after us. You young guys don't understand. When teams and coaches wrestle us, it's their chance to shine. They'll tell their grandkids about the night they wrestled Oklahoma

State. But you stand there with your feet together and let him hit a desperate shot and double leg you? Double leg you! Twenty-five seconds left in the match, and you're behind 5-4 and you aren't going bezerk? What are you waiting for? A stalling call?" You have to score points, son! You never got a takedown in this entire match, and you're not going to get one with your forearm resting on your knees. You're going to win by going after them. You have several good scoring positions from your feet and if you don't use them, you're not going to win. Several times in that match tonight your guy was ready to break and you backed off. You need to push through it. That guy shouldn't beat you in a hundred tries."[23]

Smith's voice lowered an octave as he turned his gaze to Chris Pendleton. "One seventy-four, outside of getting thrown on your back and almost getting pinned you didn't have a bad match. You won tonight and it wasn't pretty. But often you want your performance to be perfect, and sometimes it just can't be. Sometimes when you're wrestling guys who try to keep the score down, like this guy tonight, you have to take risks to make something happen, and sometimes you get caught like you did tonight. He 'high-flyered' you…no way you get 'high-flyered' with your head up. You're the best offensive wrestler in the nation. Stay in your stance."[24]

Smith's mood darkened once again as he looked down at Clay Kehrer. A burly airport employee who heard raised voices coming from the usually quiet haven for tired pilots, meekly looked around the corner into the lounge, but quickly withdrew down the hallway when he saw Coach Smith bearing down. "One eighty-four, that match is 4-2 in the third period and you get majored! You're riding the hell out of him and he's dead tired and ready to break in the third period and you end up getting majored? We don't get majored…especially under those circumstances. You're behind, and you crack in the end? You locked your hands twice! That's what a third grader does. I don't like what I saw. I'm not sure about this weight right now. I've got to make a decision."[25]

Jake Rosholt sat expressionless against the wall. "One ninety-seven. You stepped up tonight in a tough situation and got the job done, but it never should have come to that. How does he have almost three minutes riding time going into the third period? I know the crowd is roaring, but you should never be in that situation with that guy. He took you down and rode you out the entire first period. That should never happen to you! I want to see my guys step up in a cracker box gym full of people cheering against us and not choke or feel pressure, but get the job done. That's what it's going to take to win the title this year in March, and that's what you did tonight, Jake."[26]

The meeting continued as the clock inched past midnight, but Smith had words for even Mocco, whose 12-2 victory at the time seemed enough to seal the Cowboy victory. "Heavyweight, you score 10 points and then you stop wrestling! To hell with getting the major decision. I would rather you go after it and make a mistake and win by seven then stop wrestling. That is not your style, Mocco. Maybe you saw the rest of your teammates giving half-ass efforts and you decided to do the same. I don't know."[27]

Smith sighed and stood silently for several seconds, and then spoke in a soft, conversational tone, ignoring several wrestlers who were covering up yawns with scabbed and cold hands. "Over the past couple of weeks I have seen too many guys who are hoping things work out for them, instead of taking their destiny in their own hands and taking responsibility to be a champion. I see too many worrywarts…guys worrying about little stuff. I've seen crybabies whining and moaning about how your back hurts or how your legs hurt. I've seen guys worrying about their national ranking. It's not a disadvantage to be number one and having everyone give us their best effort. It is a privilege. So start training like a champion…like you're going to win every match and kick everybody's ass."[28]

"Tonight some of you were exposed as individuals and as wrestlers. In this sport, guys, you can run but you can't hide. Ultimately, you'll be exposed for what you are."[29]

With that said, Smith walked out of the lounge. Some of the team followed him out while others sat and stared ahead. Smith then abruptly ordered his team back into the lounge for more. No one groaned as they sat back down on the hard, gray carpet. "We are not in an ideal situation tonight. We'll get in at 2:00 a.m., get up, and go to class and then practice tomorrow afternoon. But don't let these circumstances give you a reason not to perform. If we can perform under these circumstances, we can perform anytime."[30]

With his sleep-deprived bloodshot eyes riveted on the floor in front of him, Smith seemed to be talking to himself as an airport official signaled the plane was ready. "When I wrestled in Russia I heard my teammates complaining constantly. The rooms are too cold. The gyms are freezing and I can't sleep. They convinced themselves there was a reason not to perform. They gave themselves an out. They negotiated themselves into a frame of mind that allowed defeat."[31]

Finally, the meeting concluded and the plane lifted off from Lincoln Airport, making a broad circle around the capitol city of Nebraska and headed south for the 80-minute return flight to Stillwater. For the first 45 minutes of the return flight Smith made detailed notes in his black leather binder.

At 1:20 a.m. he flipped off his light and slept softly as his team returned to Stillwater with their 18th consecutive dual victory of the year.

Friday morning, the NCAA upheld the Cowboy's 19-18 victory, citing NCAA rules that require corrections to be made by the referee before the start of a subsequent match. Thus, under the rules, the scoring mishap in Kehrer's match should have been reported to the officials before the 197-pound bout began. In a telephone interview an NCCA administrator commented on the snafu. "The rule is very, very clear. It was a dumb mistake, and it wasn't fair to Nebraska. Nebraska should have tied the dual, and that's too bad. I don't like what's happened, but my hands are tied because of what it says in the rulebook. The mistake was not caught at the appropriate time for it to be changed. That is a rule we need to revisit after the season."[32]

Two days later Nebraska would visit the University of Oklahoma for a dual match in Norman. The competition began nine minutes late after the Nebraska coaches refused to allow its team to wrestle on a smaller-than-regulation mat the Sooners sometimes utilized when they wrestled at the local high school. The Nebraska head coach was adamant in asserting NCAA regulations. "It's really important at this level. They were upset at me, but that's the rule."[33]

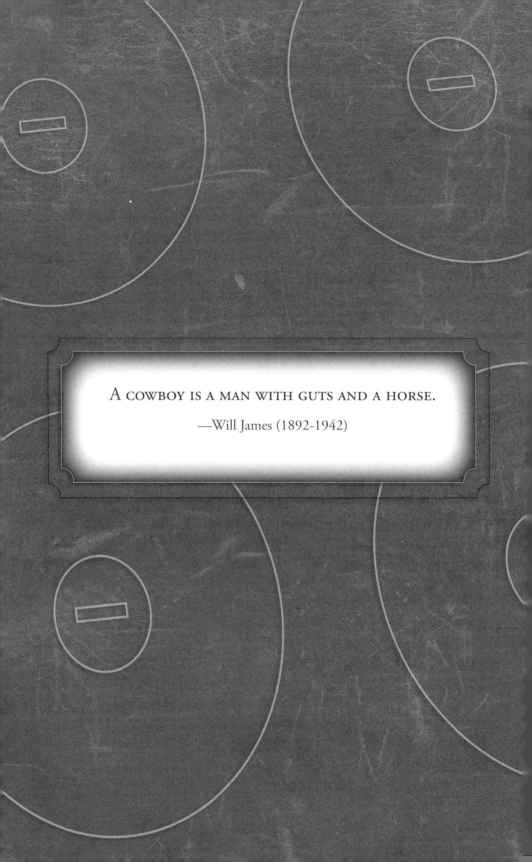

A COWBOY IS A MAN WITH GUTS AND A HORSE.

—Will James (1892-1942)

fifteen

the eastern invasion

02.13.05

TWENTY-EIGHT HOURS after returning from Lincoln, the Cowboys would embark on a weekend trip to Long Island, New York and Bethlehem, Pennsylvania, where they would face east coast wrestling powers Hofstra and Lehigh for two Sunday matches. After sleeping a few hours, the team trudged to morning classes and dragged themselves to the wrestling room, where they packed their gear for a ninety-minute van ride to the Tulsa airport before sunup the following morning. That Saturday they flew from Tulsa into Newark, rented two vans, inched through the Queens Midtown Tunnel, and continued along the Long Island Expressway toward Hofstra University located on Long Island, New York, some 1,393 miles from Stillwater.

Along the way the wrestlers sat in the crowded vans with backpacks resting in their laps as they peered outside, passing along the Hudson River by the Statue of Liberty and into the heart of the city through busy Saturday afternoon traffic, down Fifth Avenue by the Empire State Building, and through the city toward Long Island. Some talked on cell phones as they related the sights to family members back home, while others snapped pictures with digital cameras. Steve Mocco spent a portion of his childhood just miles away and proudly pointed out landmarks and highlights. "I was born right over there," he pointed. "This is my town."[1]

Earlier, Mocco's father had rendezvoused with the Cowboys at the Newark airport to lead a caravan through the city. On the way, another

Mocco vehicle joined the quixotic caravan as Steve's older brother Joe pulled behind one of the vans and joined in. At a stoplight he climbed out of his vehicle and weaved on foot through a routine traffic jam back to his father's car for a short conversation. Not to be outdone, a grinning Pat Smith jumped out of the white van at three successive stoplights, playing musical chairs in downtown New York traffic. At one stop he calmly spoke through the window to Cowboy radio voice J. Carl Guymon as both waited for the light to change. "If they can do it, so can we!"[2]

The motorcade crawled through the heavy city traffic and arrived at their hotel as the sun began to drop. They took vans to the Hofstra campus, worked out, and checked their weight. The Hofstra wrestling room, a dark, rectangular chamber with low ceilings and no windows, was consigned in the depths of Hofstra arena. It sported two blue mats with gold circles in the center. Plaques commemorating conference champions and All-Americans lined one wall just above the wall padding. Several Hofstra wrestlers sat in the center of the mats as the Cowboy team filed in carrying their black gear bags. Seeing the OSU wrestlers enter, they stood up without offering greetings and moved out. On the way toward the door, one Hofstra wrestler walked to a black boom box located in a weight room adjoining the wrestling area and turned down music that had been blaring during their earlier workouts. Coach Guerrero sat in a folding chair against the wall. "We don't allow music during practices,"[3] likening the sounds to a false stimulant wrestlers do not have access to in live competition.

The Cowboys drilled, checked their weight, showered, and went searching for a meal. One van found a Subway sandwich shop—Smith liked their pre-determined serving sizes—while the others located a take-out Italian restaurant where the wrestlers and staff loaded up plastic containers with pasta and red sauce.

At the hotel the Mocco family prepared a crock-pot full of aromatic chicken parmesan which rested on a table among various pies, cakes, and breads. Randy Pogue traveled to a nearby market and bought more groceries than usual, for the team would require pre-match snacks twice the next day. The New York evening was unusually cold, so Pogue stored the items in the back of the van.

After checking their weight once again on the scales located in Chris Pickering's room, the wrestlers scattered. Some made surreptitious trips to the Mocco room for tastes of contraband pie, cookies, and sweet breads. Others lay in bed with their stomachs growling, waiting for sleep to console hunger pains and parched mouths.

The next morning the team gathered in the hotel lobby at 8:00 a.m. for the five-minute drive to the arena. Hofstra, a private university some 25 miles outside New York City, boasted an undergraduate enrollment of more than 8,000 students pursuing degrees in some 130 undergraduate programs of study. The Hofstra wrestlers competed in the Colonial Athletic Association, and were coached by Tom Ryan, himself a former All-American on Dan Gable's national championship teams, who had lost a narrow decision to Cowboy Pat Smith in the 1991 NCAA finals. The five-time conference Coach of the Year propelled a

Coach Smith shakes the hand of Hofstra coach Tom Ryan moments before the Cowboys' dual with The Pride. Ryan, a five-time conference coach of the year, had guided Hofstra to four straight conference championships and a 35-conference dual match undefeated streak. *Courtesy Brian Ballweg, Hofstra Athletics.*

Smith addresses a group of wrestlers, coaches and parents the morning before the Hofstra match. Incredibly, the Cowboy coach was often asked by opposing teams to give a clinic or deliver remarks before matches. *Courtesy Brian Ballweg, Hofstra Athletics.*

once-proud wrestling program out of the doldrums in the mid-'90s, and lead his squad to five consecutive conference championships. Under Ryan's watch the Hofstra Pride had advanced 48 wrestlers to the NCAA tournament and had earned four All-America designations.

A little more than a year earlier, on February 16, 2004, Coach Ryan's young son Teague died suddenly at the family home from Long Q-T Syndrome, an infrequent, hereditary disorder of the heart's electrical rhythm that usually affects children or young adults. One could still see a faraway look in Ryan's eyes as the events of the day progressed.

The match began at 10 a.m. on a bright and cold Sunday morning in the 5,124-seat Hofstra arena. Opened in 2000, the $15 million, 93,000-square-foot facility hosted men's and women's basketball, as well as wrestling, and was attached to a large gymnasium facility which served the student body and housed the visitor's locker room.

While the wrestlers lounged in the visitor's locker room checking their weight and preparing their pre-match snack, Coach Smith stood at one end of the arena and spoke to a large gathering of young wrestlers, coaches, and parents. When the Cowboys wrestled non-conference opponents far from home, Coach Smith was often asked by the head coach of the host school to conduct a short clinic before the match began. This phenomenon spoke to Smith's status in the wrestling community, for his reputation transcended school rivalries and coaches' egos. It strains ones credulity to imagine Duke basketball coach Mike Krzyzewski giving a clinic to a group of UCLA fans before an NCAA basketball game. After he introduced Smith, Coach Ryan stepped aside as the OSU coach addressed the crowd, many of whom wore blue New York Yankee baseball caps.

"To you high school coaches, technique is better now than when I wrestled. It's better now than it ever has been. The sport is changing and you must spend time keeping up with changes. Because of the advent of videotapes and Internet resources, you have more access to good teaching materials than ever before. Take advantage of those resources, but remember that teaching technique is about attitude as much as anything. Technique is not all that important unless you teach it in the context of a winning attitude. Having that drive and developing that hunger to be the best will help you master technique. Without that hunger, all the tapes and camps in the world won't help you get where you want to be."[4]

The coaches sat in rapt attention. One mother took notes on the back of a paper grocery bag as her young son leaned against her shoulder and yawned. "Remember, coaches, developing good fundamental skills is crucial. The moves you teach your wrestlers now are the moves they will use for the rest of their careers. Some of my All-Americans still hit moves they learned when they were eight years old. Develop three good takedowns. Maybe a single leg, a double leg, and a front headlock. Master a standup from the down position. When you're on top know what you want to do and do it."[5]

One coach wearing a bright red letter jacket asked Smith what routine he taught the OSU wrestlers during those few agonizing minutes before their matches began. Smith almost winced. "You will hear coaches and wrestlers talk a lot about what they do before the match, and a lot of that is exaggerated. Many wrestlers think they need to go under the bleachers and bang their heads against the wall or slap themselves in the face or slap their bodies. It you do that stuff that's fine, but pre-match preparation is about what you do three or four months before a match, and not what you do three or four minutes before you wrestle. Sure, it's important to get a good warm-up, but there is no magical formula. Your success or failure will depend on what you have done for the weeks and months leading up to the competition."6

A slender man with a white towel wrapped around his neck spoke with the thoughtful, precise bearing of one who perhaps taught science and coached wrestling. He asked coach Smith to comment on "the pressure on beginners to win."

Coach Smith nodded his head and stepped forward. "Some preach that winning at a young age is not important. I disagree. It's important to the young wrestler stepping out in that circle for the first time to walk off a winner. Believe me, because of the personal nature of the sport, it's a lot more fun to win than to lose. It's combat. It's before your friends and parents. It means a lot to win. The first five matches I ever wrestled in competition, I got pinned. It was not fun. I still remember it. It is more fun to win."

The 59-year-old owner of a car business stood up and spoke with the halted tone and pained expression of a man trying to exorcise old demons. "How do I deal with the one loss I had in high school? I couldn't escape in the last period and lost by one point. I relive that match even now."7

Smith stepped back and turned away, then faced the stocky middle-aged man who stood surrounded by children midway up the bleachers. "Every one of my losses left a scar on my soul. Even though you live it over and over, you move on. It's easier to deal with our setbacks and failures if we know we did everything we could do to prepare and we applied ourselves in the right fashion, both mentally and physically. Bottom line, someone has to lose." Smith looked up, placed his hand in his pockets, and turned away. "It's always nicer to win."8

Coach Smith apologized to the fans that still had questions, and Coach Ryan intervened to thank Smith for his participation. The Cowboy coach walked back across the arena floor to check on his team, stopping to sign autographs on singlets for young boys as the stands began to fill with early-morning fans.

The Cowboys traveled to Long Island, New York where Johny Hendricks handled Hofstra junior Mark Patrovich 8-4; Steve Mocco pinned Gian Villante in 2:05; Jake Rosholt handed second-ranked Chris Skretkowicz only his second defeat in 25 matches with a 9-5 victory. *Courtesy Brian Ballweg, Hofstra Athletics.*

By agreement of the coaches, the match began at 157 before a gutsy and crowded arena. During the late-night airport scolding in Lincoln two nights earlier Smith informed Cowboy starter Kevin Ward, who was pinned in the third period of his match, that he would stay over the weekend to search his soul. The next day Ward petitioned Smith to allow him to go east and gain redemption. Smith agreed, and Ward answered with a solid 8-2 win over James Strouse.

Hendricks and Pendleton followed with two wins over ranked wrestlers to give OSU an early 10-0 lead. After Joe Rovelli majored Clay Kehrer 12-4, Jake Rosholt scored four final period points for a come-from-behind victory over number-two ranked Chris Skretkowicz. Mocco pinned Glen Villante in just over two minutes, followed by Derek Stevens' overtime loss to Dave Tomasette. As Morgan took to the mat with Deep Purple's Smoke on the Water blaring from the public address speakers, the Cowboys held a comfortable 19-7 lead with three matches remaining.

Morgan was on a six-match winning streak since dropping three straight contests at the National Duals and had been ranked as high as eighth in the nation. He was favored against 21-4 freshman Charles Griffin who was ranked seventeenth in the country. He took a 4-1 lead into the final period, only to be muscled to his back twice in the final frame to lose 7-4. Morgan's pattern of losing early leads against highly ranked wrestlers continued. Smith jabbed his finger in the air and poured words into Morgan's ear as the Cowboy coach followed Morgan behind the bench. Smith was beginning to question his 133 pounder's ability to wrestle the second and third periods with the same aggressiveness as the first. "Nathan has to withstand and win a hard-fought match somewhere down the line. He must make the commitment to stay in the battle until the battle is won."[9]

Daniel Frishkorn faced childhood wrestling nemesis Ricky LaForge, who attempted to stare down the Cowboy 141 pounder during warm-ups. Frishkorn had wrestled LaForge during youth wrestling competition when Daniel was 10 years old, and they had not wrestled since. If Frishkorn was intimidated by his opponent's attempt to gain a mental edge, he disguised it well with a 17-2 victory.

Esposito topped the morning off with a pin over Jon Masa in 3:33, and the Cowboys defeated the Hofstra Pride 30-10 for their 19th straight dual win of the season. After the match most of the team rushed back to the locker room to shower, dress, and load into the vans. Mocco, Esposito, and Pendleton were besieged by media before being herded by Coach Smith to the locker room after he concluded his radio and television appearances. Finally the team loaded into the vans and made the four-hour trip to Bethlehem, Pennsylvania, to meet the fourth-ranked Lehigh Mountain Hawks.

To lessen the strain on visiting teams, NCAA rules declared that for teams who were wrestling more than one dual match during a single day, one weigh-in would be held one hour before the beginning of the first match. The rules also required the opposing team at the subsequent site to conduct an honor weigh-in at the same time. Furthermore, no team was required to weigh in more than once a day. Thus, the Cowboys were required to weigh in only once, one hour before the Hofstra match, while Lehigh was required to conduct their honor weigh-in at the same time.

In the van on the way to Bethlehem, the wrestlers basked in mild euphoria, knowing their next weigh-in would not be until the Oklahoma match a full seven days away. They enjoyed home-made sandwiches and bottled water provided by the Mocco family, as well as groceries passed around by the ever-resourceful Randy Pogue. Wrestlers nodded off as the van rolled up Interstate-81 onto the Pennsylvania Turnpike toward Lehigh University as rolling hills and vast meadows blanketed with trees and green foliage welcomed the tired but alert band of wrestlers and coaches as they headed for their next scheduled challenge.

Because the van was crowded with groceries and wrestlers, Cowboy radio announcer J. Carl Guymon caught a ride with former Cowboy All-American and national champion Teague Moore, then a businessman in Boston, who drove down to watch his alma mater compete. On the ride to Bethlehem, Moore reflected on the mystique of Cowboy wrestling. Looking across the green fields, the articulate history major from western Pennsylvania, who would be named head wrestling coach at Clarion University in 2006, spoke softly, "It is the power of that orange singlet. I'm telling you, it has an effect on opponents."[10] Asked to explain, Teague grinned. "Many times you would wrestle harder so you wouldn't have to face Smith and disappoint him. At some programs you're encouraged to win. At Oklahoma State you're expected to win. When I was an assistant coach at Oklahoma University, we won the Big 12 Championship one year and the school had everyone fitted for these real nice rings to commemorate our winning the conference championship. Years earlier when I wrestled at OSU we won the Big 12 conference championship, and Coach Smith let us stop at a convenience store on the drive back 'and get anything we wanted.' It's about attitude and expectations. We didn't have lots of rah-rah speeches. A couple of minutes before the matches were to begin Coach Smith would say 'get your stuff on.' Not a lot of talking and game planning and pouring over film. You just go out and wrestle your match. You know what's expected."[11]

As the Cowboy caravan rolled through the Lehigh Valley, a road sign read Lehigh University, and a bright sun illuminated green rolling hills that once contained vast reservoirs of coal that sustained the Union armies. " Everywhere OSU goes to wrestle, it's an event. They draw the largest crowds and get the best effort from their opponents. Many times we would face opponents with equal or even better talent. But we would find a way to prevail."[12]

Tonight, Lehigh would test that proposition.

Coal magnate Asa Packer founded Lehigh University in Bethlehem, Pennsylvania immediately following the Civil War. His dream was to provide a top-flight scientific and classical education to deserving Pennsylvania students, hoping they would help rebuild the war-ravaged Lehigh Valley. Considered one of the finest engineering schools in the nation, Lehigh also enjoys a reputation as a top-flight wrestling school. Coached by 2004 national coach of the year Greg Stroble, the Mountain Hawks scored the school's most points at the NCAA tournament in 2004 by placing five All-Americans, crowning a national champion, and taking third place in team standings.

Lehigh was agonizingly close to bursting to the top of the college-wrestling world when Zack Esposito and Steve Mocco almost attended Lehigh. Esposito's brother Dave, a two-time All-American who placed second and third in the NCAA tournament in 2001 and 2000, graduated from Lehigh. "I was real close," says the Cowboy 149 pounder of his decision to choose Oklahoma State over Lehigh. "Really close. For me, it came down to following in my brother's footsteps and come here or try and do something on my own. I had to make a choice."[13]

The Lehigh wrestling program also enchanted Mocco. "This is a great environment for wrestling. The people here relate. They wrestled. Their fathers wrestled. A lot of the guys [on Oklahoma State's team] never got to see this kind of crowd. This is a great part of the country for wrestling. [At Oklahoma State] I liked the coaches. I really liked the school and the campus and the wrestling program. Oklahoma State was just more similar to what I was used to in athletics. I came from Iowa."[14]

The invasion of the number-one ranked Cowboys to the hills of eastern Pennsylvania was highly anticipated. To accommodate the large demand for tickets the match was moved from Grace Hall, the 2,200-seat wrestling and volleyball arena located on the main campus, also known as "The Snake Pit," to the larger Stabler Arena. The modern basketball facility located off campus held 5,600 fans. The university, using the old fashioned marketing strategy of promoting a visiting major power, had sold out the dual for weeks, the largest advance sellout in college wrestling history.[15]

Arriving two hours before the 5:00 p.m. match, the Cowboys lounged in the small locker room and sat in folding chairs on the arena floor thirty feet from the mat as they caught their breath following the ride from New York City earlier in the afternoon. Cowboy assistant coaches Mark Branch, Pat Smith, and Eric Guerrero lounged in a circle of folding chairs and chatted with Teague Moore when a blue-suited Lehigh official carrying a walkie-talkie and sporting an earphone in his left ear briskly ordered the Cowboy coaches off the floor.

As the second match of the day grew near the Cowboy wrestlers began dressing in a dark locker room divided in half by a toilet and leaking shower. Coach Smith sat alone on a wooden bench, then walked out of the dressing room door, pacing alone under the bleachers with hands in the pockets of his navy blue suit coat. He glanced at his watch then returned to the locker room, where he gathered the team around him and began speaking loudly over the drone of a window air-conditioner that recycled the aroma of sweat, rubber, stale shower soap, and popcorn. "This is just another big match for us. We've been in these matches all year. We're believers. This team does not really believe they can beat us. The only way they can even sniff us is if we let them stay in matches. Remember, each individual just do your part. If

Lehigh fans file into sold-out Stabler Arena. Their match with the number-one ranked Cowboys had been the largest advance sellout in college wrestling history. *Courtesy Jeffrey G. Nolan.*

unexpected things happen, you be the one who steps out there and makes things right."[16] Muffled cheers from the capacity crowd bounced against the dark locker room and Coach Smith's voice reflected the moment. "If you have an opportunity to put a guy to his back, you do it. You stick him. Do not let him get off. Pin him right there! Gather around Chris. Ready. 1-2-3 Cowboys. Let's go."[17]

As the team closed in around Pendleton for the prayer, everyone else stepped back. This intimate circle was reserved for the wrestlers only. After a short prayer Pendleton walked the team out through a darkened hallway lined with tables into the well-lit area where they were greeted with that strange mixture of polite applause and guttural booing. As they took their chairs, lined up in two rows on the corner of the blue mat, a Lehigh wrestler in a warm-up suit ran back and forth waving his arms and exhorting the crowd. One Cowboy wrestler looked on, slightly embarrassed at the zealous display.

LEFT: Jake Rosholt, battling a knee injury that would require post-season surgery, takes the down position against senior Jon Trenge. *Courtesy Jeffrey G. Nolan.*

RIGHT: Johny Hendricks defends top-ranked Troy Letters' takedown attempt. *Courtesy Jeffrey G. Nolan.*

The announcer introduced the Lehigh wrestlers by name, weight, and academic major. The dual began again at 157. A frenetic and intense Kevin Ward could not overcome a first period takedown and lost 6-4 to tenth-ranked international relations major Derek Zinck for the second time. The hopeful crowd, believing an upset could be in the making, roared as top-ranked Troy Letters took the mat against a rusty Johny Hendricks. The defending national champion was so esteemed on the Lehigh campus that days after winning his title the previous season, he received a standing ovation when he returned as the conquering hero to his Engaged Buddhism class.[18] He took Hendricks down in the first period and held on for a 5-2 win, his second victory over Hendricks during the year.

Pendleton and Kehrer won by decision to tie the team score at 6-6, setting up a rematch of number-one ranked Jake Rosholt and number-three ranked Jon Trenge, who had been reinstated to his team by the NCAA after taking a swing at an opponent during the National Duals weeks earlier. The injured Rosholt gave up a takedown with 38 seconds left in the final peri-

od to lose 3-2 to Trenge, whose conservative and opportunistic style stalled Rosholt's offense.

Mocco scored a 21-6 technical fall over seventeenth-ranked Paul Weibel. The victory gave OSU a 10-9 lead. Derek Stevens, in the lineup for the injured Coleman Scott, scored two crucial takedowns to claim a 6-2 victory and extended OSU's team lead to 13-9.

Morgan, wearing white John Smith signature wrestling shoes with a white kneepad on each knee, squared off against fifth-ranked Matt Ciasulli in the eighth match of the evening. The bullying, hard-nosed Ciasulli, known for his riding ability and aggressive demeanor, had defeated a dispirited Morgan weeks earlier in the National Duals with a punishing third-period ride.

As usual, Morgan started quickly with a takedown seconds into the match, but Ciasulli's escape made it 2-1. Seconds later Morgan's nose began to pour blood, which prompted head trainer Chris Pickering to plug Morgan's right nostril with white tissue. Morgan had broken his nose in January, and bled profusely at virtually every competition.

LEFT: Lehigh fans applaud as number-one ranked Jake Rosholt hand-fights with number-two ranked Jon Trenge. *Courtesy Jeffrey G. Nolan.*

RIGHT: Junior Derek Stevens, in the lineup for an injured Coleman Scott, scored two crucial takedowns against Leigh's John Stout for a pressure-packed, 6-2 win before a sold-out, partisan crowd in Bethlehem, Pennsylvania. *Courtesy Oklahoma State University.*

BELOW: Surrounded by his wrestlers and assistant coaches, Coach Smith looks on as the Cowboys battle Lehigh in Bethlehem, Pennsylvania. *Courtesy Jeffrey G. Nolan.*

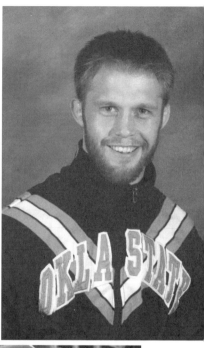

Morgan opened the second period with an escape to pull ahead 3-1. Ciasulli, with his blond curly hair protruding from his headgear like wild prairie-growth, sat back for the remainder of the period, prompting Coach Branch to plead unsuccessfully for a stalling call before the howls of the partisan crowd. Morgan's nose began to bleed again, and Pickering replaced the blood-soaked plug with a snow-white fresh one.

Neither wrestler scored again in the period, and Ciasulli led off the third frame with a quick escape. Seconds later the aggressive Morgan fired his fourth deep single-leg of the match and fought from a stacking position for almost a full minute before the official called a stalemate next to the Lehigh bench.

With 17 seconds left in the match, and both wrestlers in the neutral position, Morgan led 3-2. Off the whistle Ciasulli charged into Morgan, not with serious intentions of achieving a match-winning takedown, but rather in a desperation effort to draw a match-tying stalling call. Morgan was forced to step back each time to absorb the charge. The official had been parsimonious with stalling calls throughout the match. Mocco's opponent had pulled in like a turtle on a hot highway and still had avoided a stalling call. Morgan had been the aggressor throughout the match, and Ciasulli spent energy as he warded off Morgan's relentless low single leg attempts.

Under the rules that govern stalling, the lead seemed safe.

The clock ticked down as the frenzied crowd begged for a stalling call.

5-4-3-2.

Then as the digital clock clicked to 00:01, the official called Nathan Morgan for stalling, tying the match at 3-3.

Morgan, with blood oozing from his nose onto his upper lip, looked at the official in disbelief and shifted his gaze to the Cowboy bench. Branch and Guerrero were on their feet snarling at the official, while Coach Smith pumped his fist at his embattled freshman and pointed to the center of the mat, urging Morgan to maintain his focus and fight on. Chris Pickering came to his feet, his rubber-gloved hands holding another clean blood-plug, but Morgan's expression turned to stone. He waved Pickering off.

Morgan had lost a tough match earlier in the day against Hofstra, when his will seemed to wear down in the final period and relinquished an early lead. Now it appeared Ciasulli was reaching for that same Achilles' Heel in Morgan's newly-minted armor, his inability to wrestle tough at the end of a close match. But the time was short for analysis.

The match was now in overtime.

* * *

His teammates call him "sunshine." While Okies fled to California seeking opportunity during the dust bowl in the 1930s, the California-bred Nathan Morgan came to Oklahoma State in 2004 from Bakersfield, California, where he captured three state championships, won 166 matches, and lost only a handful during a stellar high school career.

These numbers were formidable, but he owned an even more impressive winning streak. Through a church program spearheaded in a low-income neighborhood by his father Larry, designed to assist children excel in school through developing their capacity to memorize, Nathan had committed to memory more than 1,000 Bible verses during a stretch run between kindergarten and high school.

His hero was John Smith. "I remember watching Coach wrestle on television when I was a little kid. I had my picture taken with him when I was seven years old. Now I'm wrestling for him. It's a great honor."[19]

The slender and slightly bow-legged Morgan possessed the lanky build of his head coach. He owned the technique of a surgeon, the countenance of a choirboy, the body fat of a surfboard, and the mind of a digital tape recorder. His history teacher commented that when Nathan was asked a question, he was the only student who repeated verbatim the answer from the book. But he worried that while Nathan knew the answers, he was not sure if he *understood* the context behind words he recited.

His bloodline was pure wrestling. Nathan's father Larry was a standout collegiate wrestler at Cal Poly and later served as an assistant under Bakersfield coach Joe Seay. Seay would become the wrestling coach at Oklahoma State before Smith took over the program in 1993. Larry Morgan came within one match of making the 1976 Olympic team. "I beat the guy who made the team five out of six times."[20] The defeat still seemed to haunt the memory of Nathan's father. He had trained with Dan Gable at Iowa for over a year and roomed with former Iowa assistant and now Minnesota head coach "J" Robinson. Larry hesitated when his son expressed a serious interest in wrestling. "I didn't want Nathan to go into the sport. Look what you get when you're finished."[21] But when Nathan's family traveled to Stillwater for the Iowa match weeks earlier, the trim and conditioned father, whose blond hair was lightly touched with gray, drilled with the son in the Cowboy wrestling room.

Nathan Morgan was widely recruited but returned calls to only two schools, Cal Poly and Oklahoma State. Nathan knew his father wanted him to remain in California, and his respect for his dad was a factor. "My dad was an Olympic alternate and fourth in the worlds [World Championships]. He got me into wrestling. He got me fired up about it. He has taught me so much."[22] But in the end, Nathan shook the sand out of his blond California locks and headed to Stillwater to fulfill a dream… to wear the Cowboy colors and wrestle for John Smith in hopes of one day becoming an Olympic champion. With the spirits of former Olympians populating the wrestling room, Morgan believed the Cowboy program provided the laboratory to complete that dream. "I miss my friends every once in a while, but for wrestling this is the place to be. This fits my style."[23] He was thrilled to be a Cowboy. After his first varsity match he wanted to wear home the black warm-ups reserved for OSU starters. His teammates speculated he slept in them.

Nathan relished the personal challenge wrestling provided. "We work so hard in the practice room, but the tournaments are the fun part. It shows who works hard. I just love it. I love the grind. It's just you and him. He wants to beat you and you want to beat him. That's what makes it fun." A serious engineering student with a penchant for math, Morgan carried his study habits into his wrestling preparation. "In wrestling you can never stop learning."[24]

The highly-skilled Morgan, who studied film by the hour to improve his technique, understood that flair and dexterity would only take him so far. In the toughest matches against the most obstinate opponents, technique and precision must be fueled by hard boil and gristle. Coach Smith noticed that the older, bigger and sometimes ill-tempered Daniel Frishkorn occasionally pushed Nathan around in the wrestling room, "and he lets him."[25] The head coach realized Morgan might not be frenzied and mean enough yet to win against the older and stronger wrestlers in his weight. "Slick moves won't win at this level in the heat of battle. Sometimes Nathan would as soon hug you as slap you." Nathan had memorized the correct answer to this gap in his development. "I need to get into more of that 'banger' type mentality."[26] But as his history teacher observed, does he understand the tension between Old Testament judgment and damnation and New Testament grace and compassion?

Perhaps the ensuing minutes would tell.

* * *

The crowd let out a peculiar bellowing growl as the Lehigh bench pumped fists in the air. The word was out on Nathan Morgan. He starts fast, but will stall out in the later portion of tough matches, especially from the bottom position against stronger and more aggressive opponents. The Cowboy wrestlers, led by Steve Mocco, urged their teammate on as Nathan took the center of the mat.

If matches are tied at the end of regulation, the competitors wrestle one minute from the neutral position. The first wrestler who scores a point wins the match. Morgan and Ciasulli shook hands once again and squared off. Eleven seconds into the first overtime period Morgan hit still another low single leg and controlled Ciasulli the entire period but could not break the Lehigh redshirt sophomore's desperation death-grip on his leg that prevented a takedown. The period expired and the match went to the first of two 30-second tiebreaker periods.

In the first tiebreaker Morgan chose the down position. Ciasulli broke him to the mat, sunk in two legs, and rode Morgan out, making eye contact with the crowd as he bullied the Cowboy's head to the mat.

In the second tiebreaker no takedowns were scored and the backpedaling Ciasulli was penalized for stalling as Morgan continued to move forward and apply pressure. To stem the onslaught Ciasulli slapped Morgan's nose, causing the plug to redden and fill up. But Morgan waved off the Cowboy medical staff again and walked slowly to the center of the mat. The match remained tied, and the wrestlers went to the next round of sudden death. But again, neither wrestler scored from the neutral position.

In the next tiebreaker period Morgan sunk in a deep spiral ride, fought off repeated rolls by Ciasulli, controlled his legs for the last few seconds of the period, and rode his opponent out for the balance of the period.

In the final tiebreaker period Morgan began in the down position. Because of Ciasulli's slight riding time advantage Morgan had to escape from the hard-riding Ciasulli or he would lose. Off the whistle Morgan came to his feet as Ciasulli draped around his back in piggyback position. As the sold-out Stabler arena roared for their wrestler to hang on, Morgan pried a sweaty arm under Ciasulli's leg, went to the mat, turned into his Lehigh opponent for a two-point reversal. The crowd groaned as Morgan rode Ciasulli out for the remaining few seconds.

Nathan Morgan won in overtime 6-4.

He shook Coach Smith's hand as he walked off the mat and sat down, removed the blood-plug from his nose and accepted the congratulations from smiling teammate Steve Mocco, who stood over his sweating and trembling comrade.

Morgan had theoretically known he needed to wrestle hard until the end of his matches. He had that part memorized. His performance this night indicated he was beginning to *understand.*

Lehigh fans also began to understand as they walked toward the exits while Ronnie Delk hung on to defeat Jeff Santo 14-12. Zack Esposito nailed Dave Nakasone 20-5, and the Cowboys had won their twentieth dual of the season 24-9.

After the match an excited Steve Mocco made his cameo appearance on the Cowboy post-game radio show. "We came together as a team and performed like warriors. Nathan Morgan wrestled like a champion."[27] Cowboy wrestling voice J. Carl Guymon mentioned to Mocco the controversial stalling call against Morgan. "We got an adverse call. We got an adverse situation. But we had to battle through that. Did he come through when the doors were closed in his face? He blasted through the doors. Doors can't stop him. Right through. Boom!"[28] Mocco's enthusiasm was not limited to Nathan Morgan's performance. In rapid-fire cadence he recognized the unsung heroes Derek Stevens, Ronnie Delk, and Clay Kehrer, who won clutch matches after two Murderer's Row members, Rosholt and Hendricks, lost close decisions. "Ronnie Delk slammed the door on Lehigh. Lehigh, the door was slammed on you."[29]

Guymon asked Mocco about the progress of his own season, but the Cowboy heavyweight again turned attention to his teammates. "I'm flowing. I'm in the flow. The whole team is coming together, wrestling like warriors."[30] Finally, as Mocco stood up from the press table to grant another interview, the bigger-than-life Master of Destruction, and according to *Sports Illustrated* the most feared man in college wrestling, gave his parting comments. "Colleen, I love you, thanks for listening."[31] Colleen Mocco is Steve's baby sister.

During the post-match comments Coach Smith analyzed Morgan's victory and reflected on the California true-freshman's winding journey toward maturity. "A young kid can break because of those bad calls. I think his loss this morning allowed him to stay focused in that match and find a way to win. He learned to stay focused, no matter what happens, no matter what kind of calls, get your hand raised in those tight battles."[32]

The team showered, dressed, and piled into the vans for the seventy-five mile drive to the Newark hotel. As the team filed through the hotel lobby, the dark-eyed, husky hotel concierge asked, "How did Mocco do?"[33]

Several of the wrestlers, knowing the next weigh-in was seven days away, huddled at tables throughout the hotel restaurant. Others went back to their rooms to rest. B.J. Jackson, perhaps the best natural athlete on the Cowboy squad, who had been transported to New York for possible duty in case of an injury to a teammate, sat in the Mocco hotel room on a bench next to Smith. Jackson, who had seen no action during the day, was handed a chunk of chocolate cake half the size of a small bread loaf. He looked Coach Smith in the eyes, gazed back down at the cake, hesitated barely a moment as he seemed to weigh his options, and began stuffing the cake into his mouth. The Cowboys were relaxing. The mission was accomplished. But Derek Stevens was not to be found.

The Cowboy 125-pound pre-med major, who had lost his starting job to freshman phenom Coleman Scott earlier in the year and who tonight nailed a crucial win against Lehigh in Scott's absence, realized on a pragmatic level that even though he was a junior, this might have been his last match as a Cowboy varsity wrestler. He dressed warmly, took a bus to the nearest subway stop, and sat alone on a train to Madison Square Garden. He took stairs up to Fifth Avenue where his eyes caught a neighborhood pizza shop, the same one his girlfriend had discovered while attending a cheerleading camp in New York months earlier. He bought a slice and ate it. For the first time in years he ate pizza in February without a sense of guilt. He looked down at his plate, saw a piece of crust, ordered another and ate the crust. "It was some of the best food I have ever had."[34] He then called his girlfriend and told her where he was and what he had just eaten. He got up slowly and walked onto a sidewalk still bustling at midnight on a cold Sunday evening. He walked with hands in his pockets back toward Madison Square Garden and ended up in a jazz bar where he played a game of pool and reflected on the day where his pressure-packed victory gave the Cowboys a toe-hold to pull out their twentieth straight dual victory of the season, and on a life well-lived. "I'm glad I was able to help my team win an important dual meet."[35] He continued to walk the streets of New York City. The sidewalks remained crowded as he took a deep, cleansing breath and turned home. He arrived back to the hotel at 4:00 a.m. where he slept the gloried sleep of the crowned and victorious.

The Cowboys left the next morning at 11:30 for the airport. Earlier in the morning while taping his weekly radio show in a cramped hotel room, Coach Smith commented that the travel routine the previous two days "was not as tough as I had wanted it to be."[36] As the wrestlers boarded the vans for the short ride to the airport, Chris Pendleton stood at the front desk in panic mode as he inquired whether the hotel personnel had located his misplaced wallet. His giggling teammates finally confessed they had his wallet, but enjoyed seeing him squirm.

The wrestlers, dressed in nylon black and orange warm-ups, arrived at the airport and waited by the gate. Some slept while others talked. No one dared to eat.

They finally boarded their commercial aircraft and occupied the back eight rows of the flight. As Morgan slowly walked down the aisle to claim his assigned seat, veteran Zack Esposito noticed Morgan's swollen nose and scraped face. "Your modeling days are over. Now you're starting to look like a wrestler. You have a crooked nose. You can get it fixed in 10 years when you're done."[37]

Seeing the flight attendant pass by, Esposito smiled and bellowed "Seat 28A would like an extra long submarine sandwich please."[38] An inveterate newspaper reader who has traveled across forty-five countries in connection with his wrestling pursuits, Coach Smith suppressed a slight smile as he flipped through the international section of the *New York Times*.

Morgan was asleep before the plane took off, his face bearing the bookmarks of victory. The team returned home as the sun was setting in Stillwater.

COWBOYS ARE AS DIFFERENT
AS THE STARS AND SKY.

—Kurt Markus, *American Cowboy* January/February 2001

sixteen

the oklahoma rematch

02.20.04

THEY CALLED IT *BEDLAM,* and it was the first known psychiatric hospital in the world. Founded in London in 1247, it became infamous for its harsh treatment of the insane, and by the 18th century observers could pay a penny to enter and watch confused and irrational behavior. Webster defined bedlam as a place, scene, or state of uproar and confusion.[1] By the 17th century the term was used to describe "any scene of great confusion or uproar."[2] By the mid-twentieth century, sports writers and television commentators came to refer to any wrestling competition between Oklahoma State and Oklahoma as "The Bedlam Series." It was an apt description.

In one memorable match against archrival Oklahoma, a rival wrestler's brother jumped from the stands during the heavyweight bout, ran onto the mat, and delivered a haymaker to the side of an OSU wrestler's headgear. After order was restored, the Cowboy heavyweight attacked his opponent and turned him to his back for a memorable pin. Another evening, a Cowboy heavyweight applied a crossface to his opponent, and was bitten on the arm, resulting in a disqualification, an OSU victory, and a frenzied crowd whose roar would drown out a small airliner.

The 2005 Bedlam rematch, scheduled on the Cowboy's home mat in Stillwater, would be held six days after the Cowboys arrived home from their east coast swing. Smith gave the team Monday off, and they returned to the wrestling room the next morning to prepare for the Oklahoma match with a three-day cluster of brutal practices that began at daylight Tuesday.

Stillwater News Press Sports Editor Roger Moore likened John Smith's demeanor that week to that of a "drill sergeant" during the brutal cycle of workouts, which featured sprints up stadium stairs in Gallagher-Iba Arena on Tuesday, early morning drills followed by more wrestling and stadium stairs on Wednesday, topped off by additional wrestling and drills on Thursday. "When you are asking for more you tend to get a little more involved in the workout. There is a tendency, when you've worked hard during a week, to let down at the end of that week. That is when guys have to push through tough workouts like they push through in tough matches."[3]

Smith gave the team a day off on Friday to allow torn and fatigued muscle tissue to heal. Before leaving for Tulsa in the afternoon to watch his young son Joseph participate in a youth wrestling tournament, he granted six radio interviews about the upcoming dual with Oklahoma. "The match is important for the seniors. When they turn 40 they reflect back and say, 'I never lost a Bedlam match.' I can't say that. During my time we lost two or three times."[4]

On Sunday morning the Cowboys began drifting into the wrestling room shortly after ten. The starters checked their weight, slipped into sweat gear, and began to drill and loosen up. As the Oklahoma squad strolled with a practiced nonchalance into the Cowboy dressing room in time for the one o'clock weigh-in, some momentarily held their glance toward the north corner of the wrestling room as Cowboy assistant coaches Branch, Smith and Guerrero sat and softly chatted. During their collegiate careers at Oklahoma State the three amassed a combined record of 330-36-2. They captured eight conference titles and nine individual national championships, more titles than most schools realize in their program's entire history. The tenured assistant was assistant head coach Mark Branch.

* * *

An all-purpose athlete from Newkirk, Oklahoma, Mark Branch spent his boyhood Octobers under Friday night lights. "We didn't have 22 guys out for the team, so I played offense, defense, and kicker."[5] In the winters he captured two high school state wrestling titles for the Tigers, but Newkirk

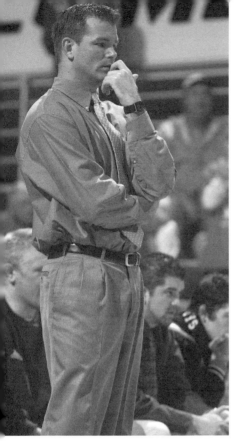

Assistant Head Coach Mark Branch looks on. Branch, a two-time national champion and four-time Academic All-American at OSU, is one of only 11 wrestlers to reach the NCAA finals on four separate occasions. His brutal mat wrestling helped transition the Cowboy style in the mid-90s. *Courtesy Dr. Jeremy Cook.*

competed in the smallest of the four high school athletic classes in Oklahoma, and Branch's raw abilities were not detected on the radar screens of many wrestling powerhouses. But the lanky, slope-shouldered Branch was a good student, and with two Oklahoma high school titles under his belt, universities did come calling. One visit started out promising, turned disappointing, but then ended up being fateful. "I took a recruiting visit to Notre Dame but days later read in the paper they were dropping their wrestling program."[6] During that recruiting visit to South Bend, Notre Dame wrestler J.J. McGrew, who later transferred to Oklahoma State, served as his host. After transferring to OSU he mentioned Branch to OSU interim coaches John Smith and Kenny Monday, who were busily working the phones attempting to assemble a team, as several Cowboy wrestlers had transferred to other schools when news of the NCAA sanctions were confirmed.

During this time the probation-racked Cowboy program was in disarray, and Branch, whose father played basketball for Henry Iba's NCAA tournament team in 1965, was offered a scholarship. "I know I was lucky. The program was in shambles."[7]

The transition from high school star to college freshman workout-fodder was not easy. "My first few weeks here were a disaster in terms of ability to compete. I went weeks without even getting a takedown. I couldn't perform the drills. I had never moved like that before."[8] He survived his redshirt year, made progress in the wrestling room, and developed a penchant for riding his opponents with an octopus-like leg ride, a process he attributed to daily, brutal workouts with stronger and older wrestlers during that first year. "I was definitely a product of the environment."[9]

Branch rotated in and out of the Cowboy starting lineup his freshman redshirt season and entered the 1994 NCAA tournament with more losses under his belt than victories, barely qualifying for the tournament by placing at the Big 12 conference meet. The nervous Branch never had attended an NCAA tournament before, but Coach Smith saw potential in the gristle-tough redshirt freshman. In his first varsity match held in Gallagher-Iba Arena weeks earlier, Branch, who had only one varsity victory under his belt at the time, pushed nationally ranked Shaon Fry of Missouri to overtime before being outflanked in a sudden-death scramble. He went on to lose several close matches, but the light seemed to come on for Branch at the NCAA tournament. Coach Smith recalled the transformation. "We got him under the bleachers before every one of his matches, telling him over and over he was capable of winning."[10]

The unseeded redshirt freshman from Newkirk with an 8-9 record, who a year earlier had experienced takedown droughts in the wrestling room that lasted for weeks, stunned the number two seed by major decision in the first round, kept grinding through the winner's bracket, and on Saturday afternoon found himself facing four-time national qualifier Laszlo Molnar of Cal-State Fullerton in the finals. "I was fine until I walked in and saw the mat sitting up on that [four-foot high] stage. I'd never seen anything like that. It made me nervous, just the setting, 11,000 people watching you wrestle up on that stage."[11] But his stage fright subsided. He nailed a takedown with 32 seconds left in the match and won the national championship as a freshman.

The following year Branch again advanced to the finals. Proving Smith's adage that it is sometimes times easier to win the first title than the second, he lost to archrival Marcus Mollica of Arizona State in the finals.

The next year Branch leveled the competition during the regular season, but during the 1996 NCAA finals against an Iowa wrestler he had pummeled 9-1 during the regular season, Branch tore the anterior cruciate ligament in his right knee. Doctors predicted he would possibly return to the mat in January 1997, but the determined Branch was drilling in the wrestling room five months later, and returned his senior year to win all 32 of his matches. He stormed to his second national title, where he defeated Penn's Brandon Slay 3-2 at the NCAA tournament held at Northern Iowa University before 17,437 fans in what was believed to be the largest crowd ever to view an amateur wrestling match,

The victory made the four-time All-American one of only 11 wrestlers to advance to the NCAA finals four consecutive years, all while earning a spot on the Academic All-American team and receiving postgraduate scholarships from the Big 12 and the NCAA. Iowa coach Dan Gable thought Branch to be "the best [wrestler] OSU had."[12]

Branch joined Coach Smith's staff the following year, and was named assistant head coach in 2000. His myriad of responsibilities included recruiting, teaching technique during practice, making travel plans for the trips, providing counseling to homesick or discouraged wrestlers, reviewing film, coaching during competition, and often wrestling full speed in the wrestling room, where he routinely manhandled the toughest and most accomplished Cowboy varsity wrestlers, including national champions and All-Americans. A NASCAR fan and mechanic by heart, he could be found helping Cowboy wrestlers repair their vehicles when he and his wife Susan were not caring for their daughter Maggie Bell and newborn son Mason Lane.

When Coach Smith was out of town recruiting, Branch conducted practice. Businesslike and stingy with words, he barked out the singular word "running" and the wrestlers began their running drills, or he let fly the word "track" and the team descended to the running track downstairs. During the workouts he stood with his arms folded, head swiveling from right to left as he observed the wrestlers drill and wrestle. One afternoon the middleweights rested their hands on their knees between periods. "Get your hands off your elbows. I've never seen so much of this as I've seen today. It's becoming a habit."[13] With the other Cowboy assistants, he constantly moved from group to group and offered instructions, demonstrated technique, and offered encouragement.

The prototype Cowboy wrestler of the early John Smith era was known, correctly or not, for cobra-like quickness, relentless motion, and elegant leverage. This contrasted with the aggressive and pounding style of chief rival Iowa, which had captured NCAA team titles during seven of Smith's first 10 years as Cowboy coach. Branch represented the evolution of this Cowboy prototype, adding brutal mat skills and gristle-like toughness to the exquisite technique and unyielding fluidity of early John Smith teams. A new paradigm was being cast, and its archetype was the pride of Newkirk, two-time national champion and four-time national finalist Mark Branch.

* * *

As two-o'clock approached, the Cowboy starters were engrossed in their pre-match routine. Pendleton ghost-wrestled on his feet on the north mat. Mocco ran sprints. Coach Guerrero paced about as Morgan and Scott drilled on their feet. Smith sat on a chair against the wall as his eyes shifted from wrestler to wrestler. Three minutes before match time Coach Smith stood. "Let's get suited up." The team gathered around Pendleton on the south mat, and some giggled as a frantic Mocco, who had lost track of time while warming up, rushed into the locker room to pull on his singlet. Morgan ghost wrestled by himself on the north wall as they waited on Mocco. After the team prayer they gathered around Coach Smith, who stood at the mouth of the hallway leading into the arena. As usual, words were minced. "Early victories. You guys get us started here."[14] Scott and Morgan's eyes widen slightly as the team jogged into the arena to the roar of the Cowboy fans.

Moments earlier three seniors received recognition for their quiet and unseen, but nevertheless crucial, contribution to the Cowboy's accomplishments over the recent past. All three had been high school stars who would have made the starting lineups of many Division I teams across the nation. Mike Christian, a highly-decorated high school wrestler from Lynnwood, Washington who compiled a 30-16-lifetime career record at Oklahoma State, was Steve Mocco's daily workout partner. An economics/pre-law major headed for a career in banking and finance and a first-team Academic All-Big 12 honoree, Christian chuckled when he thought of his afternoons in the Cowboy wrestling room where he faced off with Mocco. "His reputation precedes him a little bit. people get kind of psyched out when they wrestle him."[15]According to Coach Smith, Christian's dedication was "unbelievable."[16]

Also honored was senior Clark Shouse, one of only 18 Oklahoma high school wrestlers ever to win four state titles, compiled a 29-19 record as a Cowboy. The hard-nosed finance major who hunted and fished in his free time, often battled NCAA champion Johny Hendricks to a standstill in the wrestling room. In the classroom he garnered first-team academic All-Big 12 honors, regularly made the Dean's Honor Roll, and was named a USAA All-American Scholar.

Brett Munson, a Kansas state champion who went 24-22 as a Cowboy, was often asked to wrestle up a weight where he regularly performed with characteristic toughness and tenacity. He was awarded the top Academic Freshman Wrestler Award, was named a USAA All-American Scholar, and made the Dean's Honor Roll and Big 12 Honor Roll four times. His brothers were Division 1 wrestlers.

After those introductions, former Cowboy wrestlers who returned to Stillwater for a recognition ceremony encircled the orange mat. The youngest honoree was from the previous year's squad, while the oldest was born more than 90 years earlier. During that stretch 77 Cowboys had captured 125 individual NCAA championships. The NCAA tournament had been held 69 times and OSU had 32 first-place team finishes.[17] After introductions, former Cowboy wrestling coach Tommy Chesboro gently rolled legendary Cowboy coach Myron Roderick onto the mat in a wheelchair. Roderick, a former Cowboy national champion who coached OSU to seven NCAA titles during his 13 years at the Cowboy helm, was recovering from an illness and received a warm ovation from the crowd of 8,697. But the loudest applause was reserved for Cowboy assistant coach Pat Smith.

* * *

To win an NCAA wrestling title is a monumental accomplishment, a task that afforded only the slightest margin of error. Dozens of world-class wrestlers, many of whom stormed on to Olympic glory, never stepped onto that first place podium at an NCAA tournament, and often grieved their failure to claim that most coveted of titles for the rest of their lives. For some, the pain of loss was so cutting that they could not attend the NCAA tournament again, even as a spectator.

But to win two NCAA titles was more than monumental, it is Herculean. After winning that first championship, complacency often caused the

Cowboy assistant coach Pat Smith, one of only two four-time national champions in college wrestling history, stands and offers encouragement. Smith coached the Cowboy middle weights. *Courtesy Dr. Jeremy Cook.*

athlete's motivation to slip. Some repeated their title, but it was a remarkable achievement. Just like a major league pitcher attempting to toss two consecutive no-hitters, eventually a bloop single fell in the gap.

To win the NCAA title three consecutive times was more than Herculean, it virtually transcended all laws of probability. There were too many unseen land mines to avoid. An injury. A bad call. A tough or unknown opponent hiding like a sniper in the grass, marking his target, wanting to write his own history. But to win four NCAA titles lies somewhere between absurd and preposterous.

Pat Smith was pulled out of redshirt status after the holiday break of his freshman year, and proceeded to lose five matches during his first year of competition. But he avoided early-round upsets which had stunned brothers Lee Roy and John in their early NCAA tournaments and recovered to capture his first NCAA title weeks later as a freshman, taking Navy's Scott Schleicher down in just four seconds on his way to a 11-7 win. In the finals the following year he hit Iowa's Tom Ryan with a low single leg with 35 seconds left to prevail 7-6 before 13,223 hostile fans in Iowa City, Iowa.

The next year brother John was named co-coach of the Cowboys pending the NCAA investigation, and Pat returned to Oklahoma City, host city of the tournament that year, to pursue his third title before family and friends. "You're going to have to shoot me if you're going to beat me."[18] A determined Smith slipped past former Oklahoma high school nemesis Ray Miller from Arizona State 3-1 off a first period takedown for his third title. The Cowboy team, in an effort to soften the body blow due to come from the NCAA, did not accept its second-place team trophy.

The Cowboys were barred from competing in the NCAA tournament in 1993, but Pat Smith chose to remain at Oklahoma State, took a redshirt year and returned in 1994 in his quest for what for years before had been unthinkable.

In the days leading up to that fourth NCAA tournament, the issues were clearly framed. "I've lived with the fact for four years, that I'm shooting for four national titles. Every day I run into somebody who talks about four national titles. I'm more excited for it to be here than anyone."[19]

In his final match as a collegian, held in the Dean Smith Center on the University of North Carolina campus, Smith led 3-0 after a first period takedown and second period escape. He was taken down later in the second period, but quickly escaped and held on for a 5-3 victory. The win was a family affair. "I've always dreamed of winning four national titles, but I never really pictured my brother in the corner being the head coach. He's the coach of a national championship team, and I've won my fourth title; it's a dream come true for our family."[20]

His relationship with brother and coach John Smith had been simple. "When we're out of the wrestling room, we've got a great relationship. When we're out of the wrestling room we're brothers. We act like brothers, we enjoy being around each other. But when we're in the wrestling room, it's business. He's the coach and I'm the athlete and what he says goes."[21]

Fellow Cowboy Kenny Monday defeated Pat in the final round of the 1996 Olympic trials, and the four-time national champion returned and joined his brother's staff in Stillwater.

He lived outside of Stillwater near family. He liked to hunt, fish, and ride horses for days along the sand and brush of the Cimarron River south of town. He enjoyed reading, spending time with family and friends, and still loved everything about his sport, although sore knees limited his action.

During practice he walked about the Cowboy wrestling room in a long-sleeve t-shirt and black warm-up pants offering instruction and barking encouragement. When the tempo of practice needed quickening he leaned against the wrestling room wall and pounded the orange padding with the palm of his hands. The team listened.

He did not need to talk and brag. He had a gentle bearing that was prone to laughter, and when he entered any room his friends smiled and his rivals whispered. He was the man who won four titles. He was Pat Smith of Oklahoma State.

* * *

The Cowboys entered the Oklahoma match with a 115-24-9 series advantage. OSU had captured 21 straight duals against OU, with the last loss coming in 1995 when the Sooner heavyweight won an overtime match to give Oklahoma a rare victory. Coach Smith understood the importance of this contest against his team's home-state rival in terms of recruiting, bragging rights, and national perception. "It's not just another dual meet. In the end, what you do at nationals is how you're judged no matter what kind of regular season you had. But beating OU…they know it when they beat us."[22]

Before the match Oklahoma coach Jack Spates seemed to attribute much of the Cowboy's success to having recent signee Steve Mocco in the lineup. "Look at the impact Mocco has made on Oklahoma State's team. All three teams that have given OSU a close match [Illinois, Lehigh, Nebraska] would have won if it hadn't been for Mocco."[23]

The Cowboys were attempting to claim their twenty-first consecutive dual win on the season, but once again they faced the prospect of falling behind early. Coleman Scott, in redshirt status when the Cowboys met OU earlier in the year, faced Oklahoma's best hope for a national title in number-one ranked and undefeated Sam Hazewinkel. The Florida native, whose father and uncle were Olympians, earlier told a sports psychologist utilized by the Oklahoma wrestling program that he pictured himself not as a "panther" or "machine gun" like some of his teammates had described themselves, but rather as a "child." The 32-0 Sooner All-American explained. "Because a child's main thing is go out and have fun. When you lose, it doesn't matter. "[In college] when you wrestle, you have everything to lose. I do not need that extra pressure. I'm a child."[24]

An early head snap gave Hazewinkel a 2-0 lead. Scott quickly escaped, but a textbook arm drag registered Hazewinkel's second takedown of the period, followed quickly by another Scott escape. The Sooner then applied an unforgiving second period ride, and began the third period in the down position leading 4-2, when he turned into Scott and elevated his leg for what appeared to be a certain reversal. But Scott applied his uncanny ability to wrestle aggressively with his leg hoisted in the air and above his head, and managed to wrap up his opponent and regain the top position. Hazewinkel escaped seconds later, fought off Scott's fireman's

Sam Hazewinkle controls Coleman Scott during their first of three encounters. Possessing the balance of a tightrope walker, Scott often scored from this position. *Courtesy Mika Matzen.*

carry and double leg attempt in the last few seconds of the match to capture a 6-2 victory.

As Scott walked off the match Coach Smith sat motionless and said nothing, but followed his 125 pounder with his eyes as the panting and sweaty freshman walked away from his teammates and coaches to a sanctuary behind a section of bleachers, only to be interrupted moments later by an encouraging but intense Eric Guerrero's admonitions and remarks.

A well-meaning Cowboy fan yelled to Scott as he sat on the floor with a white towel draped around his head, "Good try, Coleman." Coleman Scott's chest heaved. He closed his eyes and pretended not to hear.

Scott's loss was reported as an afterthought in the media accounts the following day. As expected, he had avoided humiliation and had lost in a respectable fashion to the top-ranked wrestler in the land. From the most gratuitous fan, "Scott is destined for second place

Assistant Coach Eric Guerrero, a three-time national champion and 2004 U.S. Olympian, looks on during the Oklahoma match in Norman. Guerrero, who posted a 110-12 record at OSU, trains the lower weights. *Courtesy Dr. Jeremy Cook.*

as long as Hazewinkel is around."[25] Perhaps Coleman Scott's opportunity would come sometime later. But for now, the talented and experienced Hazewinkel was the class of the nation and the man to beat at 125.

Morgan put the Cowboys back on track with an 8-4 victory over Joe Comparin. Coach Smith was displeased that Morgan failed to ride Comparin out in the final period. Branch joined in, and then passed him on to Eric Guerrero, the Cowboy assistant in charge of the lighter weights.

* * *

In the early to mid-90s OSU bled you out with paper cuts. As the years progressed they bloodied your nose as well. If this gradual evolution of Cowboy wrestling was embodied in middleweight champion Mark Branch, it was passed on to the lighter weights in the form of touchstone Eric Guerrero, whose virulent aggression and nimble methodology firmly tied down the Cowboy Way that evolved during the decade of the '90s.

Eric Guerrero competed for Oklahoma State from 1996 to 1999 at 126 and 133 pounds. The dark-haired California native was only one of nine Cowboys to earn four-time All-American honors. He compiled a 110-12-career record and captured three NCAA titles, making him the 13th three-time NCAA champ in OSU history. An expert freestyle wrestler who made the USA freestyle team from 1998 to 2004, Guerrero represented the United States in the 2004 Olympic Games in Athens, Greece.

He joined the Cowboy staff in 2000 as strength and conditioning coach, and had a straightforward approach to the sport he took up while a young boy growing up in California. "I enjoy wrestling. If you get bored with a hobby, you need to stop. It's fun to get motivated. It's fun to get nervous. I have the same amount of nervousness as I did when I was eight years old."[26] It was now his job to teach and manage the young and talented stable of talent Coach Smith stockpiled over the past two seasons at the three lowest weights. "In the lighter weights the body structure is different. More flexibility. More quickness. Lots of technique."[27] He spoke and moved in staccato motions as he taught and exhorted his young titans, "When the whistle blows, you're in a fight."[28] To Delk, "Stalk your opponent."[29] He worries that Morgan was not "intense enough today."[30] He worried about Coleman Scott's injuries. He fretted about Derek Stevens getting discouraged, and Derrick Fleenor having his opportunities to succeed. "The media likes to write about different styles of particular schools or styles. But in the end it's about wrestling. Sometimes your style will change and you will pull something out from years back that's not necessarily your style, but you find a way to win. It's about takedowns, escapes, and turning people. It's about wrestling."[31]

The expressive and well-spoken education major spoke with the precision and anticipation of a young engineer working on a structure in progress. His speech was sprinkled with adverbs and gestures, and his dark eyes communicated a singular passion for The Cowboy Way. "It is more difficult to coach kids who for whatever reason you don't connect with or communicate easily with. Every young man needs to be handled differently. But you hope they all take pride in wearing the orange singlet. You hope they all want to be a part of our tradition of excellence and training and commitment that hopefully will one day allow them to achieve their goals as wrestlers and individuals."[32]

The young Olympian, still raw from a 2004 defeat in Athens, found the transition from competitor to coach and teacher to be difficult but always rewarding. "When I competed I only had to worry about my own weight and my own training and my own motivations. That inward focus created a form of self-absorption that borderd on selfishness. Coach Smith constantly told us that it's not about us, but rather the wrestlers. I understand that better now."[33]

Guerrero and his wife Malia were devoted and sensitive parents of Kaitlyn, their pre-school daughter. "My experience as a father hopefully has made me a better coach. And perhaps my experiences with wrestlers will help me develop my parenting skills. Coaching and parenting require the same aptitudes. Patience. Selflessness. Love. Commitment. The dedication to create something beyond myself. Dealing with disappointment and failure. The experiences complement one other."[34]

His penchant for wrestling came from his father, a former collegiate wrestler at Fresno State. He shared an attention to detail with his older sister, a graduate student at Berkley who studied ancient biblical languages and who spent hours a day translating text from the original Greek. The precise and organized Guerrero maintained a spreadsheet that tracked wrestlers' weight and progress. "Weight management at this level is such a science. I give the young guys diet plans with hopes they will stay within three or four pounds of their competitive weight. If they weigh 133 during competition, I want them drilling and competing in the wrestling room at 133. Otherwise they

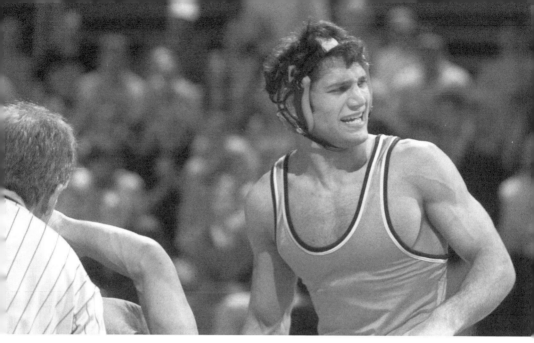

Zack Esposito gets direction from the bench against Matt Storniolo from Oklahoma. *Courtesy Mika Matzen.*

are working out in a false reality. I want their workouts and the physical demands on their bodies during practice to replicate competition as much as possible."[35]

The transition from pupil to teacher, from center of attention to behind-the-curtain supporter, is a new reality, but a necessary segment of the journey. "I want to be a head coach in due time, but I know I have to earn that privilege. For now, I wake up and think about what I can do today to help make our guys more successful? How can I help my guys progress both as individuals as well as wrestlers?"[36]

In the end, his guiding metaphor was family. "I come from a really large family, but at the same time it's extremely close. It's a cultural thing. Family is very important to me." He reflected on the painful loss of his grandmother during his junior season and concluded "…I promise you I would not [had been] wrestling in the national tournament if the funeral had been that week."[37] He received this devotion to family from his parents Sebastian and Virginia, and was intent on handing it off to his own. "As parents and coaches we assume a lot of responsibility, whether we want it or not. Take my daughter Kaitlyn. She models my behavior. I see her copying my gestures and my facial expressions and the way I speak.

The stand-up was the signature Cowboy move in the 50's and 60's. Kevin Ward executes his version during a 6-2 victory over Charles Jones of Oklahoma. *Courtesy Mika Matzen.*

I know our wrestlers look to us for how to train and wrestle and how to act. Eyes are always on us."[38]

* * *

The Cowboy coaches continued to deliberate who would carry the Cowboy orange into post-season at the 141 weight class. The experienced and dedicated but low-scoring fifth year senior Ronnie Delk, or the explosive but young and sometimes brooding Daniel Frishkorn. On the final night of the dual season Coach Smith gave Ronnie Delk one more opportunity. A Delk victory over his longtime nemesis Teyon Ware would make the decision even more difficult for an agonizing coaching staff, who balanced senior loyalty against "who gives us a better chance to win in March?" The crowd came to its feet as Delk exploded with an early takedown, but the second-ranked Ware's second period ride and final period takedown handed Delk a 7-3 loss. Ronnie Delk walked off the mat, picked up his warm-ups, and sat alone as sweat dripped from his chin onto the arena floor for the last time.

Esposito followed with a freewheeling 11-6 victory over fourth-ranked Matt Storniolo. After the match he reflected on his 28th win of the season.

"The first match [against Storniolo] I wrestled more his style, I think I was a little too conservative. I wanted to let it fly and really keep the pace up. Those guys can be dangerous because thy are funky and they can get you in some tough positions, but we are coached to be aggressive and not put ourselves in those situations."[39]

Kevin Ward, 16-9 and at risk not to qualify for the NCAA tournament and in the doghouse since the Nebraska dual, used a late takedown to put away Charles Jones 6-2. Johny Hendricks seemed to be wrestling himself back into form by shutting out Wes Roberts 4-0. Those four consecutive wins gave the Cowboys a 12-6 dual lead and set the table for Chris Pendleton's final home match against E. K. Waldhaus, who had handed Pendleton his only defeat of the year the previous December.

The crowd cheered heartily as Pendleton slapped Smith's hand and stepped before the home crowd for the final time in an OSU singlet. It had been a long and winding road for the number-one ranked leader of the team. Coming into the Cowboy wrestling room was an eye-opener. "I seemed like I was getting pounded on by somebody different everyday."[40] He was injured his freshman year during the Big 12 Championships, and lost to a Lehigh wrestler in his second NCAA tournament, where he finished third. "I have a lot of big-time regrets about that sophomore season. Taking third may have helped me grow as a person, but I still wish I could have won

Chris Pendleton rides E. K. Waldhaus in a revenge win at Gallagher-Iba. *Courtesy Mika Matzen.*

first. Seeing the guy I beat five times [OU's Robbie Waller] that year win it all was a dagger in my heart."[41]

He recovered to win his first NCAA title the next year, and stood out as one of Smith's favorites. "He's somebody that anybody would want as a son and a kid you want to be around every day that has a great attitude and cares for others."[42]

As the long-muscled and slender Pendleton faced off against the stocky Waldhaus, the fans chanted "Orange Power" while the Cowboy bench sat unusually still, knowing this was the Cowboy captain's last home match.

Pendleton hit a first period takedown that he almost transitioned into back points, but the stout Waldhaus broke the inside cradle attempt and escaped seconds later. Pendleton escaped just seven seconds into the second period, continued to apply pressure, and hit his second single leg of the match, again almost sinking in an inside cradle, but Waldhaus found his base and countered. As Pendleton rode him out for a 5-1 lead after two periods, a fan in the stands dressed in orange demonstrated a maneuver on a companion in the next chair, causing the spectators seated behind them to lean around to see the action.

Waldhaus escaped to begin the final period to make it 5-2, but Pendleton scored his third single leg takedown of the day for a 7-2 lead. He received a

RIGHT: Team leader Chris Pendleton, the sole senior in the Cowboy's NCAA tournament lineup, acknowledges the crowd's stand-ing ovation after a final appearance in Gallagher-Iba Arena. His revenge vic-tory over Waldhaus was his 108th as a Cowboy. *Courtesy Mika Matzen.*

ABOVE: Blackmon hangs on against Joel Flaggert from Oklahoma.
Courtesy Mika Matzen.

cue from the Cowboy bench to cut Waldhaus in an attempt move toward a major decision, but time expired. The appreciative crowd roared as Pendleton walked to the center of the mat and had his hand raised for the 107th time as a Cowboy. He stayed in the center of the circle for an extra beat, made eye contact with the crowd, and acknowledged the Cowboy ovation.

In his earlier defeat to Waldhaus, Pendleton relinquished two rare last-period takedowns. In this match he gave up none. "I've always taken pride in coming back and beating somebody who beat me and I've never lost to somebody two times in a row."[43]

Backups Jack Jensen and Rusty Blackmon, substituting for injured Cowboy starters, lost their matches as the score narrowed to 15-13. But Mocco, with the laces of his wrestling shoes tied secure with white trainers tape wrapped around his ankles, scored a foot sweep within seconds and went on to control Joel Tapler 10-3, handing the Cowboys a methodical 18-13 win.

In his last collegiate match, senior Ronnie Delk presses Teyon Ware during the season's final dual against Oklahoma. Ware prevailed 7-3. *Courtesy Mika Matzen.*

In the media room after the match Pendleton was in a reflective mood. "I have done a very good job all week of not letting it sink in that this would be my last time to wrestle in front of the Gallagher crowd. There was one second left on the clock and I could see everybody stand up and start cheering. That is when it sunk in. This meant a lot to me. It really did."[44]

Oklahoma coach Jack Spates was less philosophical about his eighteenth consecutive loss to the Cowboys. "We had our chances. Frankly, coming into this meet, I thought we were going to win…bottom line is that we had our opportunities to win and didn't make it happen."[45]

Cowboy Ronnie Delk wrestled his final match in Gallagher-Iba Arena and his last match as a Cowboy. His dreams of a national championship, held in his heart since childhood, would not be realized. In his last interview as a varsity wrestler, the Cowboy fifth year senior did not dwell on his final match as a Cowboy. Rather, he talked softly about his friend and teammate Chris Pendleton. "I expect nothing but what he's been doing. He'll go out there, dominate through the finals and he'll be a national champion again."[46]

Delk and his wife Stacy had a routine before a home dual match. Two days before a competition, Ronnie would wrestle down to within three to four pounds of his regulation weight. The next day he would burn down to one-half over. On match day he would delight in a short stack of pancakes for breakfast, attend class, then go home to weigh on the digital scales Stacy had purchased. If he was still under weight, he could eat a small sandwich and drink a few ounces of liquid. He would arrive at the wrestling room a couple of hours before weigh-in where he and Esposito would warm up for ninety minutes.

On this day that routine ended. He would now join the ranks of the human family that ate three meals a day. According to Stacy, "I'll have to start cooking differently now."[47]

THERE NEVER WAS A HORSE
THAT COULDN'T BE RODE.
THERE NEVER WAS A COWBOY
THAT COULDN'T BE THROWED.

—Old Cowboy Saying

seventeen

the big 12 tournament

03.05.05

DURING THE 2004-2005 REGULAR SEASON
the Big 12 Conference established itself, from top to bottom, as the toughest wrestling conference in the nation. A proven commodity, the conference failed only once since 1946 to crown at least one individual NCAA champion. Big 10 teams captured 13 of the previous 20 NCAA team titles, but with Iowa's recent descent, the Big 12 flexed its muscle. Only five schools in the conference sponsored wrestling teams, but as the Cowboy team bus departed from Stillwater on Thursday morning, bound for the Big 12 Tournament, all five squads were ranked in the top 12 in the nation. OSU, Iowa State, and Nebraska were ranked 1-2-3.

The Big 12 tournament was a valued ritual in the progression of the season, both for fans and competitors. Core supporters from each school's wrestling community turned out for the one-day uprising. Twenty-five hundred tickets were sold in advance of the event, mostly to Nebraska and Iowa State faithful, giving the wrestlers an opportunity to make progress and mark achievements against conference adversaries, many of whom they had faced several times before.

The event also served as the procedure whereby wrestlers qualified for the NCAA tournament held two weeks later. To determine those qualifiers, the NCAA applied a formula to determine how many qualifiers each conference received. The protocol was based on the number of wrestlers each conference had advanced to the round of 12 in previous NCAA tournaments, one step away from All-America status. The Big 12's number of qualifiers was capped by a percentage limit on the number of eligible participants from any given conference. No conference could be awarded fewer than 11, nor lose or gain more than three any given year.

Under the formula, the Big 12 was afforded 36 slots. For a Big 12 wrestler to qualify, he would need to place third or better in the conference tournament, or receive one of six "at-large" selections awarded by the five conference coaches immediately after the finals concluded on Saturday evening.

Even though several conference wrestlers had enjoyed a national ranking during some portion of the season, because of the 36-wrestler limit, a small number of capable wrestlers would not qualify. The six at-large slots afforded protection against top-rated wrestlers getting upset or injured during the tournament, but inevitably the 36-wrestler limit caused a wrestler from a weaker conference to slide in front of a better wrestler from a tougher conference.

Every year, Coach Smith observed inequities in the selection process. "We have had to leave kids at home who have potential to be All-Americans. Leaving one of our kids at home could cost us a national [team] championship. We have five of the toughest programs in the country. We are off the charts with our percentage of All-Americans. No other qualifier is even close. We should be awarded more based on that."[1] He argued on behalf of his own conference as well as the overall strength of the NCAA field. "I'm for making sure that every conference has its share. We're leaving some 12-13-15-16-ranked kids in the country at home and we want the best wrestlers in the country at the NCAAs."[2]

Oklahoma coach Jack Spates agreed. "…not having more qualifiers is 'ridiculous'… The Big 12 coaches are contemplating boycotting the National Duals unless something is done about the number of qualifiers we get. We need three to five more qualifiers, that's the bottom line."[3]

Four Cowboys had work to do to ensure an NCAA berth. Coleman Scott (23-7) was ranked seventeenth in the country and seeded third in the Big 12 tournament. Daniel Frishkorn (12-4) was ranked twelfth in the country and seeded fourth. Kevin Ward (17-9) and Clay Kehrer (15-13) were both unranked nationally and seeded fourth and fifth respectively. If the seeds held, only Scott would automatically advance. The others would have to wrestle their way to at least a third place finish in the tournament, or hope for an at-large bid on Saturday night. But when the coaches met to vote on at-large slots, no one was inclined to do the Cowboys any favors.

* * *

The OSU bus arrived in Omaha around midnight Thursday. After a full night's sleep, the squad awakened on Friday morning, studied and rested into the early afternoon, and bussed to a local high school for a workout and weight check the day before competition.

At five o'clock, Coach Smith rushed from his hotel lobby, across the street to the tournament arena, where the conference coaches and their assistants met for the ritualistic seeding meeting which determined the tournament bracket. As he approached the meeting room, his steps echoed through the empty arena as one Nebraska wrestler in a worn gray sweat suit ghost wrestled around the outside of a red mat placed on the empty arena floor. Black curtains dropped down from the rafters, which the following day would pour fans to the lower section of the arena closer to the mats.

The seeding meeting, held in an empty restaurant tucked away in the convention hall, did not start off smoothly. To determine the seeds, coaches examined three factors: head-to-head competition between the wrestlers, common opponents they might have faced, and individual national rankings. Nebraska coach Mark Manning had inserted a wrestler into his line-up who had not competed for several weeks. Smith's eye-teeth glared as he smiled. "You threw him in there. We should have known about this two weeks ago [when pre-seedings were submitted]."[4] Under conference rules, coaches submitted their proposed seedings two weeks before the tournament begins so disagreements can be hashed out during the intervening days.

The snappish Manning accused Oklahoma coach Jack Spates of violating a rule of coaching etiquette when Spates offered an opinion on the quality of an opposing wrestler, instead of promoting his own grapplers. "Do not talk about my program. Evaluate your own wrestlers."[5] A Nebraska assistant coach joined in the debate, which prompted Spates to retaliate, "Only one person can advocate for their team."[6] Spates then argued for his heavyweight to receive a number three seed to avoid facing Mocco in the semi-finals. Spates argued with the élan of a defense attorney, while Smith advocated like a grizzled corporate CEO. Manning was emotional.

After the meeting the coaches gathered at the end of the dining hall and broke bread. The tenor of the meeting changed, and the five competitors related like a group of tired and hungry chieftains sharing common frustrations at the end of the day.

Following the seeding process, Coach Smith joined Doc Allen for dinner in the hotel restaurant. Smith slid his fork into a piece of rare steak and fretted about the next day's competition. "This tournament is different. Only five teams compete."[7] After the dissolution of the Big 8 conference in 1996, only five wrestling squads remained in the newly-formed Big 12 conference, which had been infused with four Texas schools, none with wrestling teams. "Weaker teams can advance. Other teams are not around to knock them off."[8] He chewed his steak and put down his fork. "We could lose this tournament. Our five studs should advance, but if others lose early, it could be all up in the air. If the seeds hold, without bonus points, we win 68-60. But nothing's a shoe-in."[9]

Smith rose from the table and corralled his team in the hotel hallway. "Wake-up call at 7:45 a.m. Be ready to walk over at 8:00 for the medical check. That will give you 45 minutes if you have a weight issue. Their scales are one to two tenths lighter than ours, so take that into account. Weigh in at 9:00. Then come back here for breakfast. There's a buffet downstairs."[10]

Coach Smith looked toward Johny Hendricks. "Will anyone have a weight issue?"

Kevin Ward: "I might."

"How much time will you need?"

"I don't know. I'll see how much I float tonight."[11]

Each bracket contained only five wrestlers. The four and five seeds squared off in a morning preliminary match called a "pigtail." The winner advanced to the semi-finals later in the afternoon, while the loser would be forced to forge through the consolation bracket in order to win a medal.

"Consolation matches begin at 4:00. If you're in the consolations, check the time and decide whether you need to return to the hotel and rest. As soon as your match is over, and if you're in the finals, grab your gear and come back. Make sure you eat lunch. Your instinct during tournaments is to eat and drink less because of anxiety. Make sure you force liquids down. Make sure you eat well."[12]

Smith stepped back from the wall and turned toward the wrestlers. "When you win your semi-final match, you won't wrestle again until 7:00. When we return to the arena, your warm-up will be a real key. Those of you to wrestle in the pigtail match, that's going to be very important. Get your ass ready to win."[13]

Coach Smith peered down the hallway at his wrestlers as they sat with knees tucked under bony chins. "Daniel and Kevin, you have tough matches. Take on the responsibility that you're going to wrestle. Be ready to win the match. Put some liquid back in. Rest a little bit. Get ready to go after it. Do your thing. Get ready to go hard for seven minutes. We are well prepared. We are in shape. Your legs are underneath you. You can push as hard as you want to push."[14]

Team meetings in hallways, held on cheap carpet of faraway hotels, were a familiar scene for the travel-worn Cowboys. "We have an opportunity tomorrow to win the tournament in the first round. I don't need to beg you to do something special out there today. Just do it. You're well prepared and well conditioned. Those stadium stairs we ran will kick through. The practices we have had, take them into the match. Leave nothing out there, and we will be picking up majors and pins. If we meet our capabilities we're going to put up some big points today, and that's what we're here to do."[15]

"This time of year, you run a great risk if you have a poor match. Don't take that risk. Assume the responsibility of being a winner. Let's have a great tournament. We are ready. Now go to bed."[16]

The wake up calls erupted at 7:45 a.m. The team walked across the street to the arena, and were approached by security officers who checked the credentials which hung around the wrestlers' necks. Then they made their way into an exhibition hall large enough to punt a football. Frishkorn peered across the brightly lit and slightly chilly area at clusters of wrestlers from each school, huddled together, waiting for their weight to be called. "The number one, two and four-ranked guys in my weight are at this tournament. I have nothing to lose. I'm leaving my balls on the mat."[17]

The Oklahoma University team lounged in folding chairs next to the Cowboys. A gray t-shirt worn by one Sooner wrestler read *God, Family & Wrestling.* Sooner coach Jack Spates sat, reading from a large black Bible.

At 9:00 a.m. sharp, tournament officials called the wrestlers, weight by weight, into a small adjoining room. The five wrestlers competing at 126

Kevin Ward, ambling with the gait of a cattle-puncher, takes the mat for the Cowboys.
Courtesy Jim Bowen

hurried in, stepped on the scales, and ran back out, headed for breakfast. A serious woman in her thirties, with eyeglasses resting on the tip of her rounded nose, and a Big 12 credential hanging from her neck by a red cord, stood outside the weigh-in area and stared intently at a clipboard, not seeming to notice as wrestlers roamed past her in various states of undress.

Johny Hendricks emerged smiling. "I cut that close. 165 naked."[18] Smith and Branch didn't return the smile as Hendricks walked away carrying his warm-ups.

After the wrestlers weighed in and devoured breakfast, they returned to their rooms, dressed out, gathered in the lobby, and walked to the arena. Fans stole glances and some gawked as they walked.

Seven of the 10 Cowboys were seeded directly into the semi-finals, but three would have to wrestle through preliminary matches to reach the semi-final round. In his preliminary match, unseeded Daniel Frishkorn majored his Missouri opponent. Kevin Ward defeated an OU wrestler 6-1, but Kehrer lost. Frishkorn and Ward advanced to the semi-finals, while Kehrer dropped to the consolation round.

In the semi-finals, the Cowboys flexed their muscles. Coleman Scott overcame a leg cramp and an early takedown, but stormed back and flattened eighth-ranked Matt Keller from Nebraska at 6:21. Morgan and Esposito won handily. Frishkorn lost to number-one ranked Nate Gallik but returned to wrestle later in the day. As Frishkorn wrestled, Kevin Ward looked on. Ward was on the bubble. His victory in the preliminary round earlier in the day lifted his record to 18-9, but he needed to place third to advance to the NCAAs. Otherwise, his collegiate career was over.

* * *

Kevin Ward's father introduced him and his brother to wrestling, and the sport soon became a neighborhood affair, with several neighborhood buddies winning state titles. Ward captured three Tennessee state championships for Soddy Daisy High School and amassed a glittering 183-8 high school record. He was on the verge of signing with Virginia Tech out of high school but changed his mind after a visit to Stillwater.

Ward's main competition in the wrestling room the previous year was Cowboy freshman Johny Hendricks. Ward, proficient at scouting and neutralizing his opponent's strengths, maintained an edge over Hendricks throughout the fall, and began as the Cowboy starter at 157. Early on he registered solid victories over wrestlers from Oklahoma, Oregon State, and Cal Poly. But when he lost to Scott Roth of Cornell in the first round of the National Duals, Coach Smith inserted Hendricks in the lineup. Hendricks proceeded to defeat two top-five ranked opponents that weekend, including a defending national champion. Hendricks won his last six dual matches of the season, placed second in the Big 12 tournament, and garnered fifth in the NCAA championships. Since then, the confidence level of the two wrestlers diverged. During crucial matches Hendricks prevailed, while Ward competed vigorously, but fell just short.

During the transition, Smith took note of Ward. "We live in an 'I' world, but Kevin Ward exemplifies the type of guy that cares about his teammates. Last year he was our starter in the first semester. I replaced him with Johny Hendricks, but he continued to practice hard and really stuck it out. Ward made a difference for guys ahead of him like Esposito, Tyrone Lewis, and Johny Hendricks at the NCAA tournament. He is a guy who is respected in this room."[19]

Ward, an Academic All-American, majored in applied sociology. He practiced well, and possessed lightning-quick penetration from his feet, but Smith fretted that he sometimes circled too much, and had a tendency to get crushed by his opponent's hips in crucial situations. "Kevin has good motion, but he needs to work on finishing his moves. Completing moves is not a strength issue. It's a matter of will. You will yourself to get the takedown, or get off bottom, or ride out the shot."[20]

Smith liked Ward's work ethic, but remained perplexed at how Ward's matches progressed. "He sometimes drops his head after getting taken down. He lost several close matches. But when he wrestles hard and penetrates to the legs, no one should beat him."[21]

The hard-nosed Ward sustained a painful rib injury in December and was held out of live wrestling over the holiday break. He returned to the lineup and demonstrated flashes of brilliance, but suffered third-period pins in crucial mid-season matches against Iowa and Nebraska. A wildcard was not in the picture. He had to place third to advance.

In the semi-finals Ward faced fifth-ranked and top-seeded Travis Paulson, who had defeated Ward earlier in the year. After two periods the score was tied 2-2. Leading 3-2 off a Paulson penalty point, Ward blasted the top-seeded Paulson to his back for a 6-2 lead, held on to win 7-4, and earned a spot in the finals. The victory clinched Ward's first trip to the NCAA tournament.

Hendricks nailed two takedowns in the final 30 seconds to post an overtime win over Klein of Nebraska. Pendleton, Rosholt, and Mocco all won with major decisions. When the dust settled, eight Cowboys wrestlers advanced to the championship finals. Minutes later Frishkorn decisioned Matt Murray of Nebraska to clinch third place and a trip to post-season competition. By late-afternoon the Cowboys had clinched the conference championship, and qualified nine of 10 to the NCAA tournament.

Clay Kehrer's season ended in the consolation round with a 3-2 loss to Matt Pell of Missouri. He shook hands with his opponent, walked away from his coaches, and sat alone while he processed the reality that his first season as a Cowboy starter was over. It had been a year of challenge for the tall Texan. He had dropped down a weight class, changed academic majors, battled through ranking matches, and made the starting lineup for the nation's top team. But making the team was not enough. He still had things to prove.

After the consolation matches ended, a Nebraska wrestler clad in grey sweats stood alone in the midst of a crowded hotel elevator. He sobbed inconsolably and shook without shame as the elevator rose. Wrestling had been his constant life experience since elementary school, providing structure, friendships, educational opportunities, and a framework for self-expression and self-esteem. Fresh off a tough loss in the consolations, all he could hope for now was an at-large bid. He did not want it to end.

* * *

In the opening match of the evening Coleman Scott faced number-one ranked Sam Hazewinkel for the second time in two weeks. Hazewinkel nursed a 34-match winning streak and had not been seriously challenged all season. He was the prohibitive favorite to capture his first national championship later in St. Louis. He achieved a comfortable 6-2 win over Scott two weeks earlier in Stillwater and looked devastating in his 18-5 major decision over Grant Nakamura of Iowa State in the semi-finals.

Coach Smith, dressed in a light orange dress shirt, black vest, and pressed olive slacks, shook Scott's hand. The freshman trotted onto the mat, buttoned his head gear, and avoided eye contact with his parents Jamie and Mary, who sat in folding chairs on the first spectator's row.

Hazewinkel moved in quickly, reminiscent of his earlier victory against Scott when he took control early with two first-period takedowns. Scott blocked the initial onslaught, settled in and countered Hazewinkel's upper body tie-up attempts with vigorous hand fighting. With seconds left in the period Scott countered Hazewinkel's fireman's carry attempt and horsed his Sooner opponent to his back, but time ran out with a scoreless first period.

Hazewinkel chose the down position to start the second period. The crowd, made up mostly of Nebraska and Iowa State partisans, was eerily quiet as it looked on with interest but no vested passion. Scott stayed on top for 40 seconds, but Hazewinkel broke loose for a 1-0 lead. They circled and fought for position, but neither hit pay dirt as the period ended.

Even though Hazewinkel had applied a fierce and unforgiving ride on Scott earlier in Stillwater, the Cowboy freshman chose the down position to begin the final period. He came to his feet, hit a Granby roll to a near reversal—which Hazewinkel countered—and escaped only 40 seconds into the period. Scott then fought off a deep single leg attempt for almost a full minute before going off the mat. Seconds later, regulation time expired. Scott had fought Hazewinkel to a 1-1 tie, a respectable showing by a freshman against the top-ranked wrestler in the country who had defeated him before a home crowd days earlier. But Coleman Scott wanted more than respectability.

After a scoreless sudden victory period, Scott chose the down position for the first of two 30-second tiebreakers. If Hazewinkel, an excellent mat wrestler, could ride Scott for just 30 seconds and then earn an escape in the final 30-second period, he would avert the upset and earn his 35th straight victory. But Coleman Scott attached to Hazewinkel's back like a brown dog tick and finished the period on top. Going into the second tiebreaker, the tables were turned. The pressure had been on Scott all match, but now Hazewinkel's options were limited. He had to ride out Scott for 30 seconds, or release him and score a takedown or earn back points if the match was to continue. Scott came to his feet. In preparing for this match Scott and Coach Guerrero worked on hitting high-speed rolls from the down position to take advantage of Scott's own strength and agility. With less than 20 seconds left in the period, Scott stood, took aim, and hit a searing Granby roll, almost earned a reversal but gained an escape. He warded off Hazewinkel for the final 15 seconds and the buzzer sounded.

Coleman Scott had defeated the number-one ranked Sam Hazewinkel in a 2-1 tiebreaker. The Cowboy freshman, who began the season with four losses in his first six matches, was the Big 12 champion. "I took my lumps in the beginning of the year. I didn't prepare myself properly. Once I got some confidence, I knew I was going to be able to compete with the best."[22]

As Scott spoke to the media after the match, his mother's cell phone began to erupt as she received calls from friends and fans from Pennsylvania who listened to the match on an Internet connection. Their young hero was pleased with his victory but voiced anticipation for the next few weeks. "The ultimate goal is to win a national championship. This is a good feeling, but it's not where I want to finish. I want to be on that NCAA podium."[23]

Coach Smith was pleased and understated. "You have to find ways to win and he did that tonight. He beat a good wrestler on the mat."[24]

All day long the partisan crowd, made up mostly of Nebraska and Iowa State fans, rooted against Oklahoma State. But this evening their opportunities to cheer against the wrestlers wearing orange singlets were sparse. Throughout the day, tortured coaches from other squads, with faces reddened and veins protruding from their thickened necks, ran about the arena, screamed instructions, and gyrated in their chairs as the Cowboys' opposition, in the words of Chris Pendleton, was "dropping like flies." As Coleman Scott battled Hazewinkel in their nail-biter, Cowboy assistants Mark Branch and Pat Smith sat with Olympians and All-Americans Daniel Cormier and Jamill Kelly, three-time All-American and public relations staff member Shane Roller, and four-time All-American Johnny Thompson. They leaned back in folding chairs reserved near the mat for wrestlers and staff and observed the Cowboys demolish the competition. The six ex-Cowboys exhibited the anxiety of a pack of pond-fishing retirees. Branch heckled his teammates, "Let's hear a little more out of you guys."[25]

Each had been collegiate All-Americans, and between them collected 10 individual Big 12 titles. After Coleman Scott gathered his warm-up gear and walked toward them, the Cowboy freshman and new Big 12 champion giggled with joy.

The Cowboy victories continued. Nathan Morgan followed Scott's upset victory with a 14-6 shellacking of Moyer from Nebraska. Esposito controlled Storniolo from Oklahoma for his second straight Big 12 title. Next in line was Kevin Ward, who faced senior and 18th-ranked Brad Celeski of Missouri. The lanky Celeski had defeated Ward 5-2 earlier in Stillwater off a sloppy Ward takedown attempt late in the match.

The first period ended 1-1 after both cautious wrestlers were penalized twice for stalling. Celeski quickly escaped, but Ward countered a takedown attempt with an aggressive front headlock, and scored the crucial takedown. Celeski escaped in seconds to tie the score 3-3. In the final period, Ward escaped off the whistle to take a 4-3 lead. Seconds later, the lightning-quick Ward was in deep again. A takedown would be significant, but Ward had struggled all season translating his takedown attempts into points. Celeski, draped across Ward's back, and appeared to have blocked Ward's effort. But the Cowboy continued to scramble, gained the takedown, and held on to win 6-4. Big 12 champion Kevin Ward was bound for St. Louis.

Hendricks, Pendleton, and Mocco won handily, giving the Cowboys seven champions on the night. Rosholt, hobbled by a knee injury, could not mount an offense in his rematch with Padden of Nebraska, losing for only the second time of the season. Oklahoma State destroyed the field, tied a school record with seven champions and claimed its third straight Big 12 team title and 40th overall

* * *

The following Tuesday, with the season's end in sight, the team gathered for their afternoon workout as Coach Smith reviewed his notes. The staff had spent hours thinking about the training schedule for the next two weeks, but Smith understood the perils of rigidity. "At this time of the year you just can't plan too far ahead. A lot of it is instinctive. On some days you plan for a tough workout, but the guys just are not there. Other times you anticipate a light practice but you see something that tells you to turn up the burner."[26]

On this afternoon the wrestling room was a happy place. Mocco orchestrated a debate before wide-eyed freshmen about the relative differences in eating horse, beef, and cat, delicacies he maintained he observed while he roamed the world in competition. Delk weighed in the low 160s after making weight at 141 only eight days earlier. Kehrer gained 17 pounds in 72 hours following his consolation loss in the Big 12 tournament. But the laughter subsided as Smith drew the team in. "We really didn't wrestle that well this weekend. We crowned seven champions, and I had to say positive stuff to the media. But we have work to do. We have not been perfect all year. Now is the time to close the gap and wrestle our best. We have faced adversity all year. The travel. The tough competition. Making weight. Setting the lineup. Dealing with your own anxieties and insecurities. This type of adversity will cause most men to break. But it will cause others to break records. Which man will you be? We will find out in the next two weeks."[27]

The wrestlers listened as Smith rehashed familiar themes. "We will work on chain wrestling, because when we took that process to our opponent, they broke. And if our opponents had problems with our pressure during the season, wait until they see us at nationals. That's what chain wrestling does. That is what wrestling Oklahoma State does. Coleman scores 11 straight points after getting taken down. Ward throws the number one seed on his ass and almost pins him. People broke in our matches. But it was not us."[28]

This would be Smith's seventeenth NCAA tournament, 13 as a coach and four as a competitor. After practice, he mused, "I think it's going to be a real tough tournament. I don't like where Jake is right now. I don't know how the young guys will react. Nathan was kind of pouting this morning during his drill because of his anxiety. But I can't be soft on him right now. It's like parenting. Sometimes when our children are anxious, we are prone to be anxious. But maybe we should be holding them to standards in the midst of their anxiety. There is a tendency for a coach to take on the anxiety of his team and back off. But at this time in the season, if I cut them loose, most of the guys will do more than what I demand of them."[29]

Practice that afternoon was devoted to responding to different situations a wrestler could face during a critical and hotly-contested match. The assistant coaches roamed the wrestling room with added intensity. Smith spent much of his time on the north mat with the lighter weights. "They are the ones who may crack at nationals. They have no idea…"[30] Privately, Smith worried about the freshmen. "The young guys are not likely to be All-Americans. They have it physically, but not emotionally. I didn't place in the NCAA tournament my freshman year. I thought I was prepared, but I was not. Our job for the next few days will be to paint that picture for them of stepping out on the mat on the first day and try to avoid any mental letdowns."[31]

In the meantime, Ward took a finger in the eye. Rosholt's knee was swelling. Mocco grunted, and Hendricks limped to the center of the mat, telling the team trainers, "I need a cane."[32] The wrestlers burned through 25 minutes of live wrestling in situational contexts. "I like to concentrate on situations you're likely to be in during a match. If you wrestle 30 or 40 matches you're likely to be in certain situations. And everything we're covering in those situations are techniques we've broken down over the last month through slow, technique practices. We also use these drills to remind those that may have forgotten things over the past few weeks. I believe in drilling on situations where you are in a position to score an escape or a reversal. And you find the toughest position for young wrestlers coming in is the bottom position. It's a tougher area to teach. It's more of an attitude than anything."[33] Smith stalked about with whistle in hand as he barked out scenarios.

"You're down by one with 30 seconds left."

"You're up by one with 30 seconds left."

"You're up by one with 30 seconds left with a stalling call against you."

"The first 30 seconds of the match."

"Starters down position. Behind by one with one minute left."[34]

At five o'clock sharp Smith, still wearing no wristwatch, blew his whistle and action stopped dead. "An NCAA title does not come to you. You have to go out and take it. Now is the time to prepare to wrestle your perfect match against the toughest competition, before the most adverse crowds, with the worst officiating. Each of you knows what you need to do. You are mature and trustworthy. You can be trusted to prepare yourself for the biggest day of your lives. It's your dream. It's your future. Now you have to act on it."[35]

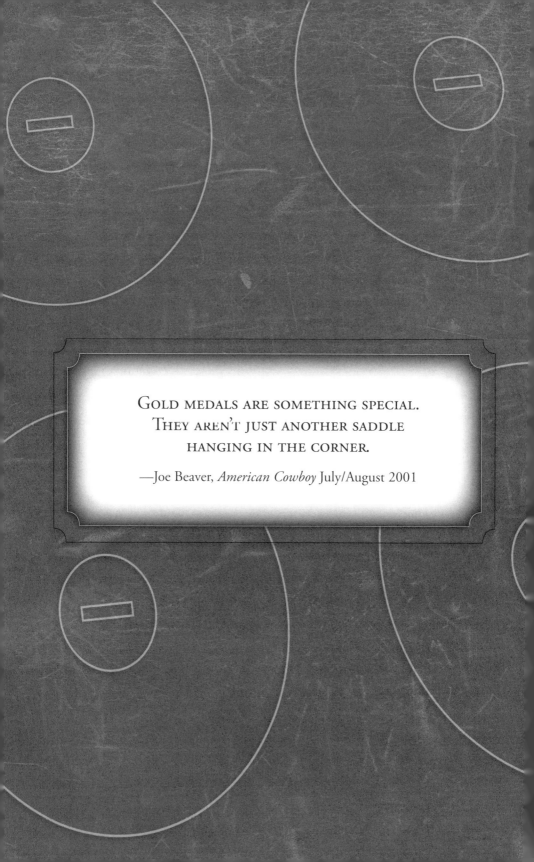

GOLD MEDALS ARE SOMETHING SPECIAL.
THEY AREN'T JUST ANOTHER SADDLE
HANGING IN THE CORNER.

—Joe Beaver, *American Cowboy* July/August 2001

eighteen

the ncaa tournament

03.17-19.05

FOUR WEEKS BEFORE the national championships, Coach Smith sat alone in his office, reviewing pages of hand-written notes compiled since his head-coaching days began some twelve years earlier. The notes, scrawled in small neat print on lined notebook paper, contained Smith's personal magnum opus detailing methods learned through trial and error. As the following sampling reflects, some were practical while others were more elusive.

1. The key right now is how we think.

2. Remind the athlete to be organized and on top of their academic responsibilities as we enter the final push.

3. In late-February into March, give guys the choice to condition on their own much of the time. That let's them know I have confidence in their maturity. Condition if you need to. If you're where you need to be today, go shower up.

4. Talk about bad practices tomorrow, not today. They recognize when they've had a bad workout.

5. Down the home stretch, what coaches say is important. Don't insult them, but motivate them. Give the work back to them. It can mean the difference between an NCAA champion and a 2-and-out.

6. Create an environment in their training where they are excited about what they are doing. Give them clarity that they are standing on the edge

of the greatest three days of their lives. Help them embrace the challenge, not dread it or be fearful of it.

7. Minimize the technical talk. At this point we're fine-tuning.

8. Tell guys in front of their teammates what you like about them. Maybe at the end of practice. It helps their confidence. It lets them know you appreciate them and that they are ready to step into battle.

9. Whoever wants it the most does not care how their arms and legs and bodies feel.

10. Remember who you wrestle for. Some teams have to rely on other teams to knock their opponents off. Not us. We control our own destiny.

11. Have more private talks with some of my wrestlers both from a technical and emotional standpoint.

12. Gently remind my accomplished veterans how painful it is to lose.

13. Accept responsibility for who you are and what you are about to accomplish.

14. Do you leave yourself any options other than winning?

15. Look back on this experience with no regrets.[1]

Smith's notes to himself had come about as a result of years of trial and error, but the journey had been long and treacherous. OSU's wrestling program is the primary repository for the university's claim to athletic prominence. The Cowboys won the NCAA team title 27 times out of 43 attempts between 1928 and 1971. Administrators and fans expected NCAA team championships. Anything less is a disappointment. But if given the choice, most college wrestlers prefer an individual NCAA title to being part of a team championship. A college wrestler who wins a national title is a "made man" in the eyes of the wrestling community. But in the eyes of athletic directors and alumni, team titles trump individual championships. This presumption is an unspoken but compulsory term of any OSU wrestling coach's contract. Violating that expectation could be hazardous.

The late Cowboy wrestling coach Tommy Chesboro, who died unexpectedly of a heart attack in 2006, won an NCAA team title in his second year as head coach, but a 17-year NCAA title drought resulted in his dismissal, even though his teams between 1970 and 1984 had posted a 227-26 dual meet record and captured 19 individual titles and eight conference championships. Joe Seay replaced Chesboro as head coach in 1985 and promptly brought home two team titles to conclude the decade. But he was ultimately dismissed for NCAA rules violations. John Smith took over in 1993 and led the Cowboys to a team title the following year, but OSU hit an eight-year drought before winning again in 2003.

Coach Smith understood this equation, and during the two-week interlude before the NCAA championships, he strained every nerve to sharpen the tip of the spear. Physical preparation was essentially complete. Most of the NCAA qualifiers were in extraordinary condition, and could wrestle several matches a day. The real "Riddle of the Sphinx" was shaping the wrestlers' state of mind, for at the NCAA tournament, competitors ruptured mentally before they surrendered physically. As writer and wrestler John Irving observed, "The mind often gives out before the body does."[2] Smith had seen the phenomenon throughout his days as a competitor and as a coach. "Guys crash at the NCAA every year due to anxiety. We take all possible measures to keep their anxiety level in check. We take them to their hotel rooms after they wrestle and encourage them to sleep or read or watch television. Sometimes they need a coach with them to keep them calm and focused. The anxiety effects their conditioning more than anything. It draws energy out of them as they sit there. It's really pretty amazing."[3]

Constructing that substructure was particularly important this year, for several well-fortified teams stood in the Cowboy's path. Minnesota qualified its entire team to the tournament, one more than the Cowboys. Illinois won the Big Ten title and propelled nine to the NCAA tournament. Iowa State advanced eight qualifiers out of the tough Big 12 tournament. On paper, Michigan was stacked. Seven Lehigh wrestlers made the grade, and their stars Letters and Trenge had posted wins over Hendricks and Rosholt during regular season competition.

As the tournament approached, Smith's coaching peers considered the Cowboys the consensus favorite. Nebraska Coach Manning said, "Ten to 12 years ago it was Iowa. Now OSU is definitely there."[4] Iowa State Bobby Douglas chimed in, "There's no way OSU is going to lose. My pick is OSU. No doubt. And I think they would be the unanimous pick."[5] Illinois coach

Mark Johnson agreed, "OSU is the favorite."[6] Lehigh coach Greg Strobel concurred that "This is the best team I've had in 10 years. But right now, OSU is the front-runner."[7] One sportswriter even characterized the season as "the golden age of wrestling"[8] at OSU. But coach Smith cast his eyes downward and shook his head slowly from side to side, "We'll have to wrestle like men, and we have to take an attitude that we have to earn everything."[9]

* * *

On an overcast Tuesday morning, the orange team bus departed Gallagher-Iba Arena without fanfare as students walked to class and athletes piled bags into the luggage compartments. On the sides of the orange and black bus, "Oklahoma State" was scripted in large white lettering, and sunken eyes in gaunt faces peered out darkened windows. As the bus rumbled north through Kansas and Missouri, Smith again considered the prospects of the team he had recruited, instructed, and nurtured during his thirteenth campaign as Cowboy coach. Eight of the nine OSU qualifiers entered the tournament seeded in the top nine spots, and if projected seeds held, the Cowboys were a 35-point favorite.

Seeding for the NCAA tournament is conducted by a committee of 20 coaches, allocated by conference from across the country. The Big 12 Conference was allotted two representatives, Nebraska and Missouri. The coaches submitted their proposed seedings to the NCAA tournament committee, who ran the pairings through a computer program designed to give equitable weight to previous performance records. A proposed bracket is then published among the coaches for review and comment. Often, changes will be made. Earlier in the week Smith had successfully lobbied for Nathan Morgan to be bumped from a number eight to a number seven seed, placing him on the more favorable side of the bracket.

But Smith placed the seeding process in perspective. "Seeds are important, but they do not determine the tournament. There are always upsets in this competition, and the team that avoids them is going to win the championship. Getting through that first day is crucial and things really get intense starting Friday."[10]

Coleman Scott was 22-6 and seeded ninth. His cautious shot-selection was sometimes a liability, and he sometimes wrestled with too much patience. But Smith liked the incongruous "nasty" attitude that had overcome the otherwise even-tempered and innocent freshman over the past few weeks. The coaches believed his best wrestling was still ahead.

Nathan Morgan was 26-4 and seeded seventh. Unlike Scott, the skilled and polished freshman was aggressive on his feet, especially early in the match, but Smith questioned his mental and physical toughness, especially against more physically dominating opponents. Said Smith, "He needs to wrestle in the second and third periods like he does the first."[11]

Frishkorn, 13-6 and seeded seventh, had developed into an explosive scrambler, capable of racking up points in bursts through a deadly arsenal of Granby rolls and throws. But after moving up a weight in December, the redshirt freshman seemed small for his weight-class. He faced taller and stronger opponents all season, sometimes to his detriment. Occasionally he takes shots that are dangerous, and he needs to protect his legs.

Esposito, 30-1 and seeded number one, was the quickest wrester in the nation off his shot, and commanded excellent control of the velocity and texture of his matches. But if seedings held, he would face Army's Phillip Simpson, the West Point senior who was scheduled for deployment to Iraq after graduation. He conquered Esposito two years earlier and would be the darling of the crowd because of his military credentials. The tempermental Esposito would need to be at his best, both emotionally and technically. Smith worried about the liabilities in being the top seed. "Once someone is recognized as the top wrestler in his weight, he has a tendency to punish himself through anxiety and worry and pressure, feelings we didn't have when we were climbing to the top. I want Zack not to dread the NCAA tournament, but to embrace it."[12]

Kevin Ward was 20-10 and the only Cowboy not to earn a seed. His weight class was considered one of the toughest in the tournament, but Coach Smith believed Ward "…has really become a mentally tougher wrestler on the mat. If he rolls that over into the NCAA Championships, he is going to have great success."[13] Coaches and teammates reminded Ward of past Cowboys who struggled through the regular season only to find their voice in March. From team captain Pendleton, "I reminded Kevin (Ward) awhile ago about what Shane Roller did."[14] Roller, a native of Bixby, Oklahoma, began wrestling at the age of four with his three older brothers and entered the Cowboy program as a confident freshman, with a bevy of high school titles under his belt. But like all highly touted freshmen that enter the Cowboy wrestling room eager to demonstrate their talents, Roller had his own "welcome to OSU" moment. "I worked out against Mark Branch and Pat Smith, and went two months without getting a takedown. That humbles you pretty quickly."[15] But his persistence paid off. He became a starter his sophomore year and advanced to the NCAA tournament seeded number 12 with just over a .500 record. He ultimately became a three-time All-American for the Cowboys. Smith wished the same for Ward. "He needs to finish his shots. It's not a strength issue, it's about the will."[16]

Johny Hendricks was 22-4 and seeded third. The sophomore's straightforward, pounding style was based on power and strength. But he had struggled with injuries in the latter part of the season, and sometimes he relaxed on his feet and gave up the easy takedown. He was a big-game wrestler who rose to the occasion but sometimes waited until deep into his matches before switching on his prodigious talent. That could prove fatal against his nemesis, number-one-ranked Troy Letters of Lehigh.

Team leader Chris Pendleton was 31-1 and seeded number one. He was relentless on his feet, and always primed for an explosive kill-shot. But he sometimes lost his train of thought during a match and become frustrated. It will take a mental letdown for Chris to lose. Pendleton would face a nemesis, the unpredictable Ben Askren from Missouri, whom Pendleton had defeated eight out of nine tries, but who beat the Cowboy in last year's Big 12 finals. Askren had 20 pins in his 34 wins during the season, with only one career loss to anyone other than Pendleton.

Jake Rosholt was 27-2 and seeded number two in another high-performance weight. He battled an injured knee, always a hindrance to a power wrestler who relied on strength as well as speed. Earlier in the year he received the ultimate compliment from Coach Smith: "Jake is a guy who trains hard and wrestlers hard every day."[17] That tenacity would be called upon if the Idaho native were to recapture his national title, for the injury to his knee came at just the wrong time in a weight class loaded with talent and experience. "Sometimes he loses focus and doesn't get his legs back when someone takes a shot."[18]

Steve Mocco was 32-0 and seeded number one. His foot-sweep take-down was deadly, he was a relentless rider, his unflagging pressure was legendary and he constantly worked for a pin. The only chink in his armor had been an inconsistency in penetrating to his opponent's legs for takedowns, always a struggle for heavyweights, but a necessity if Mocco wanted to compete on an international level. Nebraska coach Mark Manning reflected the opinion of the field, "I won't say he's unbeatable. But he's the closest thing there is."[19] According to Smith, "The only one who can beat Mocco is himself."[20]

Finally Smith put his notes aside and tried to rest, as the team bus barreled north toward St. Louis, arriving shortly before midnight. He assembled the squad in the lobby area and collected cell phones from the wrestlers while Coach Branch distributed room keys while parents, wrestlers, and coaches wandered through the hotel even at the late hour, burning energy as the day of days advanced.

Wednesday morning the squad traveled to the arena for a short workout, returned to the hotel to check their weight, and burrowed in their rooms for the final countdown. Later in the evening the team crouched in the hotel hallway as Coach Smith kneeled on one knee and spoke with a soothing intensity about weight management and match preparation. "Eat a good meal this morning and this afternoon. Keep food and liquid flowing. Every time you warm up, drink some water. You'll have more down time this week than any tournament all year. Remember, the tendency during a tournament is to eat and drink less due to anxiety. Don't worry about your weight until after your last match of the day. Try to weigh what you trained at during the year. If you're 4-5-6 pounds over, get your sweats on and get it off. There's a workout room at the hotel if you need it. Your legs are in such good shape, you could run ten miles and not even feel it. I'm not concerned about weight, and you shouldn't be either."[21]

On the first day of competition, wrestlers tend to ride the crest of anticipation and adrenalin into their first match, and do not warm up adequately, making the transition from the locker room to live competition dangerously sluggish. "Tomorrow it will be about warming up. Get up, be a man, get your ass out there and get warmed up. Put yourself through your normal routine, and don't do less out of anxiety. A bad warm-up leads to a bad match. With your level of conditioning, you can wrestle three matches tomorrow and be ready for more. Battle up."[22]

Smith also recognized there was little tolerance for public relations problems for the high-profile Cowboy squad. "There is no room for misconduct. No throwing chairs across the room or trash cans out the windows. If something doesn't go right, the coaches will protest. Just shake hands and get off the mat. Do you understand? I want to see you shake your heads up and down. Do you understand?"[23] Heads bobbed as Smith rose to his feet. "Right now you should feel relaxed. We have done everything properly this season. You should all have a good feeling tonight going to bed. We've done all we can do."[24]

So, after lifetimes of training, thousand of miles traveled, and scores of matches wrestled, there was little preparation left to do. "We have an opportunity to do something this program has not been done for 50 years, win three straight NCAA team titles. We need to put that responsibility on our shoulders and earn our way. That will help you push through tough matches. Wakeup calls at 7:45. Go get some rest. Check your weight before you go to bed."[25]

Smith and his buddies Doc Allen, George, and Chris crossed the street, braced against a cold north wind cutting through the dark streets of St. Louis, and ducked into a steakhouse for their customary late-night meal. The maitre di recognized the group from a previous year's tournament and seated them at their customary table. Smith's friends noted the Cowboy head coach carried an aura of both apprehension and anticipation that evening, and gently probed his mind. Smith watched as his waiter crushed pepper onto a Caesar salad for almost 45 seconds…perhaps a carryover from two decades of rationing food and making weight. Each bite had to count, and flavor was at a premium. "Some of my wrestlers have trained with only one option in mind, and that's to be a national champion. It's a big risk for me to foster that situation emotionally, to let them put their heart and soul on the line for only one option. For if they lose in an early round, they still have to come back [through the consolation rounds] and wrestle." He gestured with his fork as his voice lowered. "Most athletes look in the mirror and negotiate with themselves a way out. They allow themselves to consider an option other than victory. But a very small number negotiate no option other than winning. No prisoners. That is treacherous emotional ground."[26]

How would Smith deal with losing the NCAA tournament? "I'm not preparing to lose, so I don't know. Losing would be devastating. I know I would put my personal pain aside for the team I have coming back. Rest assured, there is a young guy out there right now from some other school, a green kid barely 18 years old, who wakes up every day and thinks about winning this tournament. He can feel how close he is. This may be his one shot at a lifelong dream, one he has fostered since he was a little boy. His coach knows how close he is."[27] He then allowed a knowing grin to crinkle the small scar between his eyebrows. "There are coaches in this hotel right now convincing themselves that this is their week to stun the nation and upset Oklahoma State."[28]

He finished his steak without speaking another word, almost as if merely voicing the possibility of defeat to even his close friends might coalesce the thought into reality. "I don't even want to talk to you anymore about the possibility of losing."[29] After making the final bed check, Smith found an Internet connection in his room and studied into the night the records of a handful of wrestlers whom his team could meet in the first two to three rounds, particularly in the lighter weights. He took great pains not only to check their won-loss records, but who they had wrestled and at what time of the season. He placed his notes in his black notebook, took off his shoes, and began checking phone and email messages.

Early the next morning Coach Smith caught a glimpse, from his hotel window, of a blazing orange sun centered squarely in the middle of the St. Louis arches. Too distracted to eat the day before, he enjoyed early morning coffee as his wrestlers dressed and prepared to board the bus for the 9:00 a.m. weigh-in. He looked out the window again, and hoped the seething orange sun was an omen. Walking from his room to the hotel restaurant, Smith passed by a giant hotel ballroom. A slight sour aroma of dried sweat and hotel room service enveloped wrestlers wrapped in sweats and ghost wrestling on one of four red mats laid out across the parquet ballroom floor. One wrestler in yellow sweats leaned against the gaudy red wallpaper framed by ornate ceiling trim and stared at one of three sets of scales arranged in a row adjacent to the mats.

"In private, intimate conversations the coaches knelt down and spoke to the wrestlers' boiling souls in soothing but desperate whispers." *Courtesy Jim Bowen.*

The Cowboy bus drew stares as streams of fans walked toward the arena while the bus rolled along Lewis Avenue in heavy morning traffic for the tournament's first weigh-in. The nine Cowboys stepped off and entered a door guarded by security guards dressed in smart navy blue sport coats, who checked each coach and wrestler for the laminated credential draped around thickened necks. All 330 wrestlers scheduled to compete made weight. After weigh-in the team retreated into a small locker room in the Savvis Center. Each of the 73 teams was assigned a portion of a locker facility. The Cowboys shared one half of their 20' by 40' space with rival Iowa State. The rationed locker room had the intimate and vulnerable feel of a cramped hospital waiting area, occupied by two separate warring clans, where boredom-laced anxiety permeated the concrete walls and pumping hearts.

Closed circuit televisions bolted to the walls were tuned to the action in the arena. Sporadically, the team watched the television screen as the muffled roar of cheering fans shook the concrete floor. As his match approached, each wrestler left the lonely sanctuary of his teammates and headed for a large room, where practice mats lay and wrestlers warmed up. Coaches remained close by as the moment of moments approached. Trainer Chris

Pickering stood ready to respond to anxiety-driven requests for tape, gum, band-aids, Pepto Bismol, and other forms of distractions.

The Cowboy coaches knew through their own experiences that a lifetime of training, starving, competing, and preparing came down to the next few minutes. The nervous athletes' emotional blueprints were as varied as snowflakes raging in a blizzard. In private, intimate conversations the coaches knelt down and spoke to the wrestlers' boiling souls in soothing but desperate whispers. "If you find yourself in a tough battle, then get tough. Tough matches call for tough people. This sport is about toughness."[30] The freshmen nodded as Coach Smith's voice sharpened to a whisper. But to the battle-tested veterans his tone softened. "If we focus on wrestling smart, we will take care of business. We are exactly where we need to be. No question in my mind."[31]

The Cowboy strategy was simple: from the whistle, orchestrate the tone and pace of your match by wrestling your style. Work your moves. Do your thing. Make your opponent react to your onslaught. Esposito sat in the corner of the dressing room and stared ahead through a self-made maze. He remembered the painful NCAA loss sustained his freshman year to a more deliberate wrestler who tempered Esposito's frenetic pace. "You have to go into the national tournament ready to wrestle your style. You have to attack the guys that are funky the same way as the guys who like to stall. You really have to keep the pace up against everybody. You can't let their style dictate the way you wrestle."[32] Pendleton agreed, "That's what [head coach] John Smith always talks about...not letting your opponent control the match. We want to wrestle for seven minutes and try and score as many points as possible if we can't get a pin. We try and set the pace from the beginning."[33]

The eight mats, separate theaters where dreams came to die, covered the arena floor from baseline to baseline. Sixteen wrestlers, 48 coaches and trainers, and 16 officials would be on the floor at once, with new participants rotating on and off as matches ended and dreams collided with reality. Each of the 330 competitors, including seven sets of brothers and three sets of twins, enjoyed an outpost of support somewhere in the arena. The crowd of 16,302 sat in color-coded clusters and erupted in cheers and boos as the fortunes of their wrestlers ebbed and flowed. The Cowboys brought the largest contingent of supporters to St. Louis. Their two thousand fans occupied four sections in the arena, and spewed like orange lava when Cowboy points were scored.

OSU led off with the freshmen trifecta of Scott, Morgan, and Frishkorn. Their opening performances could establish momentum for their teammates, as well as deliver a message to opponents casting about for optimism. Coleman Scott was first. He slapped Coach Smith's hand, and stepped out to face Old Dominion's Christian Staylor, a two-time NCAA qualifier and former high school teammate of Daniel Frishkorn. Staylor had notched a win over number-one seed Sam Hazewinkel the previous season and was considered by some to be the best unseeded wrestler in his weight, and a dangerous and perhaps unlucky draw for an uninitiated freshman. Scott adjusted his headgear, placed his hands on his knees, and glanced at Coaches Smith and Guerrero. This was the Cowboy freshman's inaugural NCAA tournament match. No one was sure how he would respond.

But Coleman Scott knew. He crushed Staylor 15-2. Scott summed it up later in the evening. "We talked this morning about letting it fly. It doesn't matter how old you are, when you step on the mat you step out there to win."[34]

The onslaught continued. Morgan won by technical fall. Frishkorn and Esposito posted major decisions, as did Rosholt and Mocco. Hendricks and Pendleton recorded pins. The only loss came at 157 where Kevin Ward started strong but fell again to Joe Johnston of Iowa.

The NCAA tournament is a three-day event extravaganza beginning with preliminary matches on Thursday morning, followed by afternoon and evening rounds on Thursday and Friday, climaxing with a Saturday afternoon final, televised nationally by ESPN. An NCAA champion will win a total of five matches in three days. An early loss requires the wrestler to claw through additional consolation matches. In order to continue to qualify, he could have to string together seven to eight wins during the course of the tournament. After the morning round, the Cowboys retreated to their hotel rooms to rest before the evening round. The life cycle of a collegiate wrestler is permeated by two distinct forms of waiting: the slow-burn hiatus which stretched hours prior to the weigh-in, when stomachs groaned and parched mouths settled in like sun-baked cotton. The second is the excruciating interim, after the grub-pit is raided, when the reality of impending battle caused anxiety to replace hunger pains in the stomach's deepest cavern. During the interlude most wrestlers napped, some read, and others watched television. On the return ride to the arena Coach Smith, dressed in an orange dress shirt and khaki pants, stood at the front of the bus and counted heads while flags over Busch Stadium snapped from a cold north wind. The mood on the bus was subdued and businesslike, and Smith's voice could barely be heard at the back of the bus over the rumble of the bus diesel. "No one wants to wrestle us tonight. No one wants to wrestle a team going for a championship. Don't give them a reason to want to wrestle us."[35] Those on the team who could grow beards rubbed sweaty palms against short stubble as the bus crawled down Lewis Avenue. "The NCAA gives everyone who qualifies for this tournament a framed picture. Most are happy with that. When we get back on this bus Sunday afternoon, take home what you want. Have what you want. If you want a picture, fine. Some of you want more. Go out and get it."[36]

By Thursday evening, Cowboy backups and redshirts arrived from Stillwater to support their teammates. Slightly fattened from regular meals and a respite from daily workouts, they sat in the packed arena with friends and girlfriends in choice seating close to the mat, as the eight Cowboy winners from the morning matches faced off in the tournament's second round. A win in that rotation guaranteed a slot in the quarterfinal matches on Friday morning. Winners there would achieve All-American status and earn a place in the coveted Friday evening semi-finals.

Cowboy fans roared as Scott and Morgan won tight matches. Pendleton was sluggish in his 14-10 win, but Esposito, Hendricks, and Rosholt won by major decisions. Mocco pinned his opponent, as did Frishkorn, who looked up at the cheering Cowboy crowd while holding a squirming Hofstra opponent to his back. Earlier in the evening Ward stormed through the consolations to nab two wins, including an impressive victory against ninth-ranked Derek Zinck of Lehigh.

On the first day, the Cowboys captured 18 of 19 bouts, posted bonus points in 12 matches, and opened up an 11-point team lead over second place Minnesota. The freshmen trifecta had defeated three former All-Americans, while Murderer's Row won 10 of 10, piling up six major decisions and one fall.

The next morning the team endured wakeup calls, slipped on shorts, and stumbled sleepily to the team scales. Morgan was one pound under after losing two and one-half pounds in his sleep. Johny Hendricks, one-pound heavy, packed extra gear in his gym bag for an early morning sweat at the arena before weigh-in.

Friday is moving day at the NCAA tournament, beginning with the morning's treacherous quarterfinal round. A win guarantees All-American status, keeps hopes alive of individual championship glory, and earns valuable team points. A loss in that round required the wrestler to win one more match later in the day to gain All-American status.

The day started well for publicity-starved college wrestling. ESPN carried the Saturday afternoon quarterfinals to a live audience which prompted the public address announcer supplied by the NCAA to urge the crowd into a frenzy as the cameras panned the crowd precisely at 11:00 a.m.. Even the officials clapped and stomped their feet.

But the day started poorly for the Cowboys. In a rematch of the Big 12 finals, the crowd erupted as top-seed Sam Hazewinkel edged Scott 2-0, and two-seed Shawn Bunch of Edinboro controlled Morgan 13-7. In the day's biggest stinger, Frishkorn had Oklahoma two-seed Teyon Ware on the ropes in the final period, but gave up a takedown in the closing seconds to fall 4-3. The Cowboy Murderer's Row all plowed to impressive wins led by Hendrick's pin over Sioredas of Tennessee-Chattanooga, avenging an earlier loss months ago in Gallagher-Iba Arena.

In the second round of consolation matches, Kevin Ward added to the Cowboy team total with an 8-2 win over Hill of Edinboro. His campaign ended in the third round of consolations when he lost to Horning of Clarion, but Ward's two wins helped OSU amass 78.5 total points. The Cowboys led second-place Cornell by 22 points as the quarterfinal round came to an end.

The bus carried Cowboys back and forth to the hotel after their afternoon matches where they rested for their semifinal match hours later in the evening. George stumbled on a heartbroken and sobbing Nathan Morgan sitting in his hallway with his head buried in a white towel. Morgan had been eliminated from competition earlier in the afternoon in the consolation matches, his dream of becoming a freshman All-American spoiled.

George's words were soothing, "If you didn't cry, you wouldn't care. The same thing happened to Zack his freshman year." Morgan's hero John Smith also had met the same fate twenty years earlier at the Meadowlands Arena in New Jersey, losing in the early rounds and failing to place in his first NCAA tournament. The loss spurred Smith on. Time would tell for the shattered Morgan.

For the five Cowboys who remained undefeated, a win on Friday evening guaranteed the wrestler a spot in the finals the next afternoon. Cowboys Esposito, Pendleton, Rosholt, and Mocco had experienced the Friday night caldron. It was the first trip for sophomore Hendricks. All five Cowboys took the mat with hopes for glory. All five won. Top seed Esposito survived an accidental but vicious first period head butt which left his eye swollen and his face a deep purple. He held on and defeated Michigan's fifth-seeded Eric Tannenbaum 7-2. While Hendricks drummed second-seeded Ryan Churella from Michigan 6-2, Coach Smith stole glances on the adjacent mat as nephew Mark Perry upset number-one seed Troy Letters, 3-0. Perry's victory robbed Hendricks of an opportunity to avenge two earlier losses to Letters, while Perry's stunning win afforded him the chance to avenge two earlier losses to Hendricks, in the national finals, no less. As the victorious Perry ran off the mat, he pumped his sweaty and clinched fist in the direction of his mother, who sat near the front row next to the OSU section. As the Cowboy fans applauded the fortune of the Stillwater native, Perry's cousin Joe, the young son of John Smith, looked up at his mother, seeking approval to join the Cowboy fans in cheering for his cousin Mark. Pendleton smoked Mazzurco of Cornell 16-1. Rosholt avenged his earlier loss in the Big 12 finals with a 10-9 win over B. J. Padden of Nebraska, and Steve Mocco shut out Indiana's Pat DeGain 4-0.

The five winners returned to the hotel, but the Cowboy trio of freshmen, having lost earlier in the day, prepared for late-evening consolation matches. Often the tournament is won or lost in the grind of the consolation bouts. Competitors defeated earlier in the day meet other vanquished wrestlers for All-American honors and team points. New emotional rules are in place and seeds became irrelevant. Tournament favorites who unexpectedly lose can face reckless fifth-year seniors making a desperate and last-ditch lunge for glory. Ironically, a wrestler who loses early in the tournament, but claws his way through the bracket and wrestles for third place on Saturday afternoon, could score more team points for his squad than a competitor who wins a national title. It happened if that wrestler rang up enough bonus points and pins as he brawled through that purgatory known as the loser's bracket.

The freshman trifecta seemed to understand. Coleman Scott edged Preston from Harvard 5-4—prompting Coach Smith to leap in the air—giving the Cowboys their first true freshman All-American since Eric Guerrero achieved the feat nine years earlier. Frishkorn pinned Lang of Northwestern, but a devastated Morgan suffered a discouraging 4-0 loss to senior Evan Sola of North Carolina. Smith sensed that the hungry 11th-seeded fifth-year senior might be a problem for Morgan. "At this time of the tournament, throw out the seeds. This was Sola's last chance to All-American. He was a fifth-year senior. He felt a sense of desperation and motivation that a young freshman just can't experience. I was once in Nathan's shoes [Smith was eliminated early in his first NCAA tournament], and I expect the pain of this loss will be with Nathan Morgan all year. Next year, watch out."[37]

Smith's tough January decision to infuse three freshmen in the starting lineup reaped benefits. "That's huge for us. That's inspiring to the next guys that step out when they see freshmen stepping up and getting all-American. All season long in some ways we've relied on the upper weights. But in the last two tournaments, the Big 12 and the NCAA Championship, those young guys down low made a difference for us. That does a lot for you as a team."[38]

After the Friday evening smoke cleared, the Cowboys had marched five wrestlers into the championship finals, and two freshmen survived to battle in the consolation bracket. The Cowboys racked up 127.5 points and extended its lead to an insurmountable 56-points over runner-up Cornell. It had been a remarkable quarterfinal and semifinal round for a program that had in recent times seen NCAA hopes dissolve on Fridays. It was unlikely that Saturday's performance could match Friday's run to victory. Competition was even tougher, the stakes were higher, and the unexpected waited around every bend.

* * *

For the Saturday afternoon NCAA finals, the eight mats were removed and replaced by a single mat rolled out on a four-foot stage, bordered by photographers, television crew, and tournament officials. The first Cowboy finalist was Zack Esposito, who ran across the floor, bounded up the eight steps, and walked to the center circle to meet Army's Phillip Simpson for the national championship. Simpson, the top high school recruit in the nation in 2001, and a four-time state champion from Nashville, Tennessee, owned a victory over Esposito two seasons earlier. The packed Savvis Center roared in unison "Army, Army" as the West Point senior, scheduled to be deployed to an infantry unit in Iraq within several weeks, buttoned his headgear. The anti-OSU flavor caused Cowboy assistant Pat Smith to smile. "Just listen to the crowd. When they root against us, we love it. I tell our guys, 'People always hate the ones who are winning.' We turn that stuff into a positive."[39] Esposito reflected on the moments leading up to the opening whistle: "…I didn't know how many Army fans there are, but all of a sudden I hear 'Army' and the whole crowd just erupts…it just wasn't a school going against me – it was kind of like a whole country."[40]

But Esposito's takedown 40 seconds into the match took an edge off the partisan crowd. He rode Simpson the entire second period, chiseled out a reversal in the final frame and gleaned over three minutes in riding time. Esposito had dominated his opponents throughout the weekend, averaging over three minutes riding time and allowing only eight points in five matches. At the final buzzer the black-eyed junior jumped into John Smith's arms with a 5-2 victory and his first national championship," "I don't care how I look. That'll heal. [The national championship] won't heal. I'm tired, my knees hurt, my leg hurts, but it's all worthwhile."[41]

Two matches later Hendricks came out against Mark Perry rumbling forward like a John Deere combine. He bore in a single leg but Perry retreated out-of-bounds. The Iowa freshman was warned for stalling at the 1:30 mark, which prompted Hendricks to hit and hold a low double leg on the mat's edge with one minute left in the period. "That first takedown was huge because it allowed me to set the pace for the match. Up 2-0, I knew that even if I make a mistake, I could scramble and still be in the match."[42] As in their earlier encounter in Stillwater, he tyrannized Perry with a second period ride, and thwarted an escape at the end of the frame by forcing a stalemate. Hendricks quickly snagged a reversal to begin the final period. Perry

ABOVE: With Cowboy fans in the background, Johny Hendricks controls Mark Perry in NCAA finals. *Courtesy Dr. Jeremy Cook.*

RIGHT: Chris Pendleton's hand is raised after defeating nemesis Ben Askren of Missouri for his second national title. *Courtesy Dr. Jeremy Cook.*

answered with a reversal of his own with 25 seconds left, but Hendricks staved off Perry's desperation tilt attempt to win 5-2.

After the match, Perry ran across the mat and shook the hands of uncles Pat and John, then donned his black and gold warm-up and disappeared into the arena with his Iowa brethren. At the post-match press conference Coach Smith answered the media's interest in the intra-family competition. "The only time that I felt that Mark Perry was my nephew and my sister's son was after the match. He showed great courage to come over and shake his uncles' hands. Before the match and leading into the match, it's about my guy winning. The guy in orange is the guy I'm going to coach. Him being a part of our family, we were very proud about what he did here. I think he showed great character on his part for coming over to shake his uncles' hands."[43]

Pendleton then faced nemesis Ben Askren for the ninth time in a repeat of the previous year's national title match. He vaulted to an early 6-0 lead, but when Askren posted four consecutive points and Pendleton took an injury time-out for Doc Allen to tend to a strained shoulder, Cowboy fans held their breath. But the Cowboy captain battled through with a late escape, takedown and riding time point to prevail 10-5, posting his 115th win while wearing the orange singlet. As time expired on their ninth and final meeting, Askren stepped back and let the clock tick down. The wrestlers shook hands and the Missouri sophomore smiled, embraced his rival, and spoke so no one could hear. "Thanks for the battles"[44] he said, as hair shot from his headgear like straw-colored laser beams.

Askren was somber as he stood center-stage and received his runner-up plaque. Choosing not to speak with reporters after the match, he sat and sobbed in a dark and private arena corridor. He lost only four matches during the season, all to Pendleton. Askren's teammate, 165-pounder Tyron Woodley, put it best, "I'm guessing he's happy [Pendleton] is gone."[45]

Pendleton reflected on his part in one of college wrestling's most durable and spirited rivalries. "Our relationship as competitors really came full circle. It started out as some punk kid who took me to overtime last year, then to someone I completely detested when he beat me in the Big 12 Tournament. This year, I looked back at it, and that's a guy that battled me every time.

Sometimes this year I didn't think guys were giving me their full effort, and that's something I can respect Ben Askren for."[46]

When Jake Rosholt took the mat, teammates Esposito, Hendricks, and Pendleton already had won their national championship matches. "Right before I went out there they said [over the public address system] that Iowa had five champs in 1997. I didn't want to be the guy [to lose]. It was a battle for me...this whole tournament was a battle for me."[47] Rosholt faced Northern Iowa's Sean Stender, whose takedown with 30 seconds left in the match erased Rosholt's riding time advantage and tied the match at 4-4. But Rosholt's escape with 13 seconds remaining gave him his second career title and boosted his NCAA tournament record to 14-1. "I didn't wrestle my best tournament at all and had a rough string of matches, but I got it done. That's all that really matters."[48]

When Rosholt injured his knee during the Lehigh match in February, Coach Smith worried the timing of the injury might hamper important tournament preparation. "The last six weeks had been a real struggle for Jake. He's been injured and missed some time in the room. But he battled through all that and won even though he wasn't at 100 percent."[49]

The final match of the tournament and the concluding match of the season for the Cowboys pitted Steve Mocco against Cole Konrad, his nemesis from Minnesota. Mocco's path to the finals had been methodical and ruthless. He posted a fall, a major decision, and two decisions, and allowed only three points to be scored against him in four matches. Now he found himself in the NCAA finals for the third consecutive year. This time he wore an orange singlet

* * *

Some called him "The Intimidator." Others called him "The Bear." Workout partner Mike Christian put it bluntly. "Some people are scared to wrestle him. His reputation precedes him a little bit."[50] Before matches he paced and pawed his feet like a rabid bull. While he warmed up, he looked at his opponent with the narrow eyes of a hungry man eyeing a succulent pot roast. After one match, a father ordered his son, who had survived a match with the Cowboy heavyweight, to call home and "Tell your mom you're okay. She's worried sick."[51] Before his matches the Darth Vader theme song was piped through Gallagher-Iba Arena. "I just come out for

LEFT: Johny Hendricks bear hugs Coach Smith moments after a dramatic 5-2 victory over Mark Perry in the national finals. *Courtesy Dr. Jeremy Cook.*

RIGHT: Coach Smith celebrates with Zack Esposito after the New Jersey native captures his first NCAA title. Esposito was Smith's 10th national champion since taking over the wrestling program in 1992. *Courtesy Dr. Jeremy Cook.*

Jake Rosholt, who battled a knee injury throughout the season, relishes his second NCAA title after defeating Northern Iowa's Sean Stender 5-4. *Courtesy Dr. Jeremy Cook.*

business. I'm here to win matches. That's my livelihood and my job. When I go out there, I'm trying to make the person never want to wrestle me again. I want them to cringe when they see me."[52] After his matches he sprinted away like a man with his hair afire and bounded for the wrestling room, where he ran sprints, hit push-ups, and pumped repetitions on a chin-up bar. "I want to keep my heart rate up."[53] Coach Smith called him the hardest working athlete his size in the world.

But the guy who "expects opponents to tremble when they meet him on the wrestling mat"[54] was a 4.0 student who enjoyed crafting ceramic bowls for fun. Late one sunny afternoon in Lincoln, Nebraska he sat with Smith, recited each of the Ten Commandments in order, and debated how they were altered and refined through the vagaries of the Middle Ages. One brother was a brain surgeon; another an Ivy-league trained attorney. Sister Katie was a world-class judo competitor who hoped to join her brother at the next Olympic games. His roommate was sister Colleen, an honor student at Oklahoma State.

Mocco's arrival in Stillwater was big news, but sometimes he was unaware of his standing on campus. When asked to serve as a celebrity waiter at a

Special Olympics fundraiser in Stillwater with teammate Chris Pendleton, he was curious, asking "Who are the celebrities?"[55]

But most of all, he was a wrestler. "I love to wrestle." After a stellar high school career at Blair Academy, where his roommate was fellow New Jersey native Zack Esposito, he pulverized everyone in sight. Major wrestling programs rolled out the red carpet, including Oklahoma State. He said no to John Smith, and chose to attend Iowa. It was a reasonable choice at the time. The Hawkeyes' pounding and relentless style, perpetuated by the ghost of Dan Gable, fit hand-in-glove with his own. According to Smith, Mocco's decision "…broke my heart."

At Iowa Mocco went 74-3 with 24 falls and a national title. He liked the wrestlers and coaches. "I only have positive memories of my experiences there. I just needed something different."[56] But at Iowa, something was just not right.

In 2004 he took a year off to train for the Olympic team. He finished third in the tryouts, and the next day asked his coach Jim Zalesky for a release. The Iowa coach was true to his word. "I promised him two things when he came here and I don't go back on my word…I promised him if he wanted to redshirt he could take an Olympic redshirt and if he wasn't happy here, I would release him."[57]

So Steve continued his search for the Holy Grail. While Mocco trained in Colorado Springs for the Olympics, Cowboy coaches and former wrestlers were everywhere, and a curious Mocco turned to his high school buddy Esposito. "I knew he would give me the real deal and wouldn't hustle me. I knew I had a guy on the inside that would tell me how it was at OSU."[58]

As it turned out, coach Smith had phoned Mocco three years earlier to wish him good luck after the devastated Cowboy coach learned Mocco had chosen Iowa over the Cowboys. It may turn out to be the most important recruiting call John Smith ever made, for after a summer visit to Stillwater, Mocco announced his intention to be a Cowboy. Mocco sensed quickly the Olympic-quality flavor of the program. "Everyone has similar goals and they're training to be world and Olympic champions. This is the ultimate place to train at. This is the best situation for my life."[59]

One sunny day in late November, Steve's father drove 30 hours from New Jersey to see Steve wrestle. In the Cowboy locker room he was introduced to Lee Roy Smith Sr., the patriarch of the wrestling Smith clan. During practice the two fathers sat with their heads close together and whispered knowingly of their sons' respective journeys. "Steve didn't want to be a doctor or a lawyer like his brothers. He wanted to be a wrestler. We weren't television people. After homework, Steve would be in our basement wrestling room. 'Dad, you shoot and I'll sprawl.'"[60] As a seven-year-old junior wrestler, while watching his older brother compete in a tournament, Steve Mocco bounded onto the mat and locked onto the leg of his brother's unsuspecting opponent.

He did not carry the ripped physique of a body builder, and many of his terrified opponents enjoyed a height advantage over the stocky, blond haired education major. When trainers instructed wrestlers in the heavier weight categories to perform cartwheels to enhance strength and balance, the 270-pounder twirled like a ballerina. Able to jump from a standing position onto a box four feet high, he drew the football coaches' endearing attention when they saw him pump weights. Strength coach Gary Calcagno observed Mocco's physical gifts. "Tremendous balance and core strength. Explosive. Docs super-sets, alternate exercises with sets of 10. Over and over. He's the most intense guy in a roomful of intense guys."[61]

Like any college student who moved to a new school, the transition was gradual. Weeks went by and Mocco still did not know the names of his teammates. He occasionally became angry when teammates teased him good-naturedly about his less-than-blinding foot speed. He hung out mostly with Blair Academy buddy Esposito and Pennsylvanian Coleman Scott, and looked primarily to his family for support and companionship. During dual matches he sometimes appeared on the bench just before his match, and sprinted off afterwards to the locker room to continue practice.

His trophy case was stocked full of individual awards, but he had never wrestled on a championship team at Iowa. Smith recognized this dynamic, for despite his own prodigious individual titles, he had never been a part of a national championship team during his years at OSU. "Individuals perform better in the context of a successful team effort. When wrestlers strive for team success, individual achievement often follows. Camaraderie and esprit de corp produce energy and motivation. The total is greater than the sum of the parts."[62]

Cowboy heavyweight Steve Mocco prepares to take the mat. *Courtesy Mika Matzen.*

So when the Cowboys battled to a National Dual title the previous month in Cleveland, Mocco watched while teammates, some who had forfeited scholarship monies to accommodate Mocco's entry into their program, competed together. Hendricks battled through injuries, backups Jensen and Lewnes supplied timely victories, and the freshmen trifecta survived its scorching baptism by fire. The value of team wrestling seemed to crystallize. The Cowboys won the National Dual championships, and for the first time in his college career Mocco was a part of a national team championship.

By the Lehigh dual, a transformed Mocco stood to his feet, pointed to his temples with his forefingers, and implored Nathan Morgan during a dramatic overtime victory to "use your head...wrestle smart."[63] Later Esposito cracked that Mocco "Put the fear of God in him."[64] In the post-game radio interview Mocco focused on his teammates' performances and not his own. By the end of February the team crowded around him at the end of a long practice and clapped in cadence and cheered as he strained on the pull-up bar. He roamed the wrestling room after practice, draped in a towel, telling jokes to all who would hear.

Coach Smith: "My heavyweight is a very unique person. With him there is no option other than being the best in the entire world." *Courtesy Dr. Jeremy Cook.*

Amidst the transformation, Mocco's game plan remained simple. "Before I step onto the mat, 10 seconds before the match, I think 'Show time.' I don't want this guy ever to want to come back on this mat with me again. I want him to fear me forever. On the top position I like to ride, always going for the pin, wearing them out. I like to take the guy down and get back points. At that point he's helpless. I am domination minded. I make it more like a fight. My strength is dominating the head position. I wear the other guy out. My favorite move from the down position is just to jump up to my feet like the other guy is holding me under water. I make it more like a fight than who has the best moves. I am more of a brawler."[65]

But as Olympic Silver medalist Jamill Kelly, who trained the Cowboy middleweights, observed, "Intimidation won't work on the Olympic level." At Iowa, Mocco's first period arsenal involved leg sweeps, sprawls, spins, and front headlocks. Mocco now received high-tech instruction from Cowboy coaches on finishing shots to the legs, an absolute necessity on the international level, and a sequence that opened up his conventional attack even more.

Always among the last to leave the wrestling room after practice, Mocco looked to Coach Smith for encouragement, affirmation, and critique of the day's workout. "My heavyweight is a very unique person. With him there is no option other than being the best in the entire world. That's not saying he will look past the NCAAs. He won't. He knows there will be threats down

BELOW: Steve Mocco and Cole Konrad hand-fight in the NCAA finals. *Courtesy Dr. Jeremy Cook*

the road and that guys will challenge him. But the best thing I can do for Steve is to help him step back and think differently about his bad days so the next day will be better. So he will understand it's not about his manhood or his gut or pride or conditioning, but rather 'My technique needs to get better.' Wrestlers get in the habit of being very robotic and not coming out of their box to explore and learn. You will see them making the same mistakes in year three as they did in year one. I'm trying to help Steve prevent that."[66]

The runaway freight train in search of the Holy Grail.

———————————

Earlier matches between Mocco and Konrad resembled cautious, low-scoring pitchers' duals. This match followed a similar pattern. In the opening period both wrestlers clutched for legs, but to no avail, resulting in a double stall warning. In the second period Mocco escaped in just four seconds, and the crowd gasped when Konrad locked a single leg and actually elevated Mocco's leg waist-high. Hopping on one leg, Mocco fought to the edge of the mat and fended Konrad off. In the third period Konrad escaped in less than 30 seconds, and neither wrestler scored in regulation time. But seconds into the first sudden victory period, Mocco momentarily posted the bulk of Konrad's weight to one foot, and at the precise moment swept Konrad's ankle away with his foot, causing the Golden Gopher to crash to the mat like a tall Norway Pine. Mocco pounced, secured the takedown, and captured his second NCAA crown and the first as a Cowboy.

Ironically, "the most feared collegiate wrestler in the nation"[67] known for his aggression and brute force, won the title with a maneuver predicated on balance and leverage. "That's the first time I hit an overtime foot sweep in competition. I drilled it a lot when I was a little boy. When you drill something over and over, it gets effective."[68] Not only did Mocco utilize the foot sweep in crunch-time, it was a variation of his normal repertoire. "It was my off side. That is the first time I've ever hit that off-side in a tournament match. I consider it a leg attack…just with the foot. It's effective because I drill it."[69]

———————————

The Cowboys were expected to capture the team title, but the relatively young team made of five underclassmen out of 10 weights, manned by only one senior, had been severely tested in close duals throughout the season. No coach or journalist predicted OSU would crown five national champions, place seven All-Americans and run away with the team title by 70 points. Top-seeded Esposito, Pendleton, and Mocco won titles, and second seed Rosholt and third seed Hendricks also won championships. During the three days of competition some 94,959 attendees, the second highest total attendance in the 75 years the tournament had been held, saw the Cowboys win 38 of their 47 matches. Eleven wins were major decisions, and six came by fall. The seventy-point margin of victory was the second largest in NCAA history. It was the most dominating performance in the gloried history of Cowboy wrestling, performed by a squad made up of only one senior. Smith knew the performance might be special after the team stampeded to the Big 12 championship two weeks earlier and doubled the combined point totals of nationally-ranked Iowa State, Nebraska and Oklahoma. "Our mission was to be the very best, and to get to the point where at the end of the season we were able to translate that belief into performance. We trained hard and pulled together. By the end of the year I had a group of true believers. I mean, true believers. They were talented and well trained. But in the end, it all came from within. It always does."[70]

The Cowboys crowned five national champions, the most of any OSU team *Courtesy Dr. Jeremy Cook.*

After pictures were taken and congratulations accepted, Coach Smith addressed the media. "It was an amazing night for Oklahoma State wrestling. To have half the champions in the field in a very competitive year, the most competitive year I can remember…it's good to know you're doing the right things."[71] Coach Smith was not ready to admit to the media this was his best team. "That's for you guys to decide."[72]

"I tell our guys that pressure is a privilege. We came in here knowing what was expected, and we accepted the challenge. Wrapping up the team title on Friday is something we're proud of, but I'm just as impressed with the way our guys responded today."[73]

To see our guys reach their individual goals today, capturing the championships they've worked for and dreamed of, it's tremendously gratifying."[74]

The tournament's Outstanding Wrestler was awarded to West Virginia's three-time national champion Greg Jones. The deserving Jones defeated a five-seed 5-2 in the semi-finals, followed by a 5-3 win over a seventh seed in the finals. In contrast, Pendleton reached the semi-finals with a fall and two decisions, and outscored his opponents 30-11. In the semi-finals he defeated a five seed 16-1, and in the finals topped off a two seed 10-5. Some argued that Pendleton deserved the award as the tournament's outstanding wrestler, but the Cowboy leader deflected such revisionism. "I approached this year with my goals laid out. I wanted to win another NCAA title. I wanted to

BELOW: Cowboy radio voice J. Carl Guymon interviews Zack Esposito and Chris Pendleton after their victories in the NCAA finals. Guymon, a nationally known wrestling broadcaster, is a walking dictionary of wrestling knowledge. *Courtesy Dr. Jeremy Cook.*

ABOVE: Five of the ten champions at the 2005 NCAA wrestling tournament hailed from Oklahoma State. *Courtesy Dr. Jeremy Cook.*

win the Hodge Trophy [for top wrestler]. I wanted Outstanding Wrestler here. After I lost a match in December and the way my teammates rallied around me, that wasn't the big picture any more. I took this year enjoying every single moment with my teammates and seeing them get their goals."[75] Mocco's analysis was more heartfelt but equally cogent, "I'd pick Esposito because he's from New Jersey."[76]

THOSE WHO STILL COWBOY, DO IT BECAUSE
THEY LOVE IT AND DO SO WITH THE HOPE
THAT THEY ARE KEEPING ALIVE A WAY OF LIFE
THAT FEW OTHERS COULD WITHSTAND AND
ABSOLUTELY CANNOT UNDERSTAND.

—Curt Brummett, quoted in *Horsing Around* (1999)

epilogue

THE SUNDAY MORNING AFTER the NCAA tournament, the Cowboy bus departed St. Louis at 11:00 a.m. bound for Stillwater. The evening before, a thousand OSU fans cheered the conquering Cowboys at the Hard Rock Café located blocks from the arena. As the fans waited for the Cowboys to arrive from their hotel, Coach Smith spoke on his cell phone, buying time from anxious athletic department administrators as his wrestlers sprinted from the bus to their hotel rooms for quick showers. The athletic department had rented the entire Hard Rock facility. It was 8:30 p.m., and the boisterous fans were anxious to congratulate the Cowboys. When the team arrived, Coach Smith stood on a stage and paid tribute to his team as fans, former wrestlers, family, and curious onlookers basked in the victory.

On the bus the next morning some wrestlers slept, oblivious as music blared from IPods through tangled wires connected to bruised and swollen ears. Coach Smith poured over tournament score sheets, napped, made notes in his black leather journal, and conversed softly with his son Joseph, who sat at his side.

The Cowboys crowned five individual NCAA champions, seven All-Americans, four academic All-Americans, seven academic All-Big 12 selections, and a 33rd NCAA national title. Since 2000, the OSU wrestling program had produced 15 academic All-Americans, the highest number among all other Division I schools in the nation. Dr. Jeremy Cook, academic advisor and tutor for the wrestling team, reflected on the year. "Everything ties together, everything works together—it's holistic. You cannot succeed on the mat and fail in the classroom. You cannot fail on the mat and succeed in the classroom. Success breeds success."[1]

How did they do it? Mocco attributed much of the Cowboy success to John Smith's ability to incite each wrestler in a different manner. "He motivated us by any means necessary. He put a fire in our bellies to train hard. He made sure we remained focused."[2] Pendleton agreed. "Some of the fans booed us, but we were the ones who traveled to their home states to wrestle in their arenas, sometimes to wrestle three dual meets in a week while juggling classes and practices. And by the time the tournament season rolled around, I swear a week in Stillwater with coach Smith was a nightmare."[3]

In reflecting on the year, some speculated the season turned on OSU's gutsy win at the National Dual Tournament, an event that rewarded team strength over individual accomplishment. Coach Smith saw the impact of this team's unity as individual goals were relegated to team accomplishment. "We had guys that had passions and drives to win a national championship as a team. These individuals were not self-centered in their individual success. In a lot of ways, they put the team ahead of themselves. That's a reason we had five champions."[4]

Team captain Chris Pendleton recognized the value of a roomful of men dedicated to a singular cause. "You could hear it in the crowd. I've never done anything to anyone in Iowa...I didn't wrestle an Iowa guy in the tournament...yet they were booing me. That's the reaction we get everywhere we go. It creates a bond with your teammates. It makes you brothers."[5]

The following year the 2005-2006 Cowboys would return 127 of the 153 points they scored at the NCAA tournament, 44 more than their nearest rival. Graduation would claim Pendleton from Murderer's Row, but title-hungry underclassmen eagerly awaited their opportunity to wear the orange singlet, and the Freshman Trifecta returned in tact.

Seven hours later the national champion Cowboys pulled into an empty Gallagher-Iba parking lot. There was no welcoming party to meet the bus as they carried bags through the arena and into the wrestling room. The team gathered one last time as coach Smith explained the dangers of complacency.

"We had a great season, one of the best in school history. But we can do better. Give your equipment to Randy. I'll see you next week."[6]

* * *

On an overcast Friday afternoon, some three weeks before the 2005 NCAA tournament, John Smith drove to Tulsa to watch his son Joseph compete in the 27th annual state of Oklahoma tournament for junior wrestlers—ages four to 11. It was sweater-weather, and the sun struggled to appear. Smith himself had wrestled in the tournament over three decades earlier. Fourteen mats covered the floor of the Tulsa Convention Center, servicing more than 1,800 young wrestlers, with the smallest competitor tipping the scales at 37 pounds. They wore tiny singlets, shiny-new wrestling shoes and headgears that seemed too large for their heads. Forty-two officials stood around the mats as an arena-wide prayer was held "In Jesus' Name," followed by a taped rendition of the national anthem.

Wrestling crowds are usually conservative, respectful of authority, and patriotic. The stands were almost full of parents, mostly moms from middle-class families talking on cell phones, pouring over brackets and socializing while dads and husbands were at their jobs. Many held video cameras. Some walked the aisles carrying bottled water and strips of beef-jerky, wearing t-shirts bearing the names of their children's wrestling teams. The young competitors waited in the stands. Some slept, others played video games, while most chatted with teammates. One wore a t-shirt that read "Hold my water while I kiss your girlfriend."

Four former Cowboy wrestlers coached the Stillwater team. All had been college All-Americans, and two had represented the United States in the recent Olympic games in Athens. Before the tournament began they were introduced, and the public address announcer proudly observed they had all been coached by "OSU Coach and Olympic champion John Smith."

During the three-hour interval, while Smith sat in the stands waiting for Joseph's three-minute match, a stream of fans approached the Cowboy coach, asking him to autograph programs, singlets, hats, or scratches of paper. Finally Joseph took the mat. Smith had not instructed or trained his young son much in the sacred art of wrestling. "When he is ready for me to help him, he will let me know."[7] At the whistle, Joseph's dad sat by his wife Toni, but moved three rows back to sit alone as the two young wrestlers began to circle. Toni moved three rows forward and grasped the brass railing. In previous tournaments, parents and wrestlers had gathered around Joseph's mat to watch "John Smith's son" compete. On this afternoon, Joseph fell victim to a headlock and back-points early, bridged off his back for a full minute, only to come back to claim victory with a takedown at the end. During the match his father looked on. He didn't stand, stomp, or scream. He did a fair amount of leaning, a good amount of laughing, and while Joseph battled off his back, his heart appeared to break.

After his son's hand was raised as the victor, Smith walked quickly from the arena. With a proud smile, he reflected on his son's match and every other match for every other wrestler who has stepped on a mat. "You cannot understand the frame of mind in one-on-one competition. There is nothing tougher. It exposes every weakness an athlete has."[8]

Smith glanced back at the arena, then walked to his pickup for the drive back to Stillwater. He had phone calls to make. Some guys had tests that day.

More personal now, Smith spoke with pride of Joseph's victory. "He did it with no fear in his eyes. He didn't stall. He had the right frame of mind in the third period as well as the first. He stepped onto the mat ready to battle."[9]

In the end, Cowboy Up.

Preface

1. Rhees, R., *Recollections of Wiggenstein* (Oxford: Oxford University Press, 1984)

One / Glory Day

1. Etling, Kathy, *The Quotable Cowboy* (Guilford, Connecticut: The Lyons Press, 2002)
2. *Tulsa World* (Tulsa, Oklahoma), November 14, 2004.
3. Interviews with John Smith, September 2004-June 2005, hereinafter referred to as J. Smith interview)
4. Interviews with Zack Esposito, September 2004-June 2005, hereinafter referred to as Z. Esposito interview.
5. *Tulsa World* (Tulsa, Oklahoma), November 14, 2004.
6. Z. Esposito interview.
7. Ibid.
8. J. Smith interview.
9. Z. Esposito interview.
10. Sportsline.com. August 7, 2001 (cited in Oklahoma State Wrestling Media Guide, 2004-05, p. 33)

Two / John W. Smith

1. J. Smith interview
2. *The Daily Oklahoman*, January 8, 1989.
3. *The Daily Oklahoman*, January 8, 1989.
4. J. Smith interview.
5. *Los Angeles Times* (Los Angeles, California), July 19, 1992.
6. *The Daily Oklahoman,* January 8, 1989.
7. Ibid.
8. *The Daily Oklahoman,* January 8, 1989.
9. *The Daily Oklahoman,* March 15, 2006.
10. *Los Angeles Times*, July 19, 1992.
11. Ibid.
12. Interview with Lee Roy Smith Sr., September 2004-June 2005, hereinafter referred to as L. Smith interview.
13. *The Daily Oklahoman*, November 20, 1983.
14. *The Daily Oklahoman*, December 8, 1983.
15. *The Daily Oklahoman*, February 27, 1984.
16. J. Smith interview.
17. Ibid.
18. *The Daily Oklahoman*, March 24, 1984.
19. Ibid.
20. Ibid.
21. *The Daily Oklahoman*, March 29, 1984.
22. *The Daily Oklahoman*, February 1, 1985.
23. Ibid
24. *The Daily Oklahoman*, February 3, 1985.
25. *The Daily Oklahoman*, February 17, 1985.
26. *The Daily Oklahoman*, March 14, 1985.
27. Ibid.

28. *The Daily Oklahoman,* March 17, 1985.
29. *The Daily Oklahoman,* March 17, 1985.
30. J. Smith interview.
31. Ibid.
32. Ibid.
33. Ibid.
34. Ibid.
35. Ibid.
36. Ibid.
37. Ibid.
38. Ibid.
39. *Los Angeles Times,* July 19, 1992.
40. J. Smith interview.
41. Ibid.
42. Ibid.
43. Ibid.
44. Ibid.
45. Ibid.
46. *The Daily Oklahoman,* March 22, 1987.
47. Ibid.
48. Ibid.
49. Ibid.
50. *The Daily Oklahoman,* July 16, 1987.
51. J. Smith interview.
52. The Daily Oklahoman, March 6, 1988.
53. *The Daily Oklahoman,* June 19, 1988.
54. *The Daily Oklahoman,* September 26, 1988.
55. *The Daily Oklahoman,* September 27, 1988.
56. *The Daily Oklahoman,* September 29, 1988.
57. Ibid.
58. *The Daily Oklahoman,* September 29, 1988.
59. Ibid.
60. Ibid.
61. Ibid.
62. Ibid.

63. *The Daily Oklahoman,* September 30, 1988.
64. Ibid.
65. *The Daily Oklahoman,* September 30, 1988.
66. *The Daily Oklahoman,* September 16, 1990.
67. Knight-Ridder Newspapers (cited in *The Daily Oklahoman*), May 29, 1991.
68. *Los Angeles Times,* July 19, 1992.
69. *The Daily Oklahoman,* December 10, 1991.
70. *The Daily Oklahoman,* May 27, 1992.
71. Ibid.
72. *The Daily Oklahoman,* September 24, 1992.
73. Associated Press cited in *The Daily Oklahoman,* June 7, 1992.
74. *Los Angeles Times,* July 19, 1992.
75. Ibid.
76. *The Daily Oklahoman,* July 19, 1992.
77. *The Daily Oklahoman,* July 1, 1992.
78. Ibid.
79. Los Angeles Times, July 19, 1992.
80. J. Smith interview.
81. *The Daily Oklahoman,* July 7, 1992.
82. *The Daily Oklahoman,* August 14, 1992.
83. Interview with Kami Barzini, April 20, 2007.
84. In April 2007 the United State government, in an attempt to foster contacts with the Iranian government

in the midst of international tensions over Iran's nuclear program, invited the top Iranian wrestlers to train in the U.S. for the 2008 Olympic Games in Beijing. (Reuters, April 25, 2007)
85. J. Smith interview.
86. J. Smith interview.
87. Associated Press cited in *The Daily Oklahoman*, August 9, 1992.
88. Ibid.
89. *The Daily Oklahoman,* November 5, 1992; Seay stayed involved in collegiate and international wrestling, and was named head wrestling coach at the University of Tennessee-Chattanooga in December 2005.
90. Ibid.
91. Ibid.
92. Ibid.
93. *The Daily Oklahoman,* November 5, 1992.
94. Ibid.
95. Ibid.
96. *The Daily Oklahoman,* February 5, 1993.
97. *The Daily Oklahoman,* January 25, 1993.
98. *The Daily Oklahoman,* January 16, 1994.
99. *The Daily Oklahoman,* January 30, 1994.
100. *The Daily Oklahoman,* December 5, 1995.
101. *The Daily Oklahoman,* March 25, 1996.
102. *The Daily Oklahoman,* July 24, 1997.

103. *The Daily Oklahoman,* February 24, 2000.
104. *The Daily Oklahoman,* March 20, 2000.
105. *The Daily Oklahoman,* December 11, 2000.
106. *The Daily Oklahoman,* February 3, 2001.
107. Ibid.
108. *The Daily Oklahoman,* March 21, 2002.
109. Dan Gable's Wrestling Essentials: Standing Position[video recording] Human Kinetics, 1999.
110. J. Smith interview.
111. Ibid.
112. Ibid.
113. Ibid.
114. Ibid.
115. *The Daily Oklahoman,* March 23, 2003.
116. *Los Angeles Times,* July 19, 1992.
117. Ibid.
118. Ibid.
119. J. Smith interview.
120. *Daily O'Collegian* (Stillwater, Oklahoma), January 20, 2005.
121. J. Smith interview.
122. At the close of the century, ESPN compiled a list of the greatest North American athletes of the 20th century. Michael Jordan, by virtue of his six NBA titles and two Olympic gold medals, was ranked number one, followed by Babe Ruth, Muhammad Ali, Jim Brown, and Wayne Gretsky. John Smith captured six world championships, and two Olympic gold medals. Smith was not included in ESPN's list. (See http://espn.go.com/sportscentury/athletes.html)
123. http://www.filahalloffame.com/smith.html
124. ESPN.com, 2/20/2007, Jerry Crasnick, http://sports.espn.go.com/mlb/
125. *The Daily Oklahoman,* March 23, 2004.
126. J. Smith interview.

Three / The Orange & Black Match

1. Ibid.
2. Ibid.
3. Ibid.
4. *Stillwater News Press,* November 4, 2004.
5. J. Smith interview.
6. Gladwell, Malcom, *Blink-The Power of Thinking Without Thinking* (New York: Little, Brown and Company, 2000).
7. Ibid.
8. J. Smith interview.
9. Ibid.
10. *Time Magazine,* March 7, 2005 (p. 60).
11. J. Smith interview.
12. Ibid.
13. Ibid.
14. Ibid.
15. Ibid.
16. Ibid.
17. Ibid.
18. Ibid.
19. Ibid.
20. Interviews with Ronnie Delk September 2004-June 2005, hereinafter referred to as R. Delk interview.
21. *Stillwater News Press,* November 5, 2004.
22. *Daily O'Collegian,* November 5, 2004.
23. J. Smith interview.
24. Ibid.
25. *The Daily Oklahoman,* November 5, 2004.
26. *Stillwater News Press,* November 5, 2004.
27. Author's observation.
28. Ibid.
29. Ibid.
30. Ibid.
31. Ibid.
32. Ibid.
33. J. Smith interview.

Four / The University of Tennessee at Chattanooga/Boise State

1. http://www.kenchertow.com/coaches_norner/title_bush_admin.html.
2. For a general treatment and review of the relevant issues, see Title IX Basics by Valerie M. Bonnette, Good Sports, Inc., 2000.
3. http://www.ncaa.org/news/2002/20021223/active/3926n02.html.
4. http://www.intermat-wrestle.com/college/dropped.aspx.

5. http://www.kenchertow.com/coachs_corner/title_ix_irving.html.
6. http://www.kenchertow.com/coachs_corner/title_ix_bush.html.
7. http://www.kenchertow.com/coachs_corner/title_ix_bush_admin.html.
8. Ibid.
9. Title IX Seminar Keynote Address delivered by Miles Brand, April 28 2003, cited at http://www.ncaa.org/gender_equity/general_info/20030428speech.html
10. Ibid.
11. Ibid.
12. Ibid.
13. The NCAA News & Features, April 29, 1996 cited at http://www.ncaa.org/news/1996/960429/active/3317n07.html
14. http://www.kenchertow.com/coachs_corner/title_ix_60_min.html., December 2, 2002
15. http://www.kenchertow.com/coachs_corner/title_ix_urgent_action.html, January 13, 2003
16. http://www.kenchertow.com/coachs_corner/title_ix_60_min.html.
17. J. Smith interview.
18 . The Daily Oklahoman June 24, 2001.
19. Cowboy Wrestling press release, November 14, 2004.

20. Author's observation.
21. Interviews with Derek Stevens, September 2004-June 2005, hereinafter referred to as D. Stevens interview.
22. Interviews with Pat Smith, September 2004-June 2005, hereinafter referred to as P. Smith interview.
23. The Daily Oklahoman, November 15, 2004.
24. Interview(s) with Taylor Hosick, September 2004-June 2005, hereinafter referred to as T. Hosick interview.
25. Author observation.
26. Ibid.
27. Ibid.
28. Ibid.
29. Ibid.
30. Ibid.
31. Ibid.
32. Ibid.

Five / Minnesota
1. J. Smith interview.
2. Author observation.
3. Ibid.
4. Ibid.
5. Ibid.
6. J. Smith interview.
7. Author observation.
8. Ibid.
9. Ibid.
10. Author observation.
11. Interviews with Daniel Frishkorn, September 2004-June 2005, hereinafter referred to as D. Frishkorn interview.
12. Ibid.
13. Ibid.
14. Ibid.
15. Ibid.
16. Ibid.

17. Ibid.
18. Ibid.
19. Ibid.
20. Author observation.
21. Ibid.
22. Ibid.
23. Ibid.
24. Ibid.
25. Ibid.
26. Ibid.
27. Ibid.
28. Ibid.
29. Ibid.
30. J. Smith interview.

Six / Oklahoma
1. Author observation.
2. Interview Dr. Jeremy Cook.
3. Author observation.
4. The Daily O'Collegian, December 10, 2004.
5. Author observation.
6. J. Smith interview.
7. Justin Porter interview.
8. Author observation.
9. Author observation.
10. Author observation.
11. Author observation.
12. Author observation.
13. Author observation.
14. Interviews with Sarah Tackett, September 2004-June 2005, hereinafter referred to as S. Tackett interview.
15. Ibid.
16. Author observation.
17. Ibid.
18. Ibid.
19. Interviews with Chris Pendleton, September 2004-June 2005, hereinafter referred to as C. Pendleton interview.
20. Ibid.
21. Ibid.

22. Ibid.
23. Ibid.
24. Ibid.
25. Ibid.
26. Ibid.
27. Ibid.
28. Ibid.
29. Ibid.
30. Interviews with Eric Guerrero, September 2004-June 2005, here-inafter referred to as E. Guerrero interview.
31. P. Smith interview.
32. J. Smith interview.
33. Tulsa World, December 13, 2005.
34. Ibid.
35. Stillwater News Press, December 13, 2004.
36. *Tulsa World,* December 13, 2005.
37. Author observation.
38. Ibid.
39. Ibid.
40. Ibid.
41. J. Smith interview.
42. Ibid.
43. Ibid.
44. NCAA 2005 Rules and Interpretations.
45 Author observation.
46. J. Smith interview.
47 Ibid.
48 Ibid.
49 Author observation.

Seven / The Western Invasion

1. Author observation.
2. Author observation.
3. R. Delk interview.
4. Ibid.
5. Ibid.
6. Ibid.
7. Ibid.
8. R. Delk interview.

9. Author observation.
10. Ibid.
11. Author observation.
12. Author observation.
13. J. Smith interview.
14. Author observation.
15. Ibid.
16. Interviews with Joe Azevedo, September 2004-June 2005, here-inafter referred to as J. Azevedo interview.
17. Ibid.
18. Author observation.
19. Author observation.
20. Author observation.
21. Author observation.
22. Author observation.
23. Author observation.
24. J. Smith interview.
25. Author observation.
26. Author observation.
27. Ibid.
28. Ibid.
29. Ibid.
30.. Ibid.
31. Ibid.
32. Ibid.
33. Ibid.
34. Ibid.
35. Ibid.
36. Ibid.
37. Ibid.
38. Ibid.
39. Ibid.
40. Ibid.

Eight / Michigan State

1. Author observation.
2. J. Smith interview.
3. Author observation.
4. Author observation.
5. J. Smith interview.
6. Ibid.
7. Ibid.
8. Ibid.
9. Ibid.

10. *The Daily Oklahoman,* January 12, 2005.
11. Ibid.
12. *Tulsa World*, January 6, 2005.
13. *Daily O'Collegian*, January 13, 2005.
14. Ibid.
15. *Stillwater News Press,* January 12, 2005.
16. Author observation.
17. Author observation.
18. Author observation.
19. Author observation.
20. *The Daily Oklahoman,* January 14, 2005.
21. *Stillwater News Press*, January 14, 2005.
22. *Stillwater News Press*, January 14, 2005.
23. Ibid.
24. *The Daily Oklahoman*, January 14, 2005.
25. *Tulsa World*, January 14, 2005.
26. Author observation.
27. Author observation.
28. http://www.nytimes.com/2006/10/29/sports/playmagazine/1029play_parcells.html?spring2007/columns/story?columnist=crasnick_jerry&id=2771923.

Nine / Iowa

1. http://www.themat.com/pressbox/pressdetail.asp?aid=7645.
2. Ibid
3. Ibid.
4. J. Smith interview.
5. *Sports Illustrated,* January 24, 2005.
6. Ibid.

7. Heifetz, Ronald A. and Marty Linsky, 2002. *Leadership on the Line: Staying Alive Through the Dangers of Leading.* Boston: Harvard Business School Press.
8. Ibid.
9. J. Smith interview.
10. Author observation.
11. Author observation.
12. Ibid.
13. *Sports Illustrated,* January 24, 2005.
14. Author observation.
15. *Tulsa World,* January 17, 2005
16. The Daily Oklahoman, February 11, 2007
17. Interviews with Johny Hendricks, September 2004-June 2005, hereinafter referred to as J. Hendricks interview.
18. Author observation.
19. Ibid.
20. *The Daily Oklahoman,* February 11, 2007.
21. J. Hendricks interview.
22. The Daily Oklahoman, January 17, 2005.
23. Ibid.
24. *The Daily O'Collegian,* June 17, 2005.
25. Author observation.

Ten / The National Dual Championships
1. J. Smith interview.
2. Ibid.
3. Ibid.
4. Author observation.
5. Ibid.
6. Author observation.
7. Ibid.
8. Ibid.

9. J. Smith interview.
10. J. Smith interview.
11. Ibid.
12. Ibid.
13. Ibid.
14. Author observation.
15. Ibid.
16. Ibid.
17. Author observation.
18. Author observation.
19. Author observation.
20. Ibid.
21. Ibid.
22. Author observation.
23. Author observation.
24. Author observation.
25. Author observation.

Eleven / Iowa State & Northern Iowa
1. *Stillwater News Press,* January 26, 2005.
2. *The Daily Oklahoman,* October 17, 2004.
3. Conversations with George Shenold, September 2004-June 2005, hereinafter referred to as G. Shenold conversation.
4. Author observation.
5. Author observation.
6. Ibid.
7 Ibid.
8. Author observation.
9. Ibid.
10. Author observation.
11. Author observation.
12. Ibid.
13. Author observation.
14. Ibid.
15. Ibid.
16. Ibid.
17. Ibid.
18. Ibid.
19. Ibid.

20. Ibid.
21. Ibid.
22. Ibid.
23. Ibid.
24. Ibid.
25. Ibid.
26. Ibid.
27. Ibid.
28. Ibid.
29. Author observation.
30. Ibid.
31. Ibid.
32. Ibid.
33. http://unipanthers.cstv. com/sports/m-wrestl/ mtt/penrith_brad00. html
34. *Stillwater News Press,* January 26, 2005.
35. Author observation.

Twelve /A Mid-season Cowboy Practice
1. Author observation
2. Author observation.
3. Author observation.
4. Ibid.
5. Ibid.
6. Ibid.
7. Ibid.
8. Ibid.
9. Ibid.
10. Ibid.
11. Ibid.
12. Ibid.
13. Ibid.
14. Ibid.
15. Interviews with Chris Pickering, September 2004-June 2005, hereinafter referred to as C. Pickering interview.
16. Author observation.
17. Ibid.
18. Ibid.
19. S. Tackett interview.

20. Ibid.
21. Ibid.
22. Ibid.
23. Ibid.
24. Ibid.
25. Ibid.
26. Ibid.
27. Ibid.
28. Ibid.
29. Ibid.
30. Ibid.

**Thirteen / Missouri,
Oregon & Oregon State**

1. Ibid.
2. Ibid.
3. Ibid.
4. Ibid.
5. Ibid.
6. Ibid.
7. Author observation.
8. Author observation.
9. Author observation.
10. Author observation.
11. *The Daily Oklahoman,* February 11, 2007.
12. Wrestling Rules Pin Harmful Weight Cutting, *The Physician and Sportsmedicine,* Vol. 30, No. 12, December 2002
13. Weight Issues in Wrestling by Mike Viscardi, http://www.vanderbilt.edu/AnS/psychology/health_psychology/Weight-Wrestling.htm
14. insert footnote
15. *The NCAA News* (Comment), March 30, 1998.
16. J. Smith interview.
17. Author observation.
18. *Tulsa World,* February 4, 2005.

19. Author observation.
20. Ibid.
21. Ibid.
22. *Tulsa World,* February 5, 2005.
23. Ibid.
24. Interviews with Clay Kehrer, September 2004-June 2005, hereinafter referred to as C. Kehrer interview.
25. Ibid.
26. Ibid.
27. Ibid.
28. Ibid.
29. *Tulsa World,* February 4, 2005.
30. *The Daily Oklahoman,* February 6, 2005.
31. Ibid.

Fourteen / Nebraska

1. http://www.okstate.com/ViewArticle.dbml?&DB_OEM_ID=200&ATCLID=7462&SPID=162&SPSID=2438
2. D. Stevens interview.
3. Ibid.
4. Author observation.
5. *Lincoln Journal Star* (Lincoln, Nebraska) February 10, 2005.
6. Ibid.
7. Ibid.
8. Ibid.
9. Author observation.
10. Author observation.
11. Ibid.
12. 2005 NCAA Rules and Interpretations, Rule 6-10.
13. Ibid.
14. 2005 NCAA Rules and Interpretations, Rule 6-18 (Penalty Table)
15. Author observation.

16. Ibid.
17. Ibid.
18. Ibid.
19. Ibid.
20. Ibid.
21. Ibid.
22 Ibid.
23. Ibid.
24. Ibid.
25. Ibid.
26. Ibid.
27. Ibid.
28. Ibid.
29. Ibid.
30. Ibid.
31. Ibid.
32. *Omaha World-Herald Bureau,* February 11, 2005.
33. *The Daily Oklahoman,* February 12, 2005.

Fifteen / The Eastern Invasion

1. Author observation
2. Author observation
3. Author observation
4. Author observation
5. Ibid.
6. Ibid.
7. Ibid.
8. Ibid.
9. J. Smith interview.
10. Interviews with Teague Moore, September 2004-June 2005, hereinafter referred to as T. Moore interview.
11. Ibid.
12. Ibid.
13. http://mcall.com/sports/college, February 14, 2005.
14. Ibid.
15. *Amateur Wrestling News,* February 25, 2005.

16. Author observation.
17. Ibid.
18. *St. Louis Post-Dispatch* (St. Louis, Missouri), March 17, 2005.
19. Interviews with Nathan Morgan, September 2004-June 2005, hereinafter referred to as N. Morgan interview.
20. Interview(s) with Larry Morgan, September 2004-June 2005, hereinafter referred to as L. Morgan interview.
21. Ibid.
22. N. Morgan interview.
23. N. Morgan interview.
24. Ibid.
25. J. Smith interview.
26. N. Morgan interview.
27. Steve Mocco radio interview with J. Carl Guymon, February 13, 2005.
28. Ibid.
29. Ibid.
30. Ibid.
31. Ibid.
32. Author observation.
33. Ibid.
34. D. Stevens interview.
35. Ibid.
36. Author observation.
37. Author observation.
38. Ibid.

Sixteen / The Oklahoma Rematch

1. *Merriam Webster's Collegiate Dictionary, Tenth Edition,* 1996, Merriam-Webster Incorporated.
2. http://word-dectective.com/112701.html.
3. *Stillwater News Press,*
February 18, 2005.
4. John Smith radio interview, February 18, 2005.
5. Interviews with Mark Branch, September 2004-June 2005, hereinafter referred to as M. Branch interview.
6. Ibid.
7. Ibid.
8. Ibid.
9. Ibid.
10. J. Smith interview.
11. *The Daily Oklahoman,* March 20, 1994.
12. *A Season on the Mat,* Simon & Schuster, 1998 New York p. 127.
13. Author observation.
14. Author observation.
15. Interviews with Mike Christian, September 2004-June 2005, hereinafter referred to as M.Christian interview.
16. J. Smith interview.
17. The NCAA did not keep official team points in 1928 and 1930-33. Team titles are considered "unofficial" during those seasons.
18. *The Daily Oklahoman,* March 20, 1992.
19. *The Daily Oklahoman,* March 13, 1994.
20. *The Daily Oklahoman,* March 20, 1994.
21. *The Daily Oklahoman,* March 13, 1994.
22. *Tulsa World,* February 21, 2005.
23. *The Daily Oklahoman,* February 20, 2005.
24. *The Tulsa World,* March 4, 2005.
25. Author observation.
26. *The Daily Oklahoman,* January 7, 1999.
27. E. Guerrero interview.
28. Ibid.
29. Author observation.
30. Author observation.
31. Interviews with Eric Guerrero, September 2004-June 2005, hereinafter referred to as E. Geurrero interview.
32. E. Guerrero interview.
33. Ibid.
34. Ibid.
35. Ibid.
36. Ibid.
37. *The Daily Oklahoman,* February 1, 1999.
38. Ibid.
39. *Stillwater News Press,* February 21, 2005.
40. *Stillwater News Press,* February 20, 2005
41. *Tulsa World,* February 20, 2005.
42. *Stillwater News Press,* February 20, 2005.
43. *Stillwater News Press,* February 21, 2005.
44. OSU Press Release , February 20, 2005 cited at http://www.okstate.com
45. *Tulsa World,* February 21, 2005.
46. *Tulsa World,* February 20, 2005.
47. Author interview.

Seventeen / The Big 12 Tournament

1. *The World-Herald* (Omaha, Nebraska) March 5, 2005.
2. *Stillwater News Press,* March 1, 2005.

3. *The World-Herald* (Omaha, Nebraska) March 5, 2005.
4. Author observation.
5. Ibid.
6. Ibid.
7. Author observation.
8 Ibid.
9. Ibid.
10.. Ibid.
11. Ibid.
12. Ibid.
13. Ibid.
14. Ibid.
15. Ibid.
16. Ibid.
17. Author observation.
18. Ibid.
19. J. Smith interview.
20. Ibid.
21. Ibid.
22. *Tulsa World,* March 6, 2005.
23. Ibid.
24. *Daily O'Collegian,* March 7, 2005.
25. Author observation.
26 J. Smith interview.
27. Ibid.
28. Author observation.
29. J. Smith interview.
30. Ibid.
31. Ibid.
32. Author observation.
33. J. Smith interview.
34. Author observation.
35. Ibid.

Eighteen / The NCAA Tournament
1. J. Smith interview.
2. *The Games Do Matter,* Brian Kilmeade, ReganBooks, 2004 p. 208
3. J. Smith interview.

4. *The Daily Oklahoman,* March 17, 2005.
5. Ibid.
6. Ibid.
7. Ibid.
8. *The Daily Oklahoman,* March 15, 2005.
9. *The Daily Oklahoman,* March 17, 2005.
10. J. Smith interview.
11. Author observation.
12. J. Smith interview.
13. *Daily O'Collegian,* March 11, 2005.
14. *Stillwater News Press,* March 7, 2005.
15. Interviews with Shane Roller September 2004-June 2005, hereinafter referred to S. Roller interview.
16. J. Smith interview.
17. J. Smith interview.
18. Ibid.
19. *The Daily Oklahoman,* March 17, 2005.
20. Author observation.
21. Ibid.
22. Ibid.
23. Ibid.
24. Ibid.
25. Ibid.
26. Ibid.
27. Ibid.
28. Ibid.
29. Ibid.
30. Author observations.
31. Ibid.
32. *Stillwater News Press,* March 14, 2005.
33. *Stillwater News Press,* March 14, 2005.
34. *Stillwater News Press,* March 18, 2005.
35. Author observation.
36. Author observation.

37. Author observation.
38. *Tulsa World,* March 19, 2005.
39. *The Daily Oklahoman,* March 17, 2005.
40. *Tulsa World,* March 20, 2005.
41. Ibid.
42. *St. Louis Post-Dispatch,* March 20, 2005.
43. *Daily O'Collegian,* March 21, 2005.
44. *St. Louis Post Dispatch,* March 20, 2005.
45. *St. Louis Post Dispatch,* March 20, 2005.
46. Ibid.
47. *Stillwater News Press,* March 20, 2005.
48. *Tulsa World,* March 20, 2005.
49. *St. Louis Post-Dispatch,* March 20, 2005.
50. *The Daily Oklahoman,* November 7, 2004.
51. Author observation.
52. *Tulsa World,* January 16, 2005.
53. Ibid.
54. *Tulsa World,* January 16, 2005.
55. Author observation.
56. *Tulsa World,* January 16, 2005.
57. *Tulsa World,* January 16, 2005.
58. *Tulsa World,* March 13, 2005.
59. *Tulsa World,* January 16, 2005.
60. Interviews with Joe Mocco, September 2004-June 2005, here-inafter referred to as J. Mocco interview.

61. Interviews with Gary Calcagno, September 2004-June 2005, hereinafter referred to as G. Calcagno interview.
62. J. Smith interview.
63. Author observation.
64. Ibid.
65. Interviews with Steve Mocco, September 2004-June 2005, hereinafter referred to as S. Mocco interview.
66. J. Smith interview.
67. *The Daily Oklahoman,* November 7, 2004.
68. *Tulsa World,* March 20, 2005.
69. *Stillwater News Press,* March 20, 2005.
70. *Tulsa World,* March 20, 2005.
71. *St. Louis Post Dispatch,* March 20, 2005.
72. Ibid.
73. Ibid.
74. Ibid..
75. *Tulsa World,* March 20, 2005.
76. *Stillwater News Press,* March 20, 2005.

Epilogue
1. *Daily O'Collegian,* April 21, 2005.
2. *Tulsa World,* March 21, 2005.
3. *St. Louis Post-Dispatch,* March 20, 2005.
4. *Tulsa World,* March 21, 2005.
5. *Stillwater News Press,* March 22, 2005.
6. Author observation.
7. J. Smith interview.
8. Ibid.
9. Ibid.

index

To order additional copies of *Cowboy Up*, please contact:

OKLAHOMA STATE WRESTLING OFFICE

Gallagher-Iba Arena
220 Athletics Center
Stillwater, Oklahoma 74078
(405) 744-3288